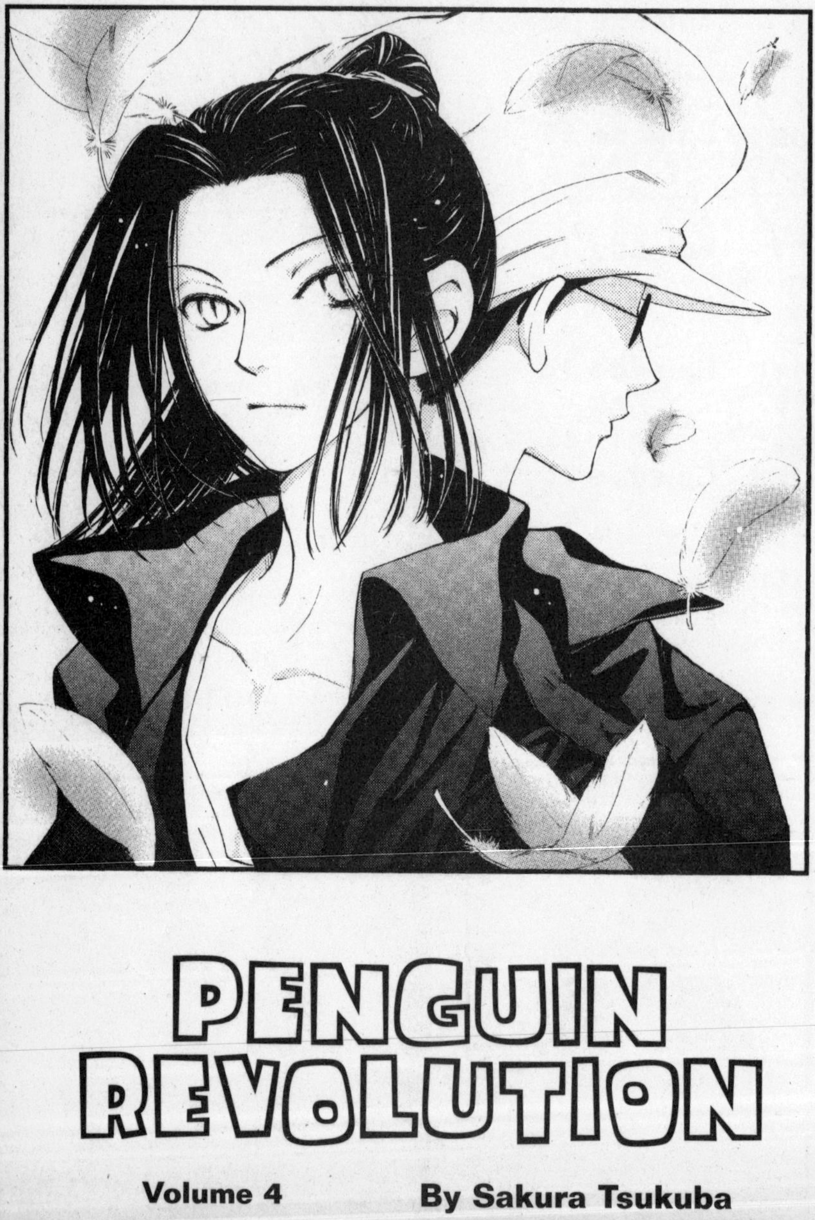

PENGUIN REVOLUTION

Volume 4

By Sakura Tsukuba

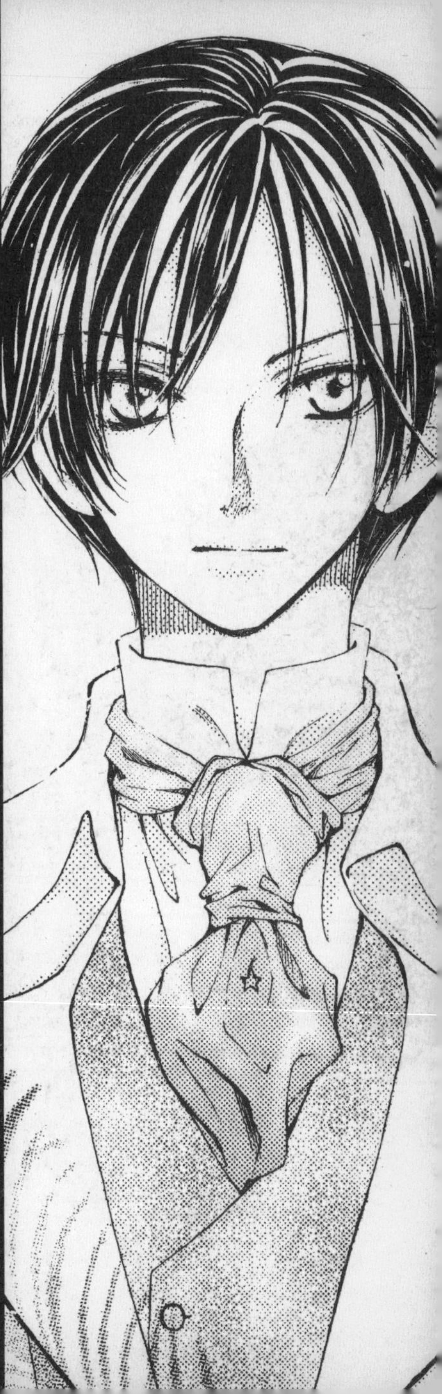

CONTENTS

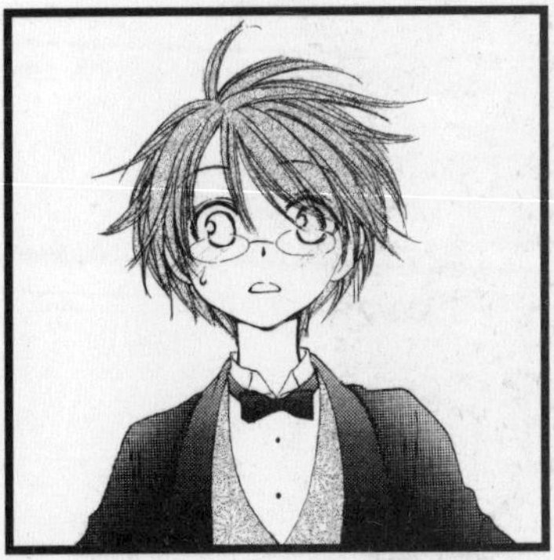

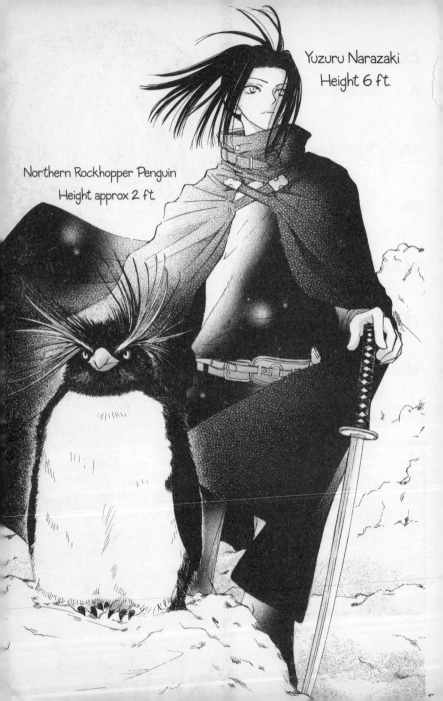

Yuzuru Narazaki
Height 6 ft.

Northern Rockhopper Penguin
Height approx 2 ft.

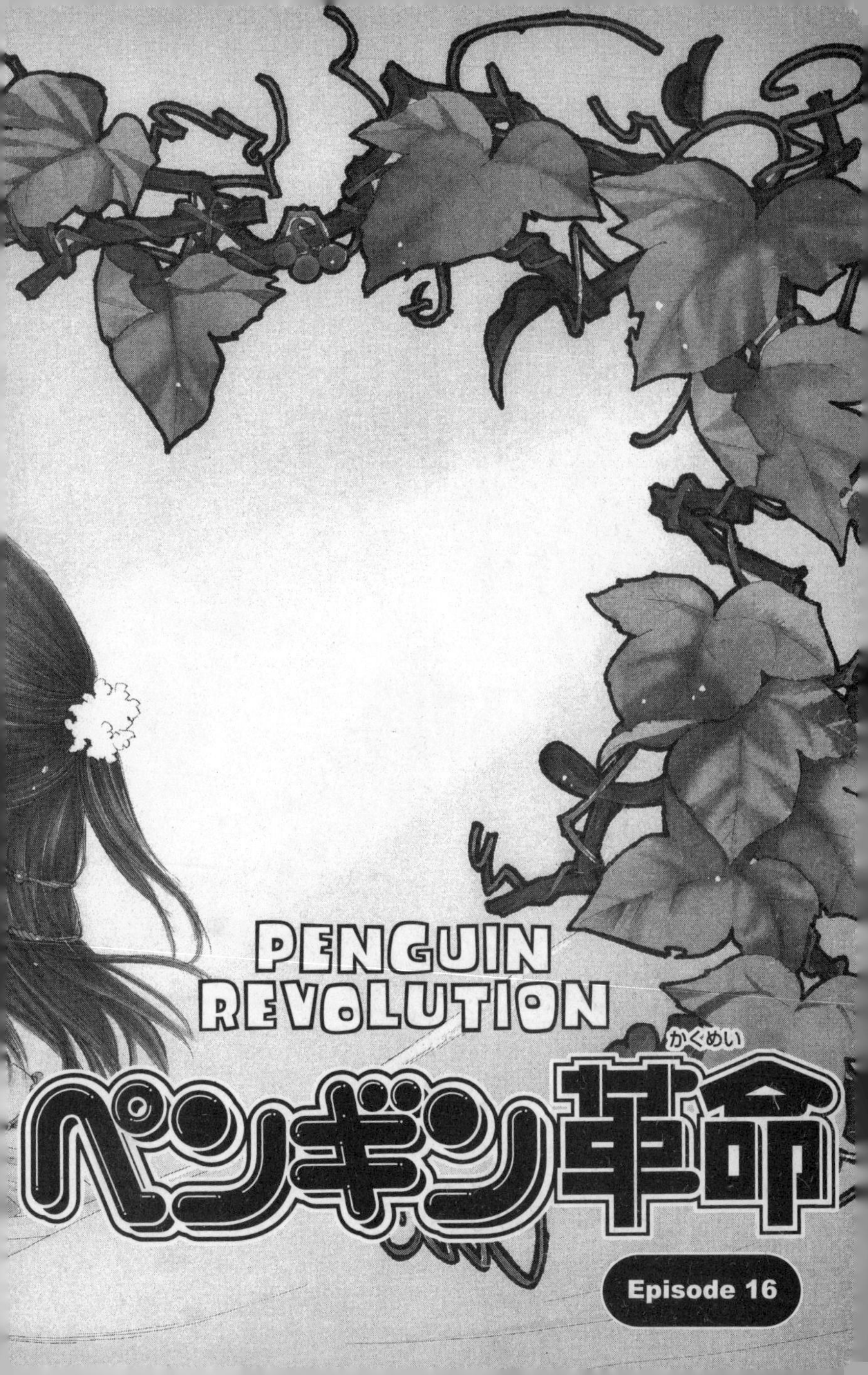
PENGUIN
REVOLUTION
かくめい
ペンギン革命
Episode 16

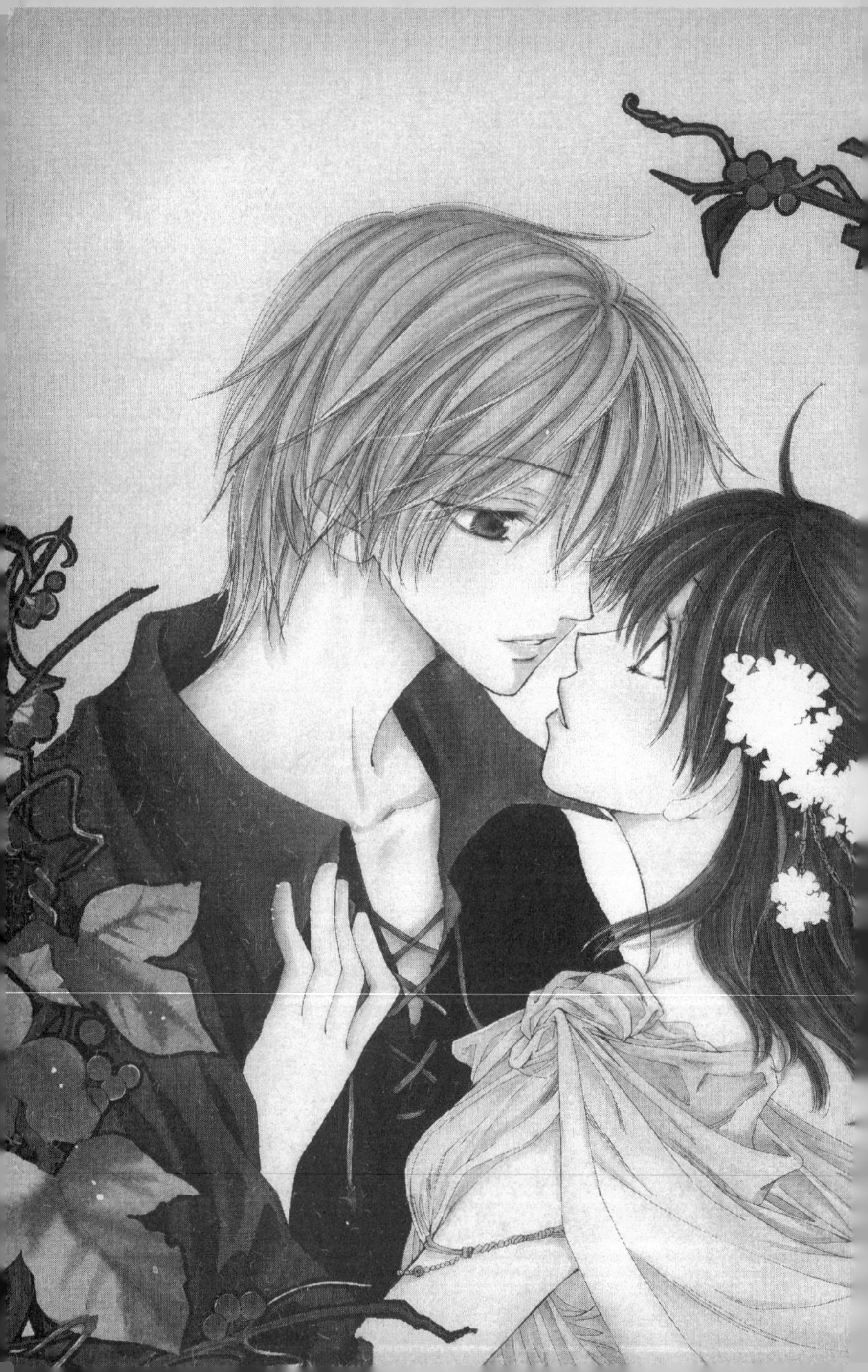

Yukari
in
battle

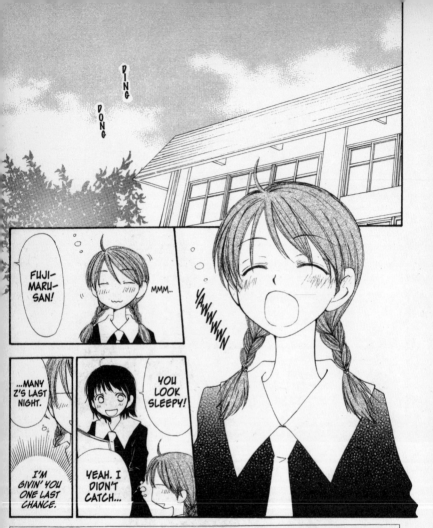

DING
DONG
YAWWWWWN
FUJI-MARU-SAN!
MMM...
YOU LOOK SLEEPY!
YEAH. I DIDN'T CATCH...
...MANY Z'S LAST NIGHT.
I'M GIVIN' YOU ONE LAST CHANCE.

1/4 Sakura Mail

Hello!! I'm Sakura Tskuba. Thanks to all of you, as always, we've reached "Penguin Revolution" volume 4. Thank you!! Yay. Yay. My plan is to work even harder so you're entertained even more.
So please keep reading!! As you can see, this volume's cover features Narazaki-san... (To be continued)

Part 1

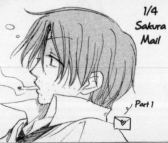

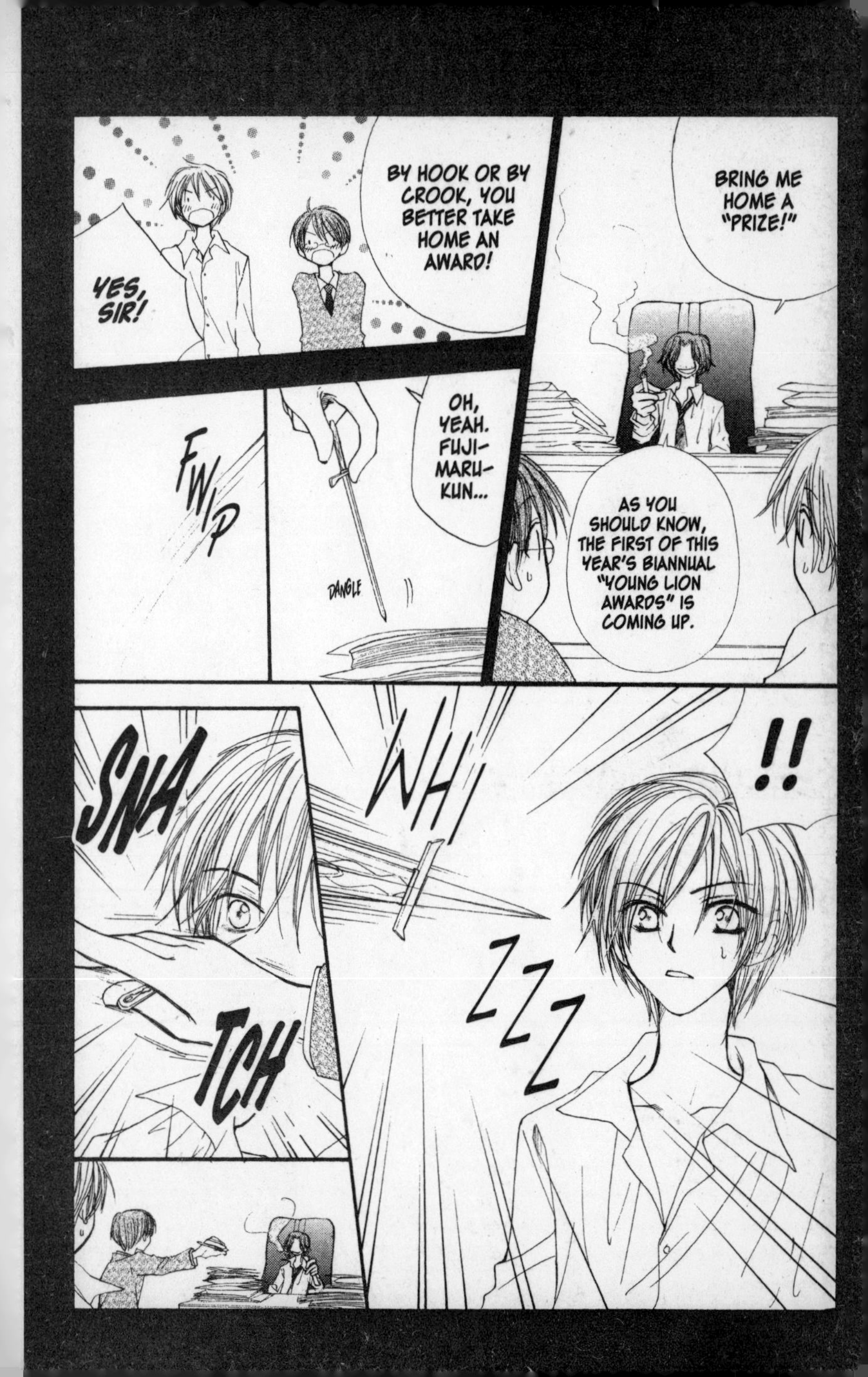
BRING ME HOME A "PRIZE!"
AS YOU SHOULD KNOW, THE FIRST OF THIS YEAR'S BIANNUAL "YOUNG LION AWARDS" IS COMING UP.
BY HOOK OR BY CROOK, YOU BETTER TAKE HOME AN AWARD!
YES, SIR!
OH, YEAH. FUJI-MARU-KUN...
DANGLE
FWIP
!!
WHIZZZ
SNATCH

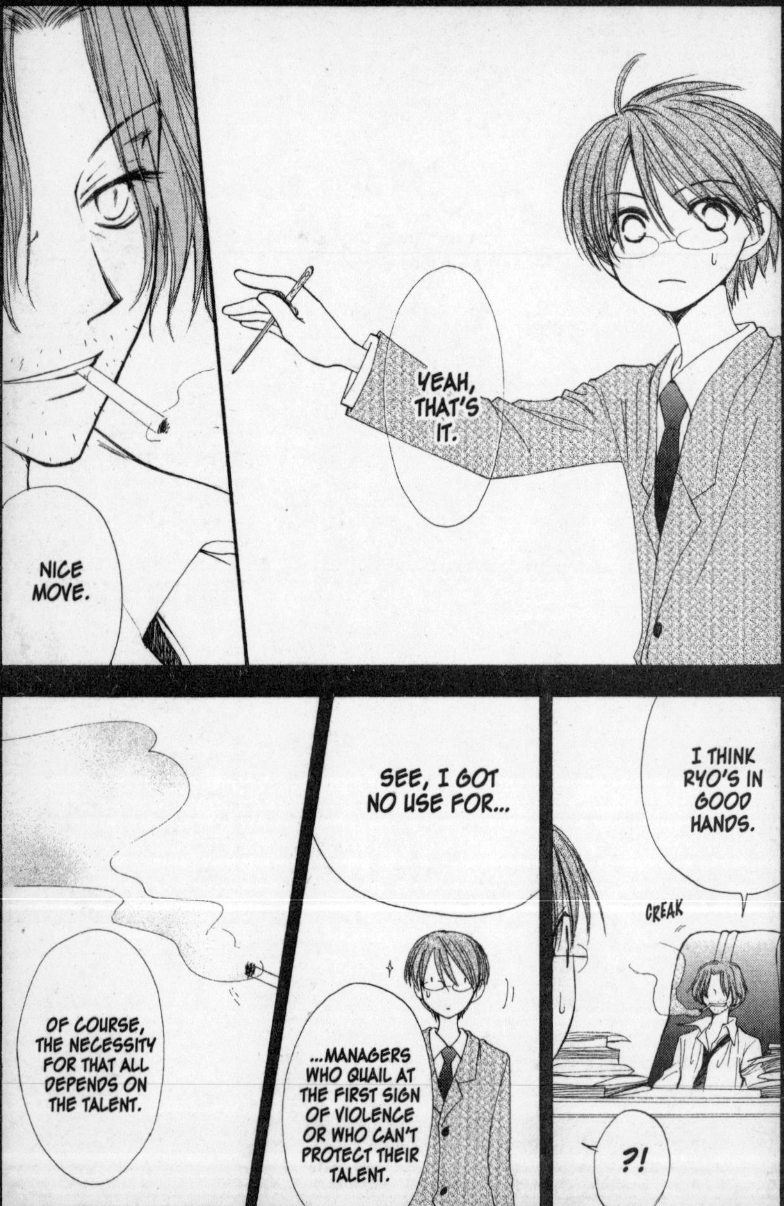
YEAH, THAT'S IT.
NICE MOVE.
I THINK RYO'S IN GOOD HANDS.
CREAK
?!
SEE, I GOT NO USE FOR...
...MANAGERS WHO QUAIL AT THE FIRST SIGN OF VIOLENCE OR WHO CAN'T PROTECT THEIR TALENT.
OF COURSE, THE NECESSITY FOR THAT ALL DEPENDS ON THE TALENT.

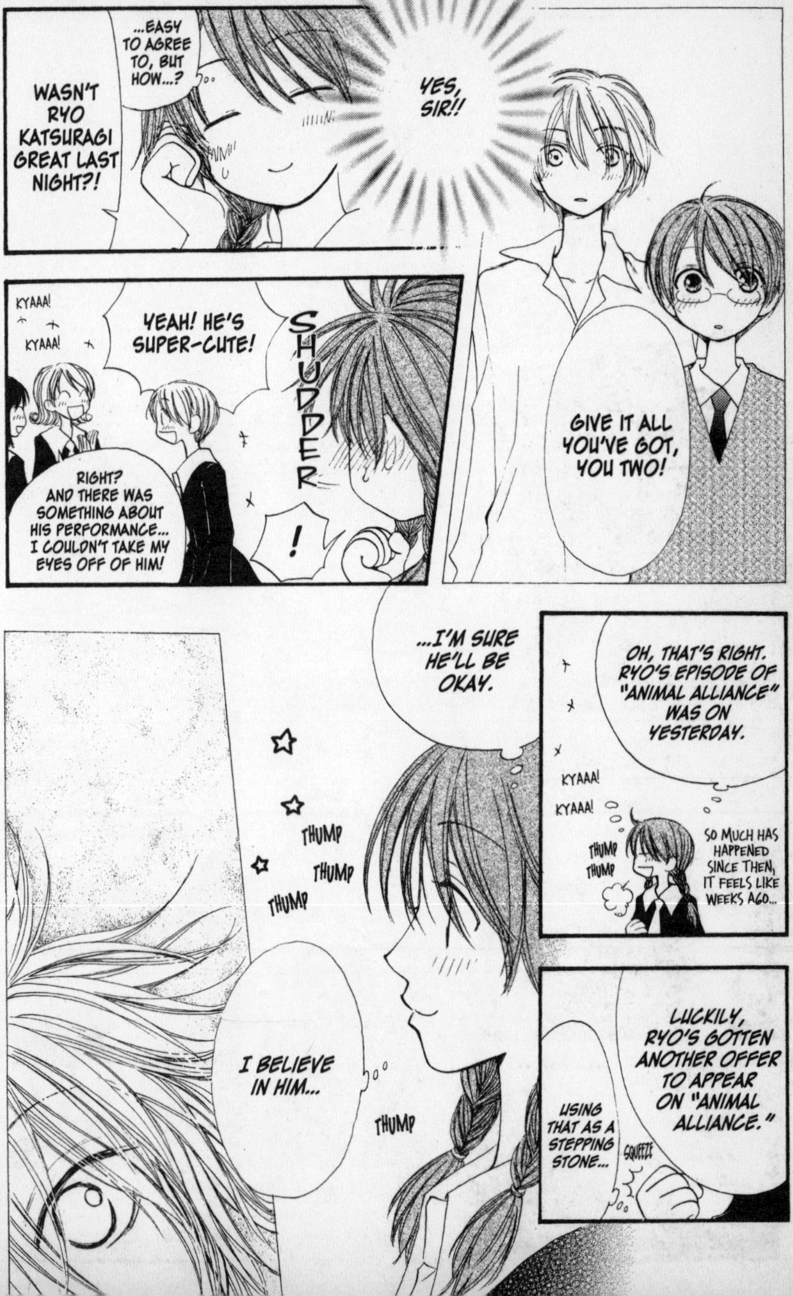
GIVE IT ALL YOU'VE GOT, YOU TWO!
YES, SIR!!
...EASY TO AGREE TO, BUT HOW...?
WASN'T RYO KATSURAGI GREAT LAST NIGHT?!
KYAAA!
KYAAA!
YEAH! HE'S SUPER-CUTE!
SHUDDER
RIGHT? AND THERE WAS SOMETHING ABOUT HIS PERFORMANCE... I COULDN'T TAKE MY EYES OFF OF HIM!
!
OH, THAT'S RIGHT. RYO'S EPISODE OF "ANIMAL ALLIANCE" WAS ON YESTERDAY.
KYAAA!
KYAAA!
SO MUCH HAS HAPPENED SINCE THEN, IT FEELS LIKE WEEKS AGO...
THUMP
THUMP
LUCKILY, RYO'S GOTTEN ANOTHER OFFER TO APPEAR ON "ANIMAL ALLIANCE."
USING THAT AS A STEPPING STONE...
SQUEEZE
...I'M SURE HE'LL BE OKAY.
THUMP
THUMP
THUMP
I BELIEVE IN HIM...
THUMP

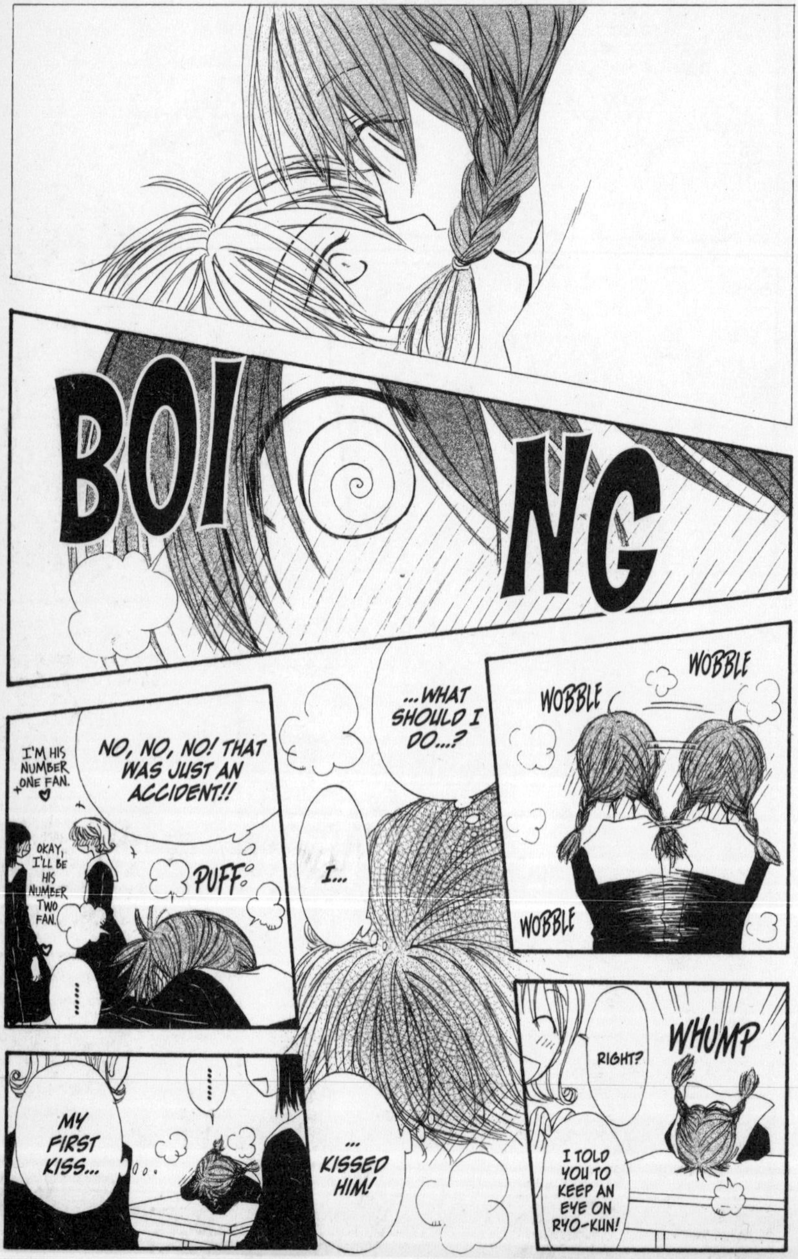
BOING
WOBBLE
WOBBLE
WOBBLE
WHUMP
RIGHT?
I TOLD YOU TO KEEP AN EYE ON RYO-KUN!
...WHAT SHOULD I DO...?
I...
...KISSED HIM!
NO, NO, NO! THAT WAS JUST AN ACCIDENT!!
I'M HIS NUMBER ONE FAN.
OKAY, I'LL BE HIS NUMBER TWO FAN.
PUFF
......
......
MY FIRST KISS...

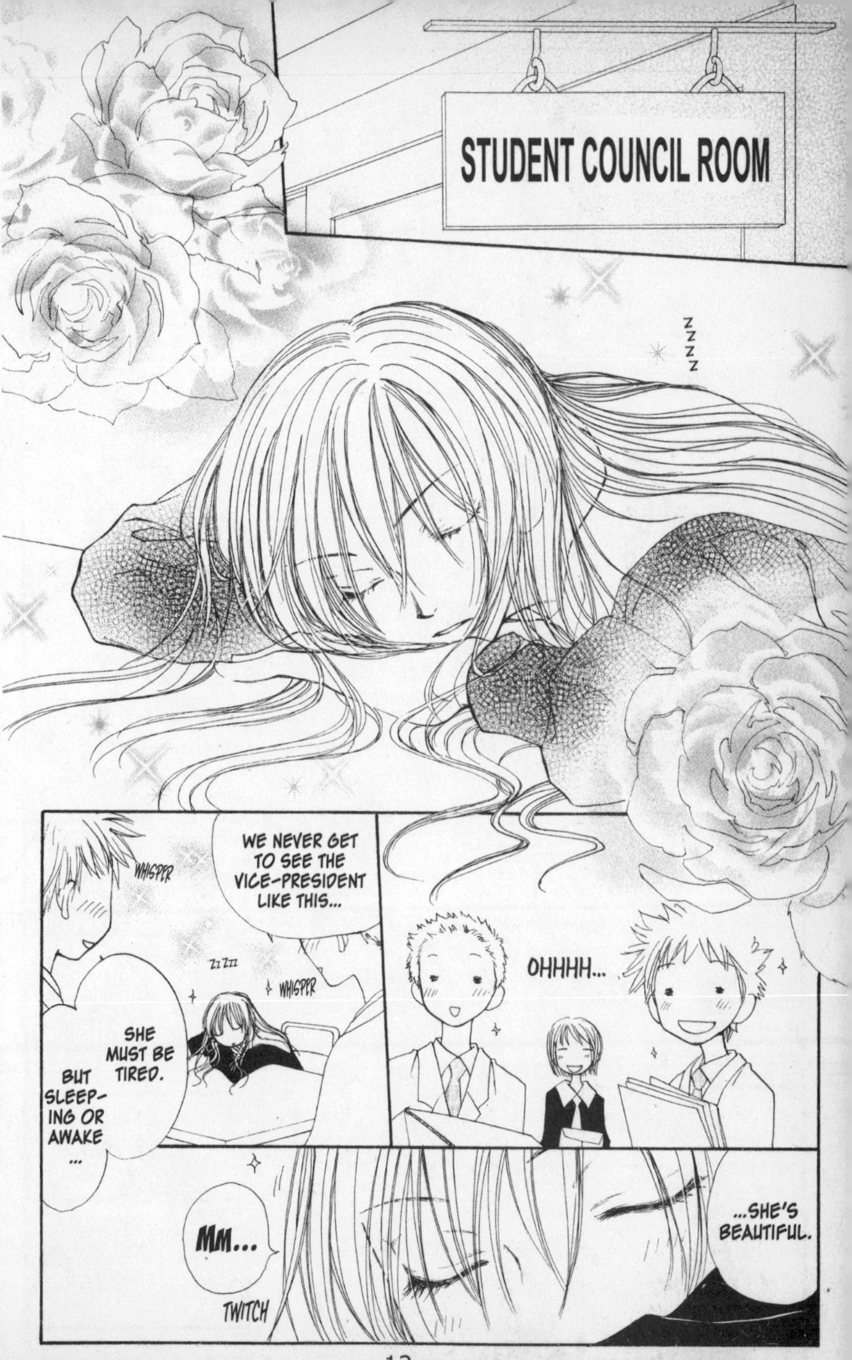
STUDENT COUNCIL ROOM
ZZZZ
OHHHH...
WE NEVER GET TO SEE THE VICE-PRESIDENT LIKE THIS...
WHISPER
ZzZzz
WHISPER
SHE MUST BE TIRED.
BUT SLEEPING OR AWAKE...
...SHE'S BEAUTIFUL.
MM...
TWITCH

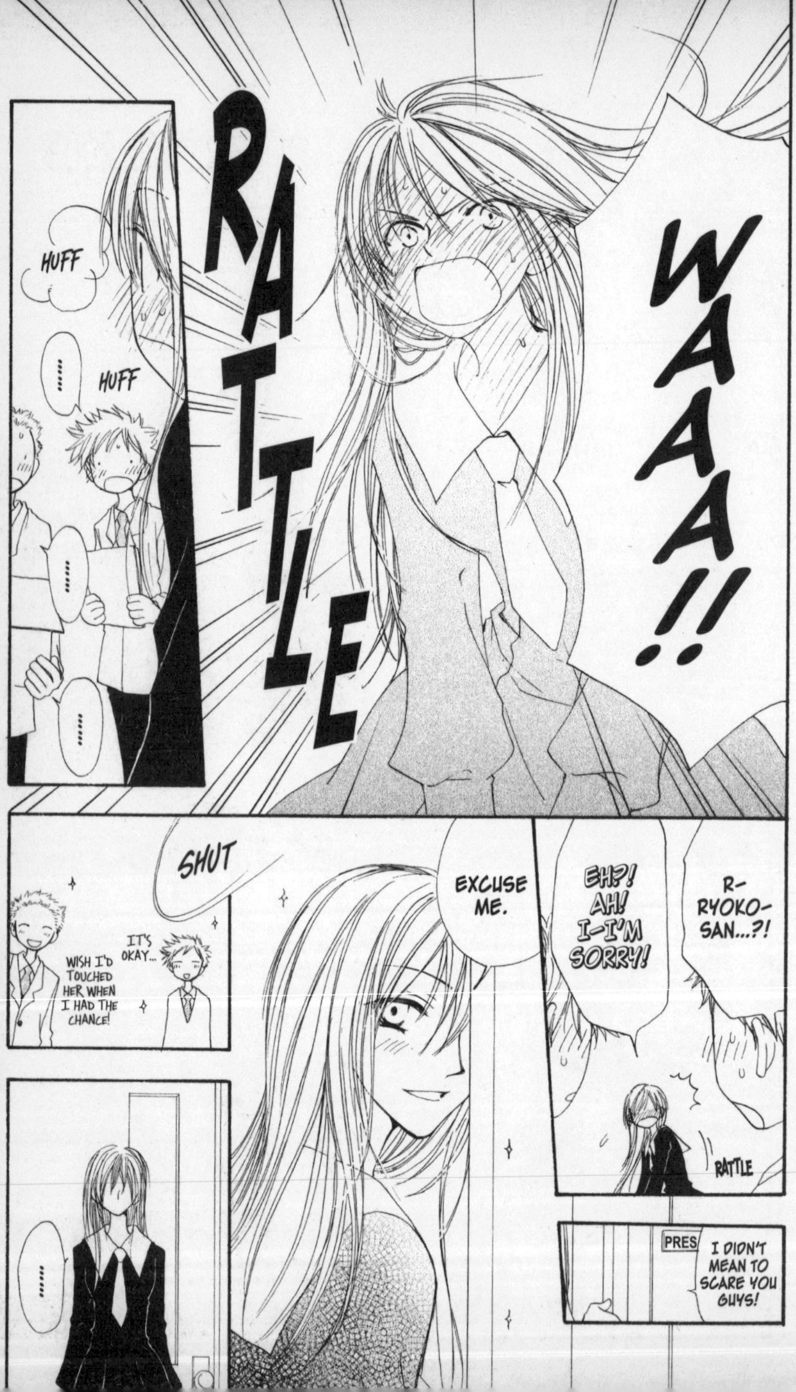
WAAA!!
RATTLE
HUFF
HUFF
......
......
......
R-RYOKO-SAN...?!
EH?! AH! I-I'M SORRY!
RATTLE
PRES
I DIDN'T MEAN TO SCARE YOU GUYS!
EXCUSE ME.
SHUT
IT'S OKAY...
WISH I'D TOUCHED HER WHEN I HAD THE CHANCE!
......

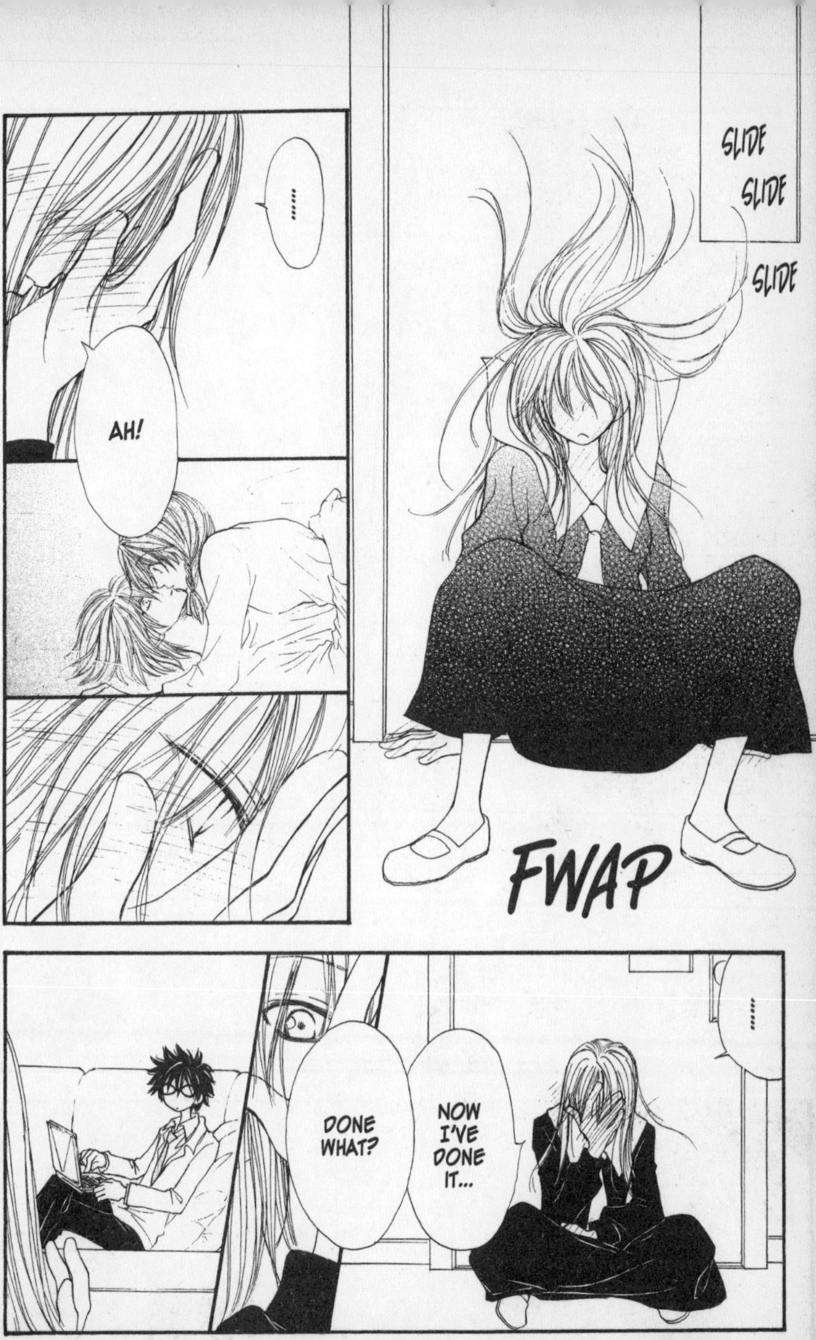
SLIDE
SLIDE
SLIDE
FWAP
......
AH!
......
NOW I'VE DONE IT...
DONE WHAT?

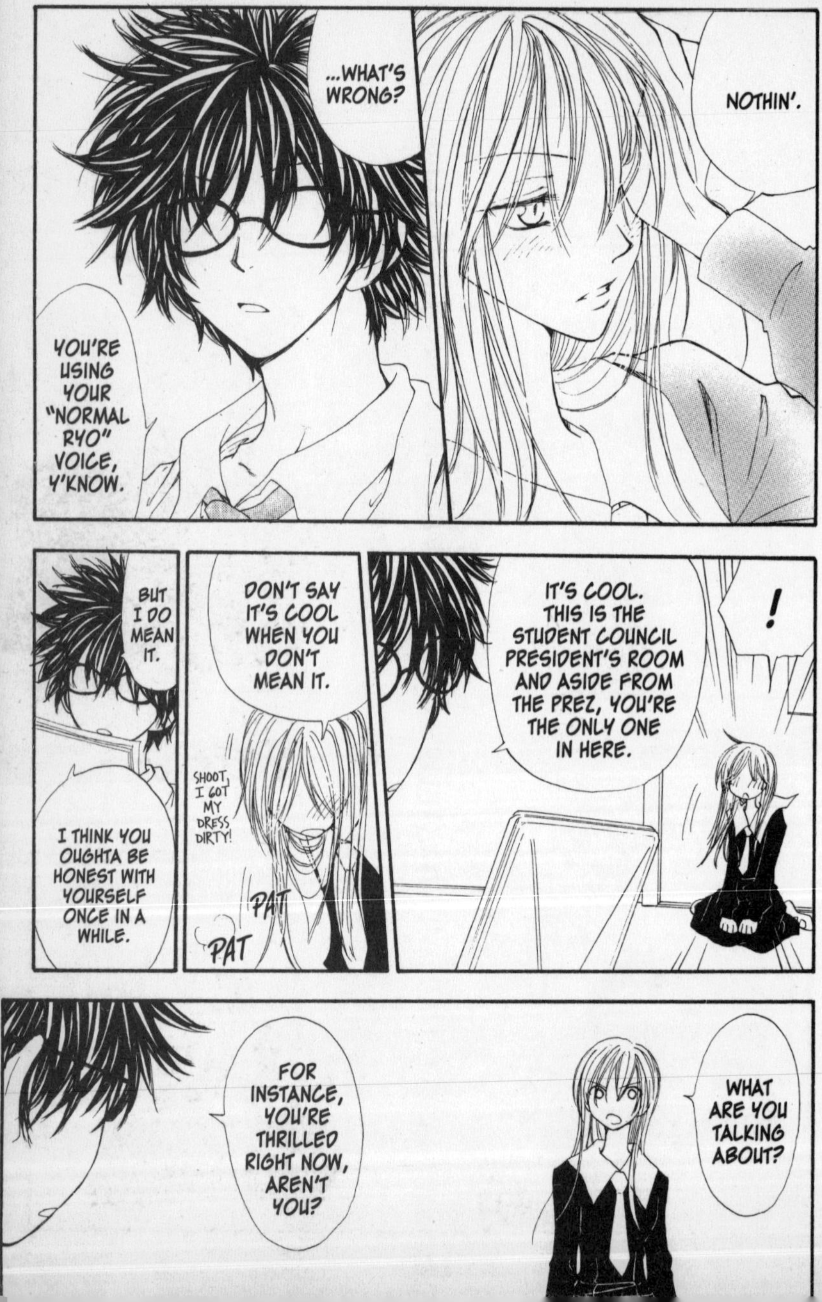
NOTHIN'.
...WHAT'S WRONG?
YOU'RE USING YOUR "NORMAL RYO" VOICE, Y'KNOW.
!
IT'S COOL. THIS IS THE STUDENT COUNCIL PRESIDENT'S ROOM AND ASIDE FROM THE PREZ, YOU'RE THE ONLY ONE IN HERE.
DON'T SAY IT'S COOL WHEN YOU DON'T MEAN IT.
SHOOT, I GOT MY DRESS DIRTY!
PAT
PAT
BUT I DO MEAN IT.
I THINK YOU OUGHTA BE HONEST WITH YOURSELF ONCE IN A WHILE.
WHAT ARE YOU TALKING ABOUT?
FOR INSTANCE, YOU'RE THRILLED RIGHT NOW, AREN'T YOU?

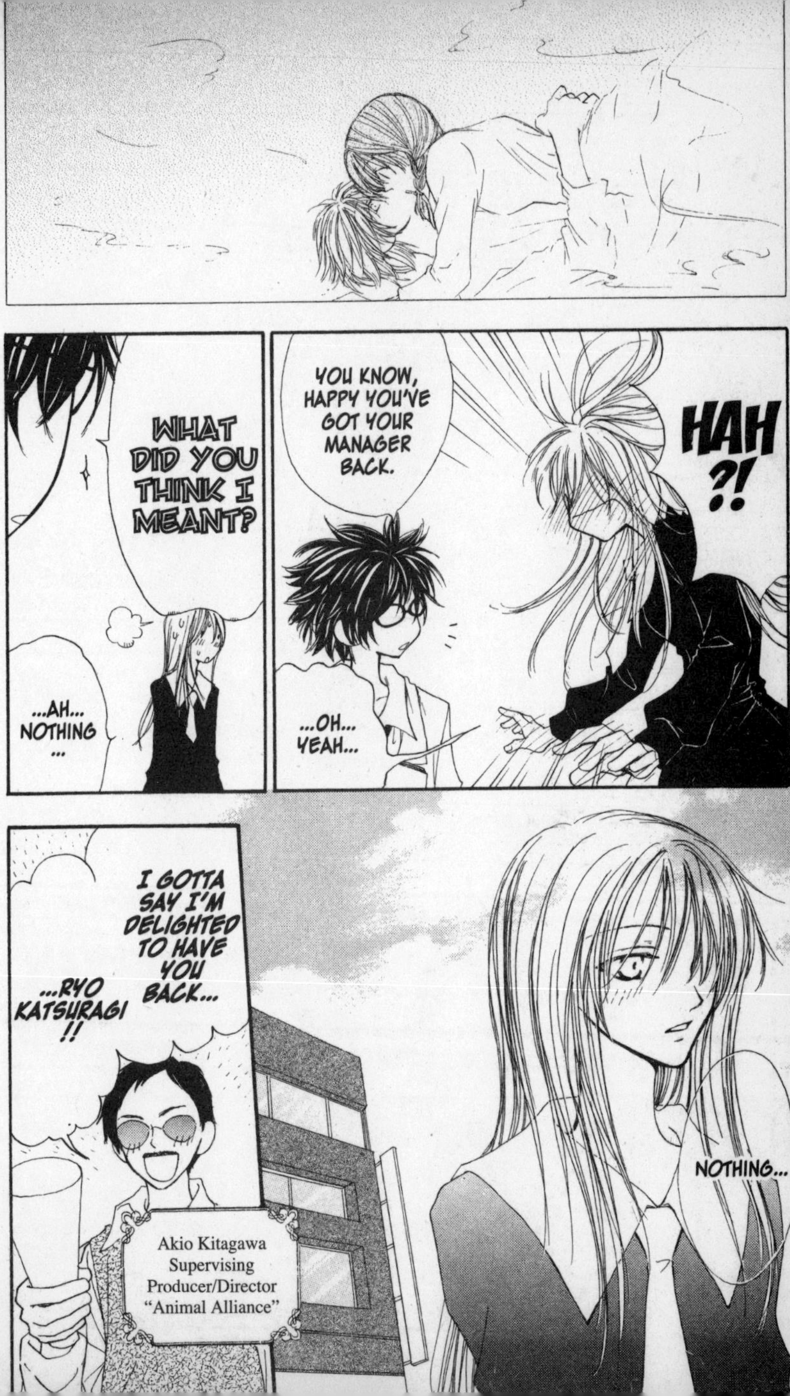
YOU KNOW, HAPPY YOU'VE GOT YOUR MANAGER BACK.
HAH ?!
...OH... YEAH...
WHAT DID YOU THINK I MEANT?
...AH... NOTHING ...
NOTHING...
I GOTTA SAY I'M DELIGHTED TO HAVE YOU BACK...
...RYO KATSURAGI !!
Akio Kitagawa
Supervising
Producer/Director
"Animal Alliance"

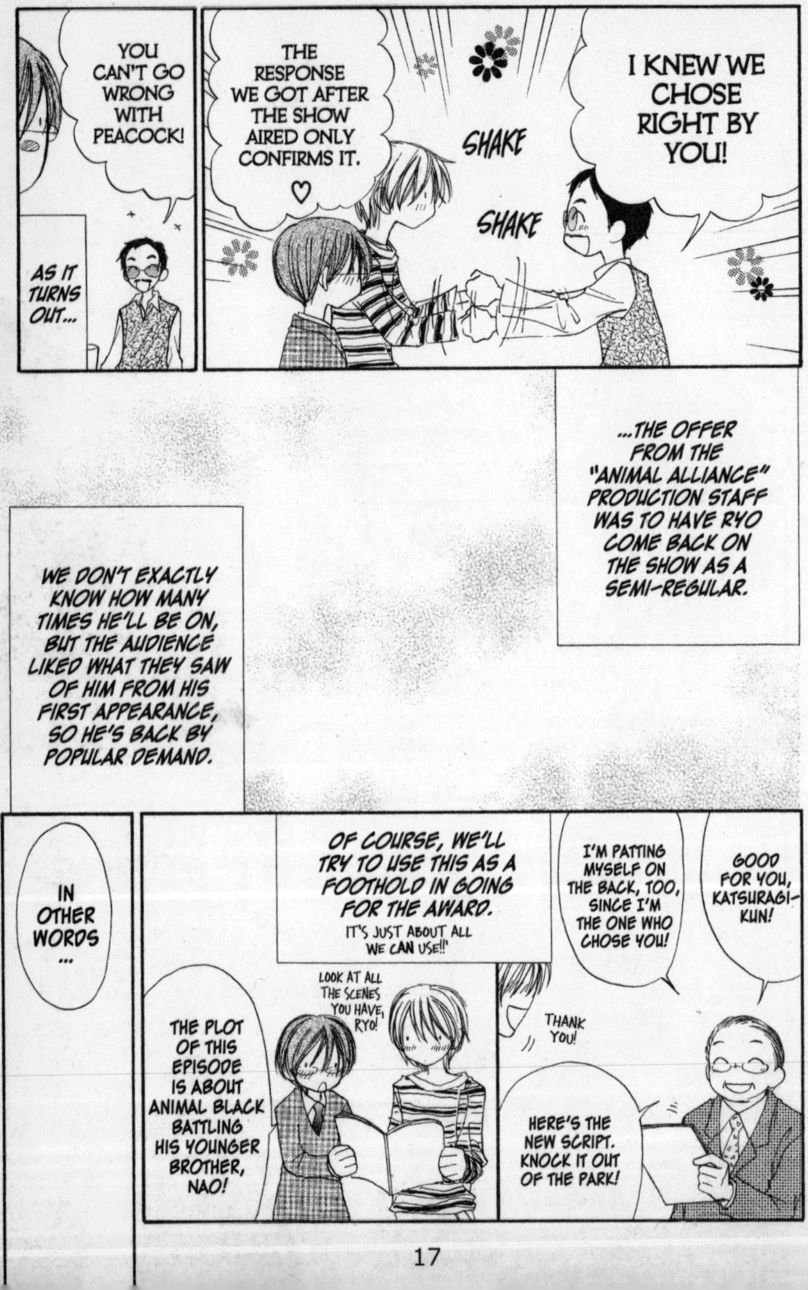

I KNEW WE CHOSE RIGHT BY YOU!
SHAKE
SHAKE
THE RESPONSE WE GOT AFTER THE SHOW AIRED ONLY CONFIRMS IT. ♡
YOU CAN'T GO WRONG WITH PEACOCK!
AS IT TURNS OUT...
...THE OFFER FROM THE "ANIMAL ALLIANCE" PRODUCTION STAFF WAS TO HAVE RYO COME BACK ON THE SHOW AS A SEMI-REGULAR.
WE DON'T EXACTLY KNOW HOW MANY TIMES HE'LL BE ON, BUT THE AUDIENCE LIKED WHAT THEY SAW OF HIM FROM HIS FIRST APPEARANCE, SO HE'S BACK BY POPULAR DEMAND.
GOOD FOR YOU, KATSURAGI-KUN!
I'M PATTING MYSELF ON THE BACK, TOO, SINCE I'M THE ONE WHO CHOSE YOU!
OF COURSE, WE'LL TRY TO USE THIS AS A FOOTHOLD IN GOING FOR THE AWARD.
IT'S JUST ABOUT ALL WE CAN USE!!
THANK YOU!
HERE'S THE NEW SCRIPT. KNOCK IT OUT OF THE PARK!
LOOK AT ALL THE SCENES YOU HAVE, RYO!
THE PLOT OF THIS EPISODE IS ABOUT ANIMAL BLACK BATTLING HIS YOUNGER BROTHER, NAO!
IN OTHER WORDS ...

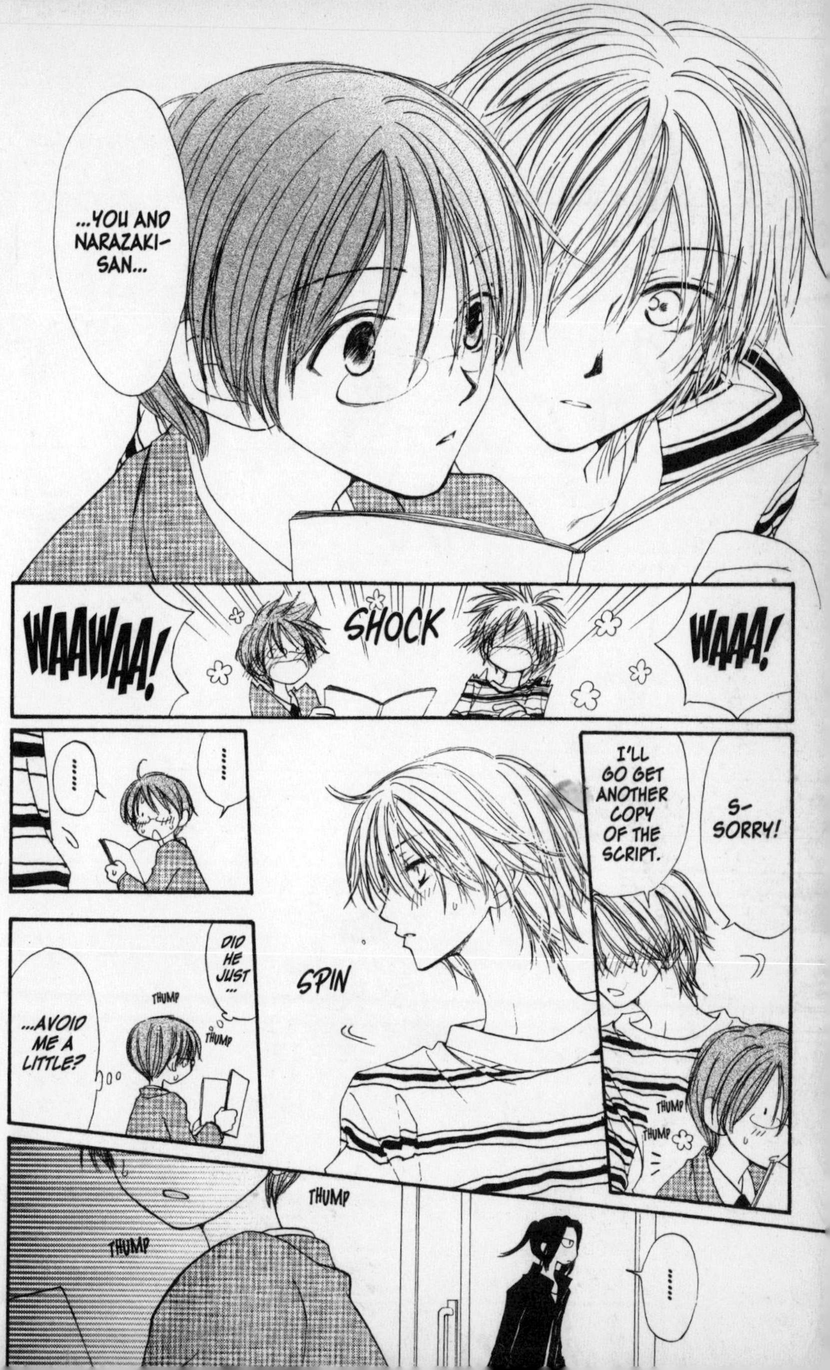
...YOU AND NARAZAKI-SAN...
WAAAA!
SHOCK
WAAWAA!
S-SORRY!
I'LL GO GET ANOTHER COPY OF THE SCRIPT.
THUMP
THUMP
SPIN
......
......
DID HE JUST...
THUMP
THUMP
...AVOID ME A LITTLE?
......
THUMP
THUMP

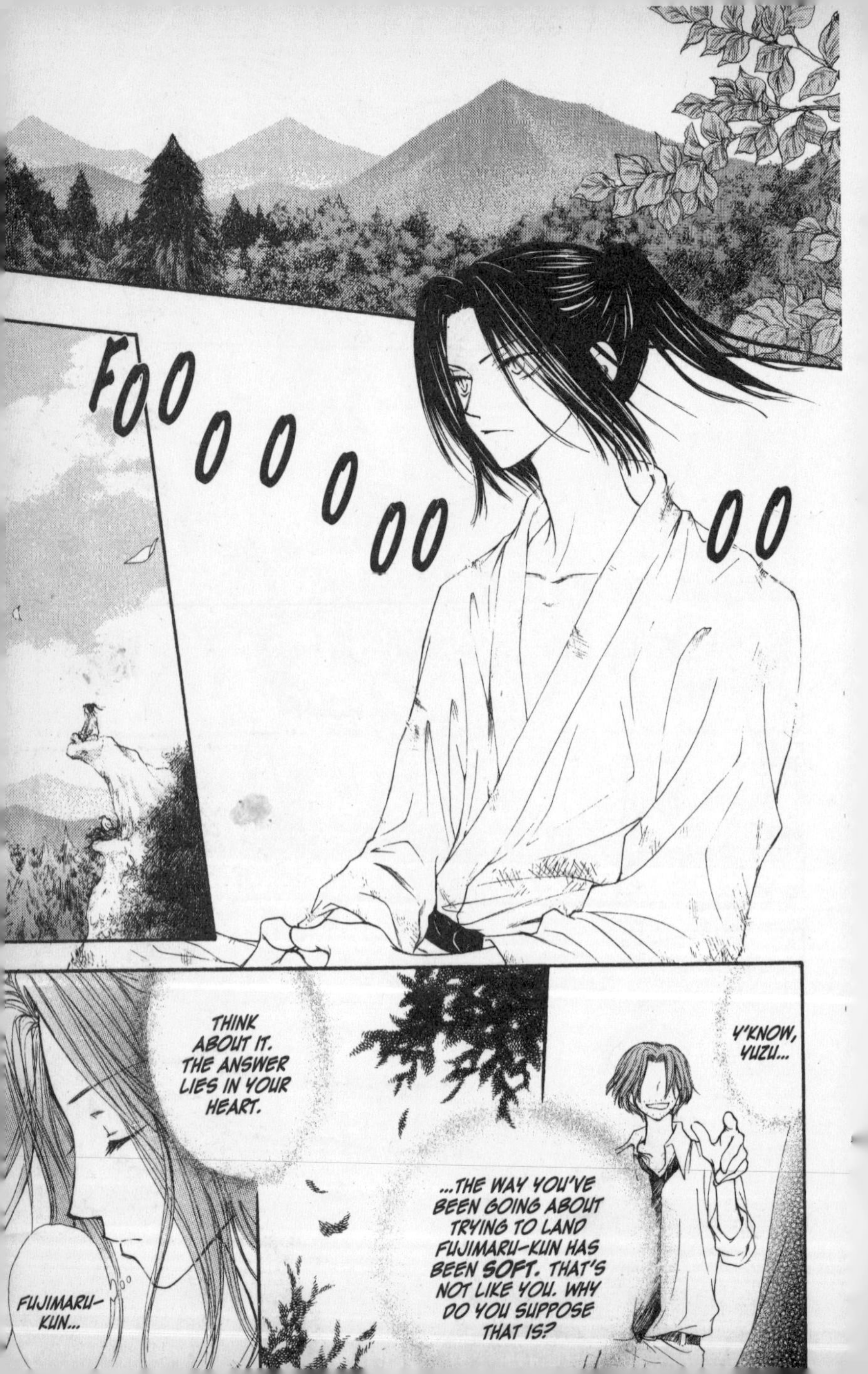
FOOOOOOOOOO
Y'KNOW, YUZU...
...THE WAY YOU'VE BEEN GOING ABOUT TRYING TO LAND FUJIMARU-KUN HAS BEEN **SOFT**. THAT'S NOT LIKE YOU. WHY DO YOU SUPPOSE THAT IS?
THINK ABOUT IT. THE ANSWER LIES IN YOUR HEART.
FUJIMARU-KUN...

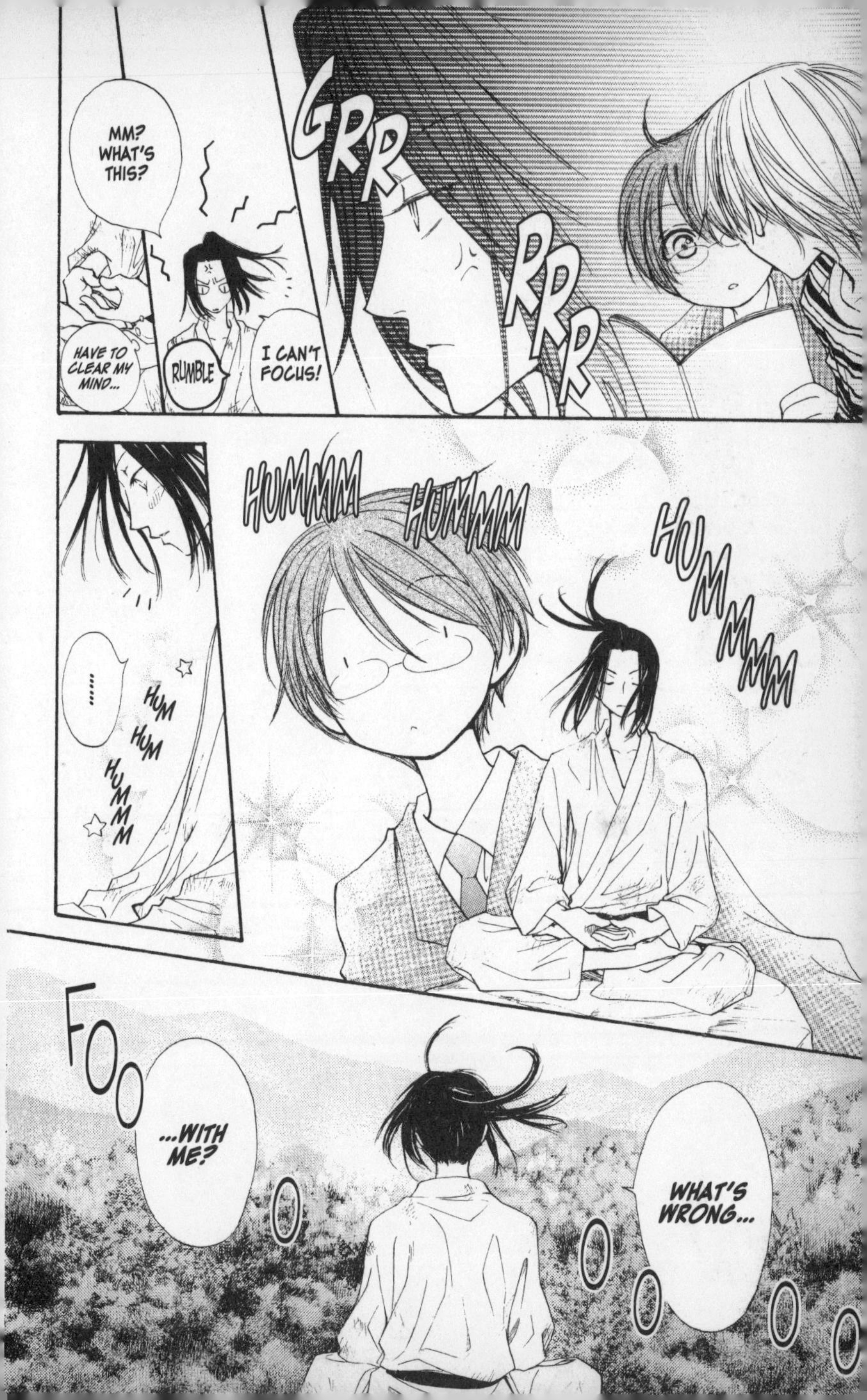
GRR
RRRR
MM? WHAT'S THIS?
I CAN'T FOCUS!
RUMBLE
HAVE TO CLEAR MY MIND...
HUMMMM
HUMMMM
HUMMMMMM
......
HUM HUM HUMMMM
WHAT'S WRONG...
...WITH ME?
FOOOOOOOOO

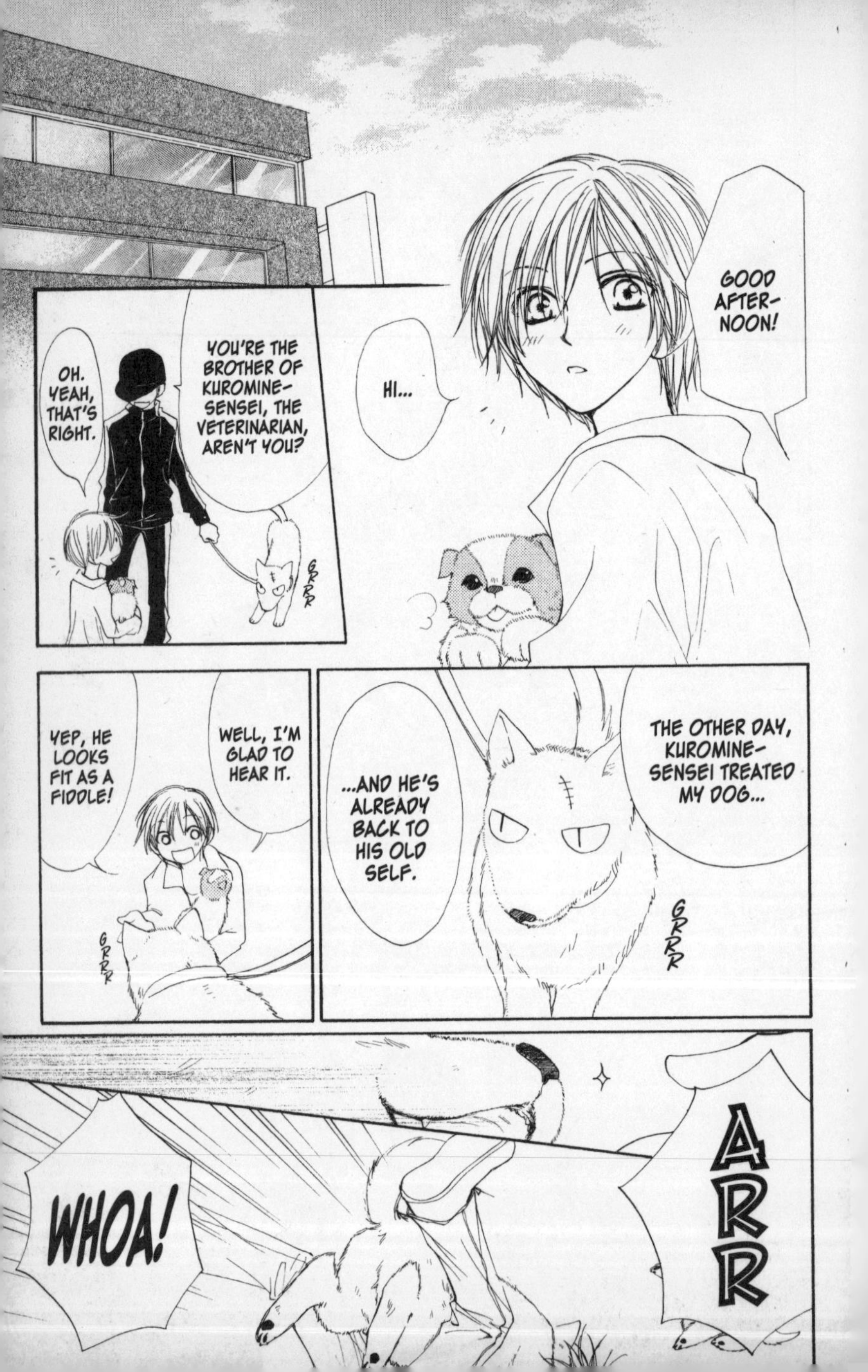
GOOD AFTER-NOON!
HI...
YOU'RE THE BROTHER OF KUROMINE-SENSEI, THE VETERINARIAN, AREN'T YOU?
OH. YEAH, THAT'S RIGHT.
GRRR
THE OTHER DAY, KUROMINE-SENSEI TREATED MY DOG...
...AND HE'S ALREADY BACK TO HIS OLD SELF.
GRRR
WELL, I'M GLAD TO HEAR IT.
YEP, HE LOOKS FIT AS A FIDDLE!
GRRR
ARR
WHOA!

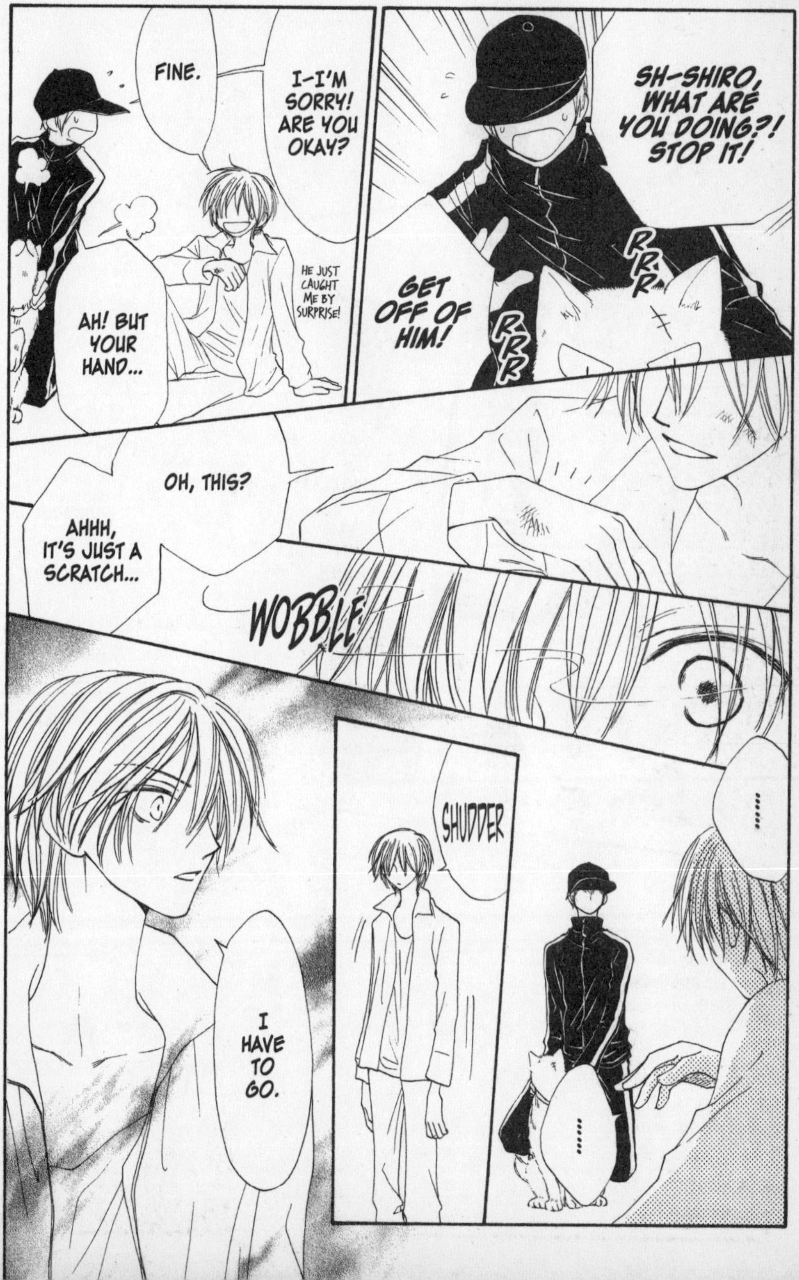
SH-SHIRO, WHAT ARE YOU DOING?! STOP IT!
RRR
GET OFF OF HIM!
RRR
I-I'M SORRY! ARE YOU OKAY?
FINE.
HE JUST CAUGHT ME BY SURPRISE!
AH! BUT YOUR HAND...
OH, THIS?
AHHH, IT'S JUST A SCRATCH...
WOBBLE
......
SHUDDER
......
I HAVE TO GO.

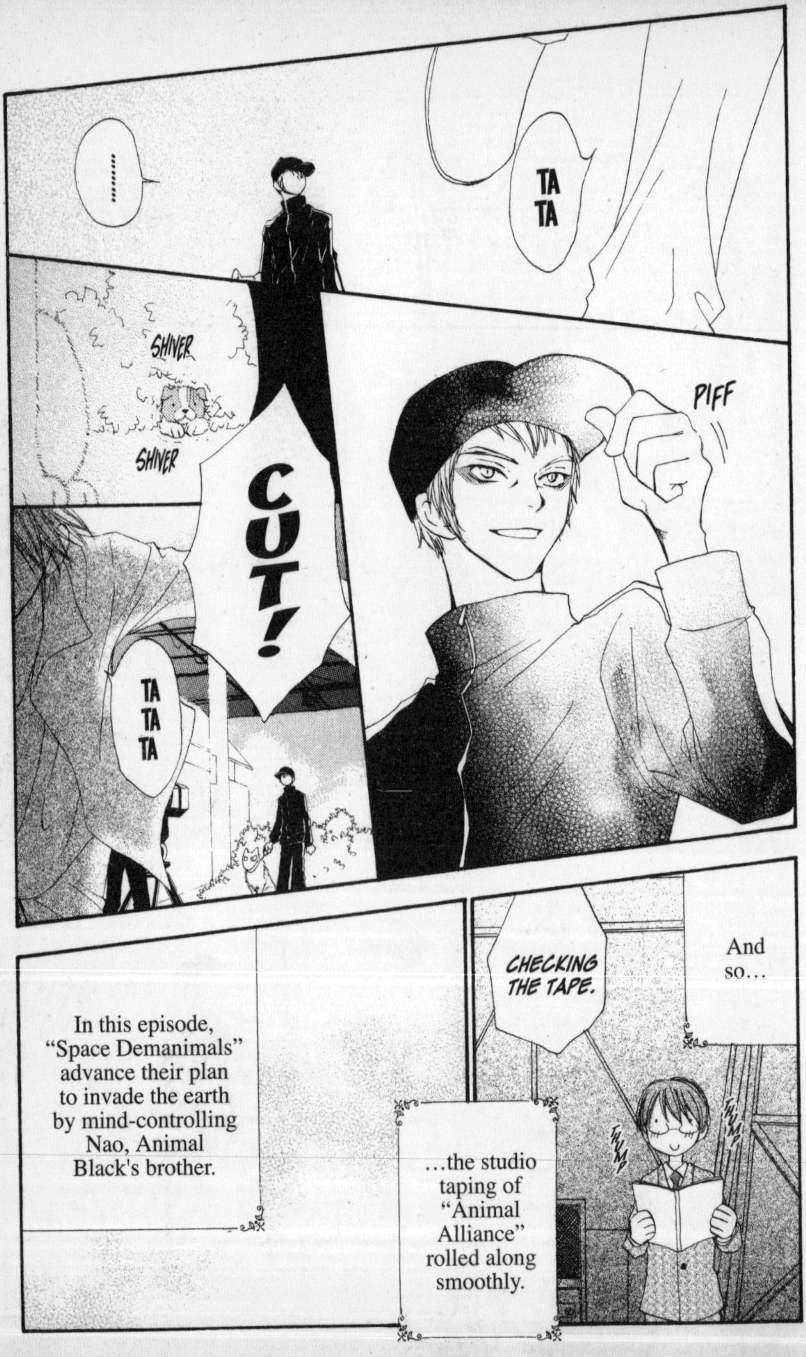
TA TA
......
PIFF
CUT!
SHIVER
SHIVER
TA TA TA
And so…
CHECKING THE TAPE.
…the studio taping of "Animal Alliance" rolled along smoothly.
THUMP
THUMP
In this episode, "Space Demanimals" advance their plan to invade the earth by mind-controlling Nao, Animal Black's brother.

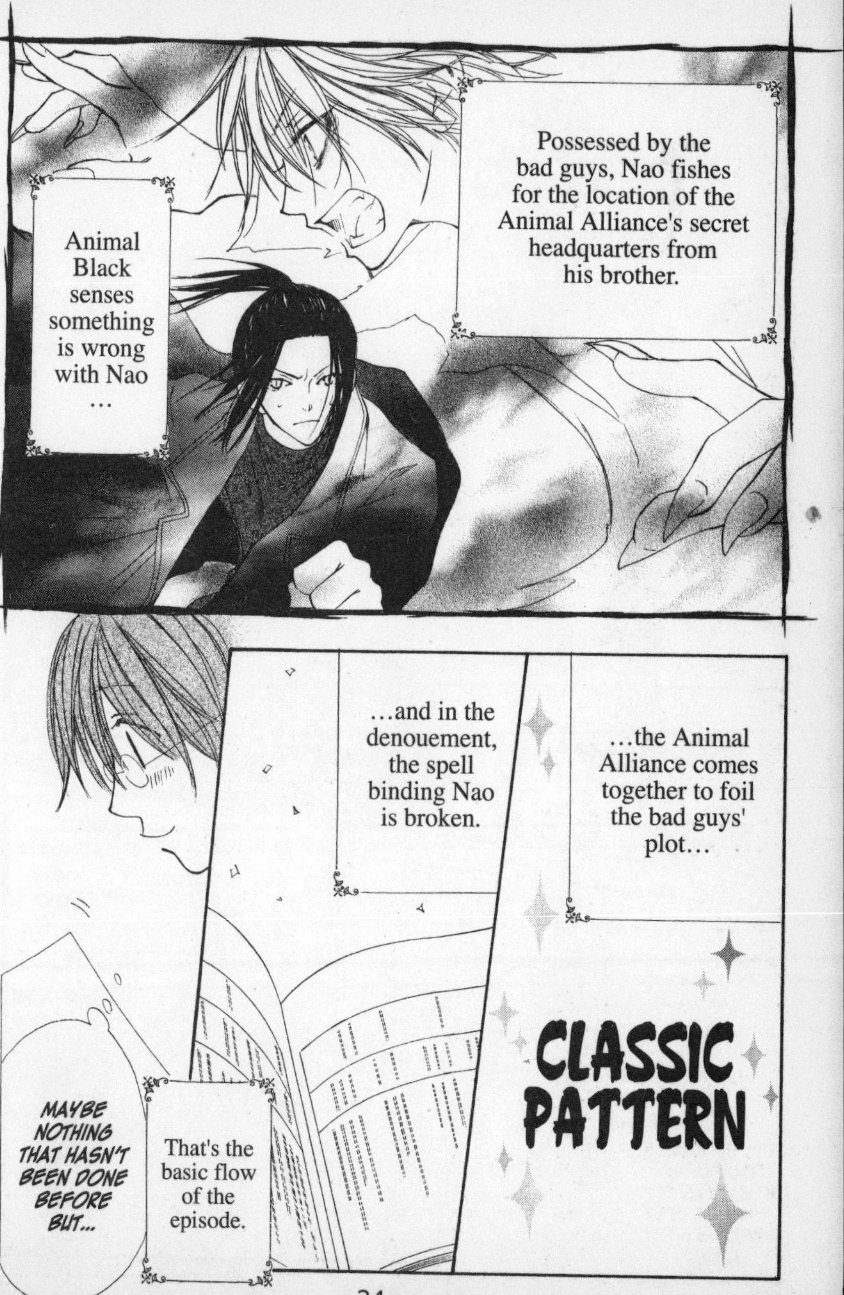
Possessed by the bad guys, Nao fishes for the location of the Animal Alliance's secret headquarters from his brother.
Animal Black senses something is wrong with Nao ...
...the Animal Alliance comes together to foil the bad guys' plot...
CLASSIC PATTERN
...and in the denouement, the spell binding Nao is broken.
That's the basic flow of the episode.
MAYBE NOTHING THAT HASN'T BEEN DONE BEFORE BUT...

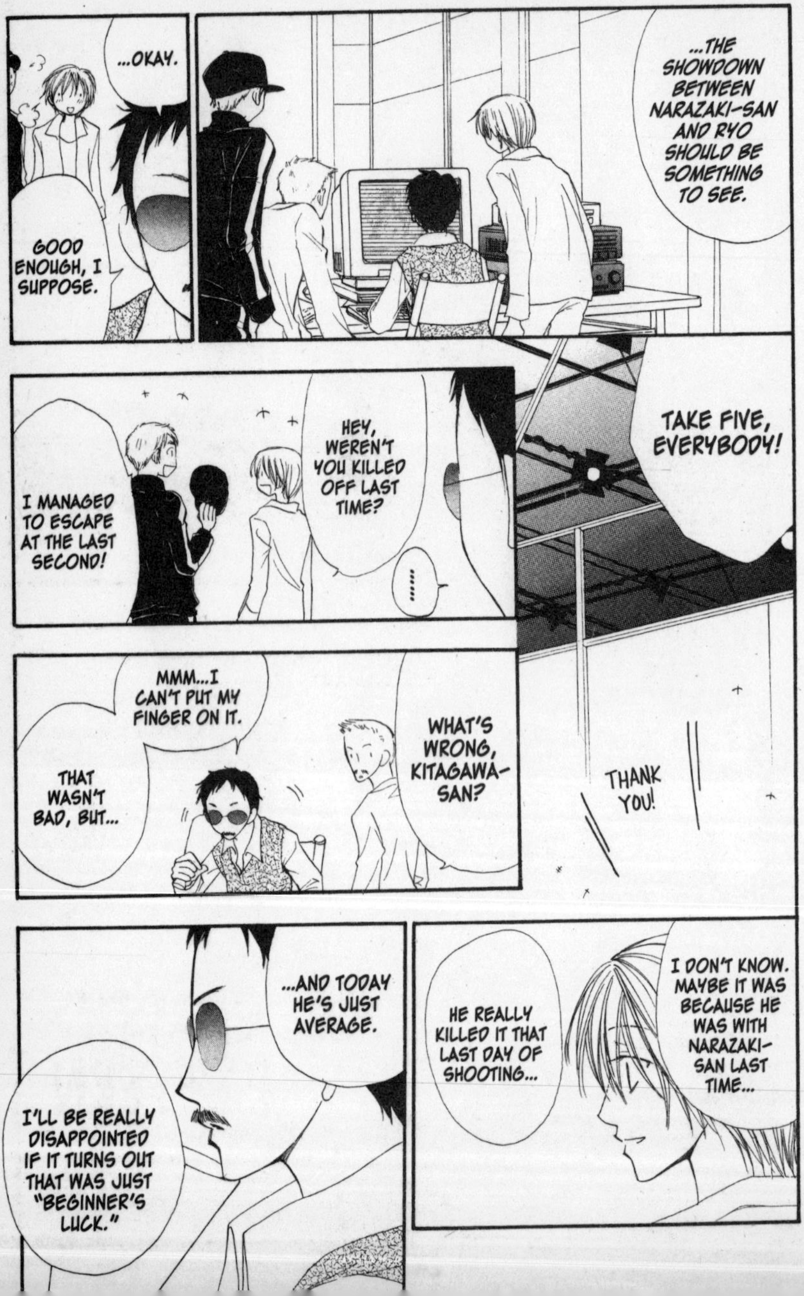
...THE SHOWDOWN BETWEEN NARAZAKI-SAN AND RYO SHOULD BE SOMETHING TO SEE.
...OKAY.
GOOD ENOUGH, I SUPPOSE.
TAKE FIVE, EVERYBODY!
THANK YOU!
HEY, WEREN'T YOU KILLED OFF LAST TIME?
......
I MANAGED TO ESCAPE AT THE LAST SECOND!
WHAT'S WRONG, KITAGAWA-SAN?
MMM...I CAN'T PUT MY FINGER ON IT.
THAT WASN'T BAD, BUT...
HE REALLY KILLED IT THAT LAST DAY OF SHOOTING...
I DON'T KNOW. MAYBE IT WAS BECAUSE HE WAS WITH NARAZAKI-SAN LAST TIME...
...AND TODAY HE'S JUST AVERAGE.
I'LL BE REALLY DISAPPOINTED IF IT TURNS OUT THAT WAS JUST "BEGINNER'S LUCK."

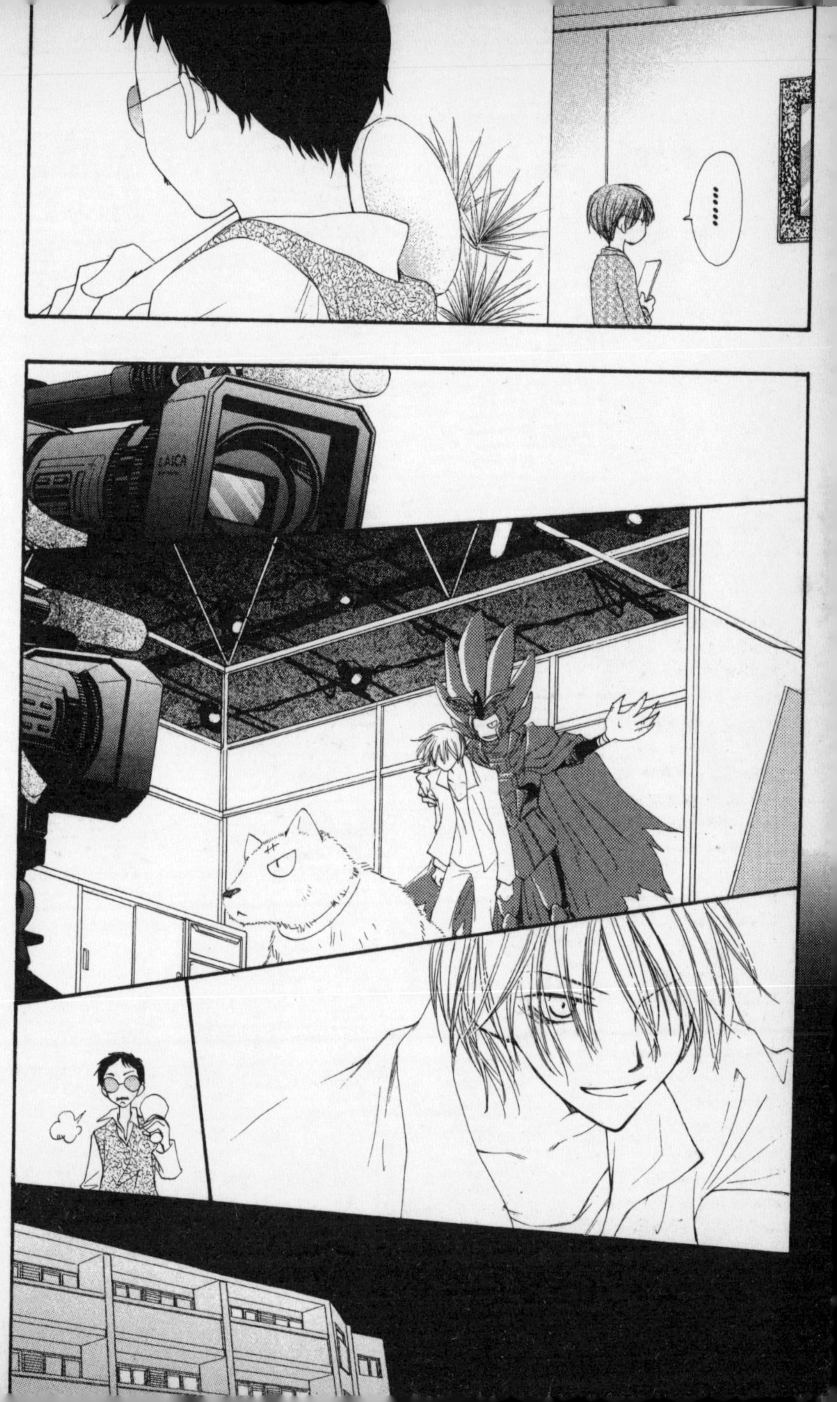
......
LAICA

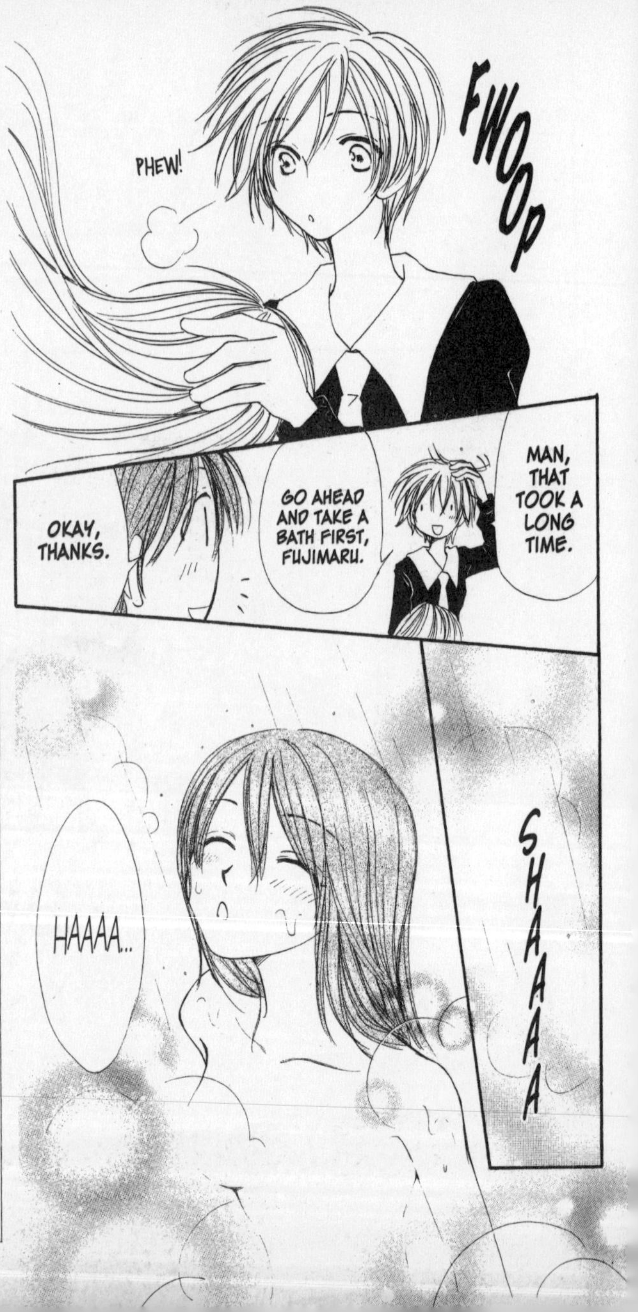
FWOOP
PHEW!
MAN, THAT TOOK A LONG TIME.
GO AHEAD AND TAKE A BATH FIRST, FUJIMARU.
OKAY, THANKS.
SHAAAAA
HAAAA...

1/4 Sakura Mail

Part 2

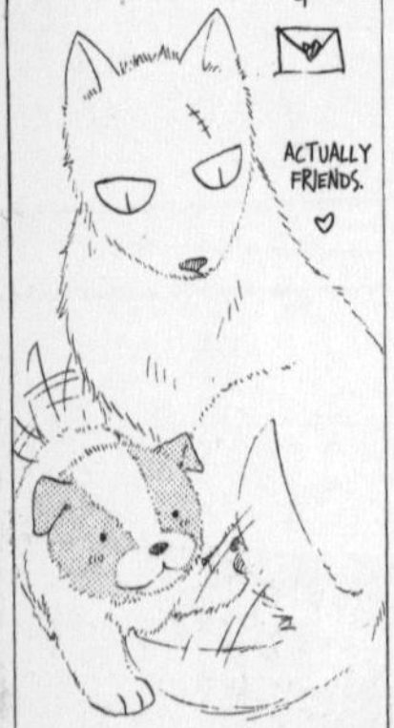
ACTUALLY FRIENDS.

(Continued)
It was my first attempt to "colorize" him, so I was extremely nervous about it. Now, I wish I hadn't colored him so plainly. Hmmm...I'm sorry, Nara-san! I've only colored two other characters outside of the three main protagonists, and they're Shacho and the back of Fukatsu-san's head. (Although I think most readers didn't notice Fukatsu-san...). If I get the opportunity, I'd love to challenge myself by drawing other characters in color as well!! Sigh...I really wanna get good at using color...

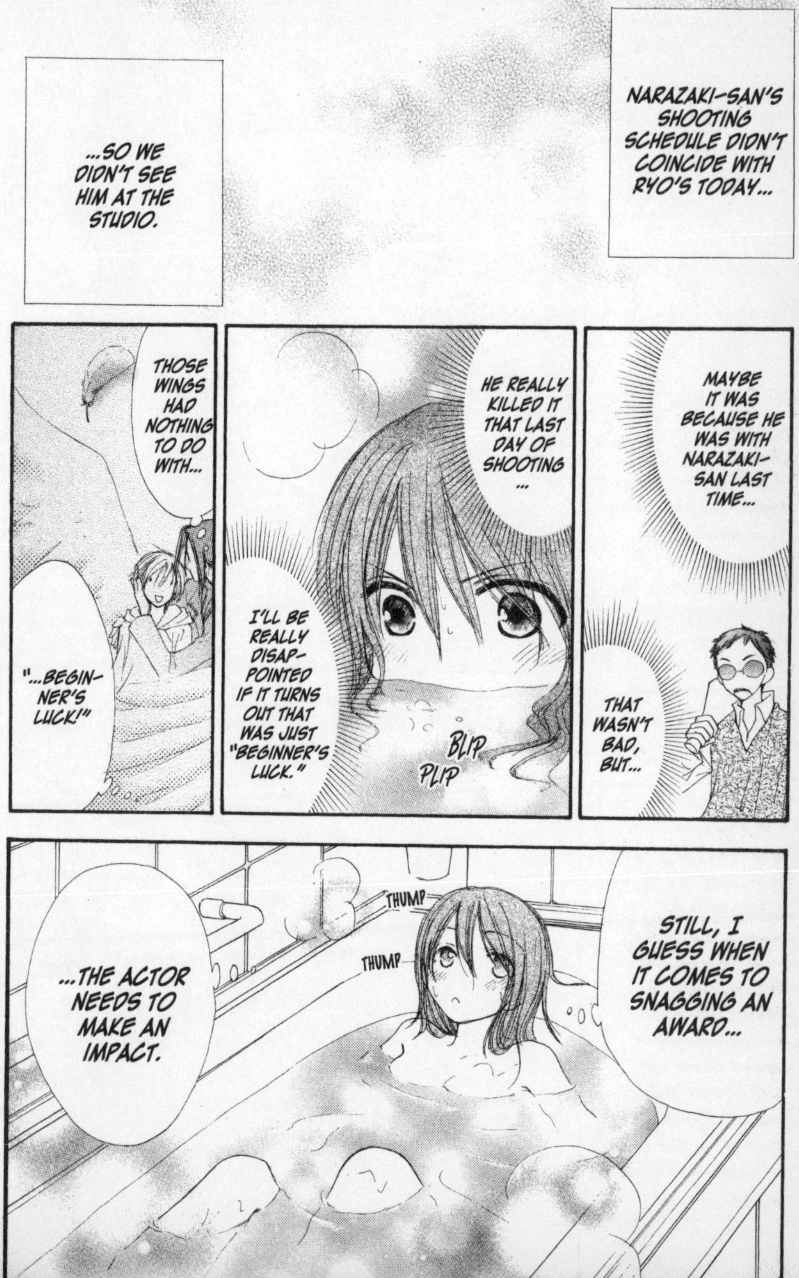
NARAZAKI-SAN'S SHOOTING SCHEDULE DIDN'T COINCIDE WITH RYO'S TODAY...
...SO WE DIDN'T SEE HIM AT THE STUDIO.
MAYBE IT WAS BECAUSE HE WAS WITH NARAZAKI-SAN LAST TIME...
THAT WASN'T BAD, BUT...
HE REALLY KILLED IT THAT LAST DAY OF SHOOTING...
I'LL BE REALLY DISAP-POINTED IF IT TURNS OUT THAT WAS JUST "BEGINNER'S LUCK."
BLIP
PLIP
THOSE WINGS HAD NOTHING TO DO WITH...
"...BEGIN-NER'S LUCK!"
STILL, I GUESS WHEN IT COMES TO SNAGGING AN AWARD...
THUMP
THUMP
...THE ACTOR NEEDS TO MAKE AN IMPACT.

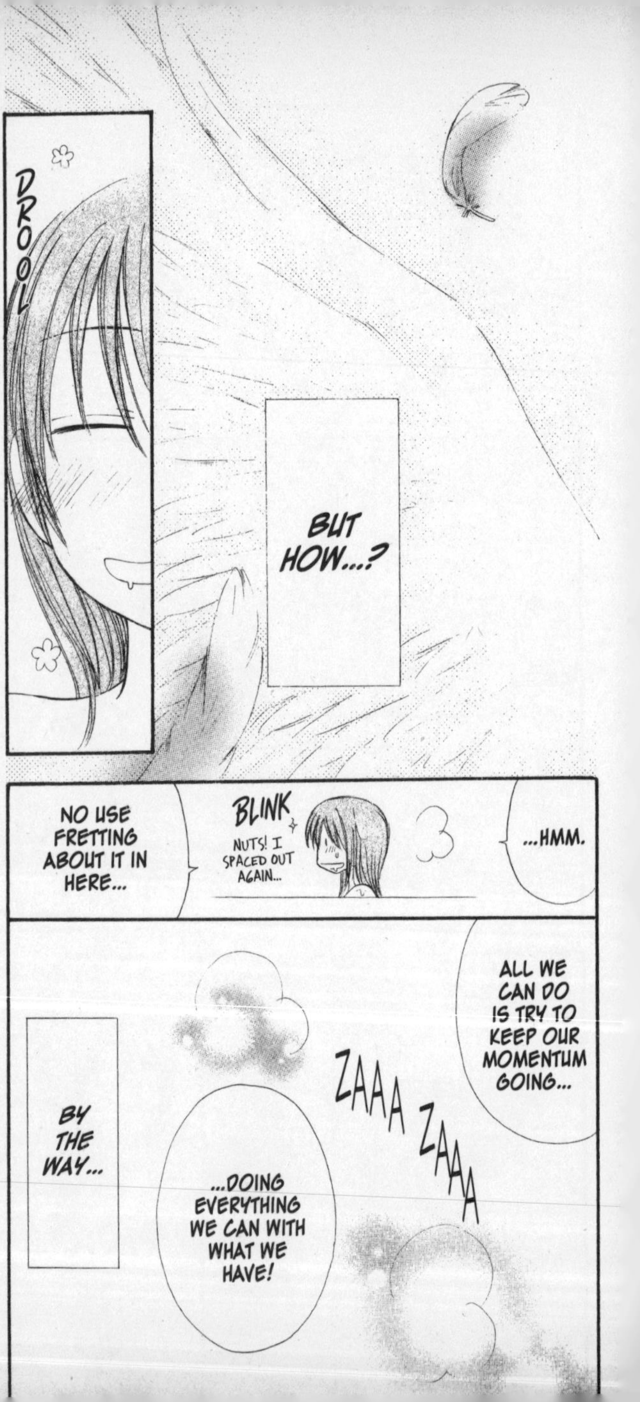
BUT HOW...?
DROOL
...HMM.
BLINK
NUTS! I SPACED OUT AGAIN...
NO USE FRETTING ABOUT IT IN HERE...
ALL WE CAN DO IS TRY TO KEEP OUR MOMENTUM GOING...
ZAAA ZAAAA
...DOING EVERYTHING WE CAN WITH WHAT WE HAVE!
BY THE WAY...

1/4 Sakura Mail

part 3

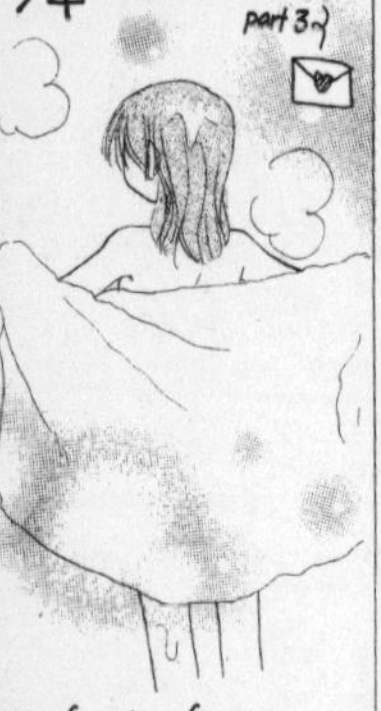

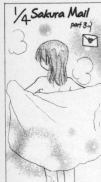

As for the first episode, let's talk about the bathroom scene. Two pages back is the panel with Yuka-chan in the shower, going, "Haaa," which I drew in a sexy style in the breakdowns. I nervously asked my editor if the panel was okay and when he looked at it, he proclaimed, "No problem!"...In fact, it was **Ryo's** shower scene that got me in trouble, since I drew his whole body (backside anyway!) in the breakdowns. in the end, it didn't matter, since I'd always planned to cover his tush with a well-placed balloon. Actually, getting that kind of reaction from my editor has become a good memory.

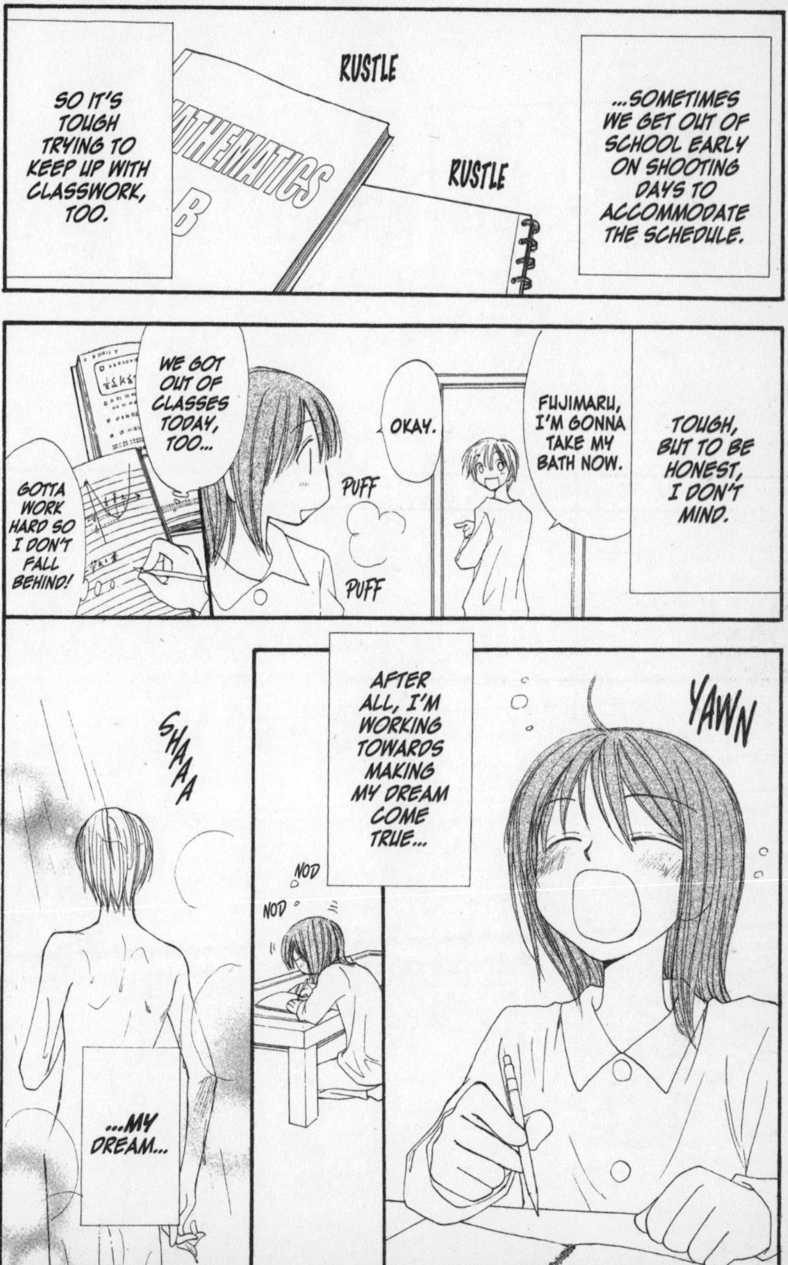
...SOMETIMES WE GET OUT OF SCHOOL EARLY ON SHOOTING DAYS TO ACCOMMODATE THE SCHEDULE.
RUSTLE
RUSTLE
SO IT'S TOUGH TRYING TO KEEP UP WITH CLASSWORK, TOO.
TOUGH, BUT TO BE HONEST, I DON'T MIND.
FUJIMARU, I'M GONNA TAKE MY BATH NOW.
OKAY.
PUFF
PUFF
WE GOT OUT OF CLASSES TODAY, TOO...
GOTTA WORK HARD SO I DON'T FALL BEHIND!
YAWN
AFTER ALL, I'M WORKING TOWARDS MAKING MY DREAM COME TRUE...
NOD
NOD
SHAAA
...MY DREAM...

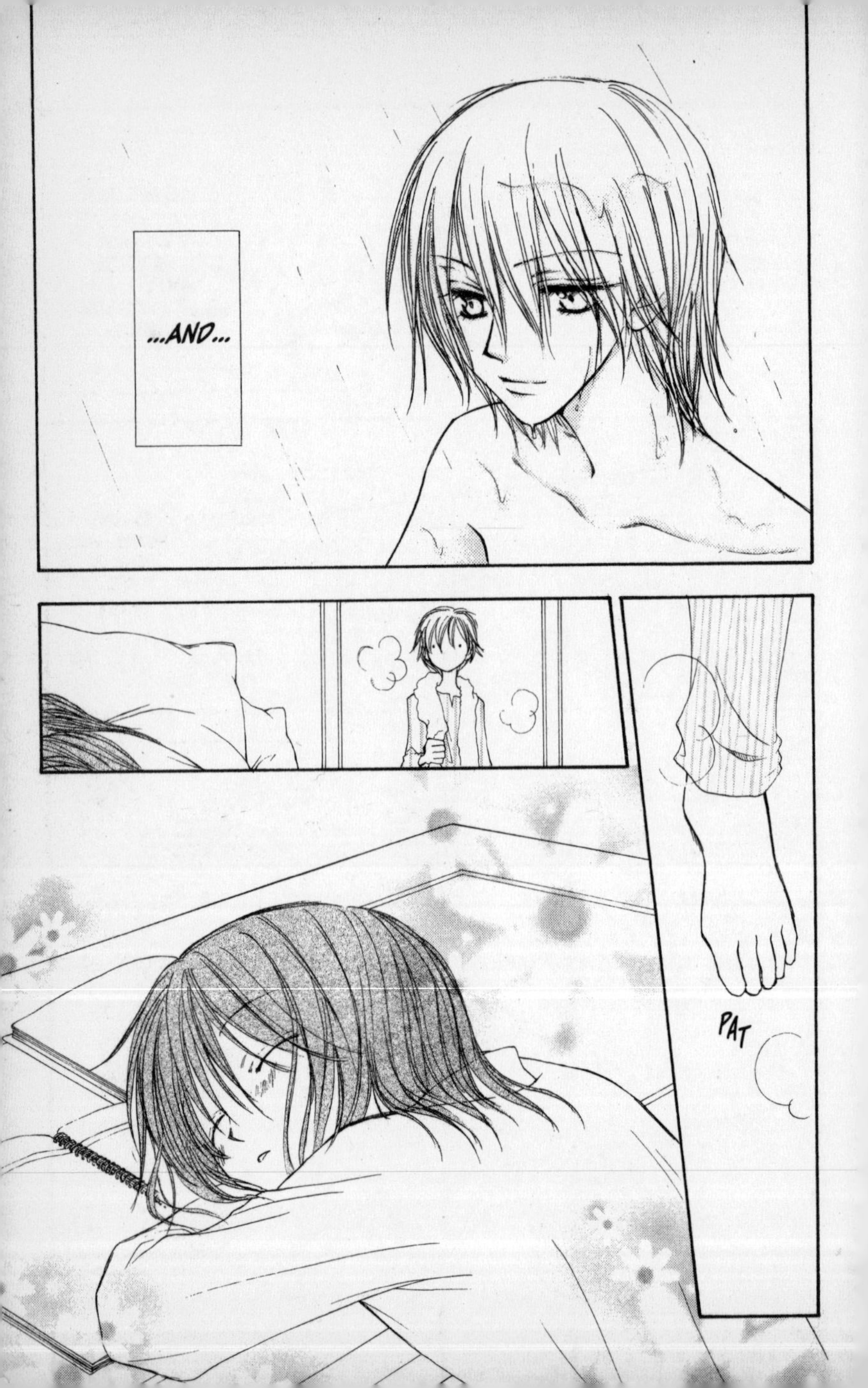
...AND...
PAT

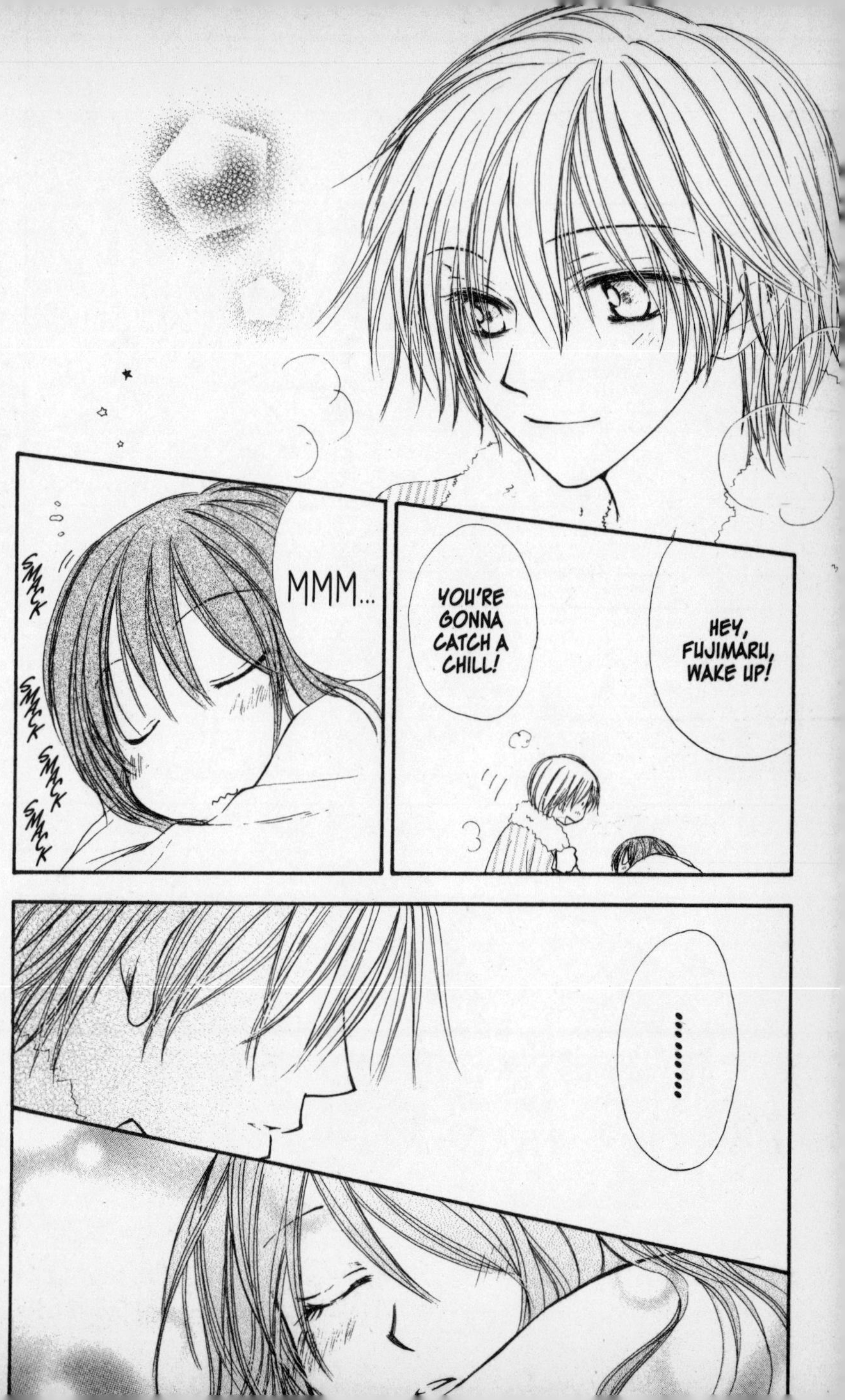
HEY, FUJIMARU, WAKE UP!
YOU'RE GONNA CATCH A CHILL!
MMM...
SMACK
SMACK
SMACK
SMACK
....

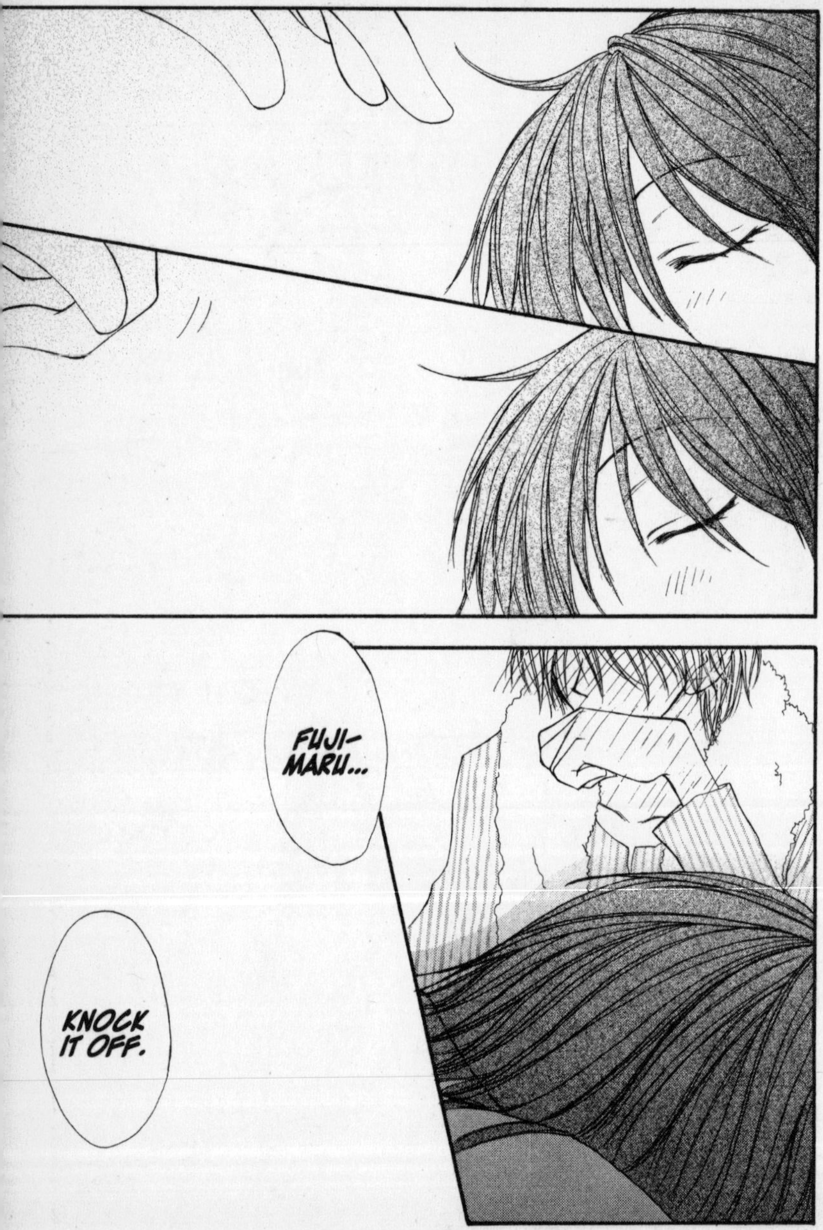
FUJI-MARU...
KNOCK IT OFF.

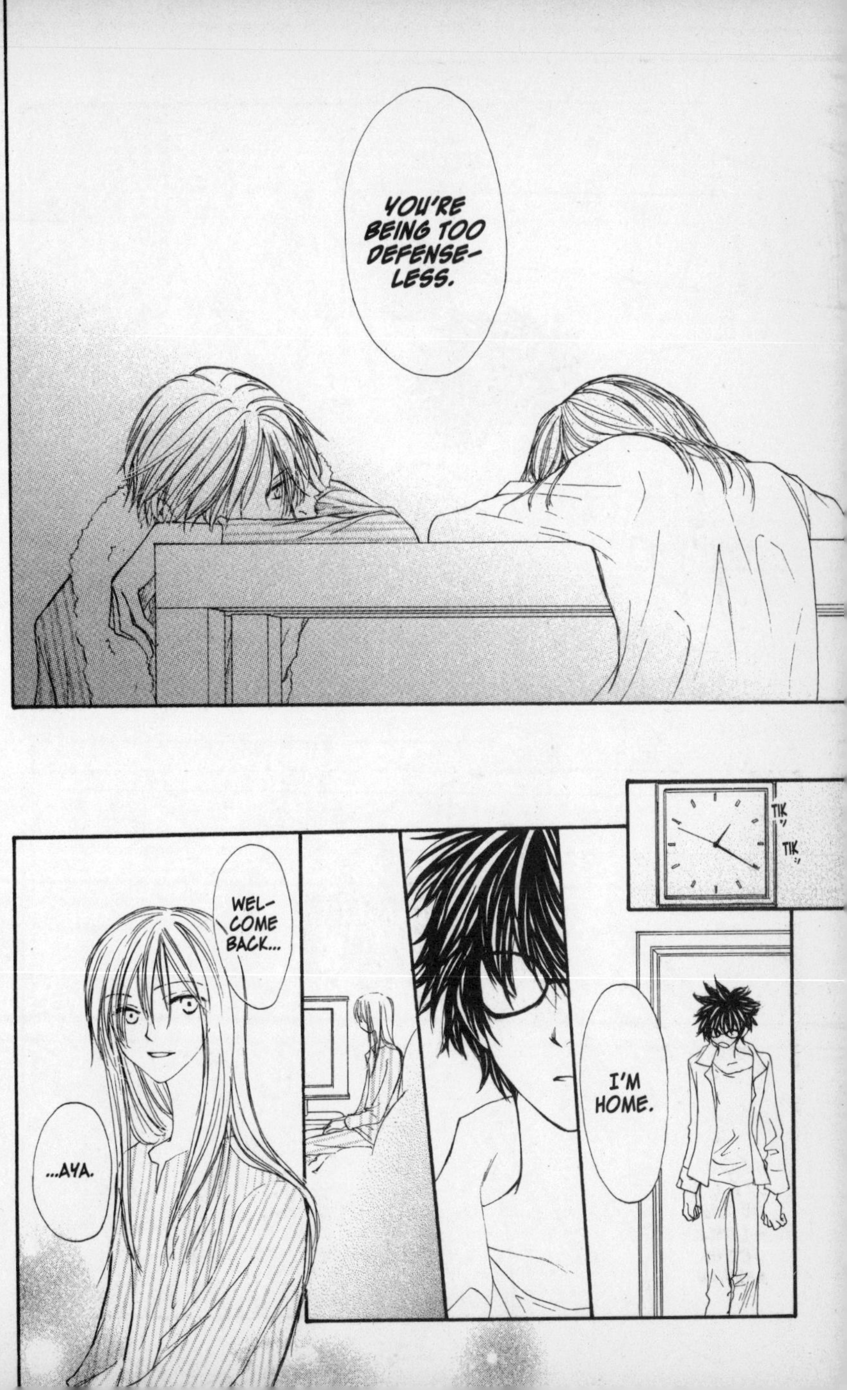
YOU'RE BEING TOO DEFENSE-LESS.
TIK
TIK
I'M HOME.
WEL-COME BACK...
...AYA.

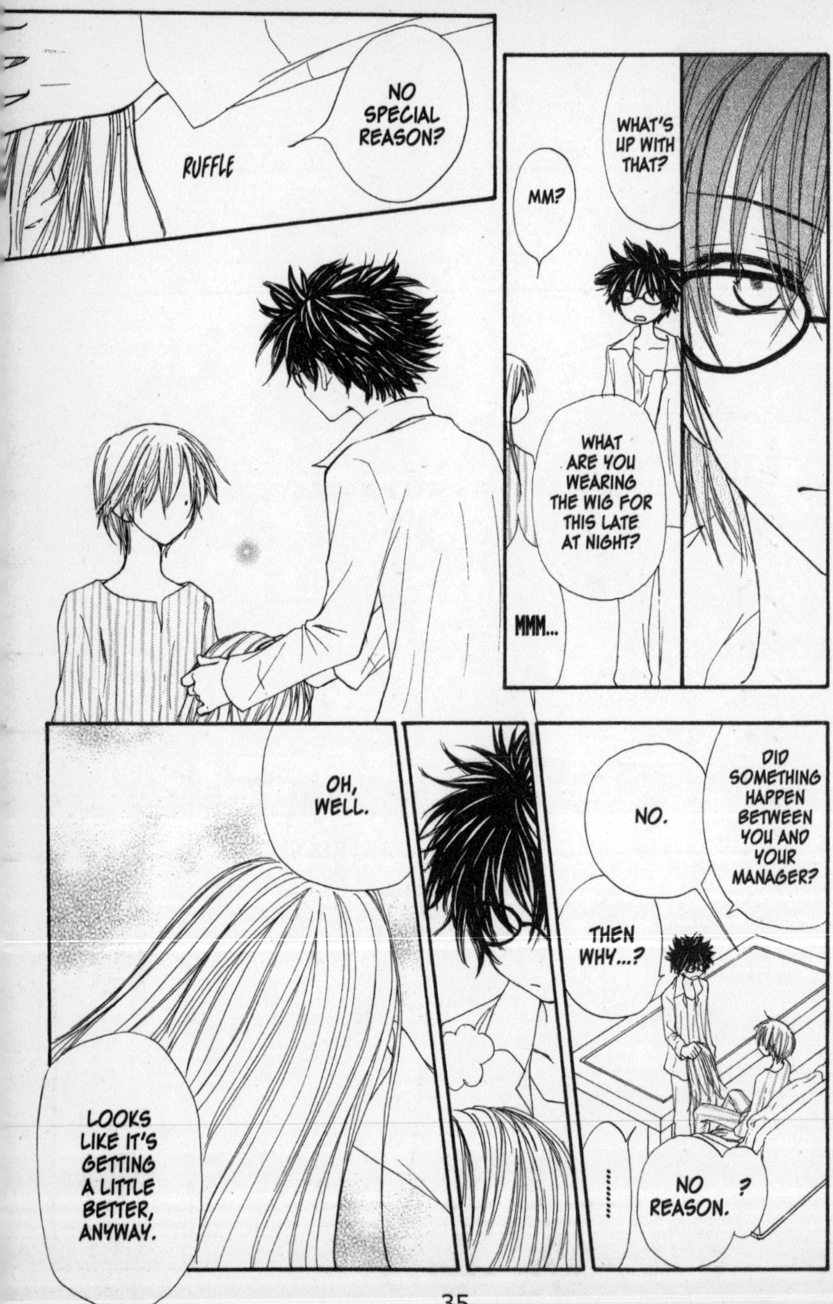
WHAT'S UP WITH THAT?
MM?
WHAT ARE YOU WEARING THE WIG FOR THIS LATE AT NIGHT?
MMM...
NO SPECIAL REASON?
RUFFLE
DID SOMETHING HAPPEN BETWEEN YOU AND YOUR MANAGER?
NO.
THEN WHY...?
?
NO REASON.
......
OH, WELL.
LOOKS LIKE IT'S GETTING A LITTLE BETTER, ANYWAY.

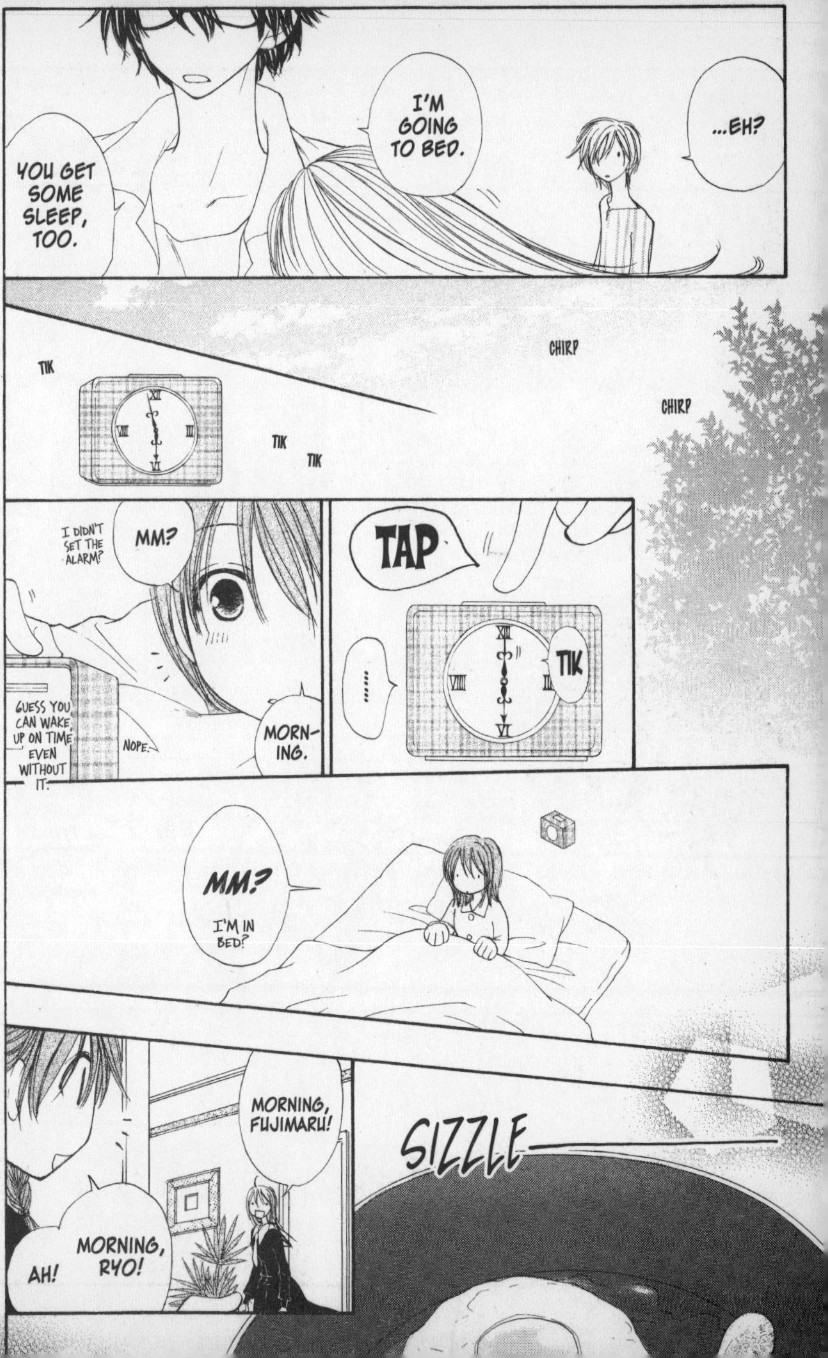
...EH?
I'M GOING TO BED.
YOU GET SOME SLEEP, TOO.
CHIRP
CHIRP
TIK
TIK
TIK
TAP
TIK
......
MM?
I DIDN'T SET THE ALARM?
MORN-ING.
NOPE.
GUESS YOU CAN WAKE UP ON TIME EVEN WITHOUT IT.
MM?
I'M IN BED?
SIZZLE
MORNING, FUJIMARU!
MORNING, RYO!
AH!

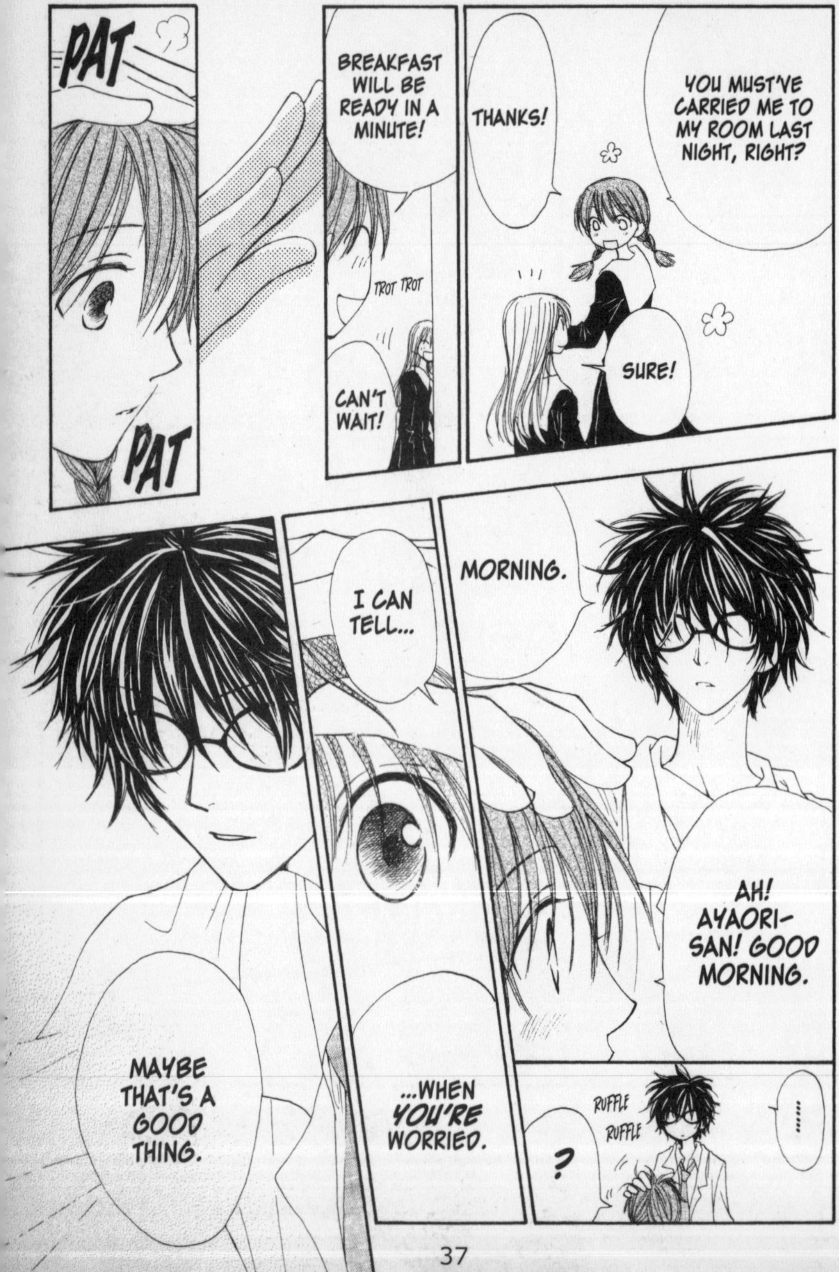

YOU MUST'VE CARRIED ME TO MY ROOM LAST NIGHT, RIGHT?
THANKS!
SURE!
BREAKFAST WILL BE READY IN A MINUTE!
TROT TROT
CAN'T WAIT!
PAT
PAT
MORNING.
AH! AYAORI-SAN! GOOD MORNING.
......
RUFFLE
RUFFLE
?
I CAN TELL...
...WHEN *YOU'RE* WORRIED.
MAYBE THAT'S A GOOD THING.

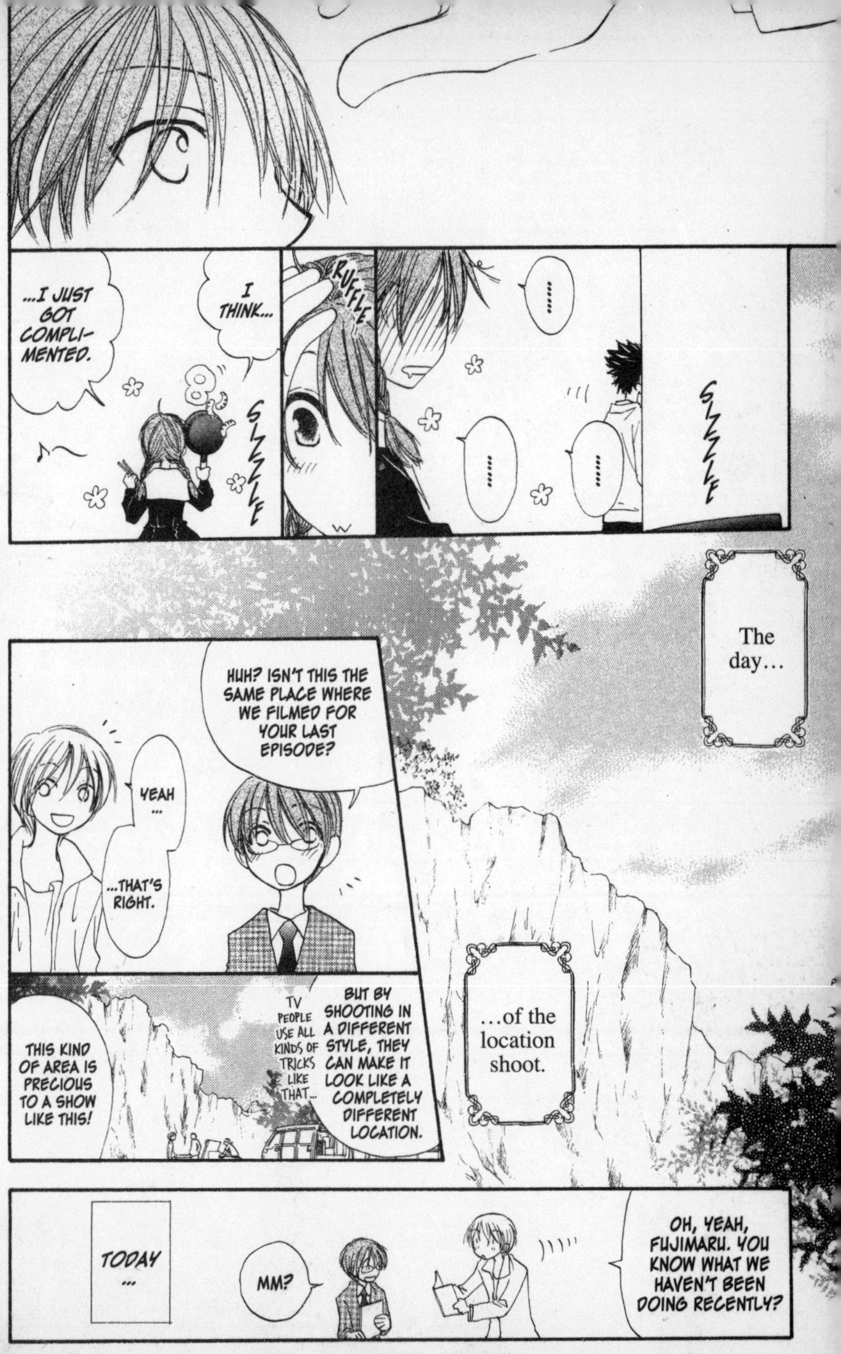
SIZZLE
......
......
......
RUFFLE
I THINK...
...I JUST GOT COMPLIMENTED.
SIZZLE
The day…
HUH? ISN'T THIS THE SAME PLACE WHERE WE FILMED FOR YOUR LAST EPISODE?
YEAH ...
...THAT'S RIGHT.
…of the location shoot.
BUT BY SHOOTING IN A DIFFERENT STYLE, THEY CAN MAKE IT LOOK LIKE A COMPLETELY DIFFERENT LOCATION.
TV PEOPLE USE ALL KINDS OF TRICKS LIKE THAT...
THIS KIND OF AREA IS PRECIOUS TO A SHOW LIKE THIS!
OH, YEAH, FUJIMARU. YOU KNOW WHAT WE HAVEN'T BEEN DOING RECENTLY?
MM?
TODAY ...

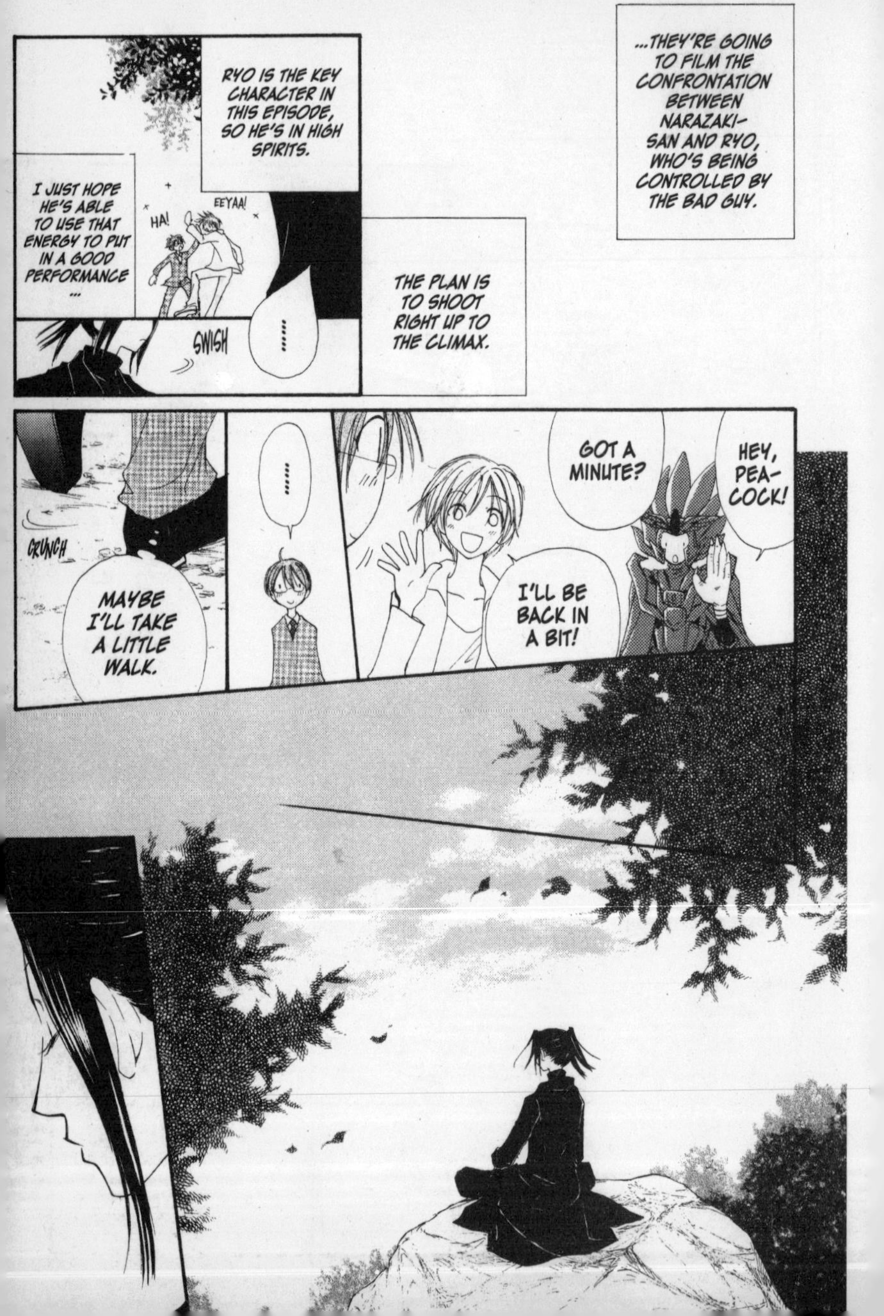
...THEY'RE GOING TO FILM THE CONFRONTATION BETWEEN NARAZAKI-SAN AND RYO, WHO'S BEING CONTROLLED BY THE BAD GUY.
THE PLAN IS TO SHOOT RIGHT UP TO THE CLIMAX.
RYO IS THE KEY CHARACTER IN THIS EPISODE, SO HE'S IN HIGH SPIRITS.
EEYAA!
HA!
I JUST HOPE HE'S ABLE TO USE THAT ENERGY TO PUT IN A GOOD PERFORMANCE ...
......
SWISH
HEY, PEA-COCK!
GOT A MINUTE?
I'LL BE BACK IN A BIT!
......
MAYBE I'LL TAKE A LITTLE WALK.
CRUNCH

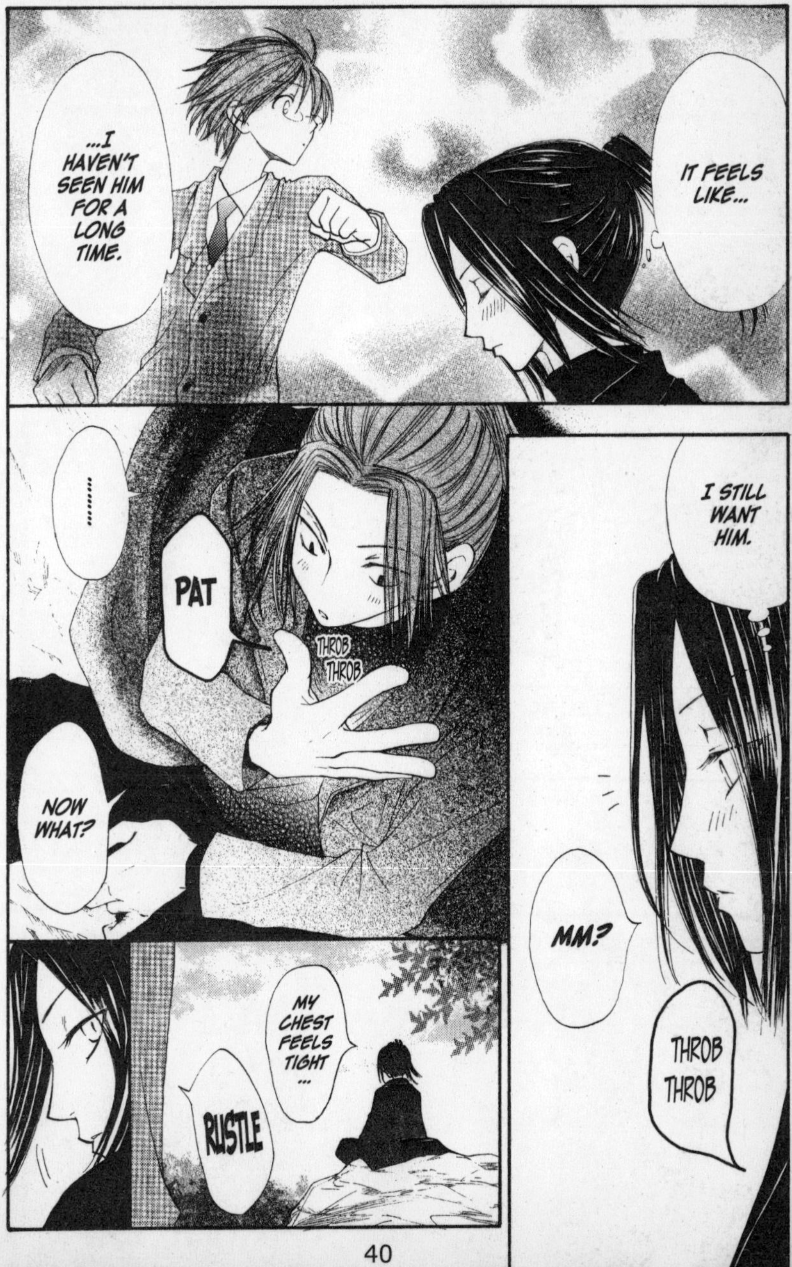
IT FEELS LIKE...
...I HAVEN'T SEEN HIM FOR A LONG TIME.
I STILL WANT HIM.
MM?
THROB THROB
......
PAT
THROB THROB
NOW WHAT?
MY CHEST FEELS TIGHT...
RUSTLE

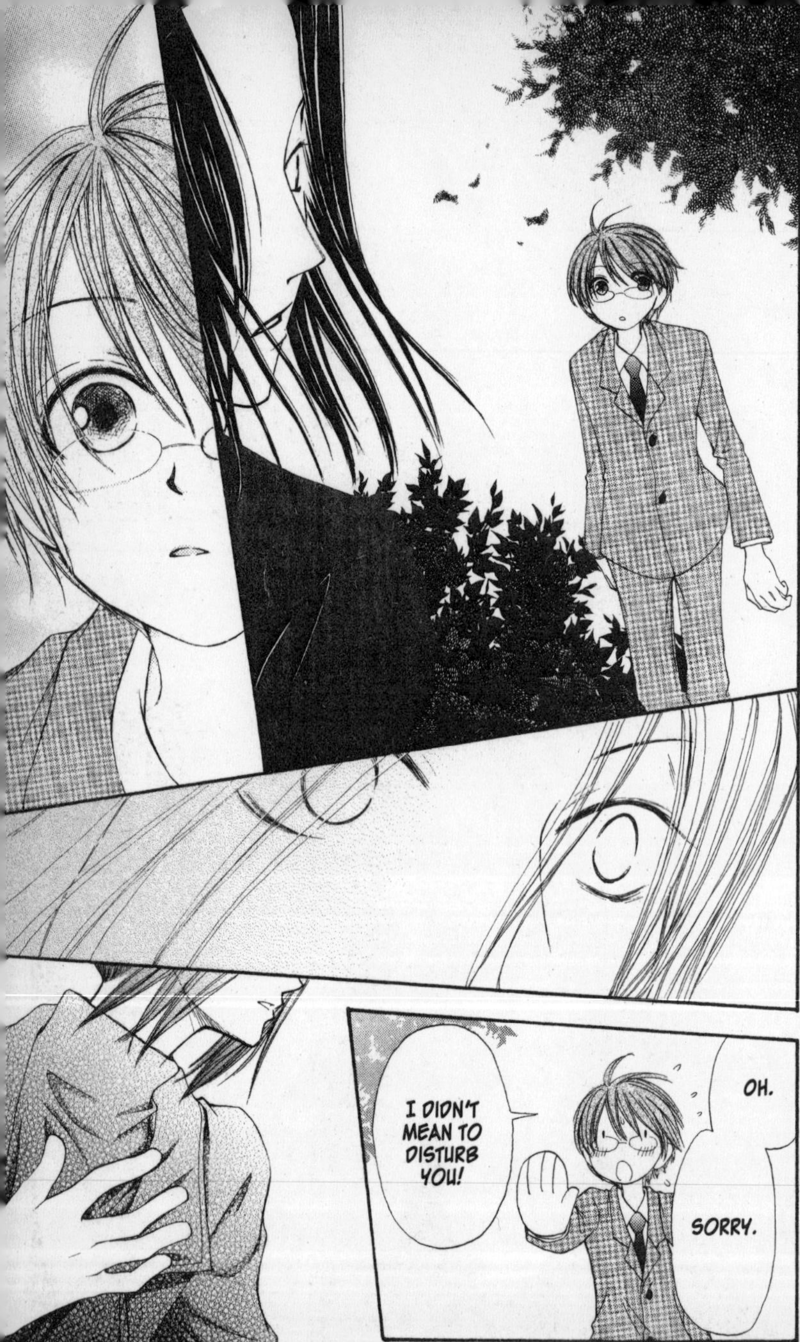
OH.
SORRY.
I DIDN'T MEAN TO DISTURB YOU!

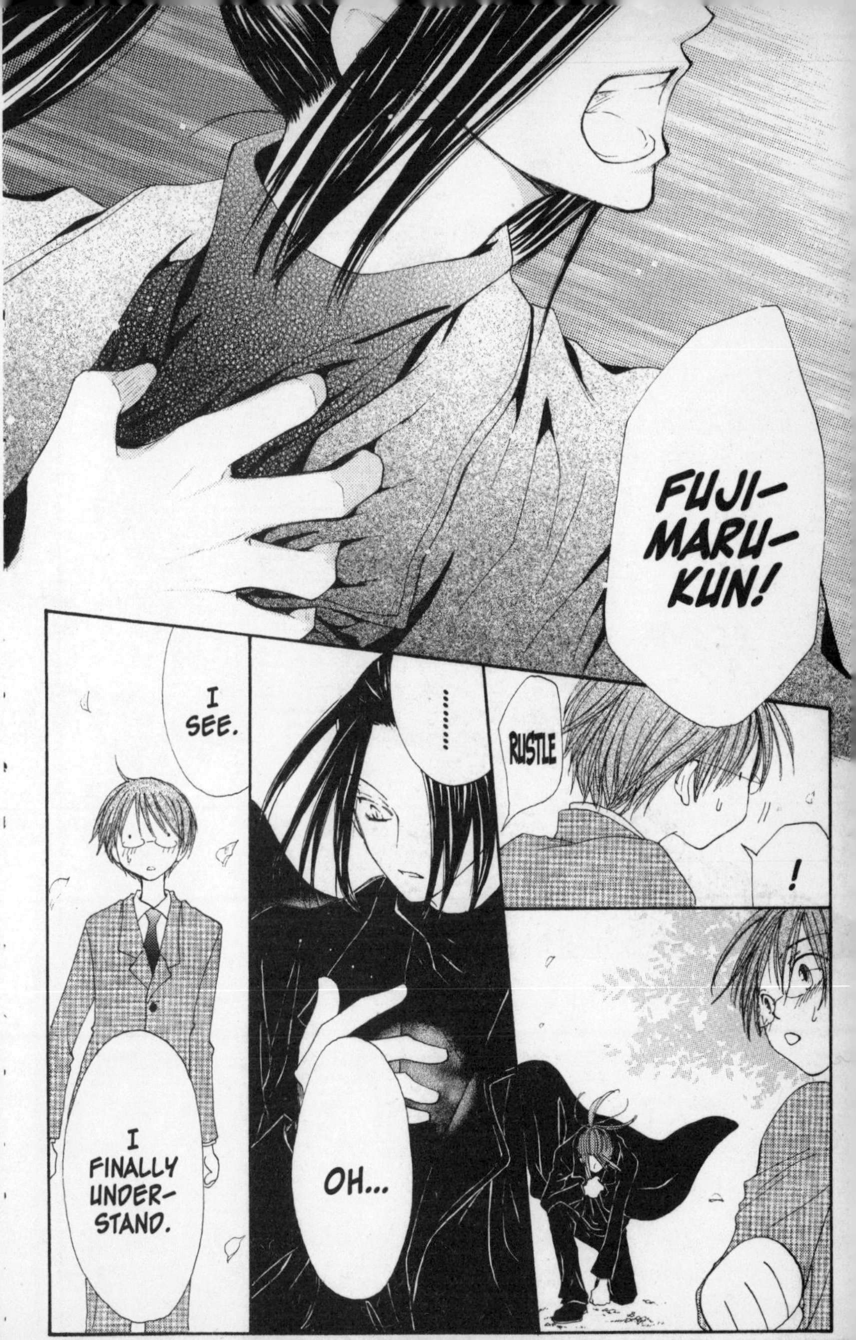
FUJI-MARU-KUN!
RUSTLE
!
......
OH...
I SEE.
I FINALLY UNDER-STAND.

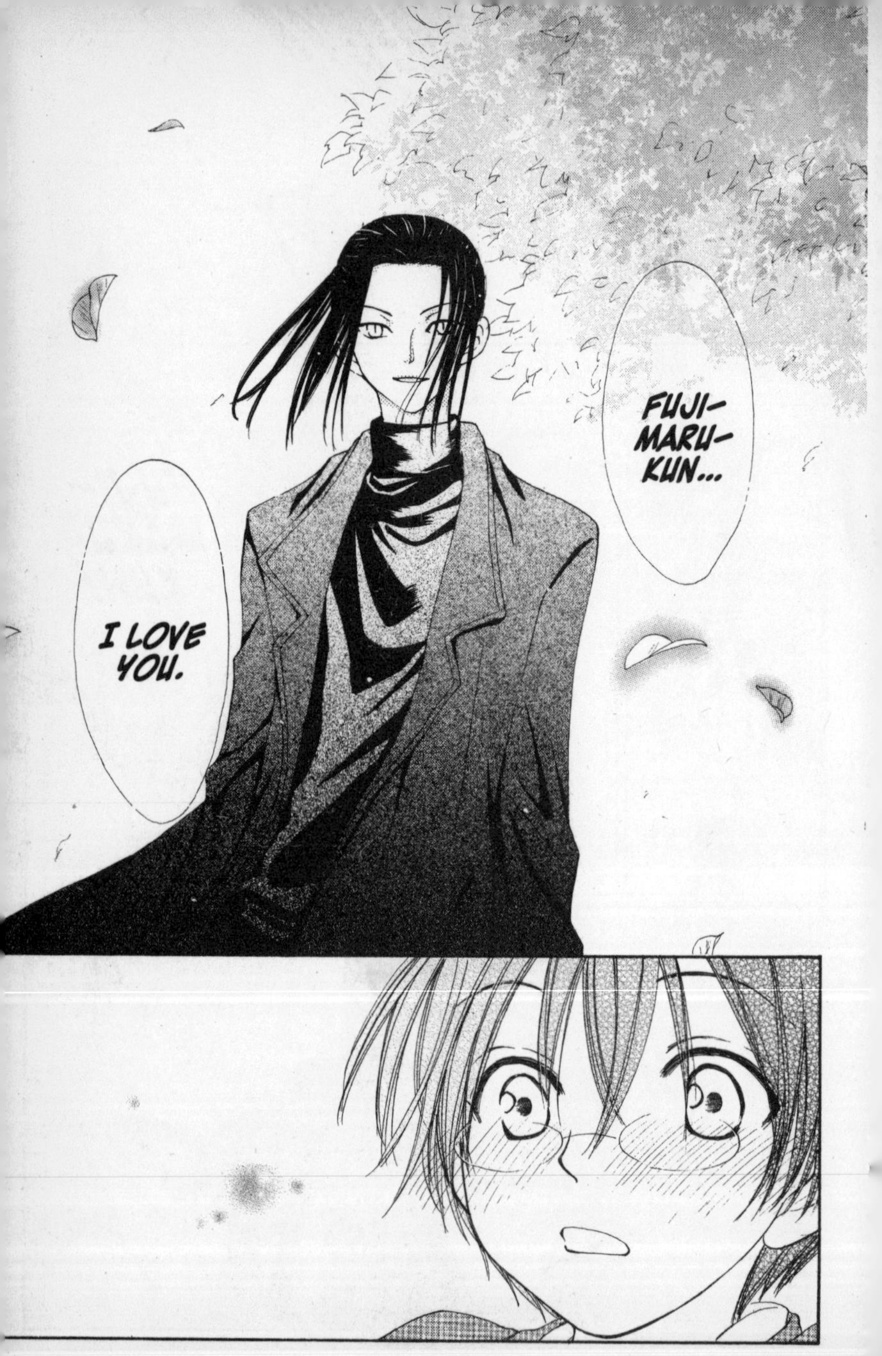
FUJI-MARU-KUN...
I LOVE YOU.

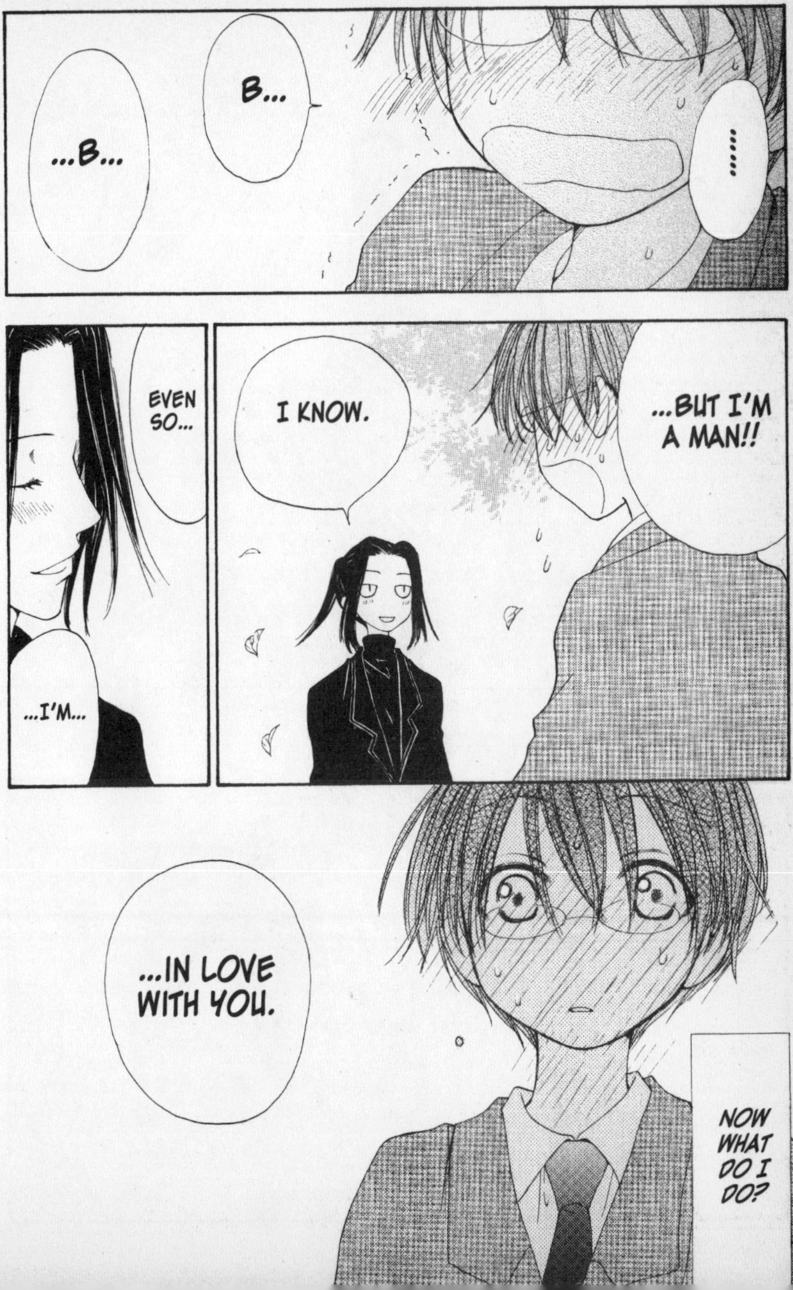
......
B...
...B...
...BUT I'M A MAN!!
I KNOW.
EVEN SO...
...I'M...
...IN LOVE WITH YOU.
NOW WHAT DO I DO?

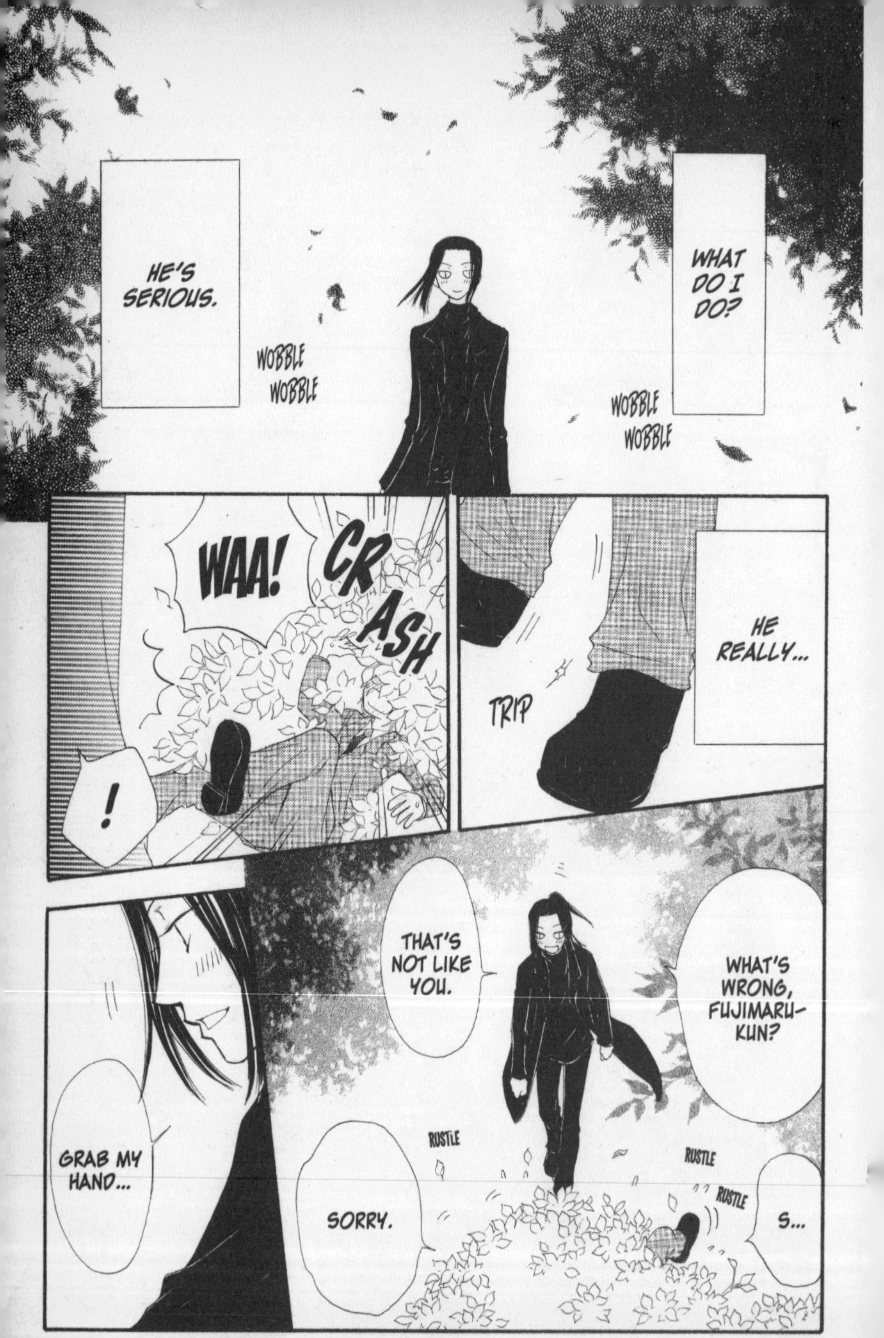
WHAT DO I DO?
WOBBLE WOBBLE
WOBBLE WOBBLE
HE'S SERIOUS.
HE REALLY...
TRIP
WAA!
CRASH
!
WHAT'S WRONG, FUJIMARU-KUN?
THAT'S NOT LIKE YOU.
RUSTLE
RUSTLE
RUSTLE
S...
SORRY.
GRAB MY HAND...

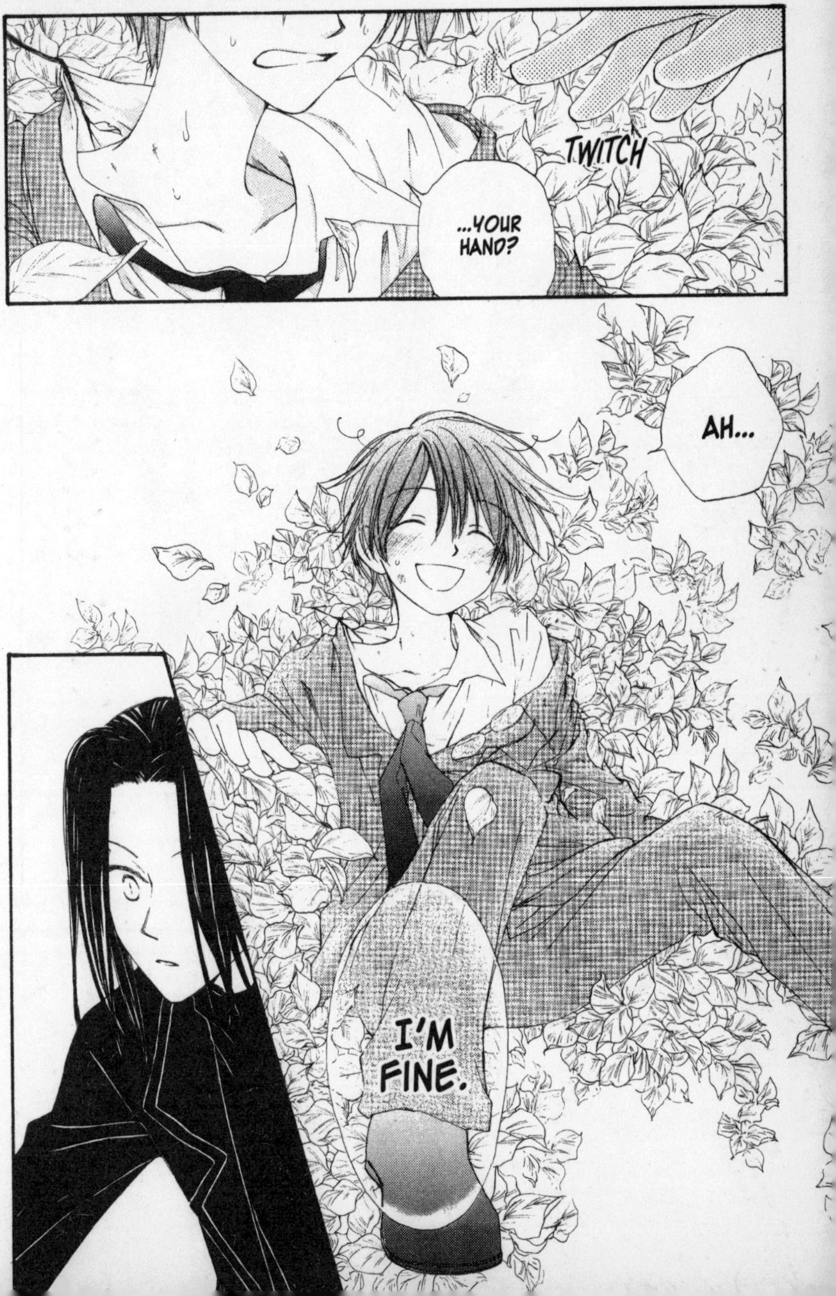
TWITCH
...YOUR HAND?
AH...
I'M FINE.

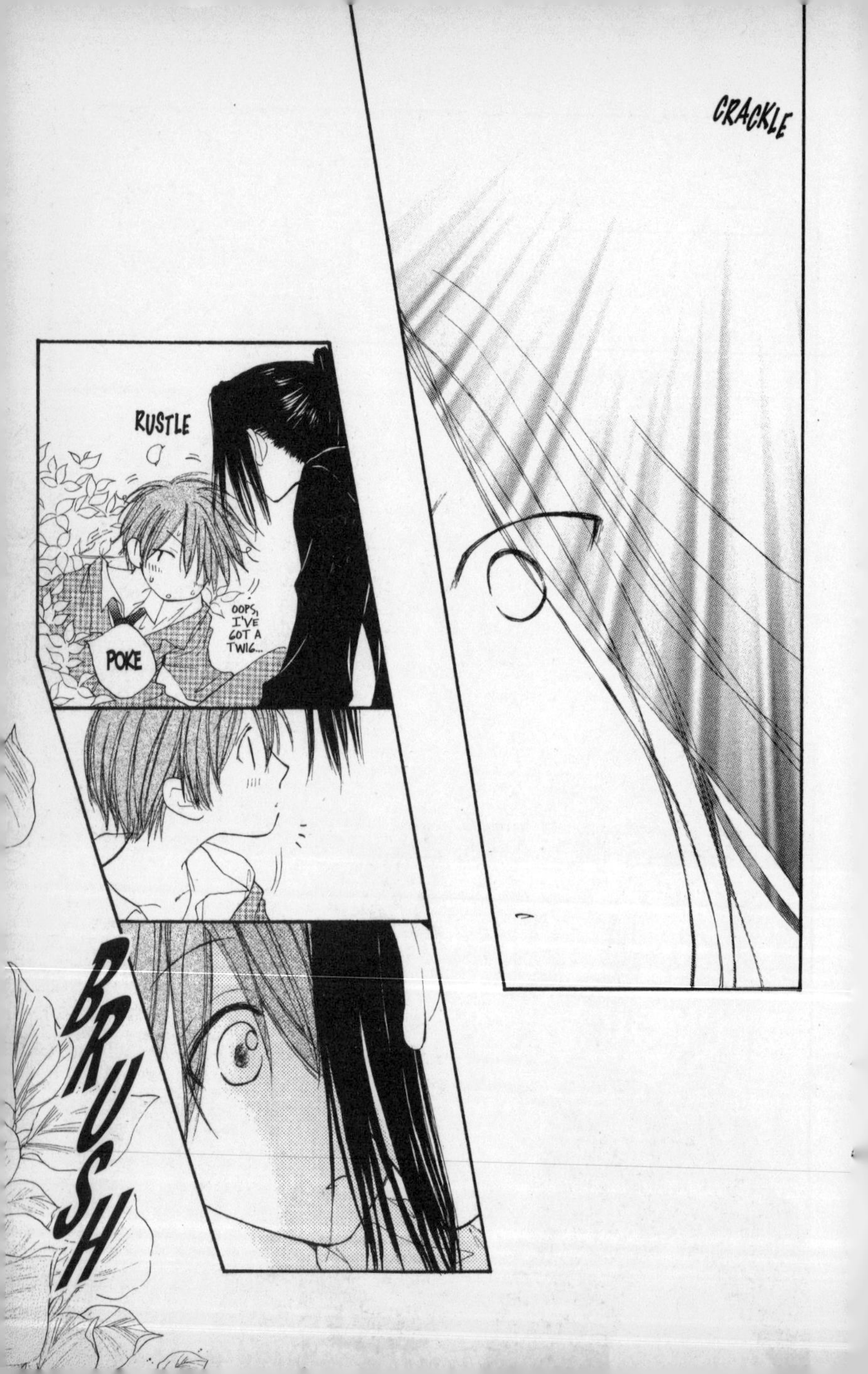
CRACKLE
RUSTLE
OOPS, I'VE GOT A TWIG...
POKE
BRUSH

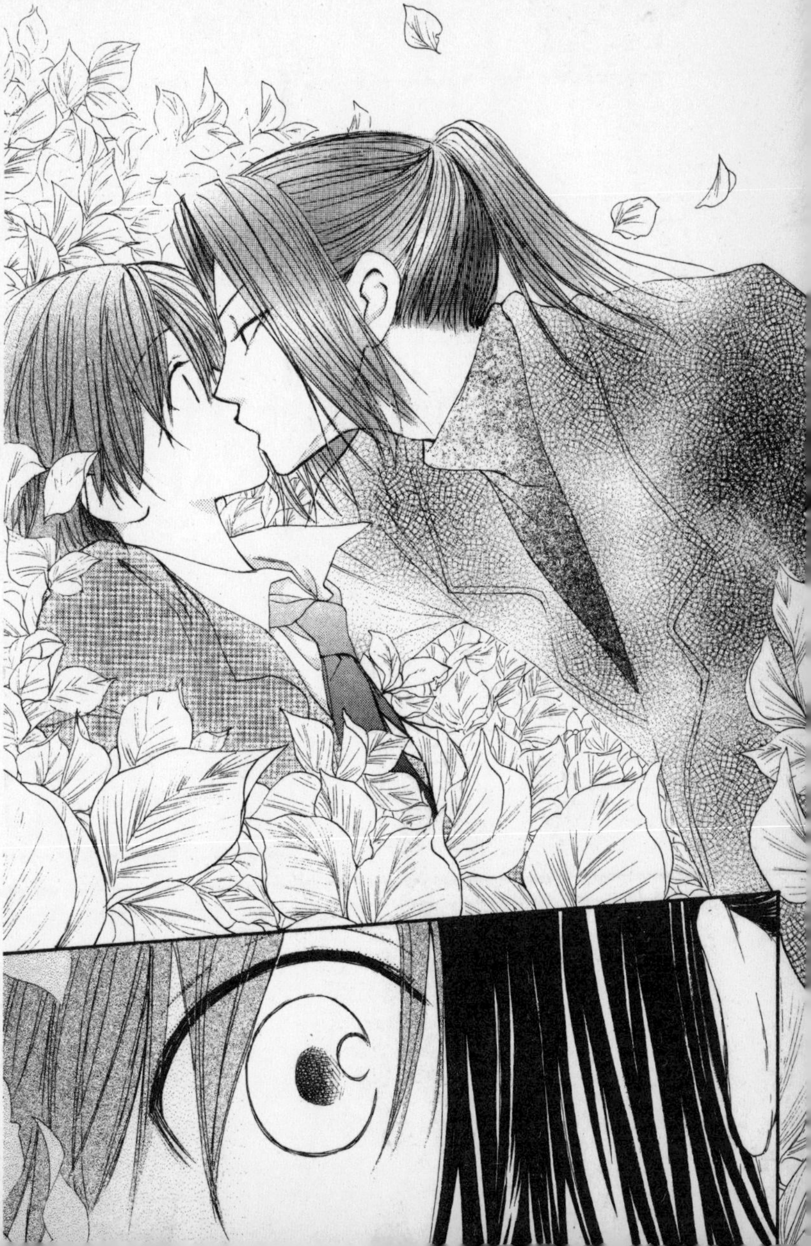

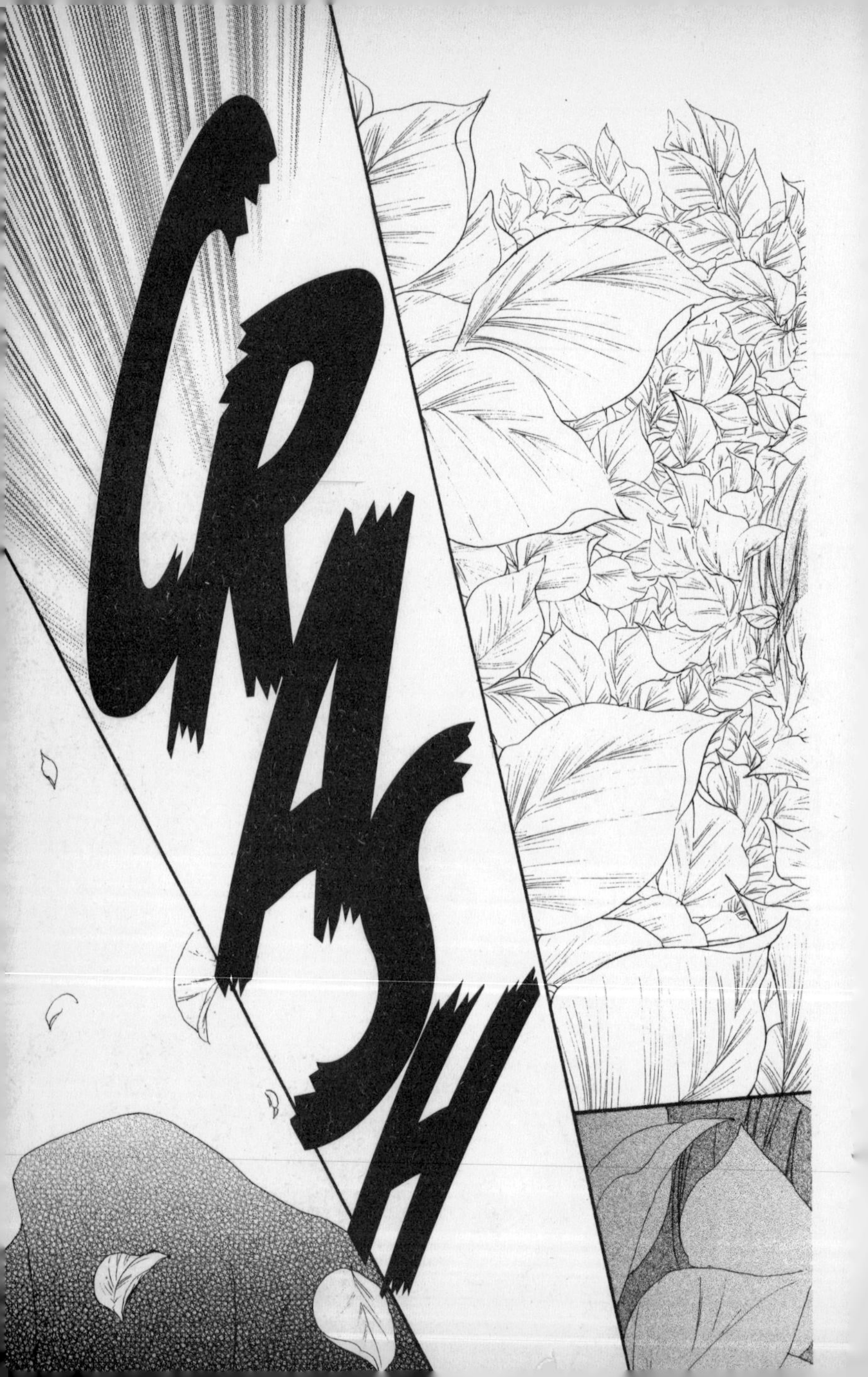
CRASH

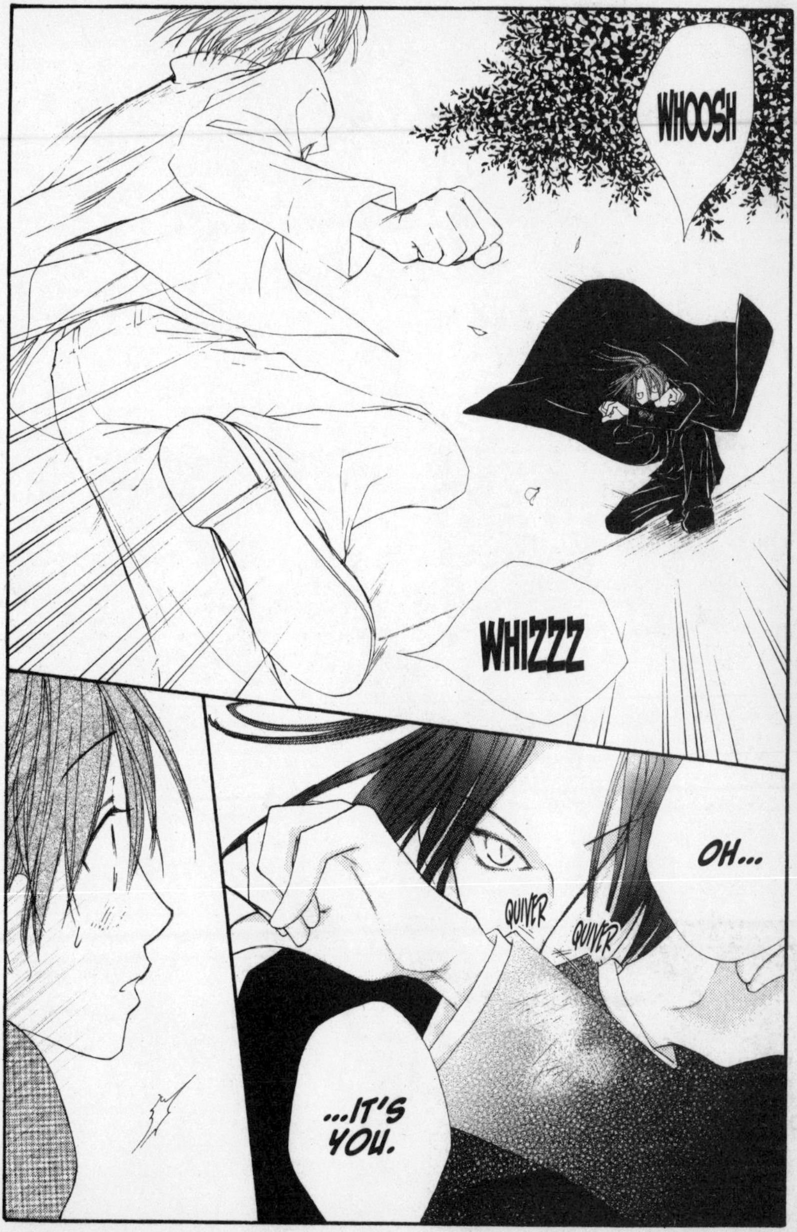
WHOOSH
WHIZZZ
OH...
QUIVER
QUIVER
...IT'S YOU.

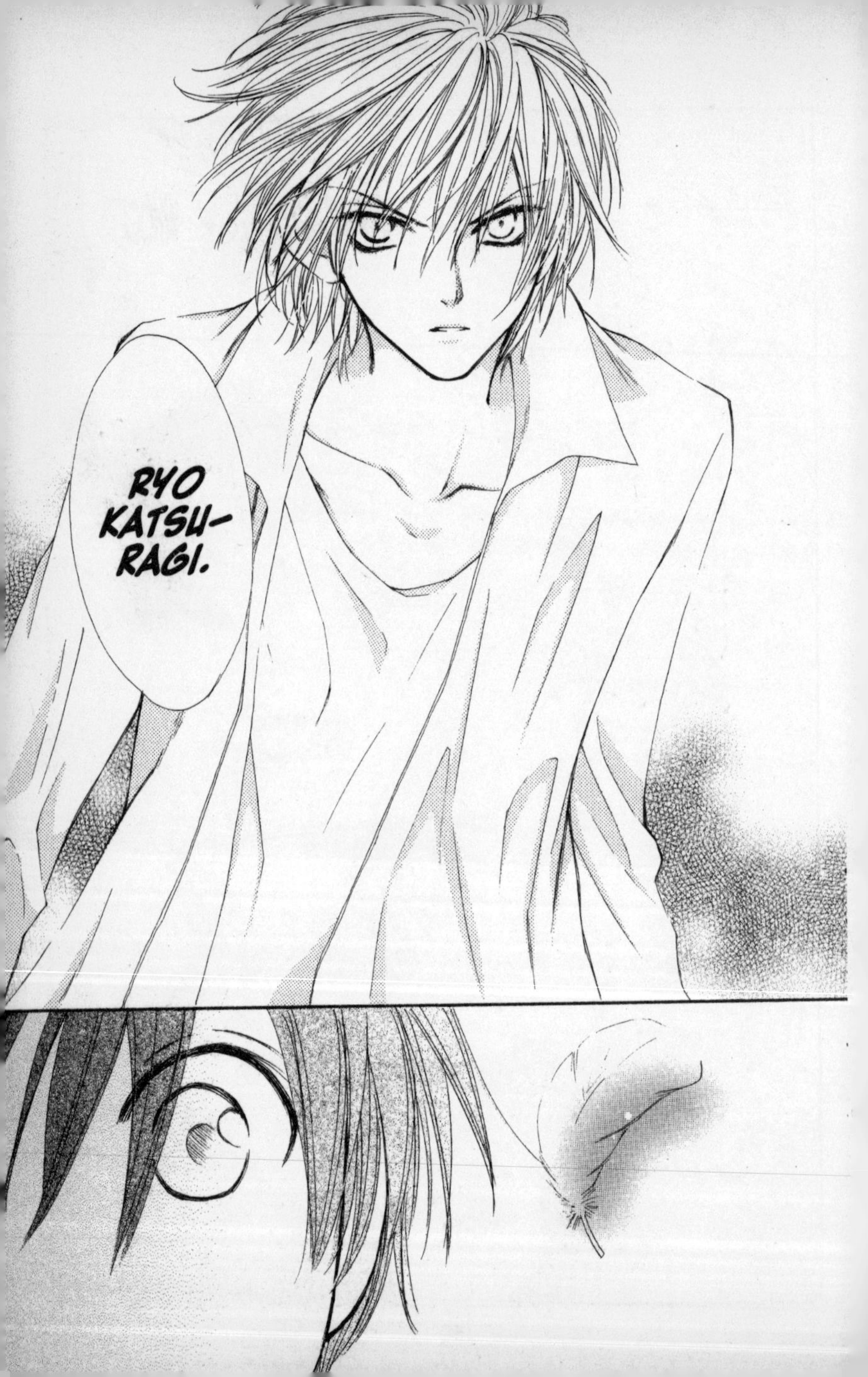
RYO KATSU-RAGI.

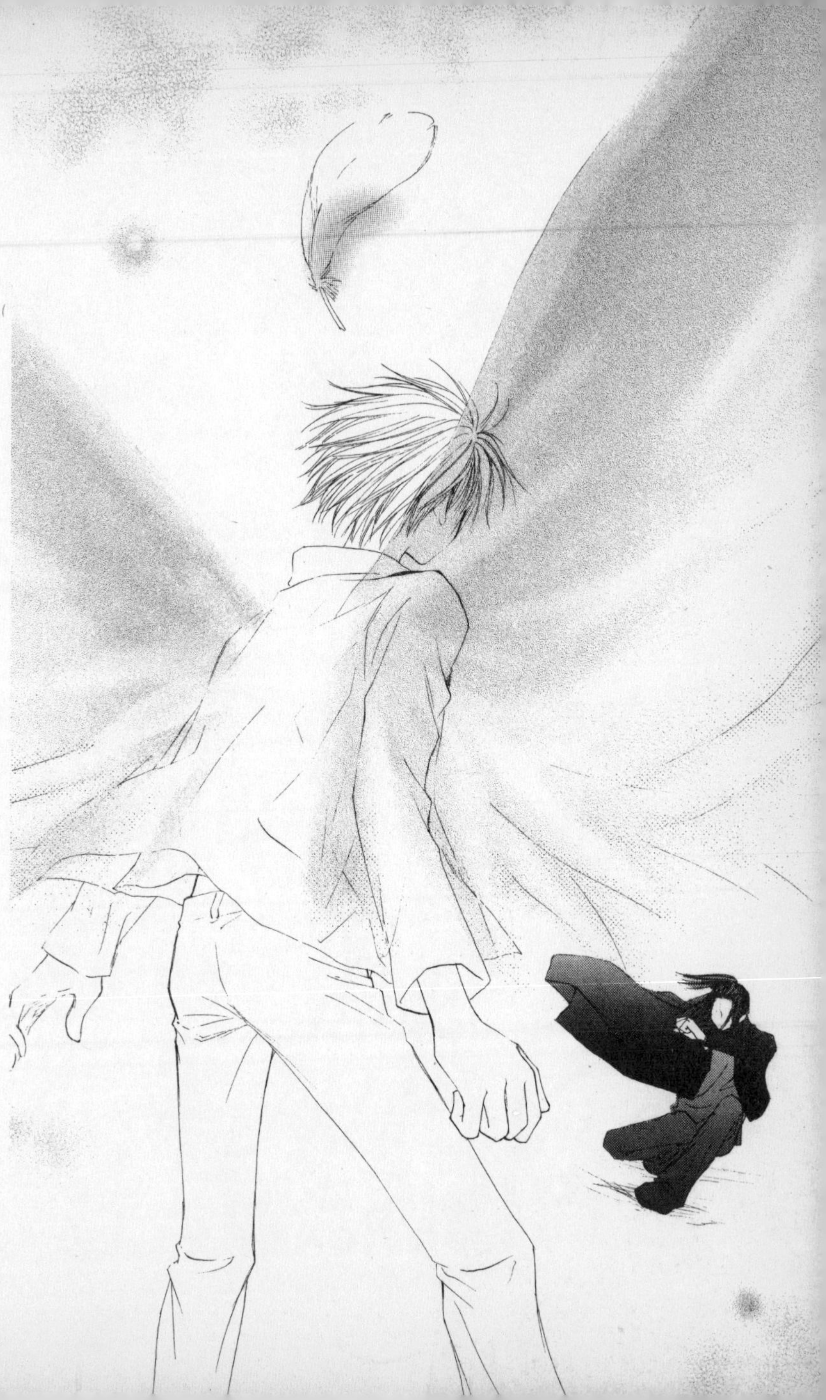

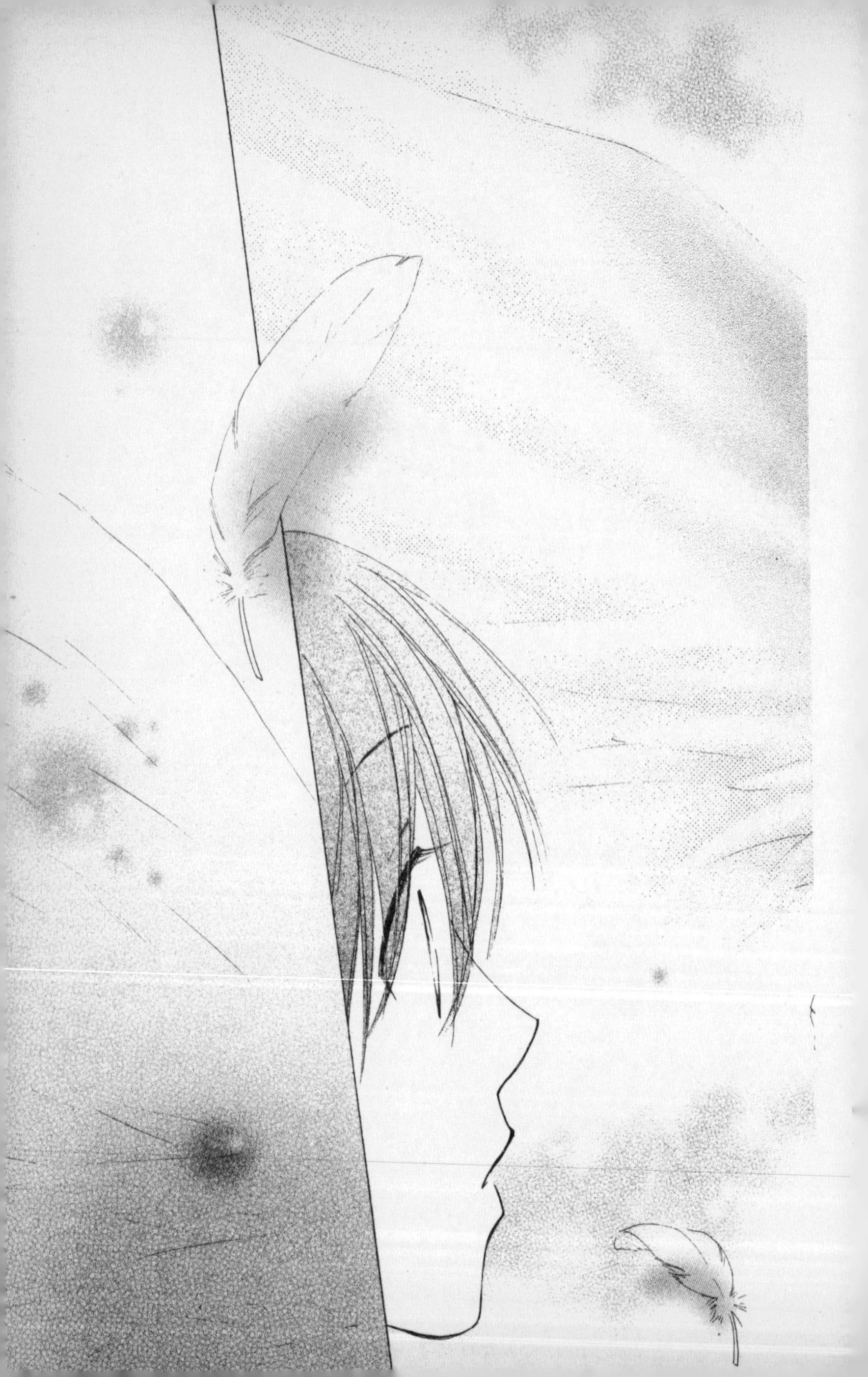

THE WINGS
WERE SO
BIG AND
DAZZLING...

...THEY
ENVELOPED
ME IN
LIGHT...

...MAKING ME
FORGET ALL
ABOUT MY
CHAOTIC
STATE OF
MIND.

Penguin Revolution Episode 16: The End

かくめい
ペンギン革命

PENGUIN REVOLUTION

Episode 17

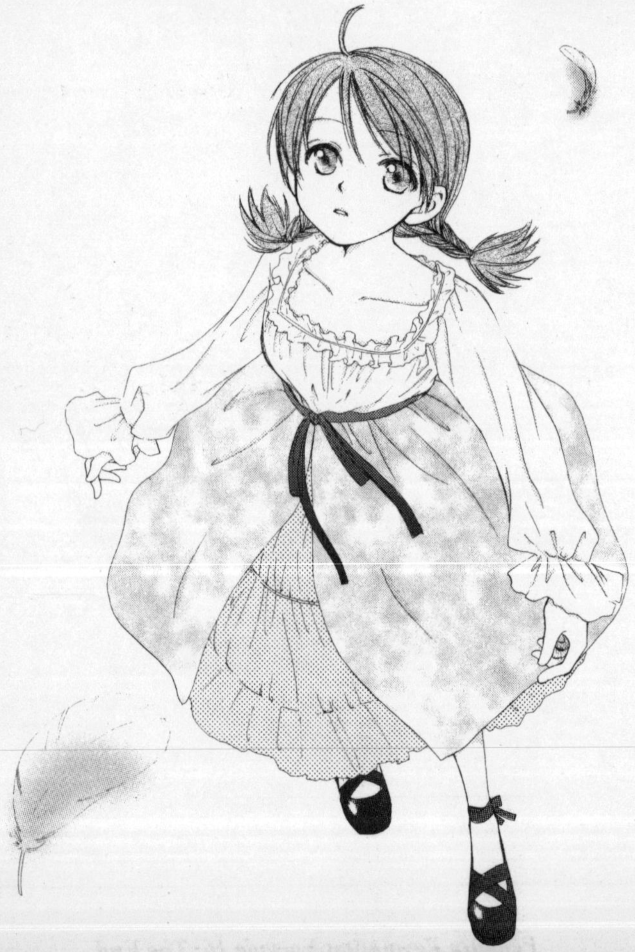

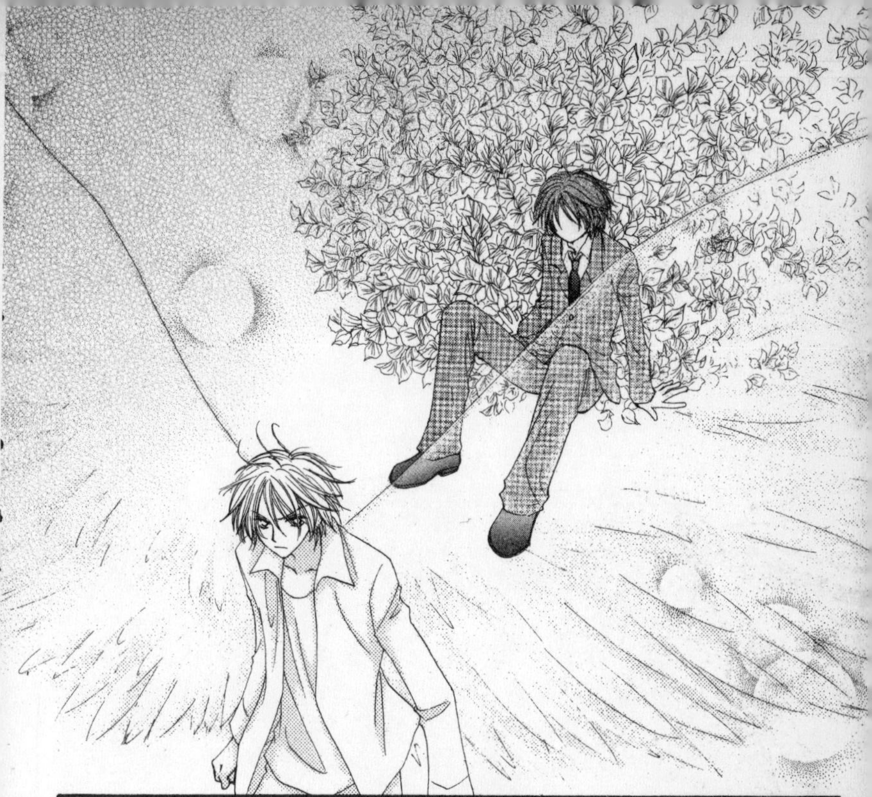

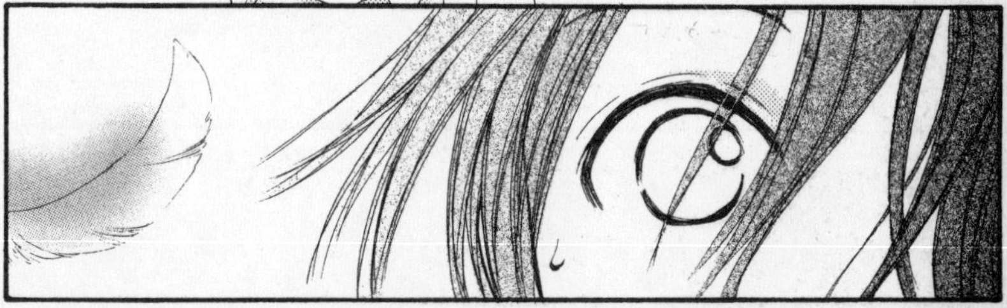

1/4 Sakura Mail

Part 4

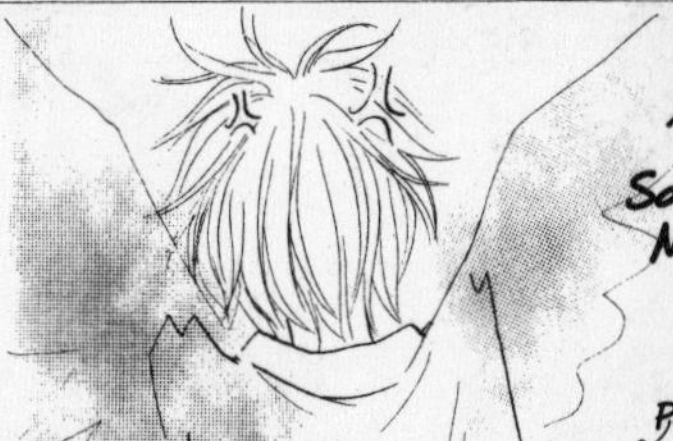

Ryo-chan is angry. Which is natural in this situation, right? If he didn't get angry, I'd be angry at **him.**
The kiss scene with Ryo and Yuka-chin was two episodes ago. Last episode had a kiss between her and Narazaki-san. I was waiting for my chance to draw both scenes. Ahhh, it was fun!! For me, I mean... Ryo and Narazaki-san are always fighting, right?

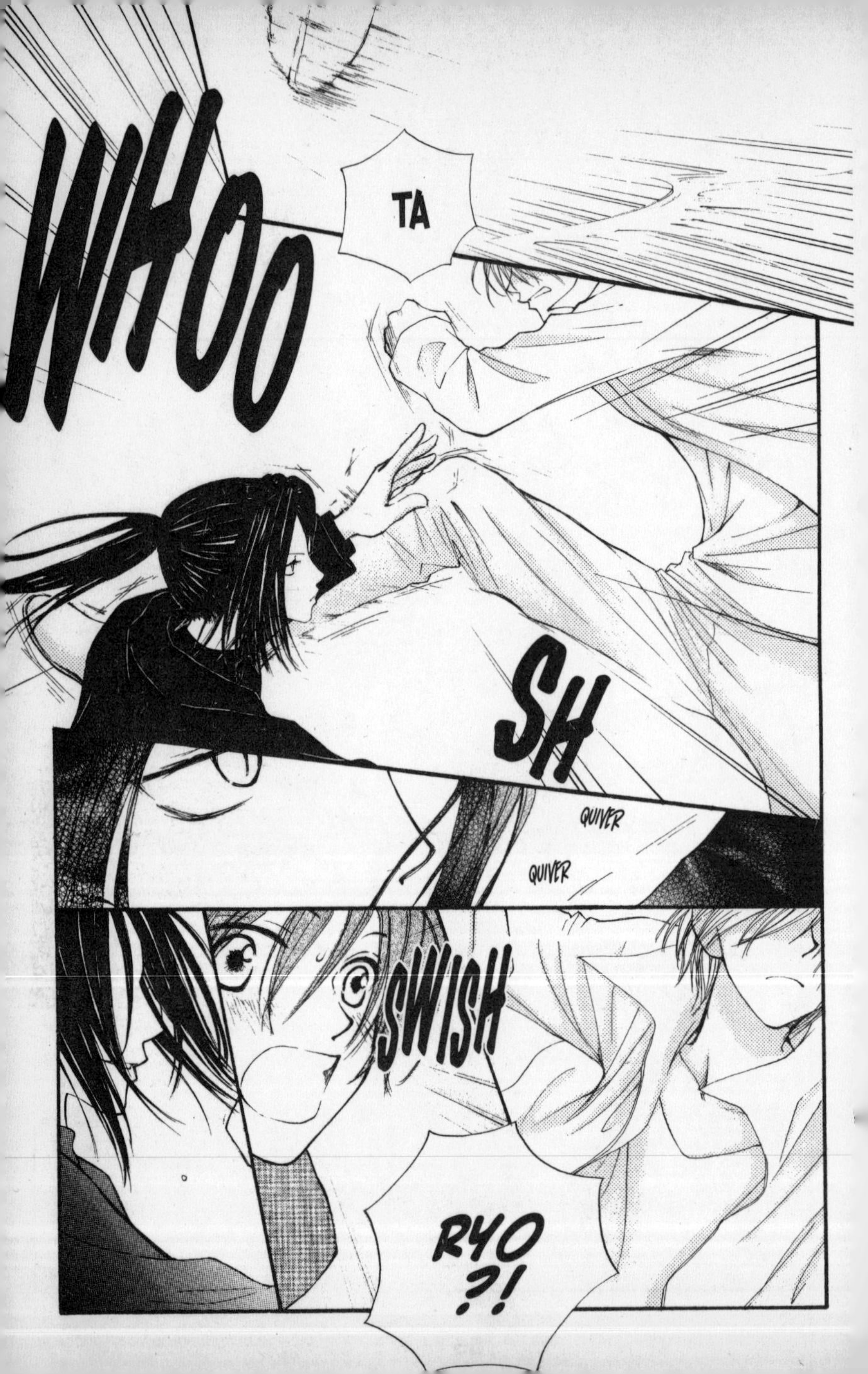
TA
WHOO
SH
QUIVER
QUIVER
SWISH
RYO ?!

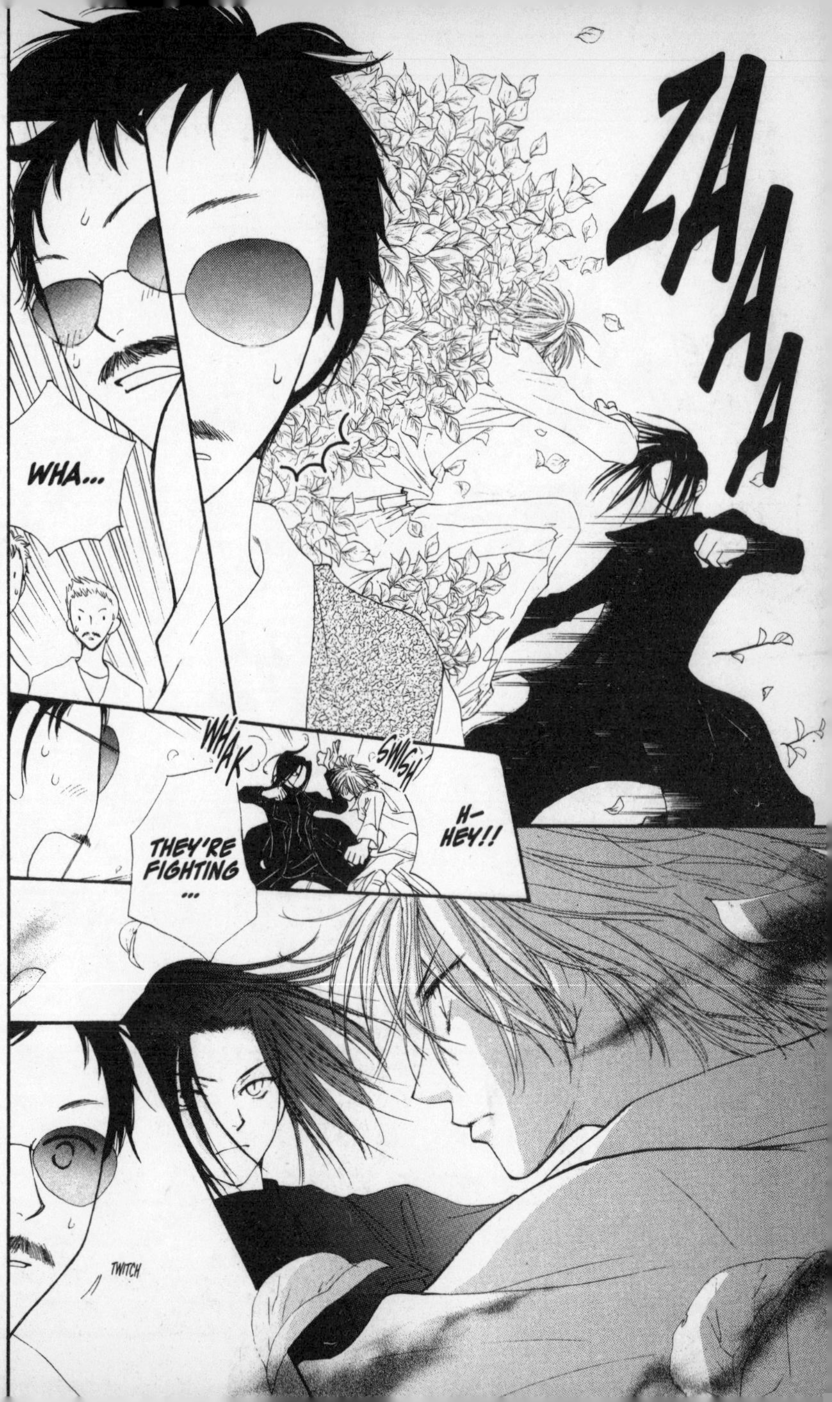
ZAAAA
WHA...
SWISH
WHAK
H-HEY!!
THEY'RE FIGHTING ...
TWITCH

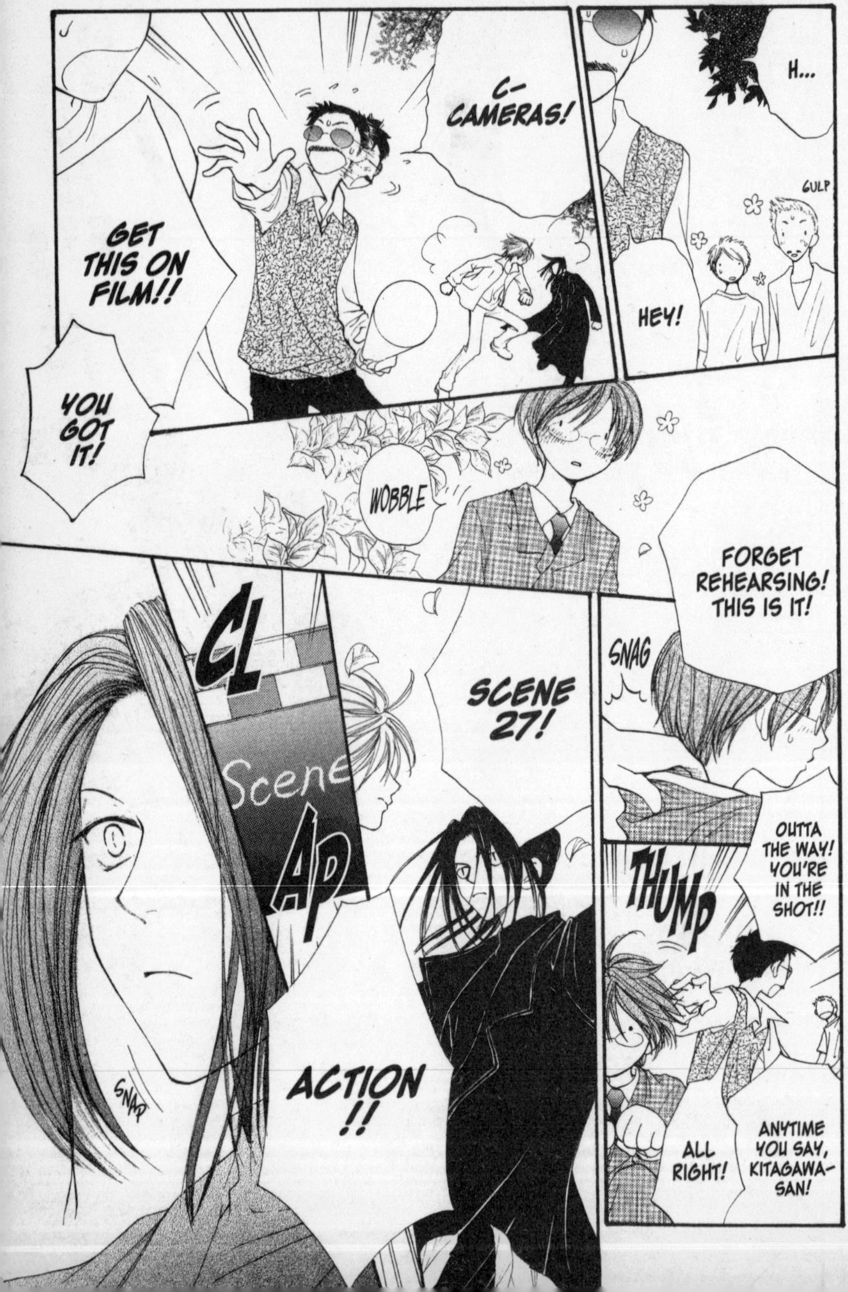
H...
GULP
HEY!
C-CAMERAS!
GET THIS ON FILM!!
YOU GOT IT!
WOBBLE
FORGET REHEARSING! THIS IS IT!
SNAG
THUMP
OUTTA THE WAY! YOU'RE IN THE SHOT!!
ANYTIME YOU SAY, KITAGAWA-SAN!
ALL RIGHT!
SCENE 27!
CL
Scene
AP
ACTION!!
SNAP

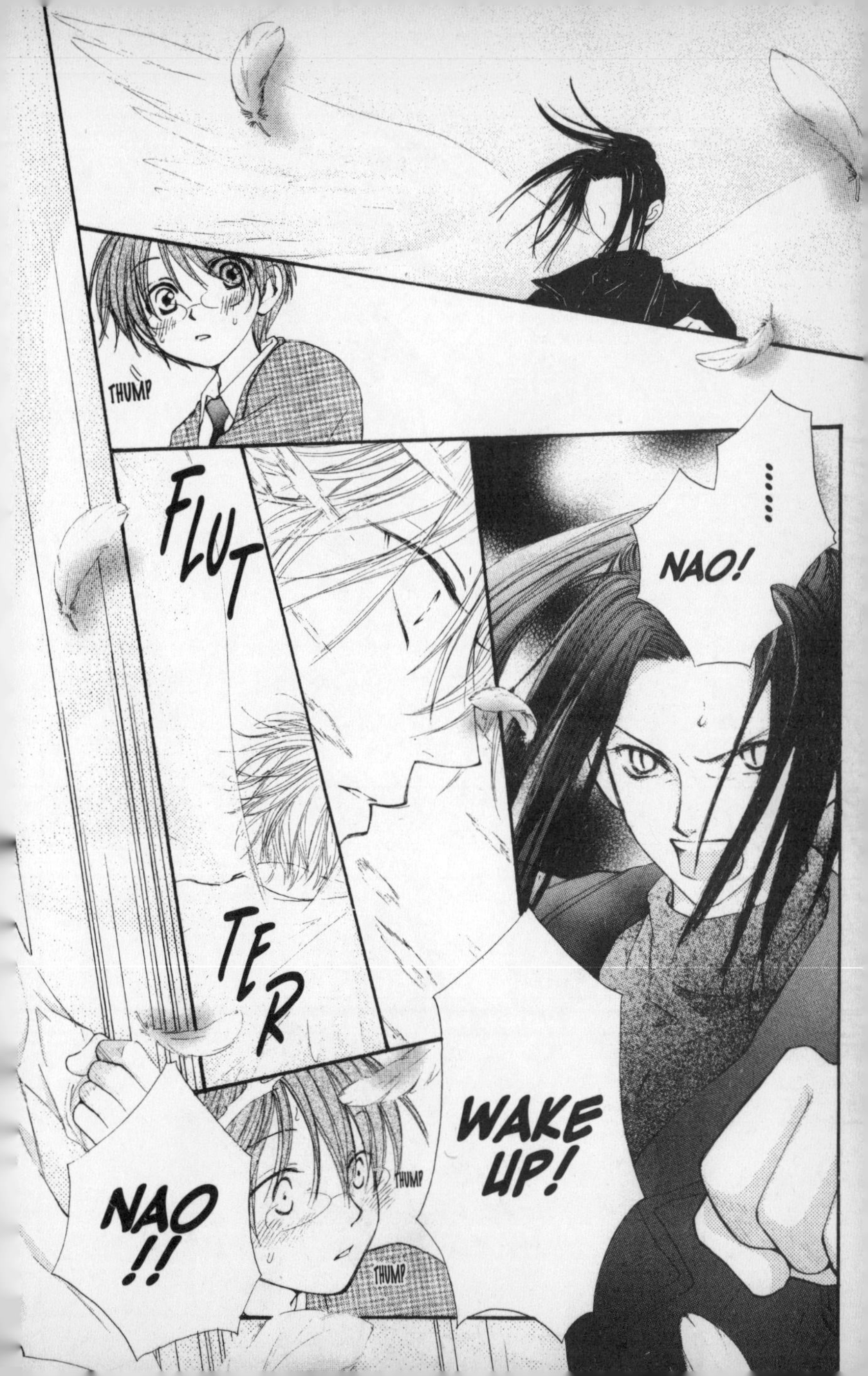
THUMP
......
NAO!
FLUTTER
WAKE UP!
THUMP
THUMP
NAO!!

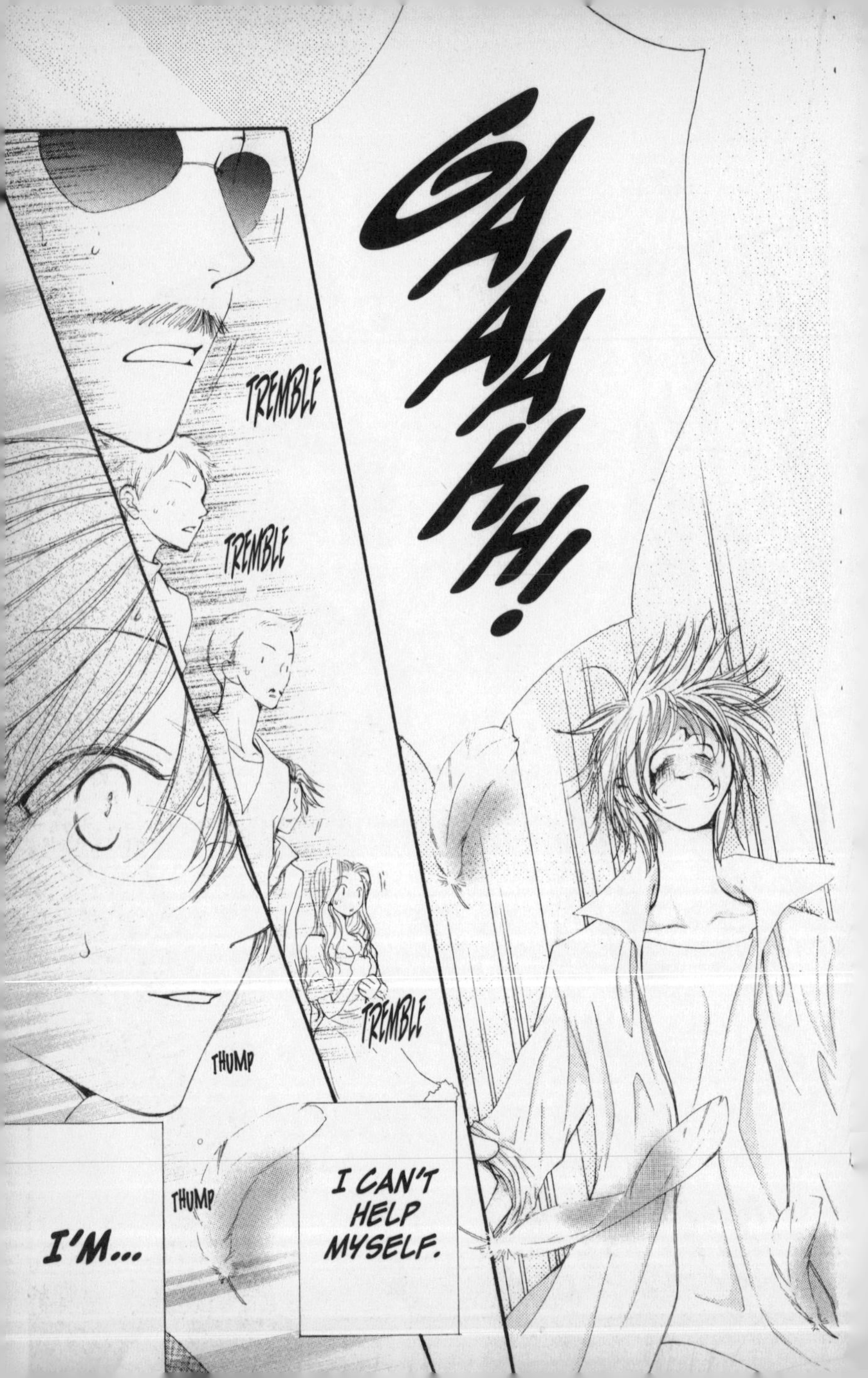
GAAAHH!
TREMBLE
TREMBLE
TREMBLE
THUMP
I CAN'T HELP MYSELF.
THUMP
I'M...

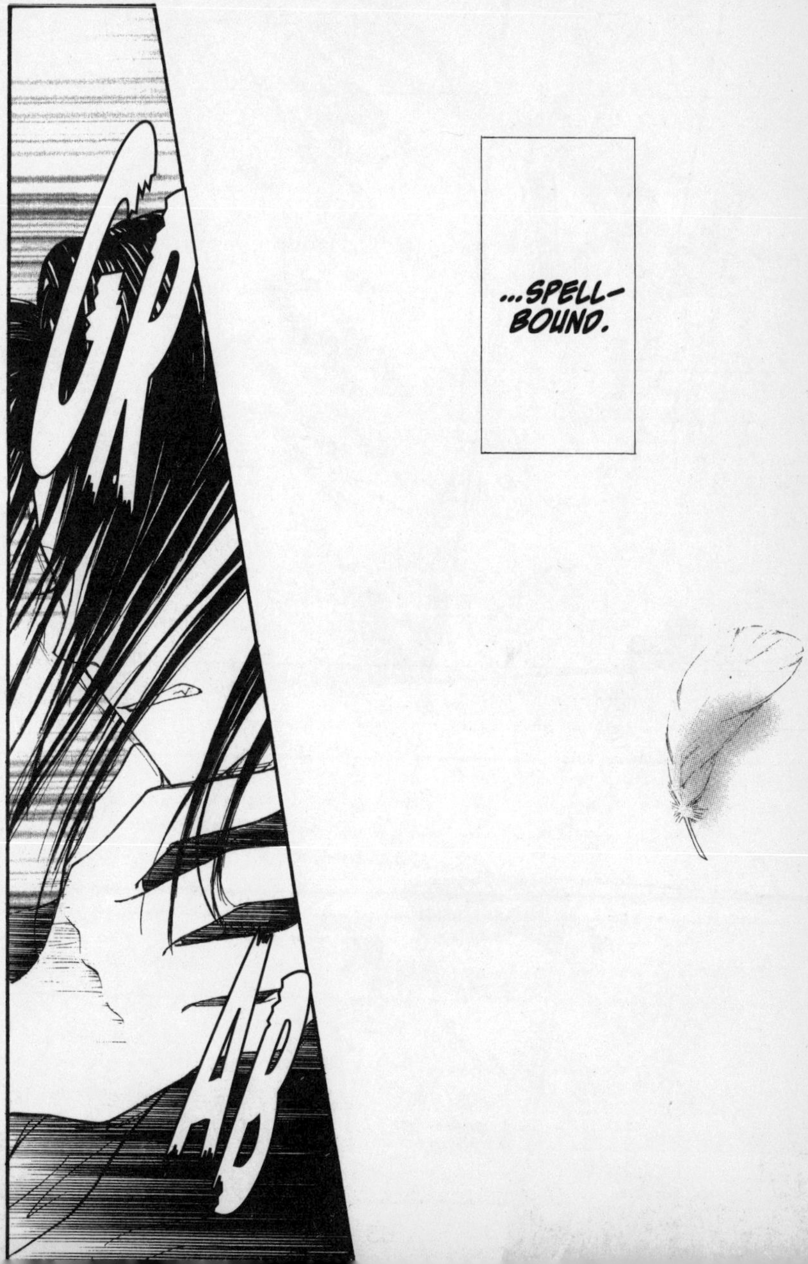
...SPELL-BOUND.
GRAB

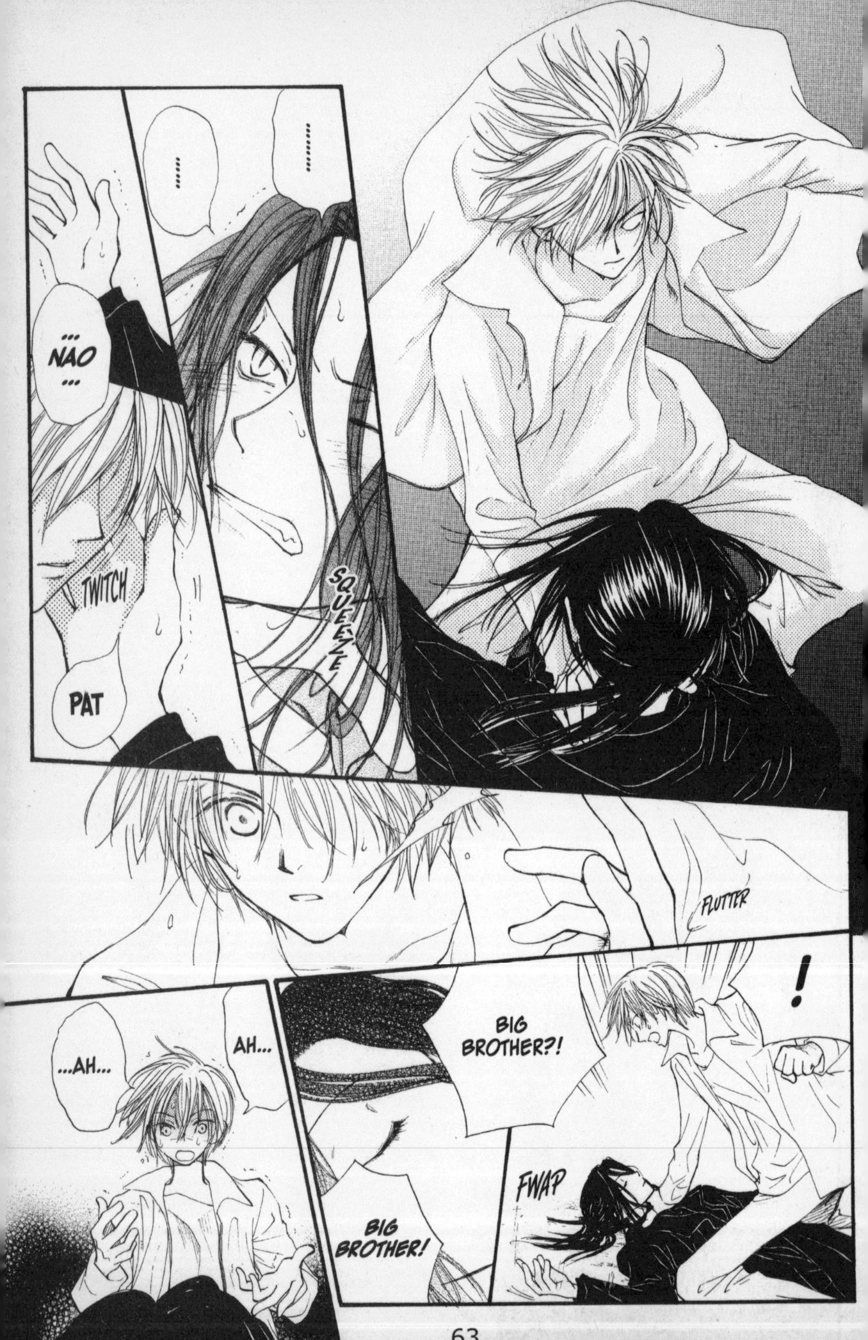
....
......
SQUEEZE
...NAO...
TWITCH
PAT
FLUTTER
!
BIG BROTHER?!
FWAP
BIG BROTHER!
AH...
...AH...

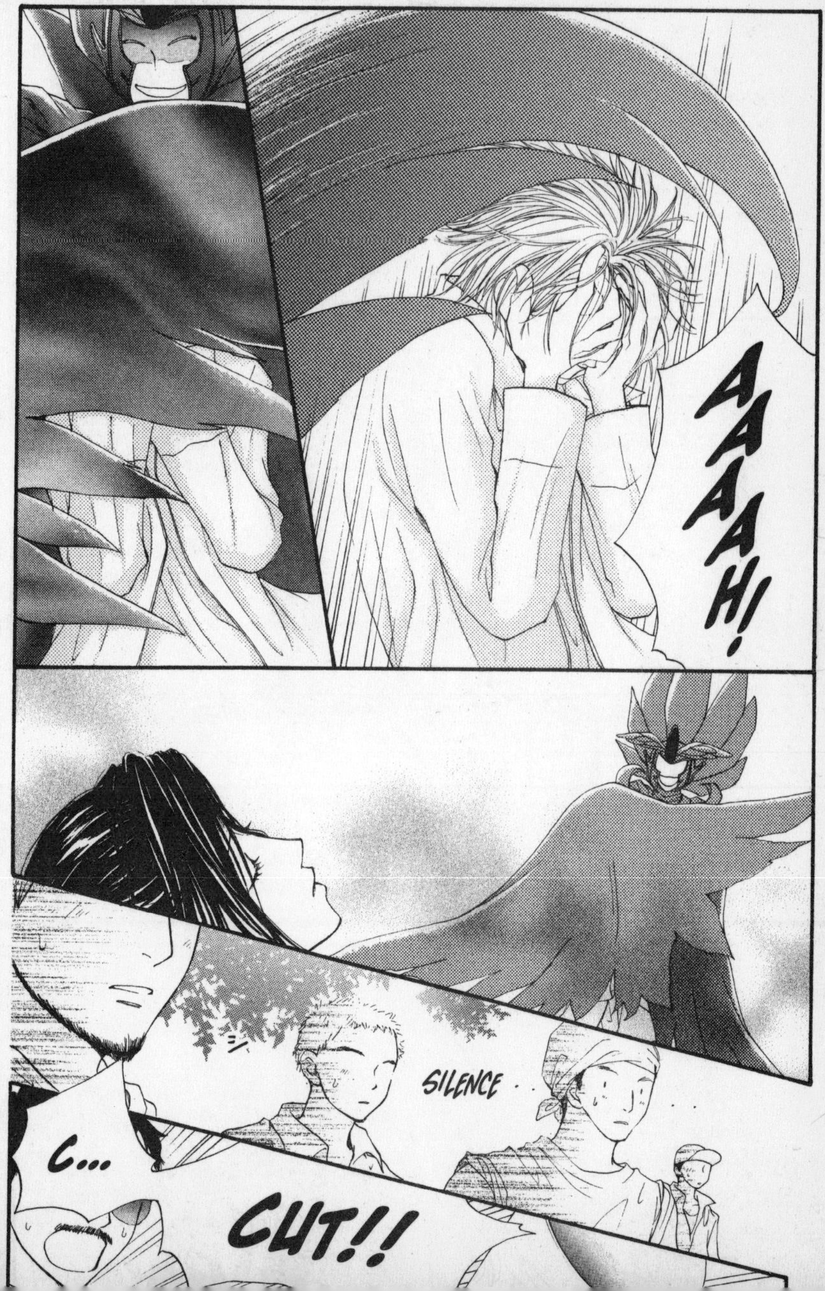
AAAAAH!
SILENCE . . . . .
C...
CUT!!

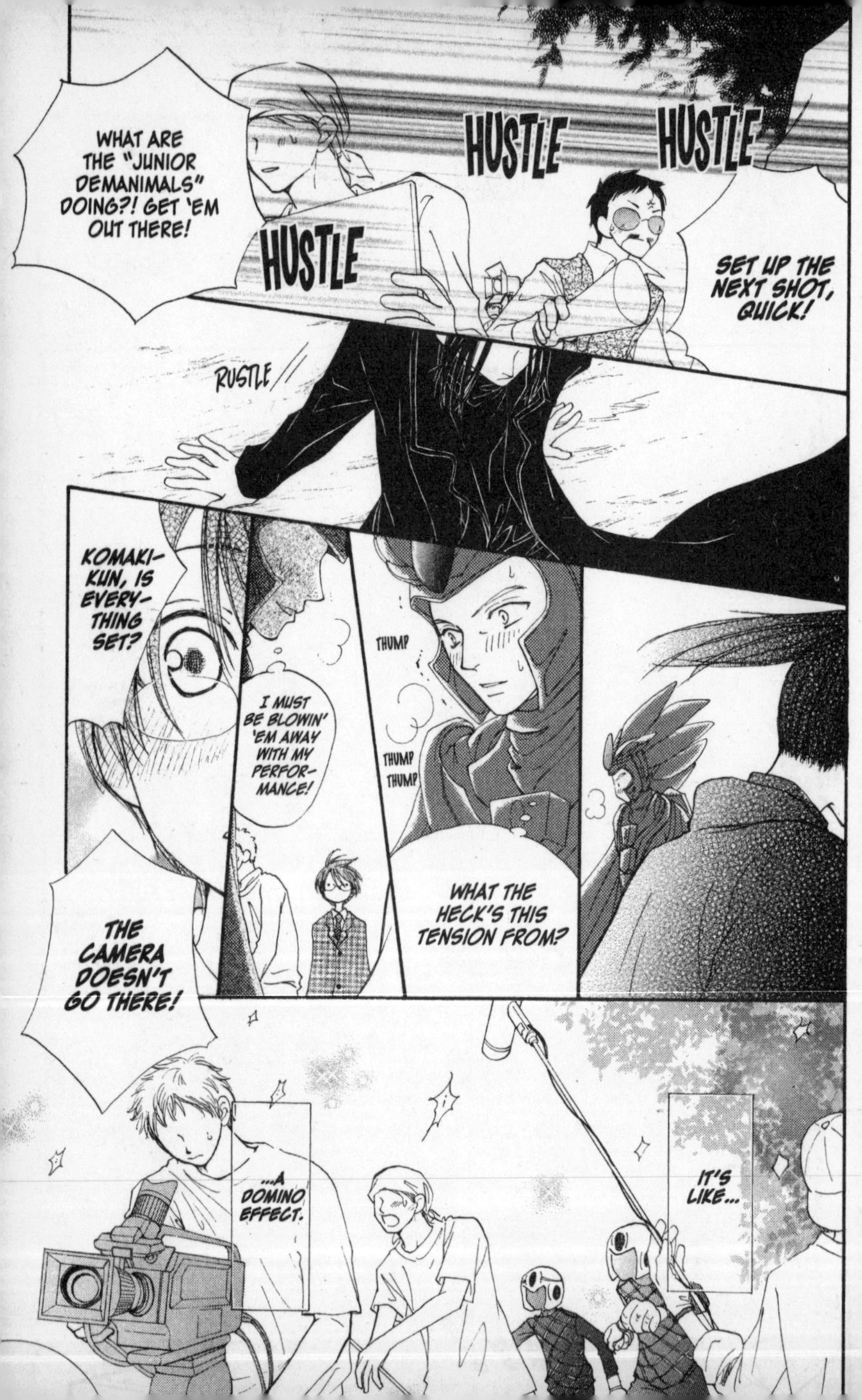
SET UP THE NEXT SHOT, QUICK!
HUSTLE
HUSTLE
WHAT ARE THE "JUNIOR DEMANIMALS" DOING?! GET 'EM OUT THERE!
HUSTLE
RUSTLE
THUMP
THUMP THUMP
WHAT THE HECK'S THIS TENSION FROM?
I MUST BE BLOWIN' 'EM AWAY WITH MY PERFORMANCE!
KOMAKI-KUN, IS EVERYTHING SET?
THE CAMERA DOESN'T GO THERE!
IT'S LIKE...
...A DOMINO EFFECT.

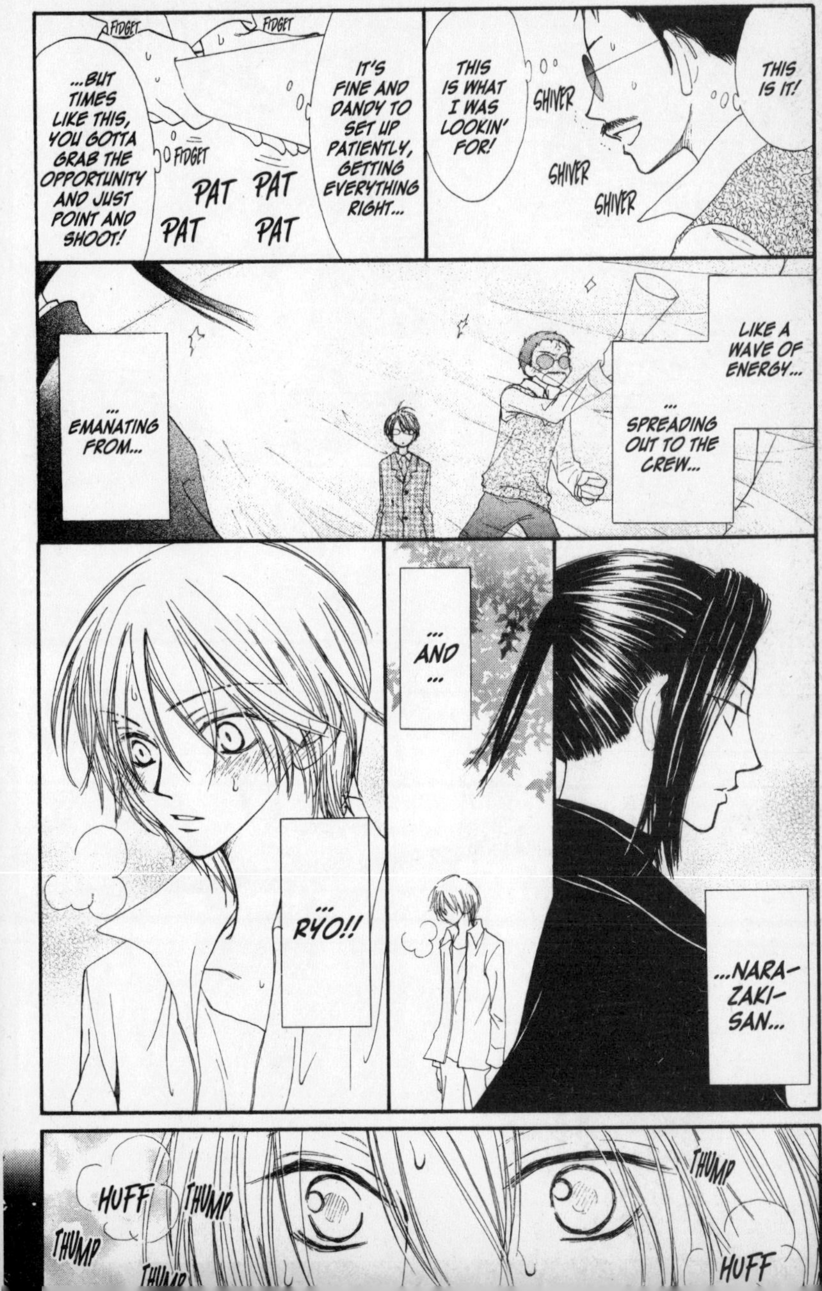
THIS IS IT!
THIS IS WHAT I WAS LOOKIN' FOR!
SHIVER
SHIVER
SHIVER
IT'S FINE AND DANDY TO SET UP PATIENTLY, GETTING EVERYTHING RIGHT...
FIDGET
FIDGET
...BUT TIMES LIKE THIS, YOU GOTTA GRAB THE OPPORTUNITY AND JUST POINT AND SHOOT!
FIDGET
PAT PAT
PAT PAT
LIKE A WAVE OF ENERGY...
...SPREADING OUT TO THE CREW...
...EMANATING FROM...
...NARA-ZAKI-SAN...
...AND...
...RYŌ!!
THUMP
HUFF
HUFF
THUMP
THUMP

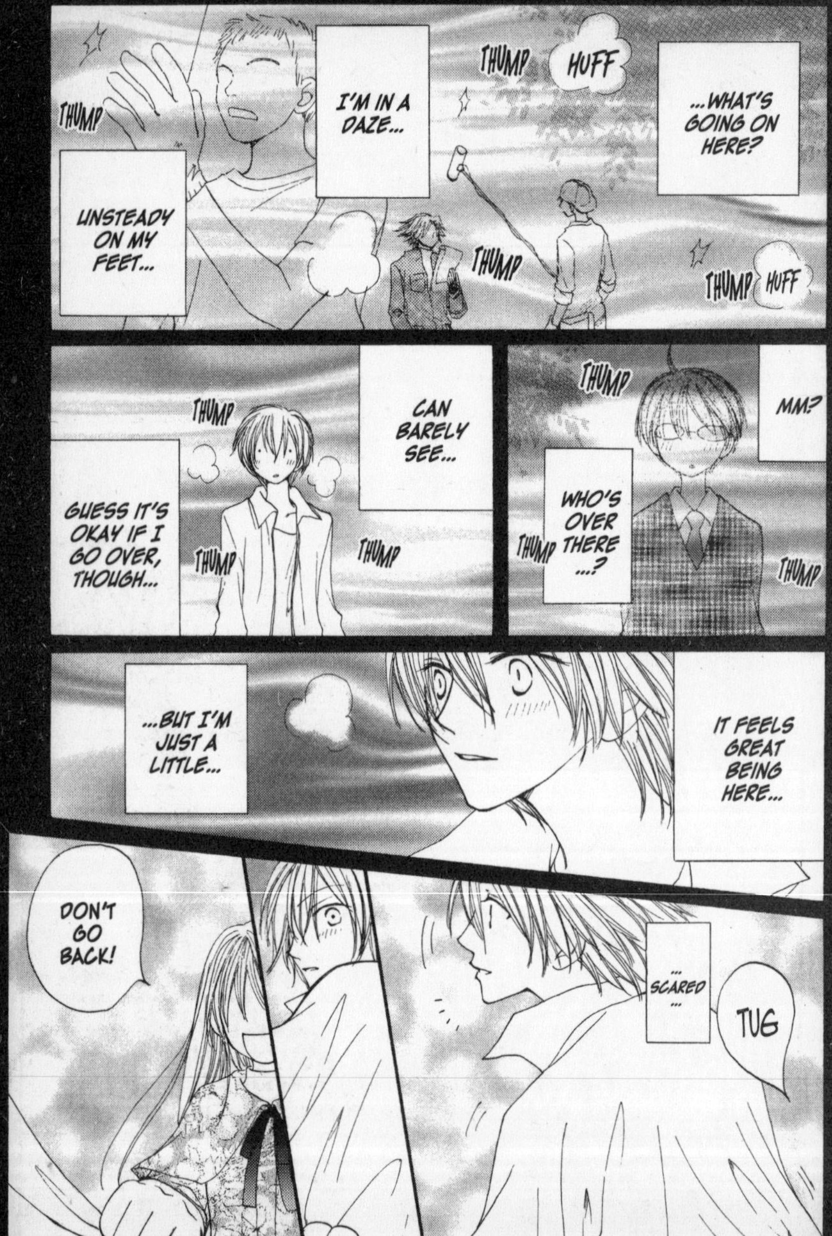
...WHAT'S GOING ON HERE?
HUFF
THUMP
I'M IN A DAZE...
THUMP
UNSTEADY ON MY FEET...
THUMP
THUMP
HUFF
MM?
THUMP
WHO'S OVER THERE ...?
THUMP
THUMP
CAN BARELY SEE...
THUMP
GUESS IT'S OKAY IF I GO OVER, THOUGH...
THUMP
THUMP
IT FEELS GREAT BEING HERE...
...BUT I'M JUST A LITTLE...
TUG
... SCARED ...
DON'T GO BACK!

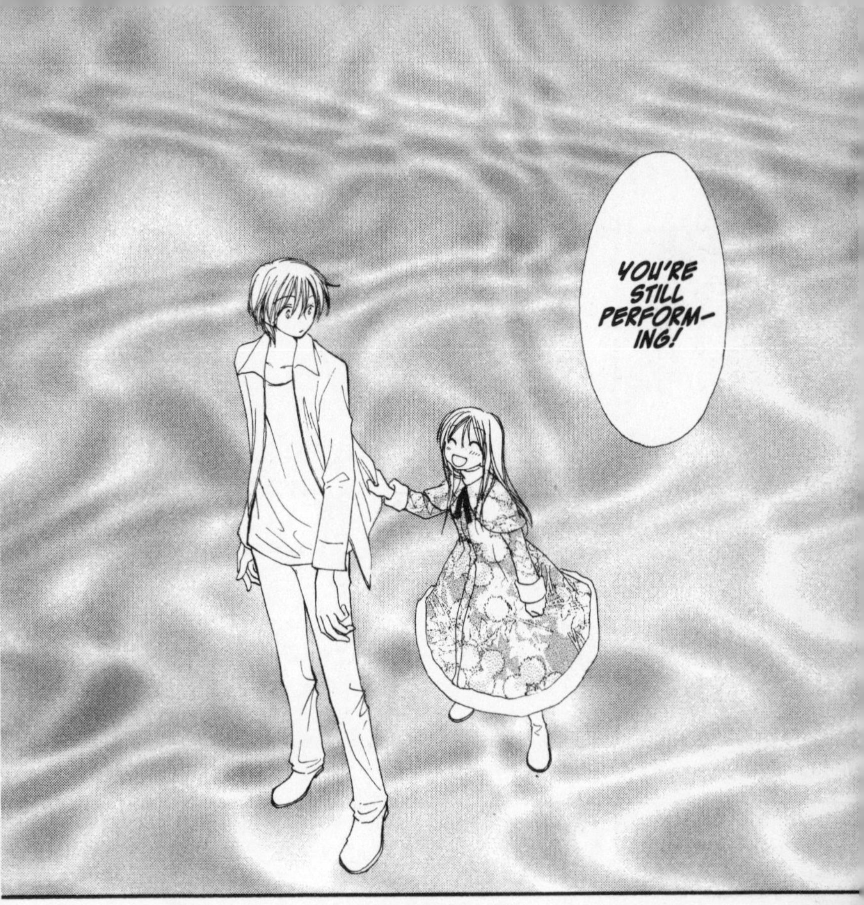
YOU'RE STILL PERFORMING!

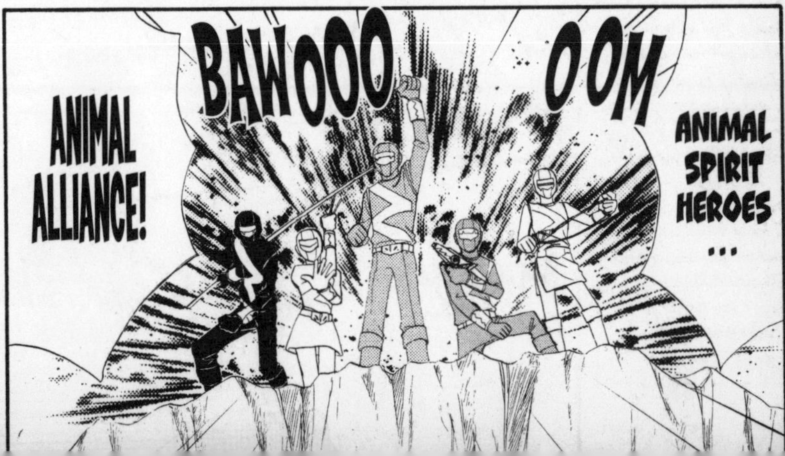
ANIMAL SPIRIT HEROES ...
BAWOOO OOM
ANIMAL ALLIANCE!

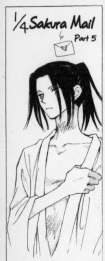

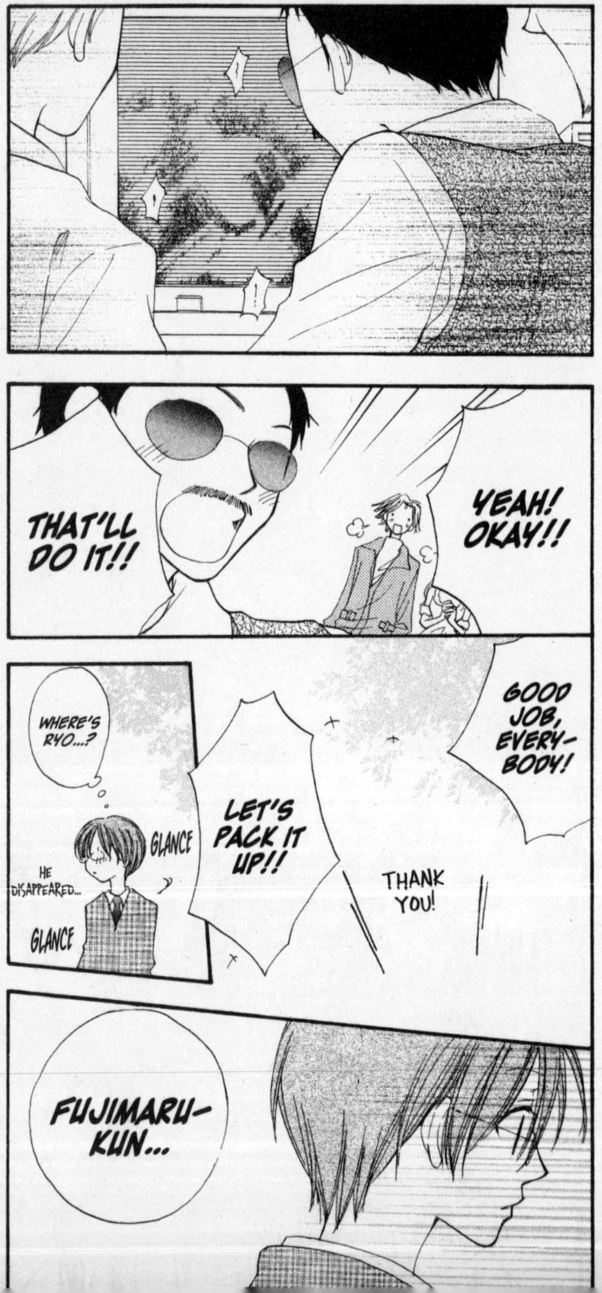
YEAH! OKAY!!
THAT'LL DO IT!!
GOOD JOB, EVERY-BODY!
LET'S PACK IT UP!!
THANK YOU!
WHERE'S RYO...?
GLANCE
HE DISAPPEARED...
GLANCE
FUJIMARU-KUN...

1/4 Sakura Mail

Part 5

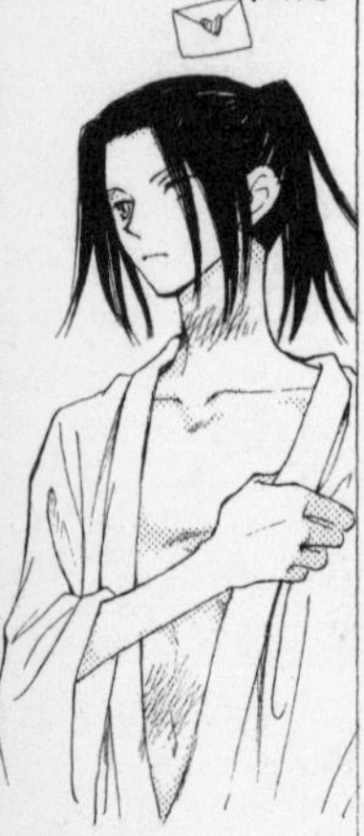

Well, in this episode, Ryo throws a whirlwind of punches and kicks at Narazaki-san, but doesn't get a single clean hit in. Guess that's to be expected, though, when his opponent is Narazaki-san. Narazaki-san doesn't fight back, but you can see he takes Ryo as a serious opponent and properly defends himself. Oh! Yuka-chin really struck me as playing the heroine in this episode. (...Of course, she is the heroine of this series.) I have fun drawing action scenes, so I hope Ryo and Narazaki-san keep fighting (good-naturedly, of course). Heehee... ...♡

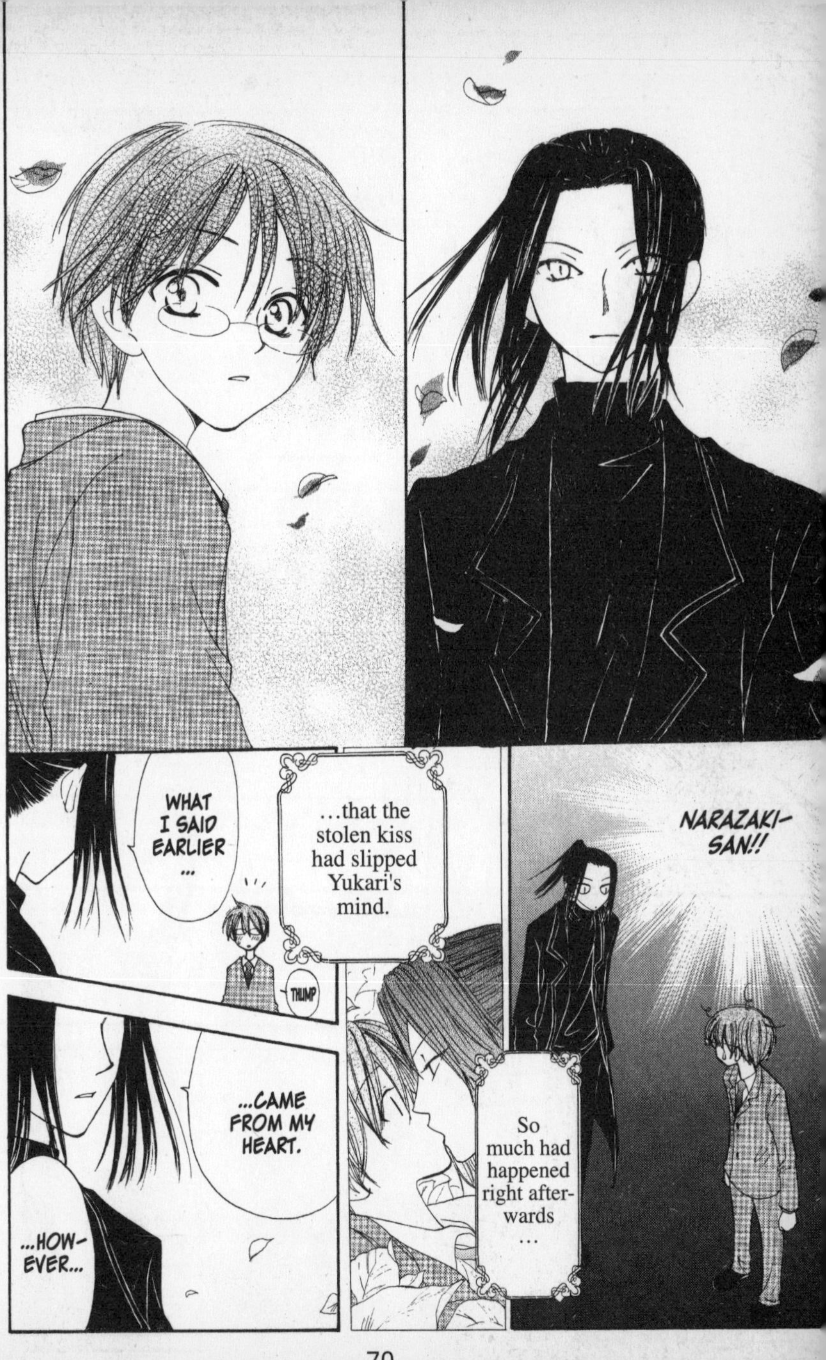
NARAZAKI-SAN!!
So much had happened right afterwards …
…that the stolen kiss had slipped Yukari's mind.
WHAT I SAID EARLIER …
THUMP
…CAME FROM MY HEART.
…HOW-EVER…

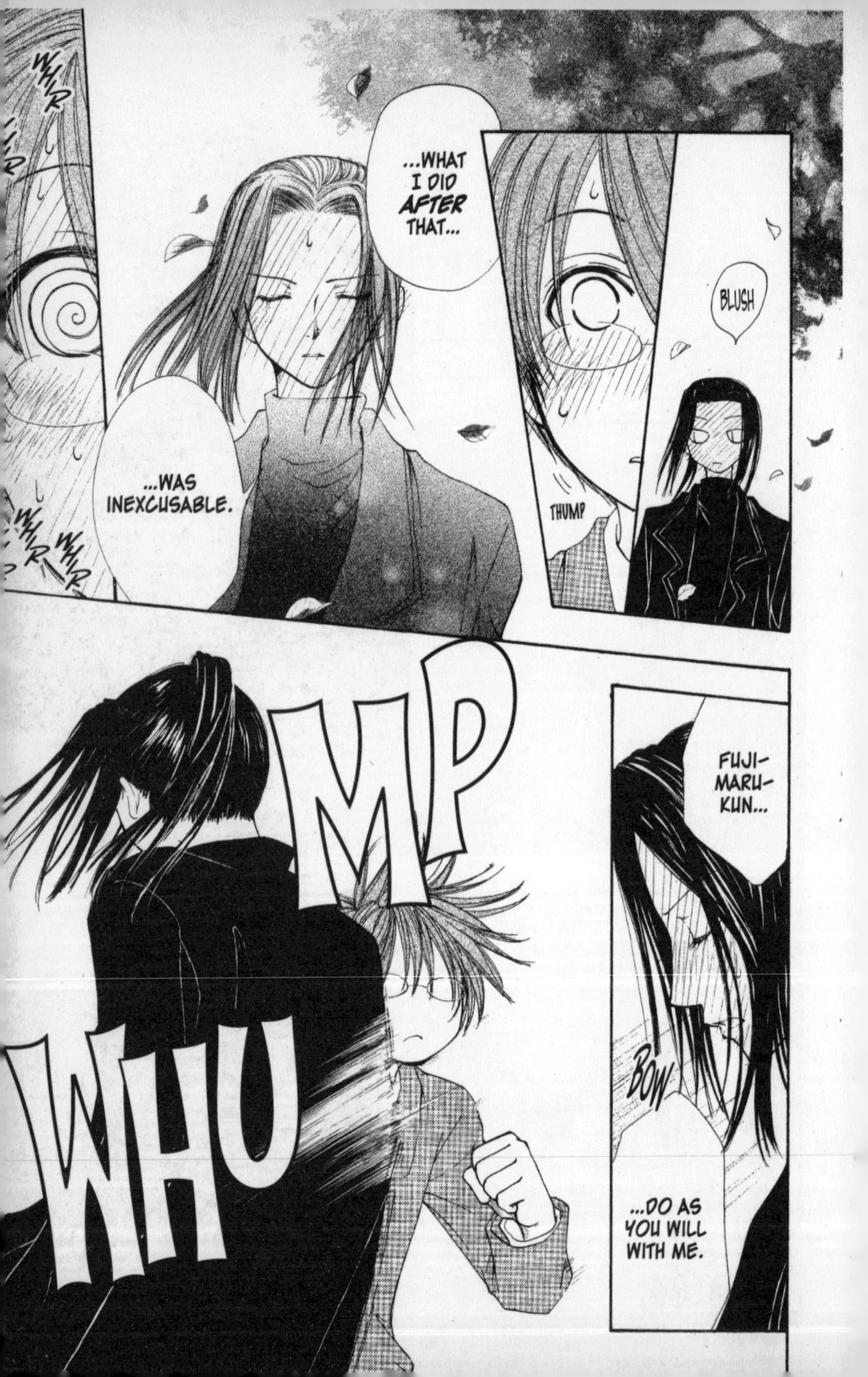
...WHAT I DID AFTER THAT...
BLUSH
THUMP
...WAS INEXCUSABLE.
WHIR
WHIR
WHIR
WHIR
FUJI-MARU-KUN...
BOW
...DO AS YOU WILL WITH ME.
WHUMP

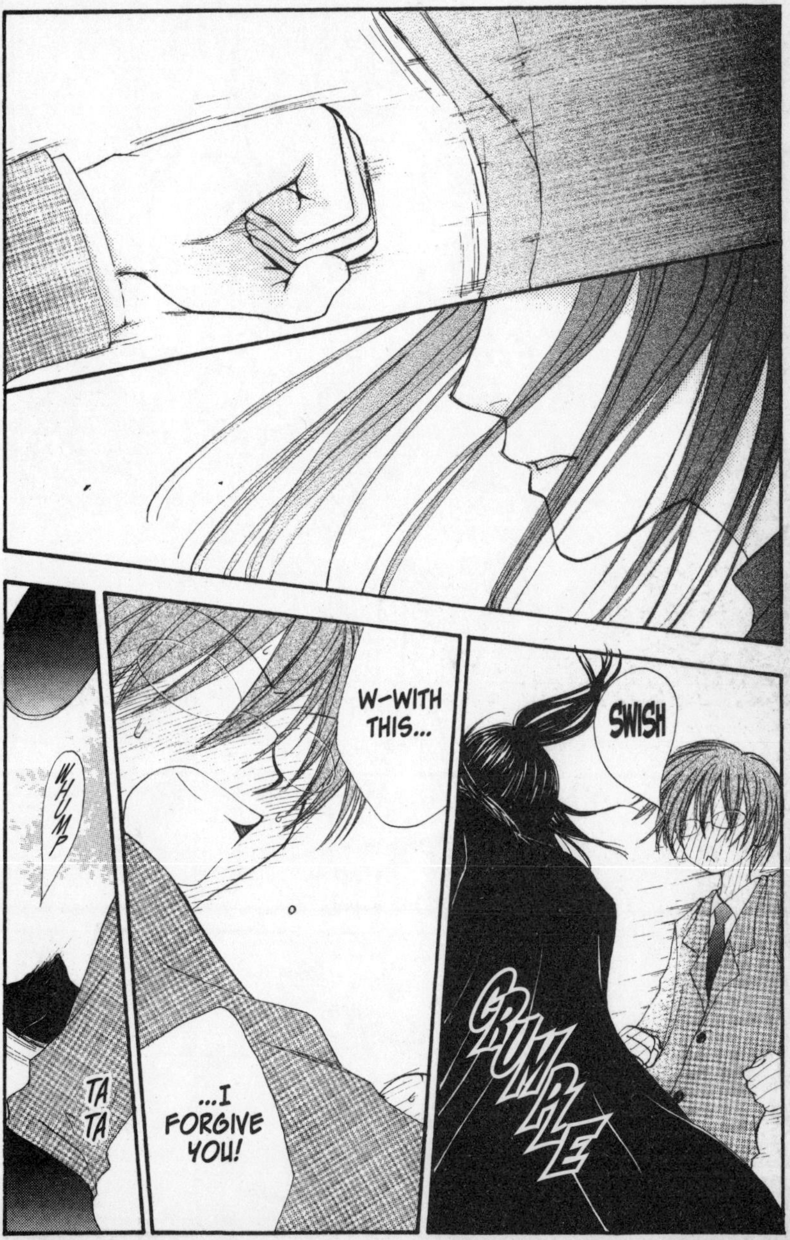
SWISH
CRUMPLE
W-WITH THIS...
...I FORGIVE YOU!
WHUMP
TA TA

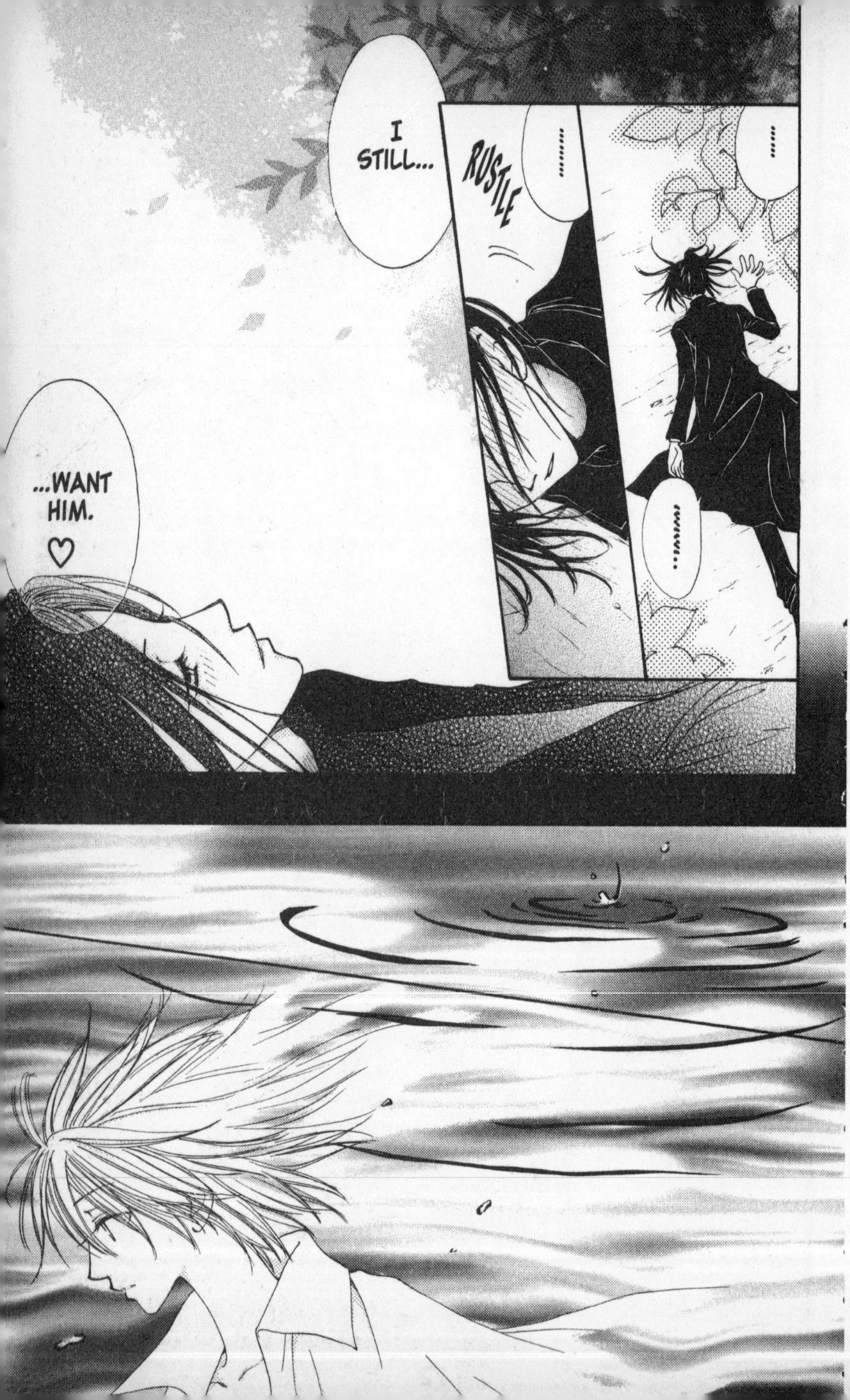
......
......
RUSTLE
......
I STILL...
...WANT HIM. ♡

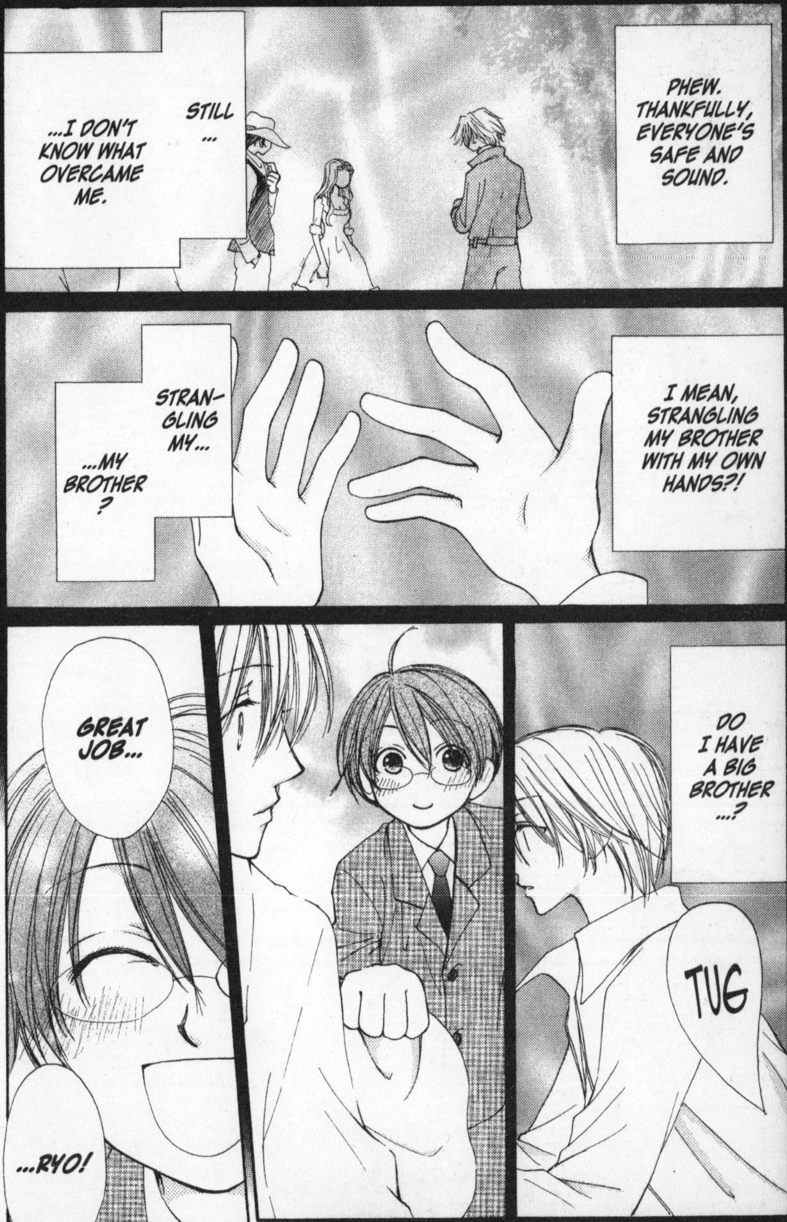
PHEW. THANKFULLY, EVERYONE'S SAFE AND SOUND.
STILL...
...I DON'T KNOW WHAT OVERCAME ME.
I MEAN, STRANGLING MY BROTHER WITH MY OWN HANDS?!
STRAN-GLING MY...
...MY BROTHER?
DO I HAVE A BIG BROTHER...?
TUG
GREAT JOB...
...RYO!

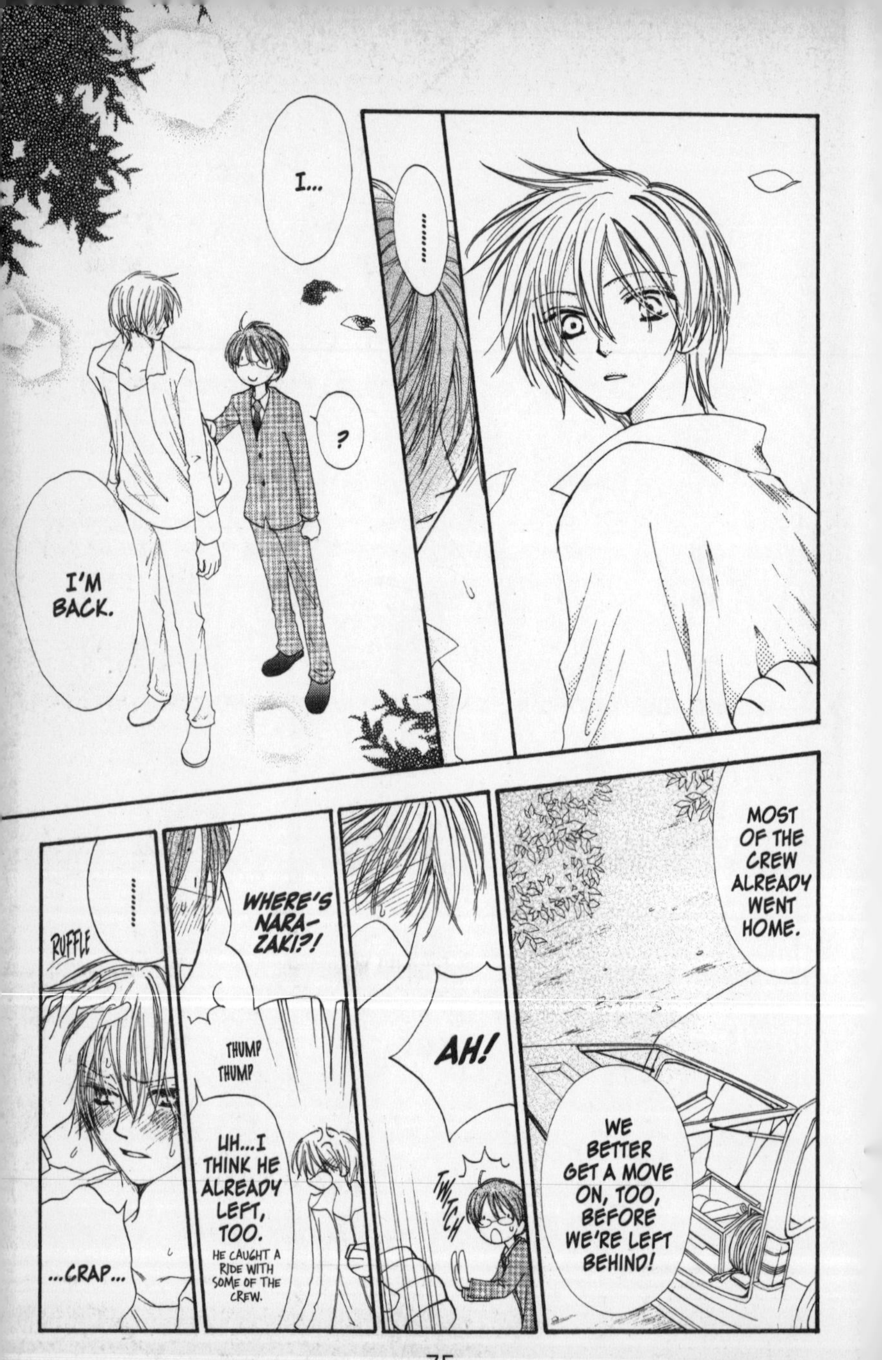
......
I...
?
I'M BACK.
MOST OF THE CREW ALREADY WENT HOME.
WE BETTER GET A MOVE ON, TOO, BEFORE WE'RE LEFT BEHIND!
AH!
TWITCH
WHERE'S NARA-ZAKI?!
THUMP THUMP
UH...I THINK HE ALREADY LEFT, TOO.
HE CAUGHT A RIDE WITH SOME OF THE CREW.
......
RUFFLE
...CRAP...

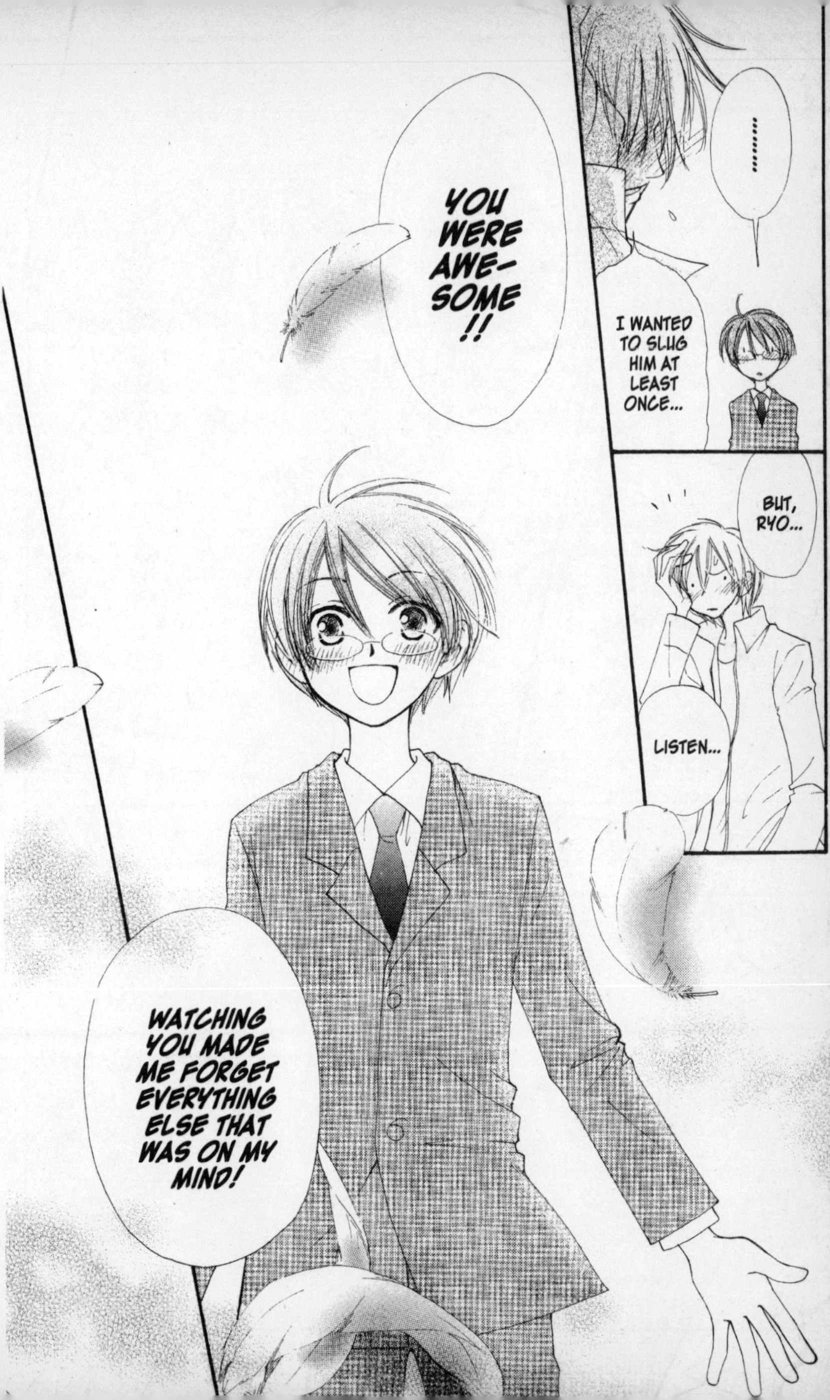
......
I WANTED TO SLUG HIM AT LEAST ONCE...
BUT, RYO...
LISTEN...
YOU WERE AWE-SOME!!
WATCHING YOU MADE ME FORGET EVERYTHING ELSE THAT WAS ON MY MIND!

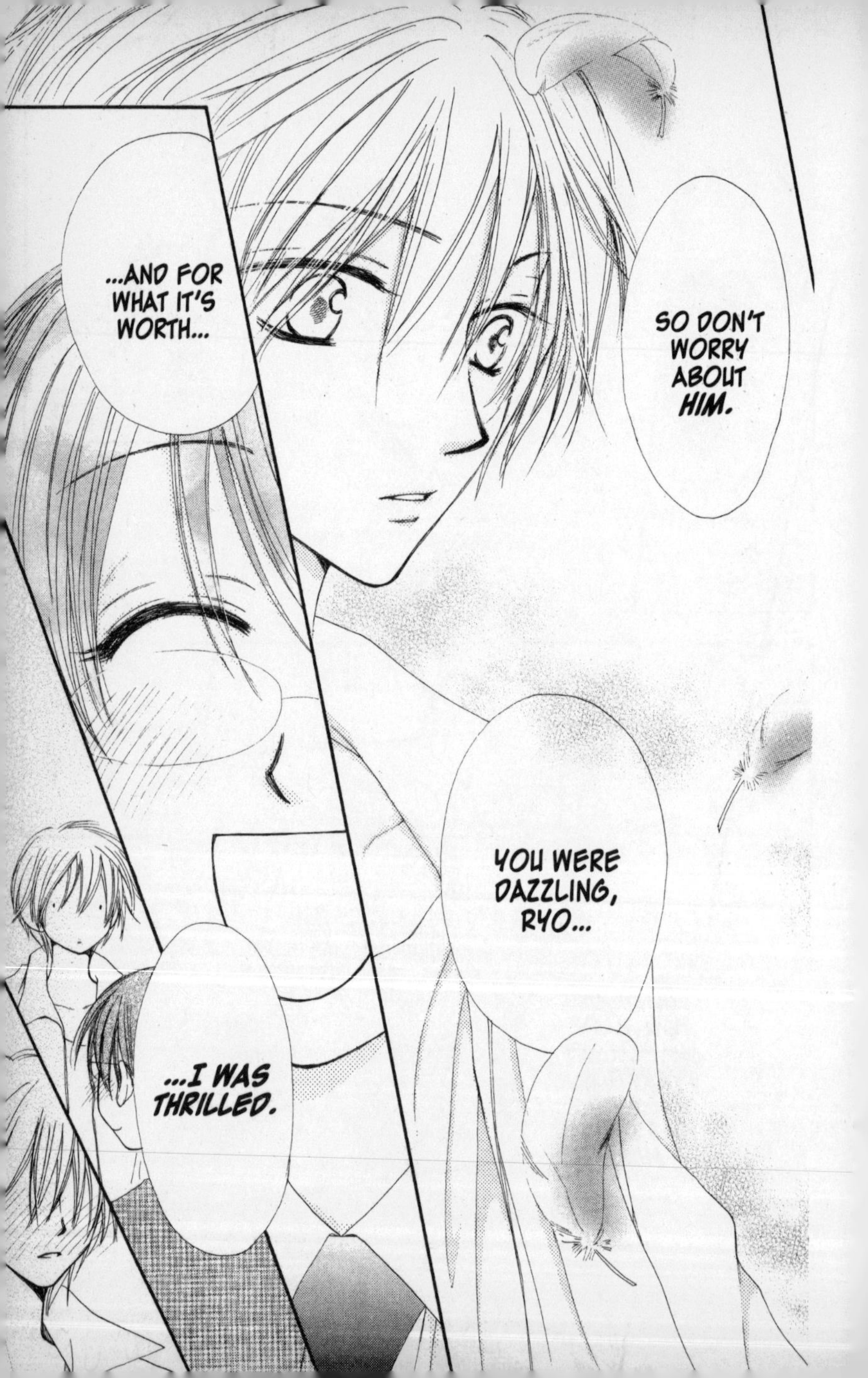
SO DON'T WORRY ABOUT *HIM.*
YOU WERE DAZZLING, RYO...
...AND FOR WHAT IT'S WORTH...
...I WAS THRILLED.

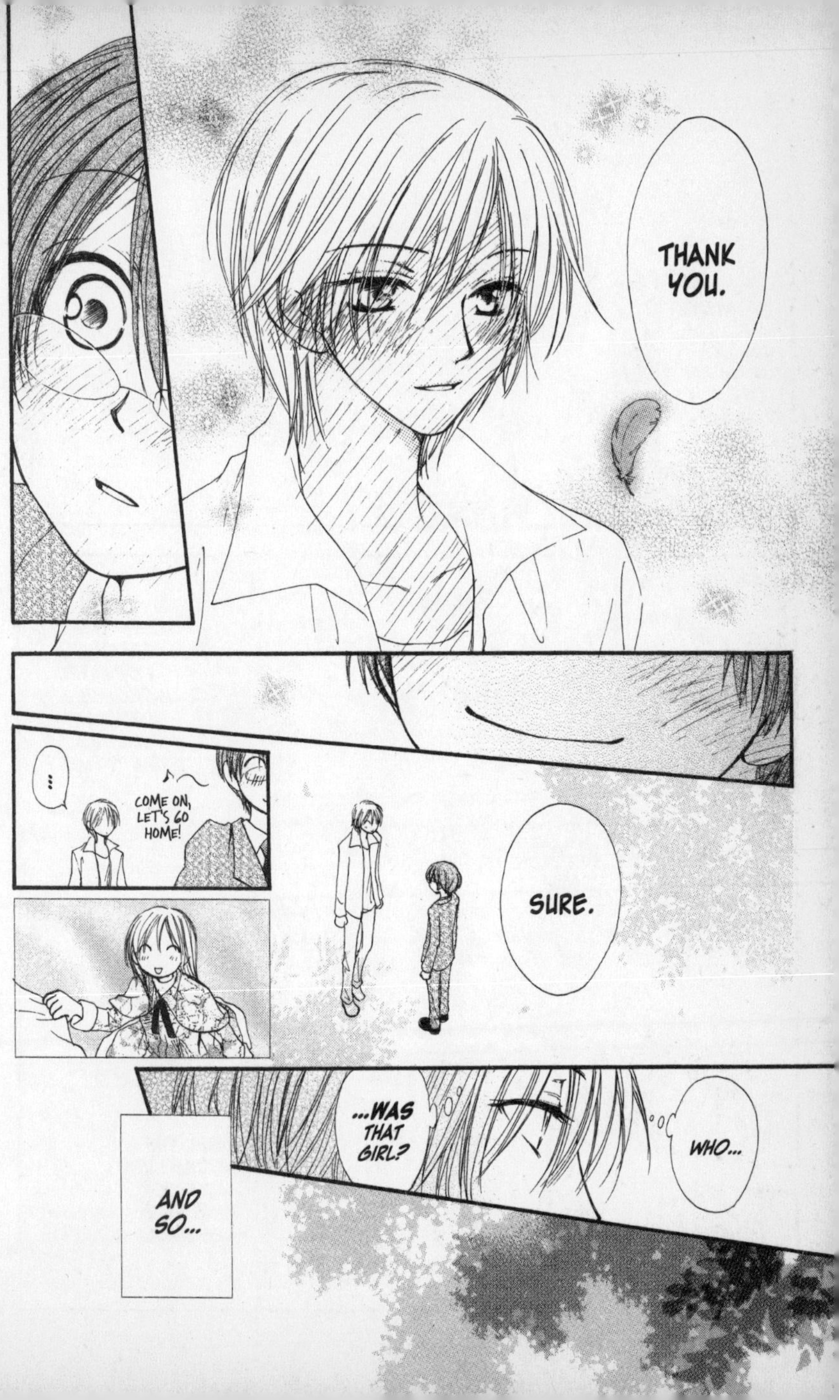
THANK YOU.
SURE.
COME ON, LET'S GO HOME!
...
WHO...
...WAS THAT GIRL?
AND SO...

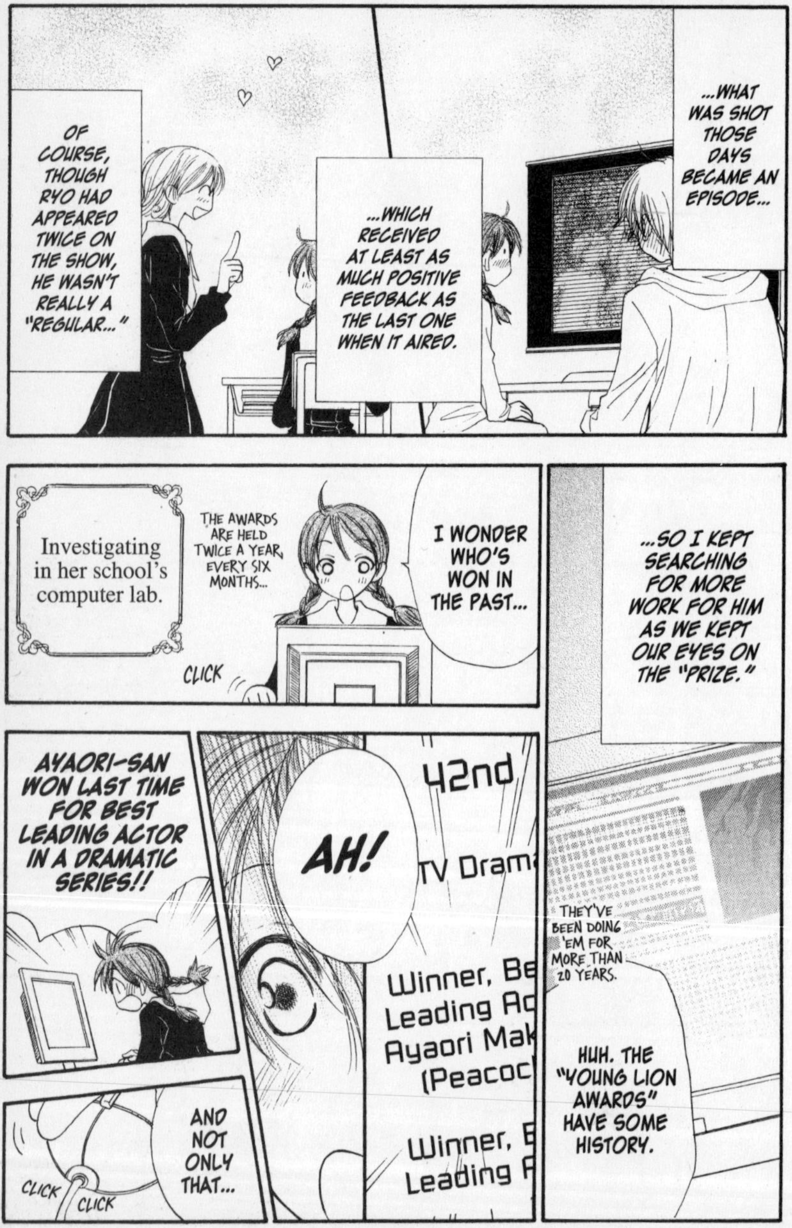
...WHAT WAS SHOT THOSE DAYS BECAME AN EPISODE...
...WHICH RECEIVED AT LEAST AS MUCH POSITIVE FEEDBACK AS THE LAST ONE WHEN IT AIRED.
OF COURSE, THOUGH RYO HAD APPEARED TWICE ON THE SHOW, HE WASN'T REALLY A "REGULAR..."
...SO I KEPT SEARCHING FOR MORE WORK FOR HIM AS WE KEPT OUR EYES ON THE "PRIZE."
HUH. THE "YOUNG LION AWARDS" HAVE SOME HISTORY.
THEY'VE BEEN DOING 'EM FOR MORE THAN 20 YEARS.
Investigating in her school's computer lab.
I WONDER WHO'S WON IN THE PAST...
THE AWARDS ARE HELD TWICE A YEAR, EVERY SIX MONTHS...
CLICK
42nd
TV Drama
Winner, Be
Leading Ac
Ayaori Mak
(Peacoc
Winner, B
Leading A
AH!
AYAORI-SAN WON LAST TIME FOR BEST LEADING ACTOR IN A DRAMATIC SERIES!!
AND NOT ONLY THAT...
CLICK
CLICK

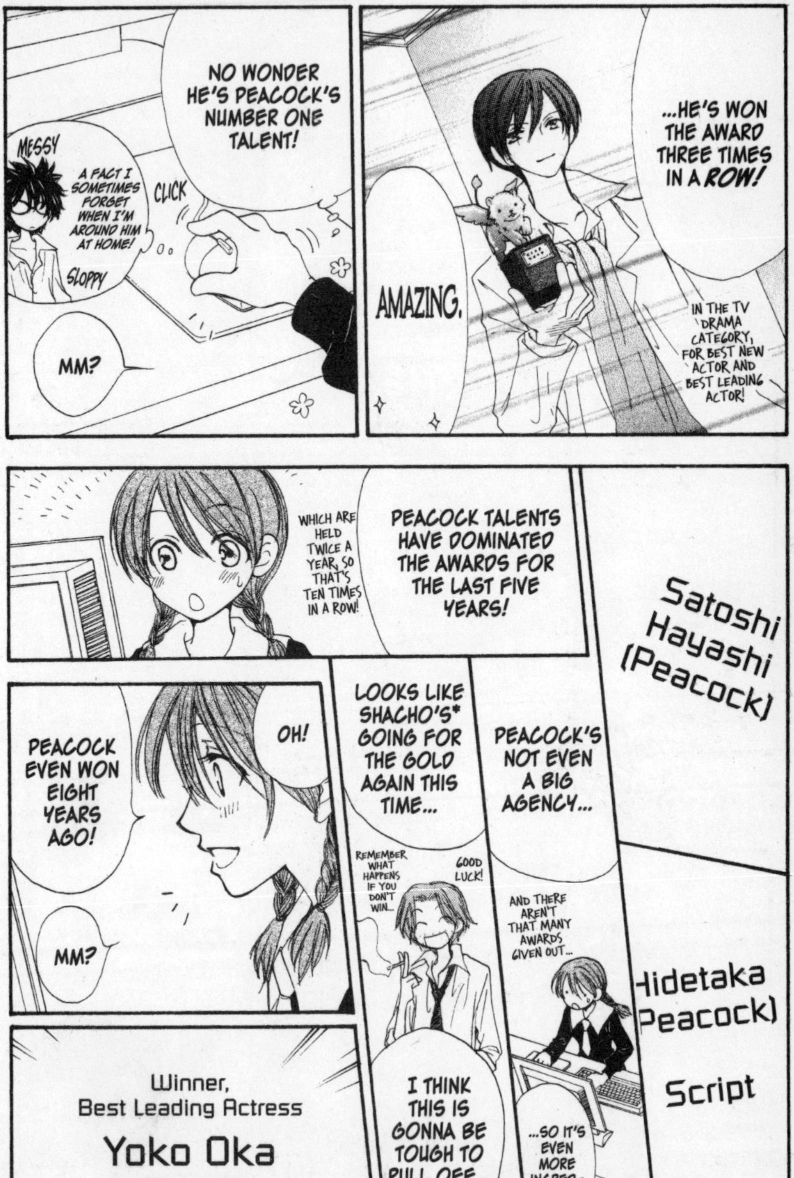
...HE'S WON THE AWARD THREE TIMES IN A ROW!
IN THE TV DRAMA CATEGORY, FOR BEST NEW ACTOR AND BEST LEADING ACTOR!
AMAZING.
NO WONDER HE'S PEACOCK'S NUMBER ONE TALENT!
CLICK
MESSY
A FACT I SOMETIMES FORGET WHEN I'M AROUND HIM AT HOME!
SLOPPY
MM?
Satoshi Hayashi (Peacock)
Hidetaka
Peacock)
Script
PEACOCK TALENTS HAVE DOMINATED THE AWARDS FOR THE LAST FIVE YEARS!
WHICH ARE HELD TWICE A YEAR, SO THAT'S TEN TIMES IN A ROW!
PEACOCK'S NOT EVEN A BIG AGENCY...
AND THERE AREN'T THAT MANY AWARDS GIVEN OUT...
...SO IT'S EVEN MORE INCRED-IBLE!
LOOKS LIKE SHACHO'S* GOING FOR THE GOLD AGAIN THIS TIME...
GOOD LUCK!
REMEMBER WHAT HAPPENS IF YOU DON'T WIN...
I THINK THIS IS GONNA BE TOUGH TO PULL OFF...
OH!
PEACOCK EVEN WON EIGHT YEARS AGO!
MM?
Winner, Best Leading Actress
Yoko Oka
(Peacock)

* Company president

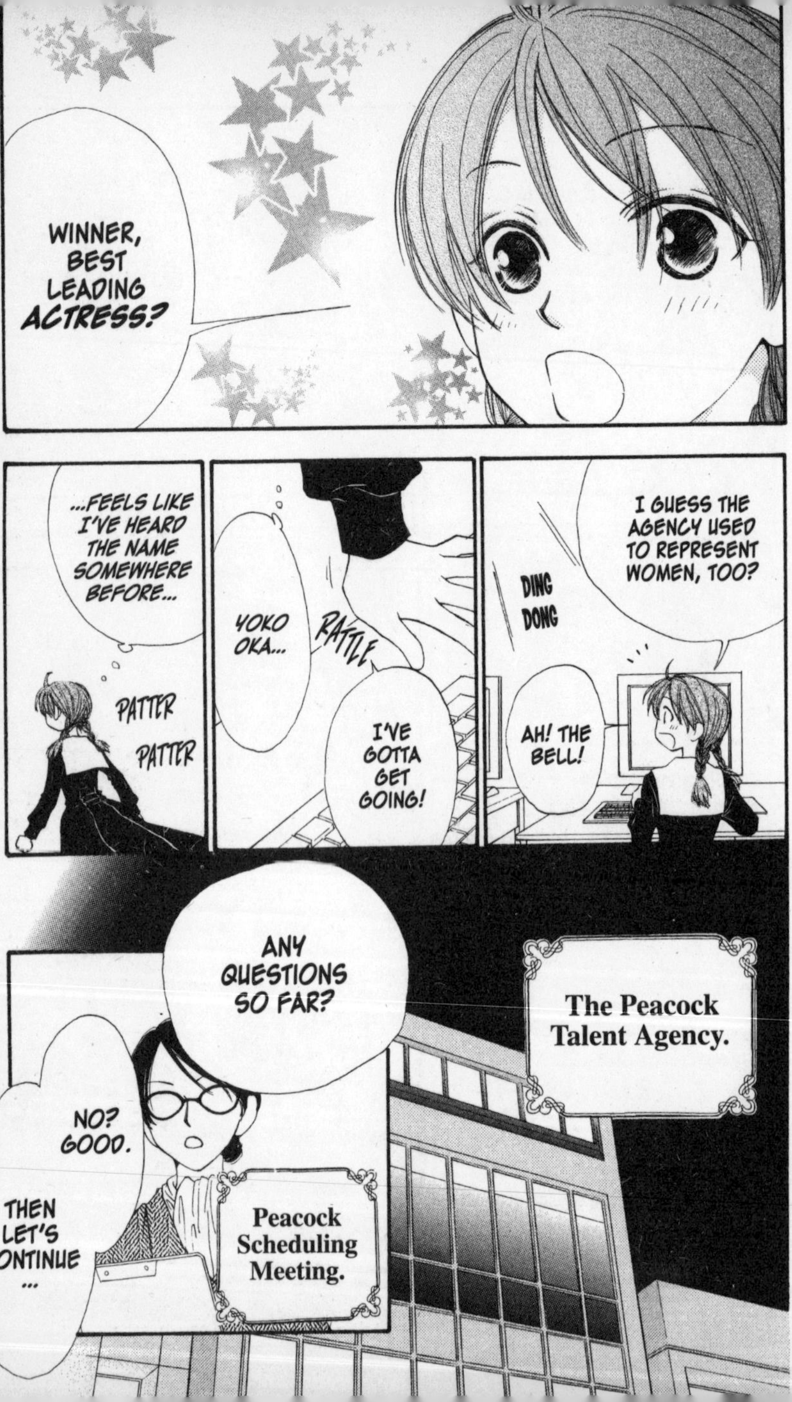
WINNER, BEST LEADING ACTRESS?
I GUESS THE AGENCY USED TO REPRESENT WOMEN, TOO?
DING DONG
AH! THE BELL!
YOKO OKA...
RATTLE
I'VE GOTTA GET GOING!
...FEELS LIKE I'VE HEARD THE NAME SOMEWHERE BEFORE...
PATTER
PATTER
The Peacock Talent Agency.
ANY QUESTIONS SO FAR?
Peacock Scheduling Meeting.
NO? GOOD.
THEN LET'S CONTINUE ...

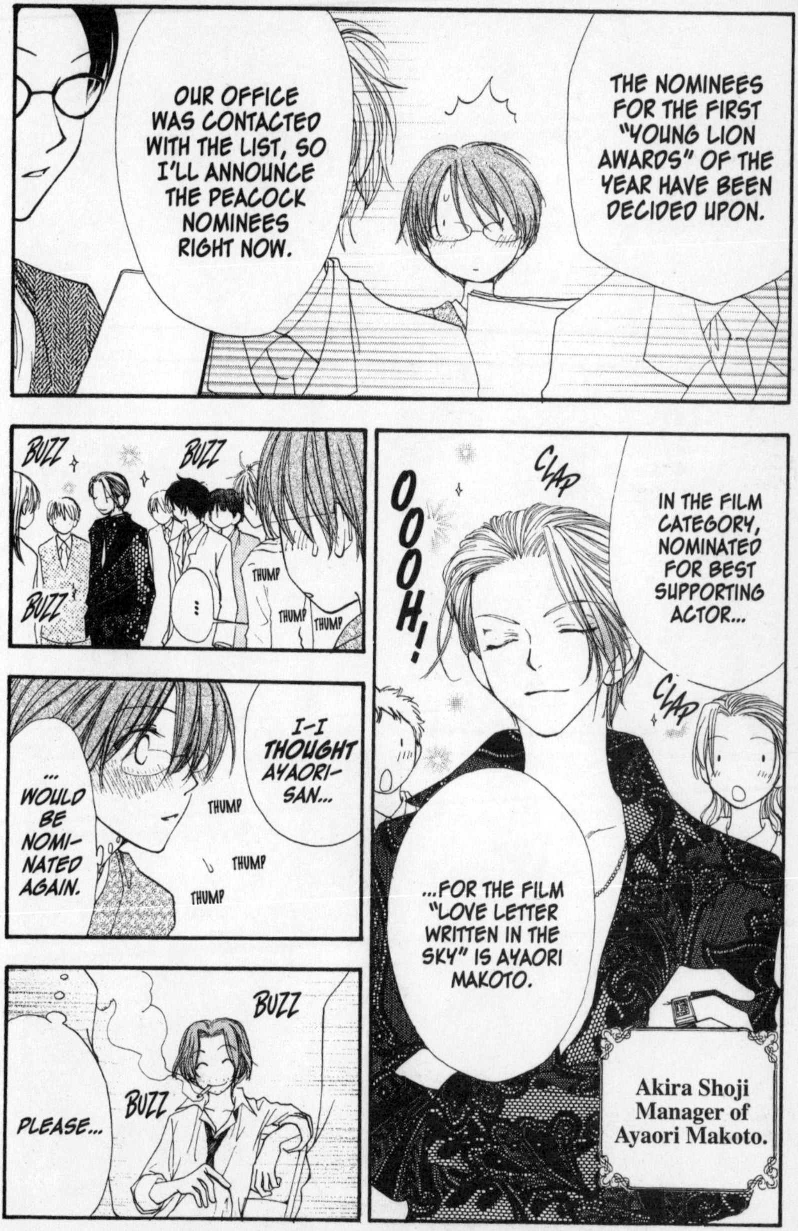
THE NOMINEES FOR THE FIRST "YOUNG LION AWARDS" OF THE YEAR HAVE BEEN DECIDED UPON.
OUR OFFICE WAS CONTACTED WITH THE LIST, SO I'LL ANNOUNCE THE PEACOCK NOMINEES RIGHT NOW.
CLAP
IN THE FILM CATEGORY, NOMINATED FOR BEST SUPPORTING ACTOR...
OOOOH!
CLAP
...FOR THE FILM "LOVE LETTER WRITTEN IN THE SKY" IS AYAORI MAKOTO.
Akira Shoji Manager of Ayaori Makoto.
BUZZ
BUZZ
BUZZ
...
THUMP
THUMP
THUMP
I-I THOUGHT AYAORI-SAN...
...WOULD BE NOMINATED AGAIN.
THUMP
THUMP
THUMP
BUZZ
BUZZ
PLEASE...

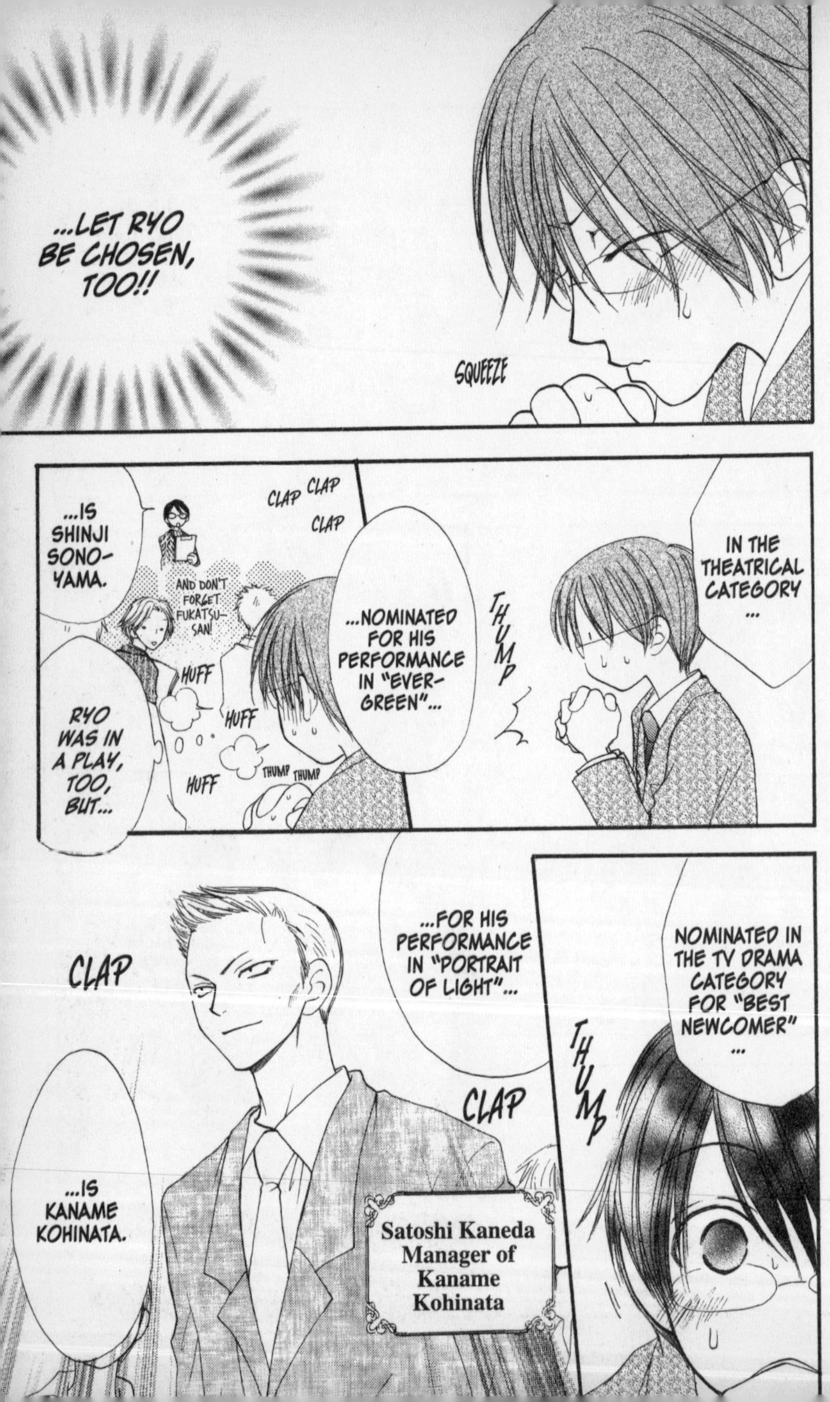
...LET RYO BE CHOSEN, TOO!!
SQUEEZE
IN THE THEATRICAL CATEGORY ...
THUMP
...NOMINATED FOR HIS PERFORMANCE IN "EVER-GREEN"...
CLAP CLAP
CLAP
...IS SHINJI SONO-YAMA.
AND DON'T FORGET FUKATSU-SAN!
HUFF
HUFF
HUFF
THUMP THUMP
RYO WAS IN A PLAY, TOO, BUT...
NOMINATED IN THE TV DRAMA CATEGORY FOR "BEST NEWCOMER" ...
THUMP
...FOR HIS PERFORMANCE IN "PORTRAIT OF LIGHT"...
CLAP
CLAP
Satoshi Kaneda Manager of Kaname Kohinata
...IS KANAME KOHINATA.

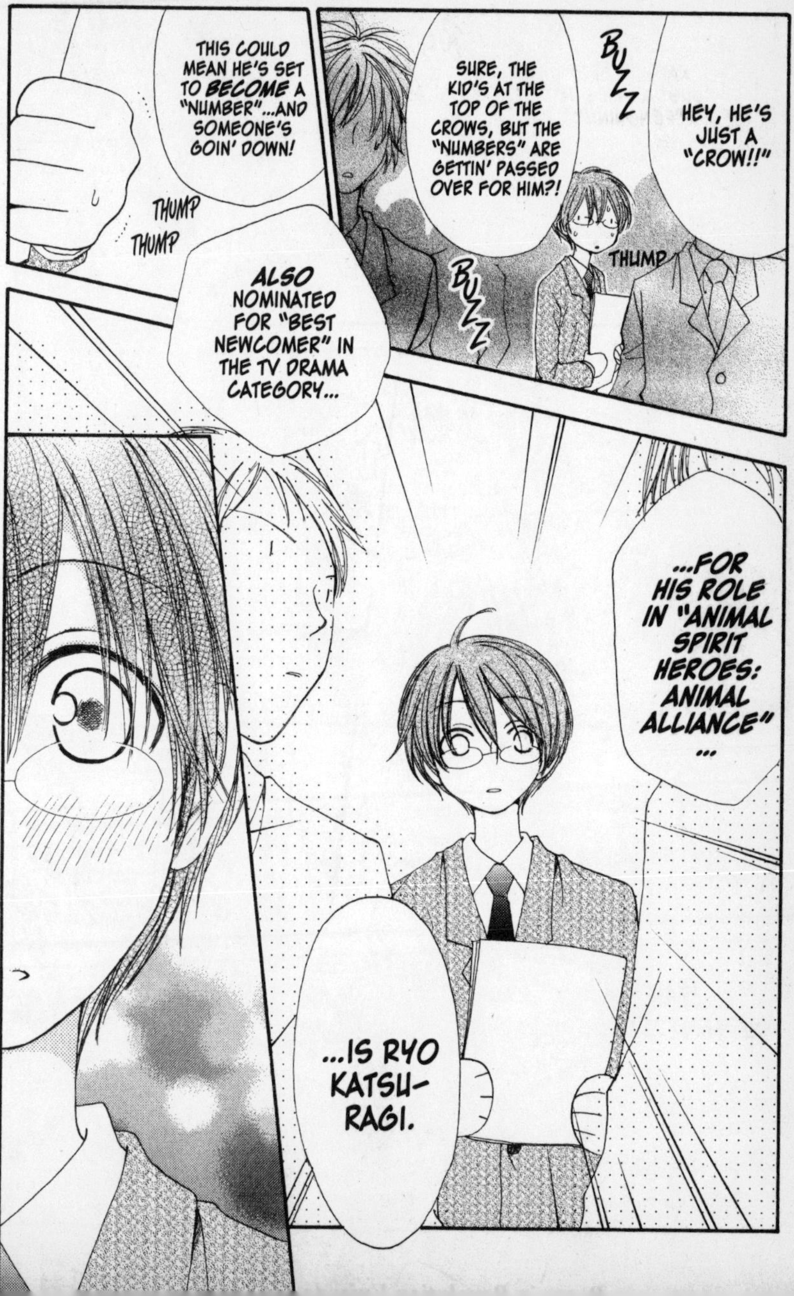
BUZZ
HEY, HE'S JUST A "CROW!!"
SURE, THE KID'S AT THE TOP OF THE CROWS, BUT THE "NUMBERS" ARE GETTIN' PASSED OVER FOR HIM?!
THUMP
BUZZ
THIS COULD MEAN HE'S SET TO BECOME A "NUMBER"...AND SOMEONE'S GOIN' DOWN!
THUMP
THUMP
ALSO NOMINATED FOR "BEST NEWCOMER" IN THE TV DRAMA CATEGORY...
...FOR HIS ROLE IN "ANIMAL SPIRIT HEROES: ANIMAL ALLIANCE"...
...IS RYO KATSURAGI.

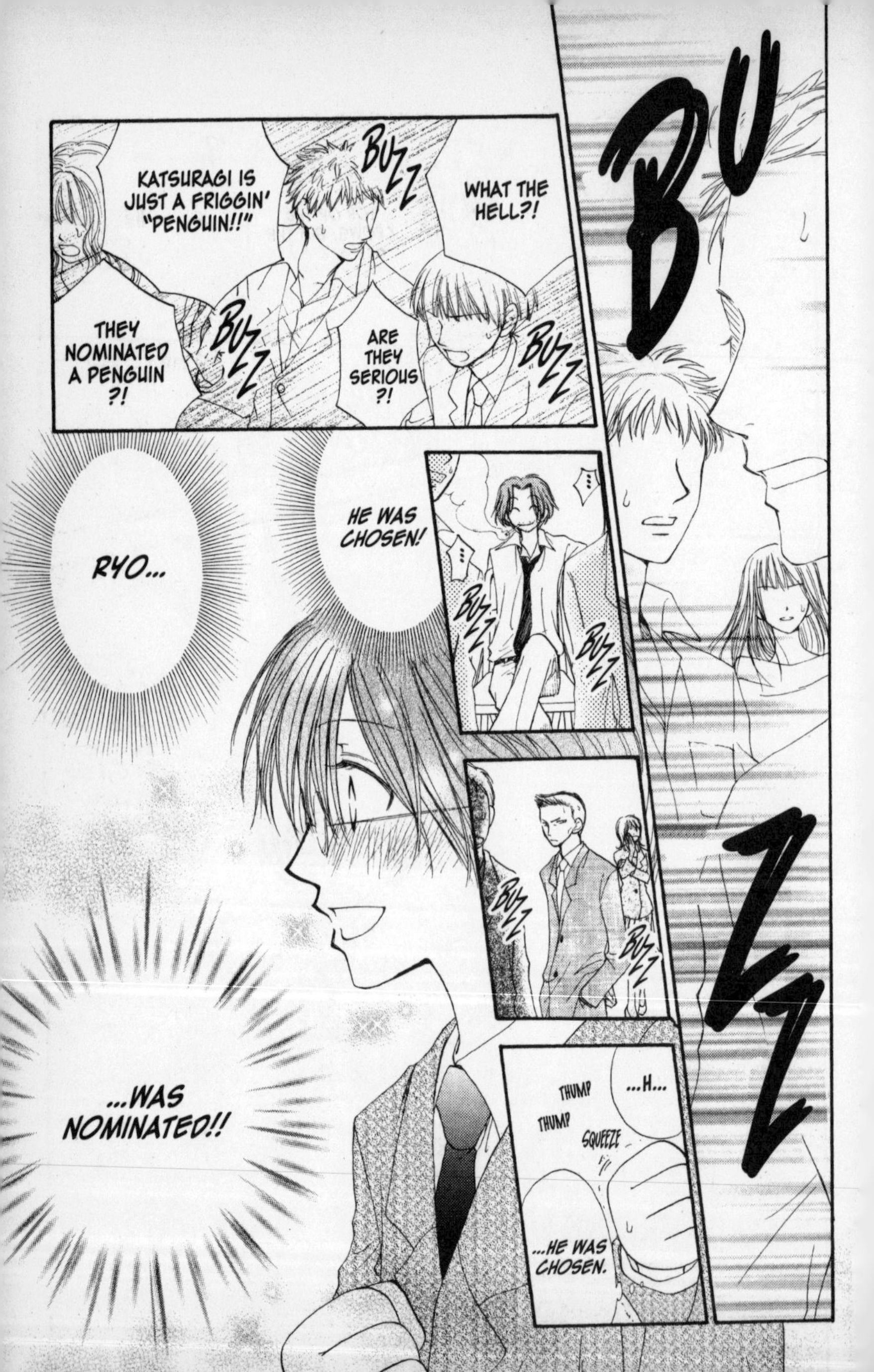
BUZZ
WHAT THE HELL?!
BUZZ
KATSURAGI IS JUST A FRIGGIN' "PENGUIN!!"
BUZZ
ARE THEY SERIOUS?!
BUZZ
THEY NOMINATED A PENGUIN?!
HE WAS CHOSEN!
RYO...
BUZZ
BUZZ
BUZZ
BUZZ
...H...
THUMP
THUMP
SQUEEZE
...HE WAS CHOSEN.
...WAS NOMINATED!!

Romeo in Revolution Episode 17: The End

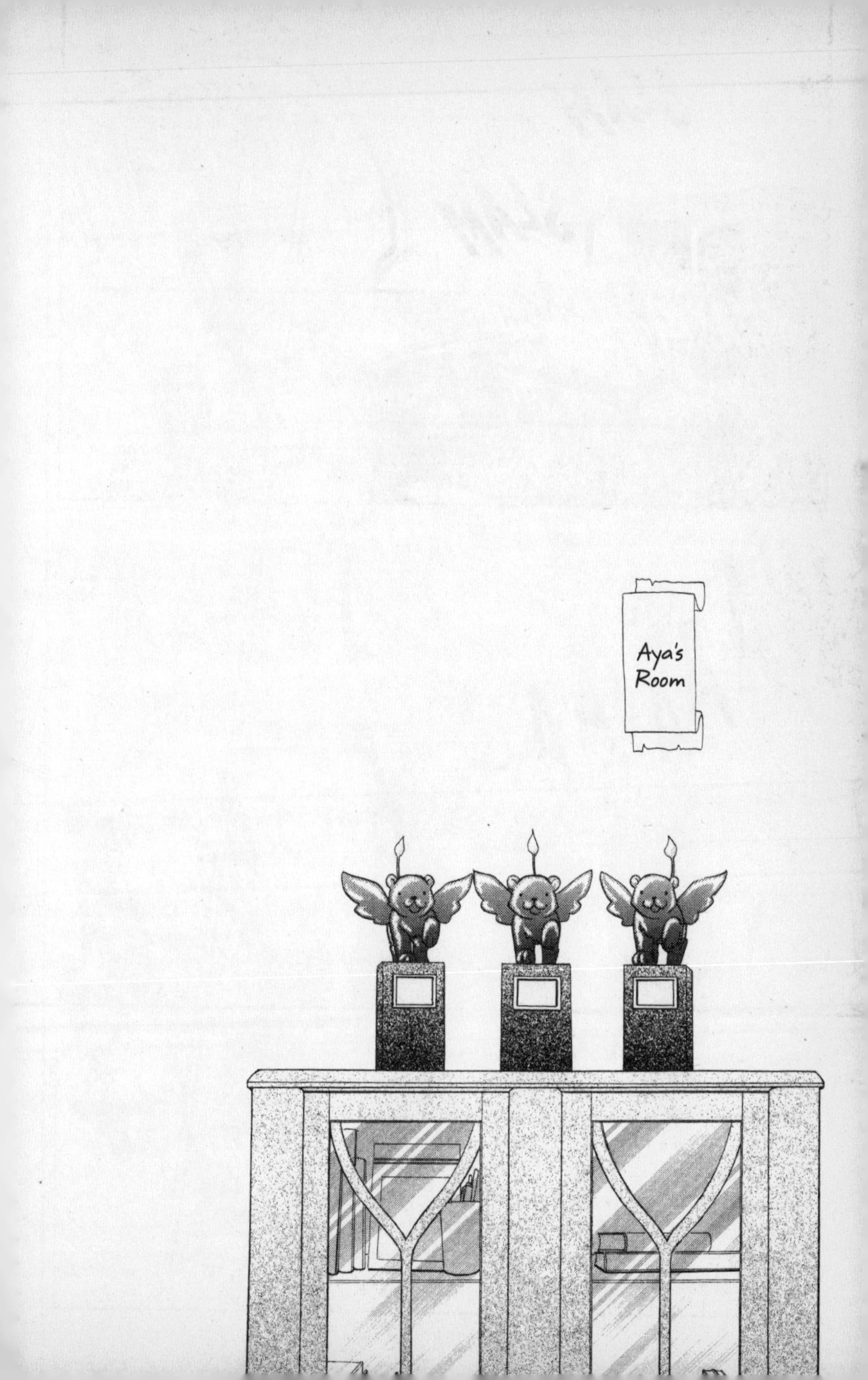

Aya's
Room

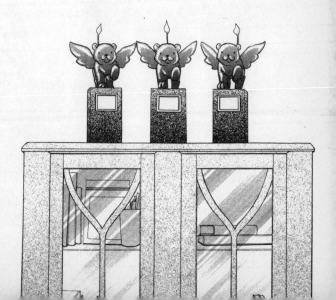

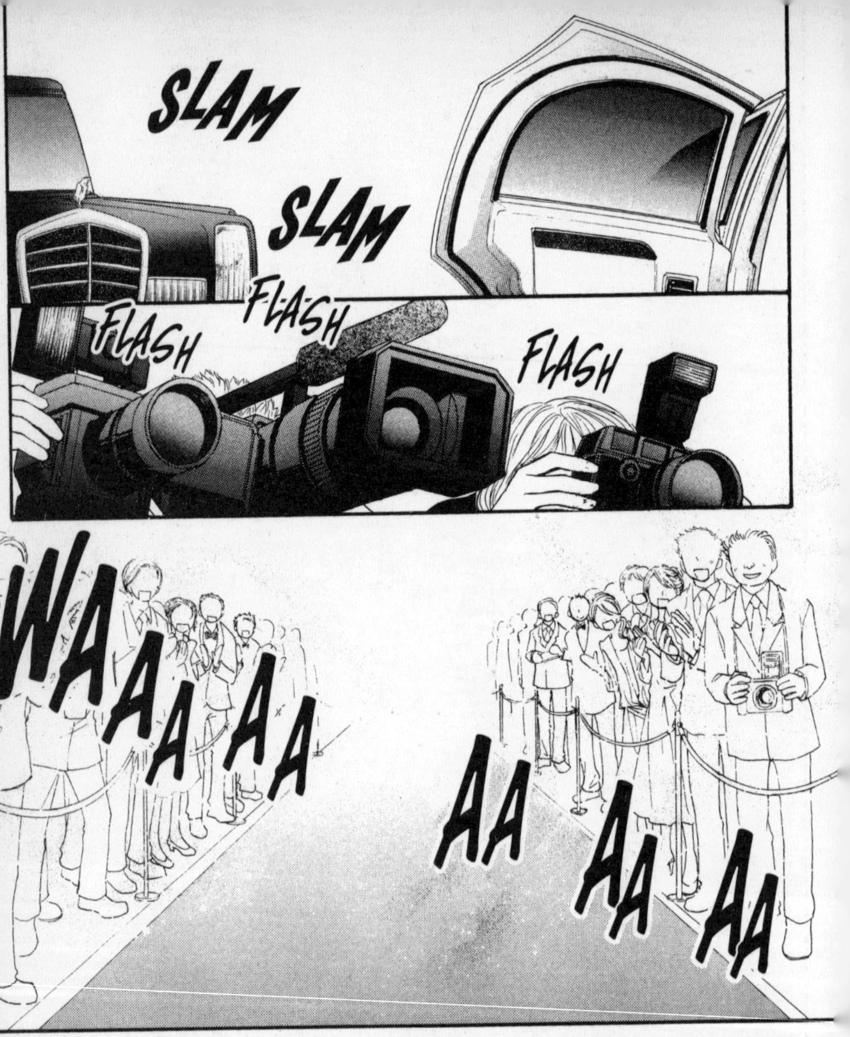
SLAM
SLAM
FLASH
F-L-A-SH
FLASH
WAAAAAA
AA AA AA

And here we are at the Young Lion Awards ceremony. I had a fantastic time drawing this!! Even my hand seems happy when it gets the chance to draw a scene in such a grand setting. By the way, the clothes the Peacock nominees are wearing were a present from Shacho. I thought maybe I should've had Yuka-chin wearing a tail coat, but oh well...
(To be continued)

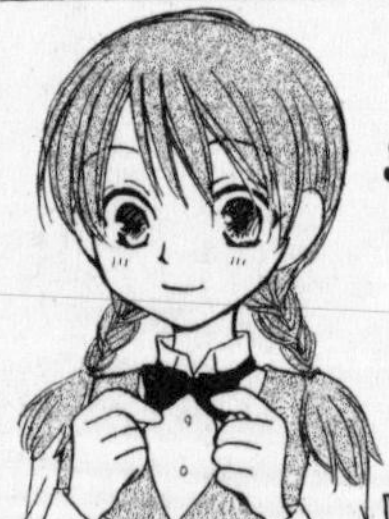

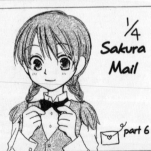

1/4
Sakura
Mail

part 6

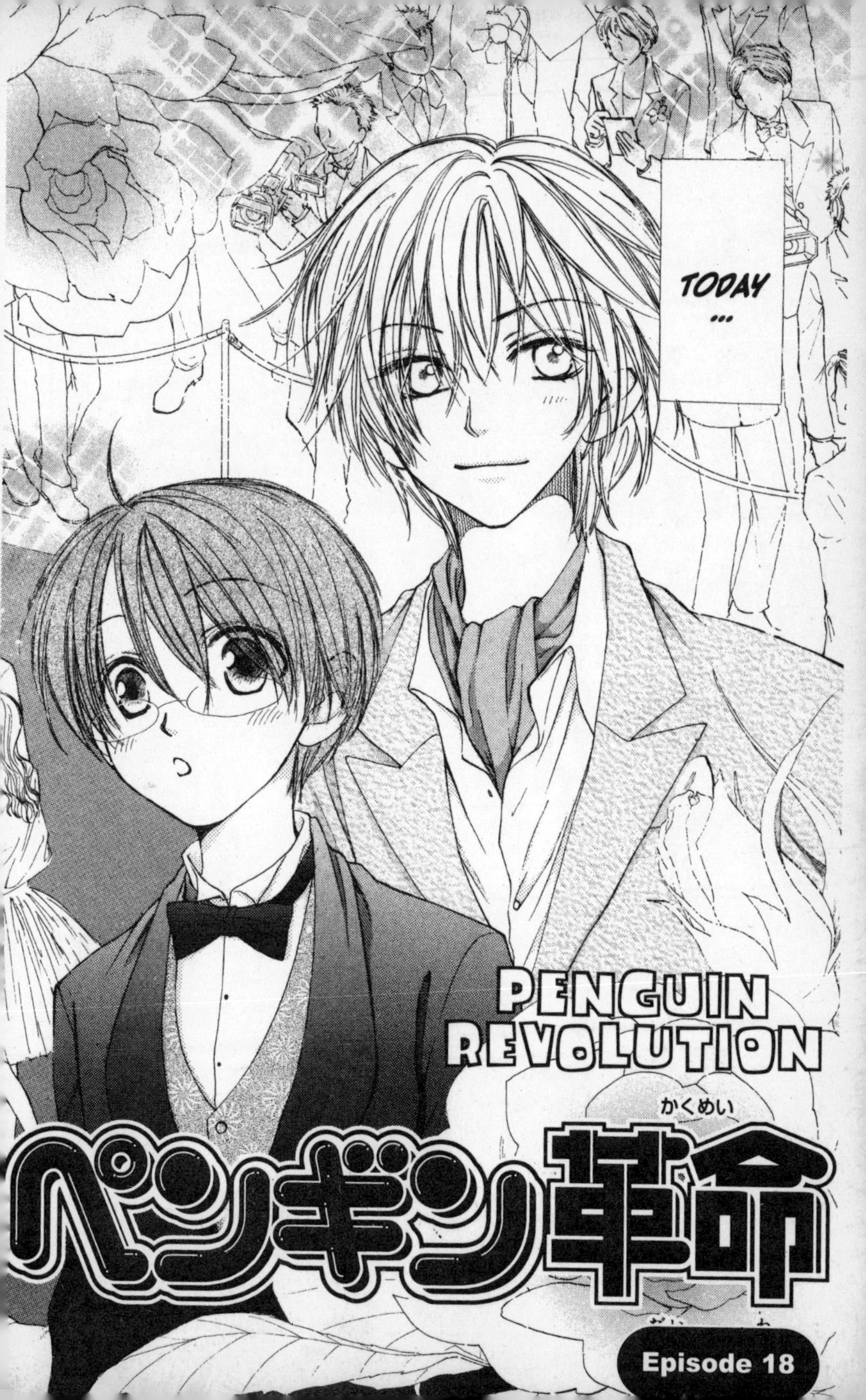
TODAY ...
PENGUIN REVOLUTION
かくめい
ペンギン革命
Episode 18

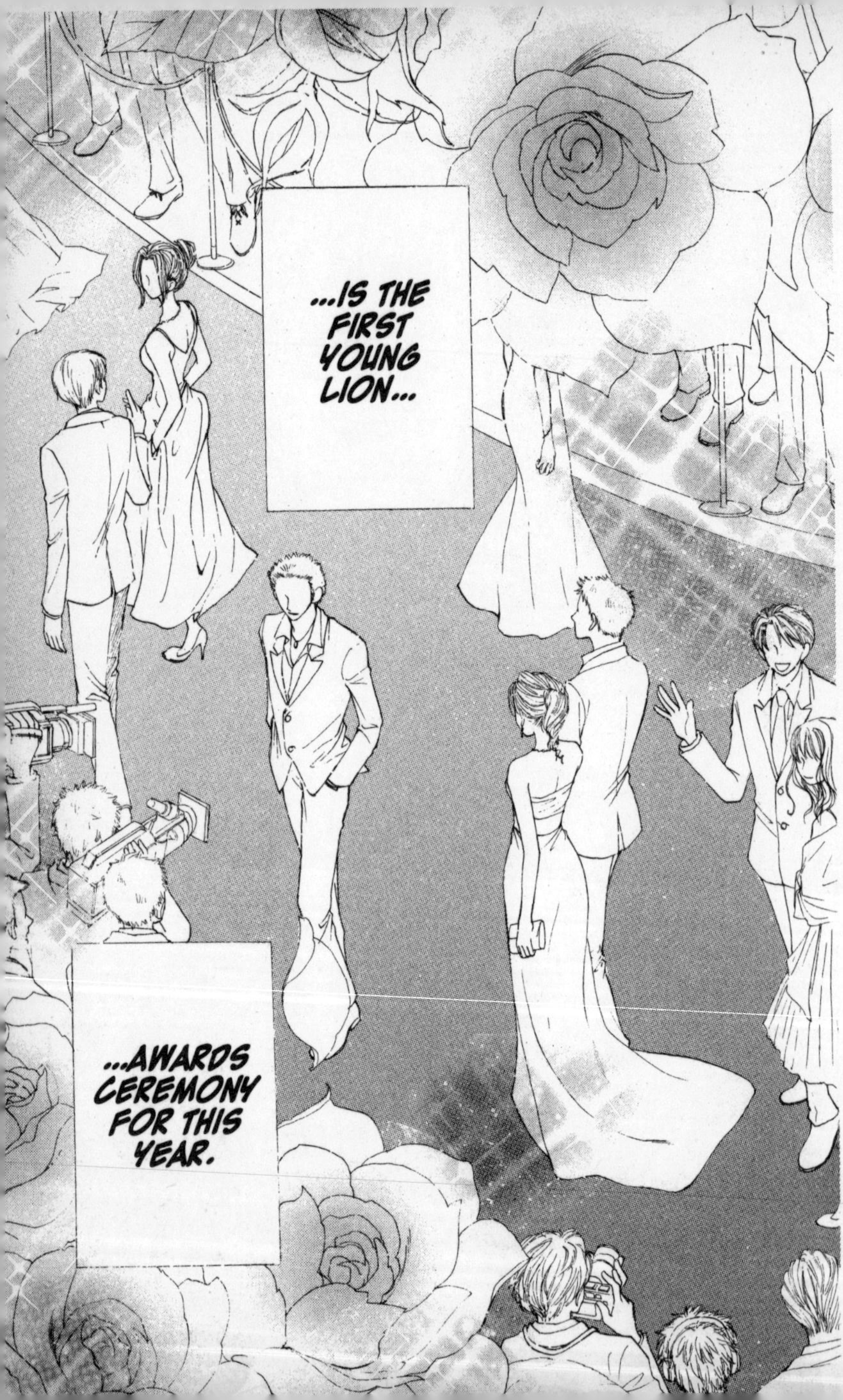
...IS THE FIRST YOUNG LION...
...AWARDS CEREMONY FOR THIS YEAR.

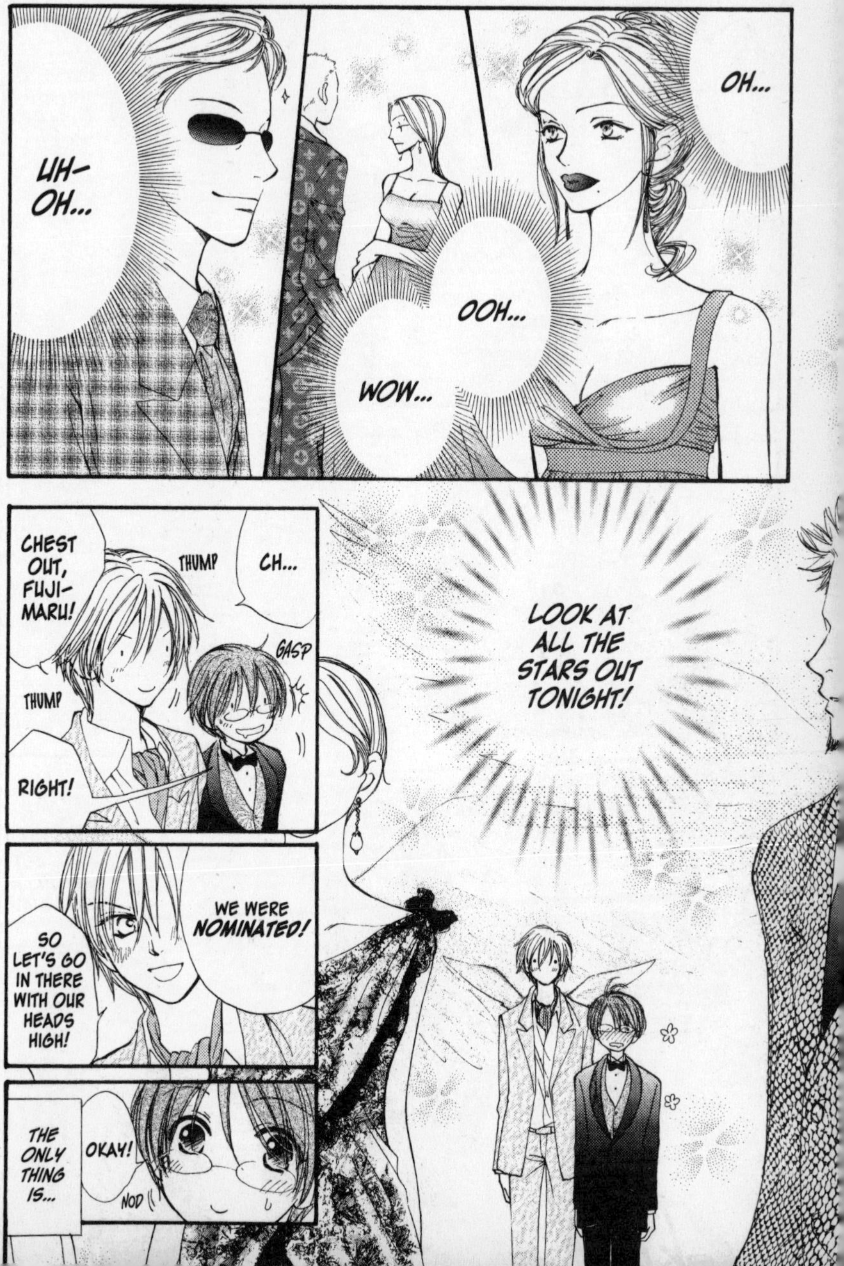
OH...
OOH...
WOW...
UH-OH...
LOOK AT ALL THE STARS OUT TONIGHT!
CH...
THUMP
GASP
CHEST OUT, FUJI-MARU!
THUMP
RIGHT!
WE WERE **NOMINATED!**
SO LET'S GO IN THERE WITH OUR HEADS HIGH!
OKAY!
NOD
THE ONLY THING IS...

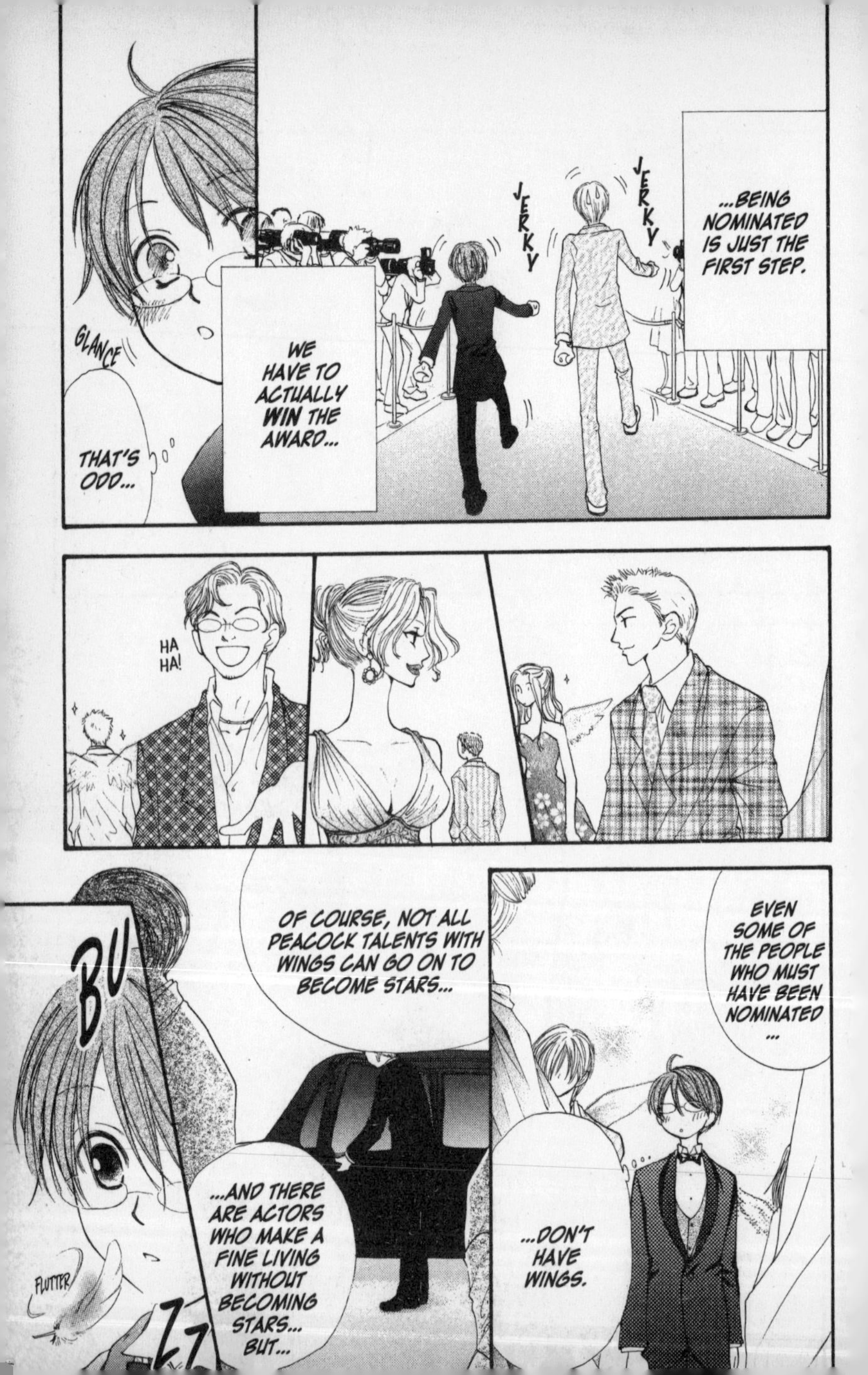
...BEING NOMINATED IS JUST THE FIRST STEP.
JERKY
JERKY
WE HAVE TO ACTUALLY WIN THE AWARD...
GLANCE
THAT'S ODD...
HA HA!
OF COURSE, NOT ALL PEACOCK TALENTS WITH WINGS CAN GO ON TO BECOME STARS...
BU
ZZ
...AND THERE ARE ACTORS WHO MAKE A FINE LIVING WITHOUT BECOMING STARS... BUT...
FLUTTER
EVEN SOME OF THE PEOPLE WHO MUST HAVE BEEN NOMINATED ...
...DON'T HAVE WINGS.

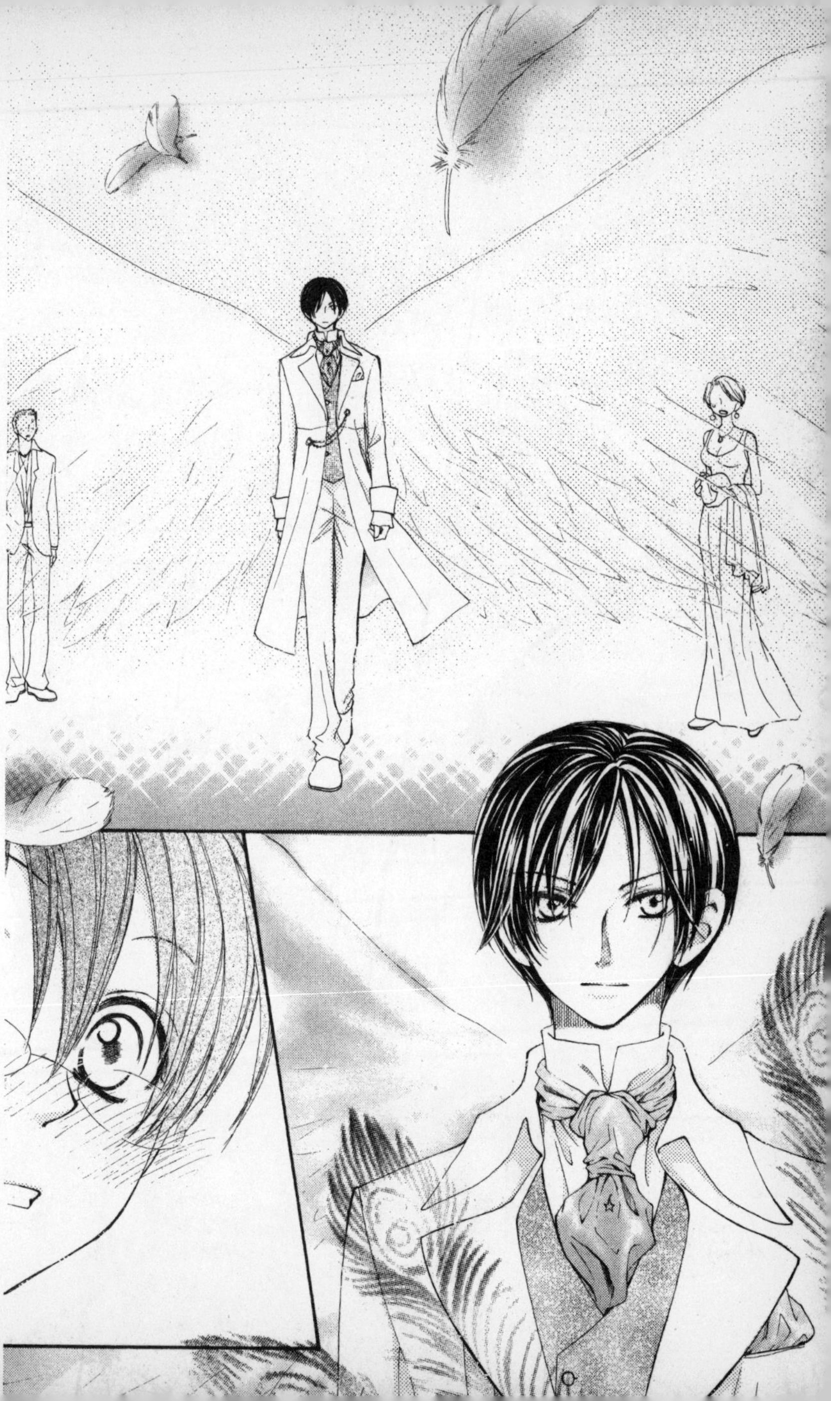

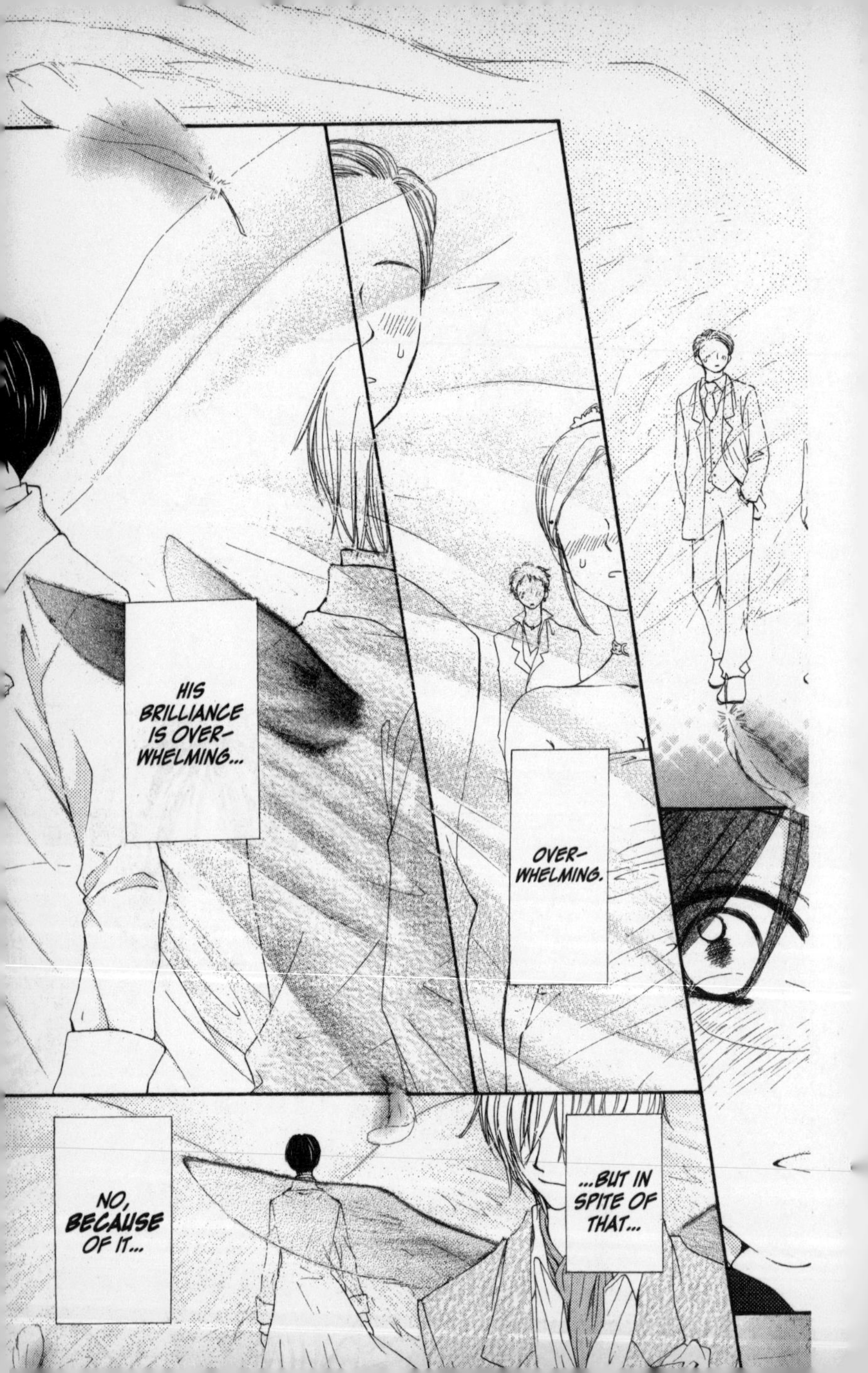
OVER-WHELMING.
HIS BRILLIANCE IS OVER-WHELMING...
...BUT IN SPITE OF THAT...
NO, BECAUSE OF IT...

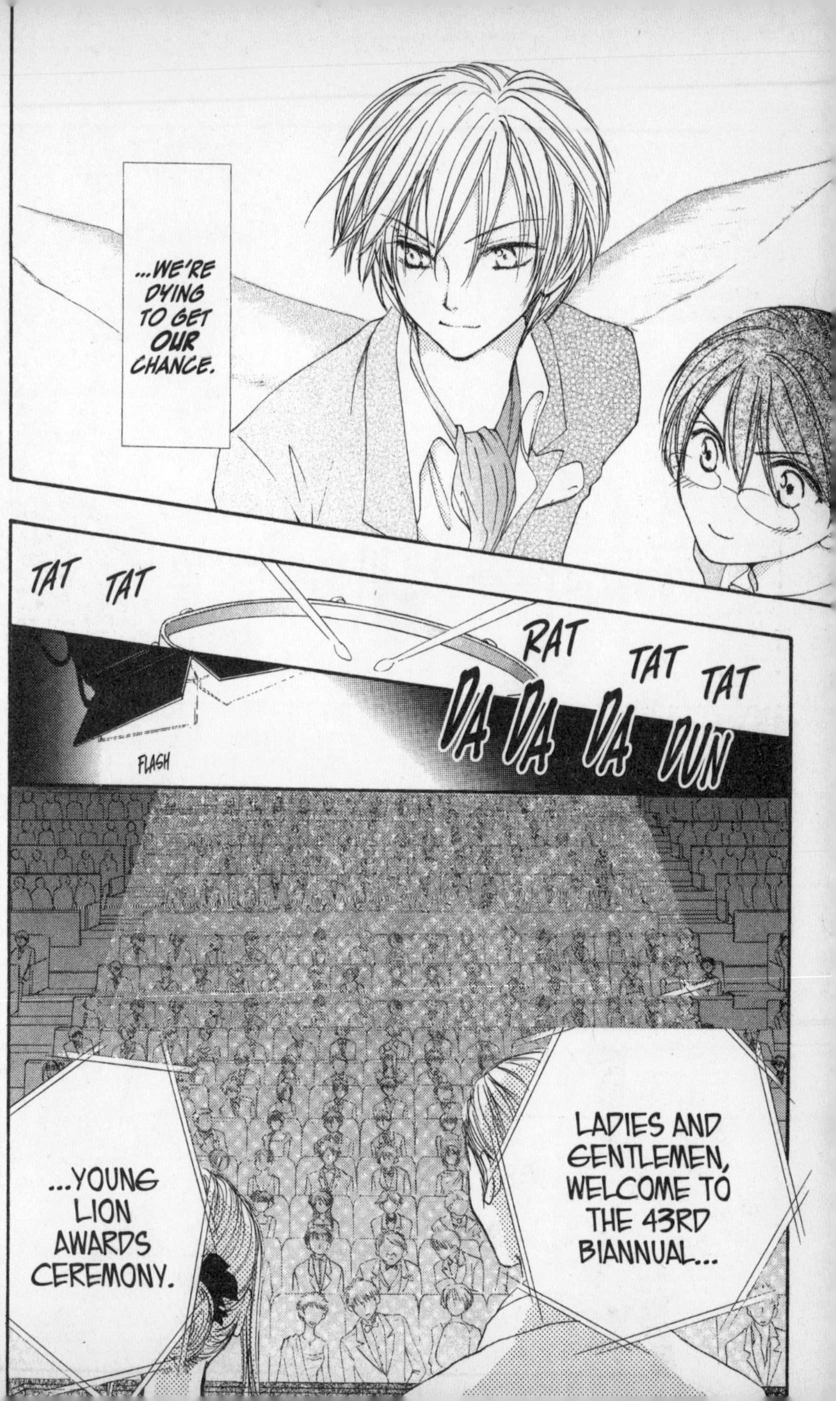
...WE'RE DYING TO GET OUR CHANCE.
TAT TAT
RAT TAT TAT
DA DA DA DUN
FLASH
LADIES AND GENTLEMEN, WELCOME TO THE 43RD BIANNUAL...
...YOUNG LION AWARDS CEREMONY.

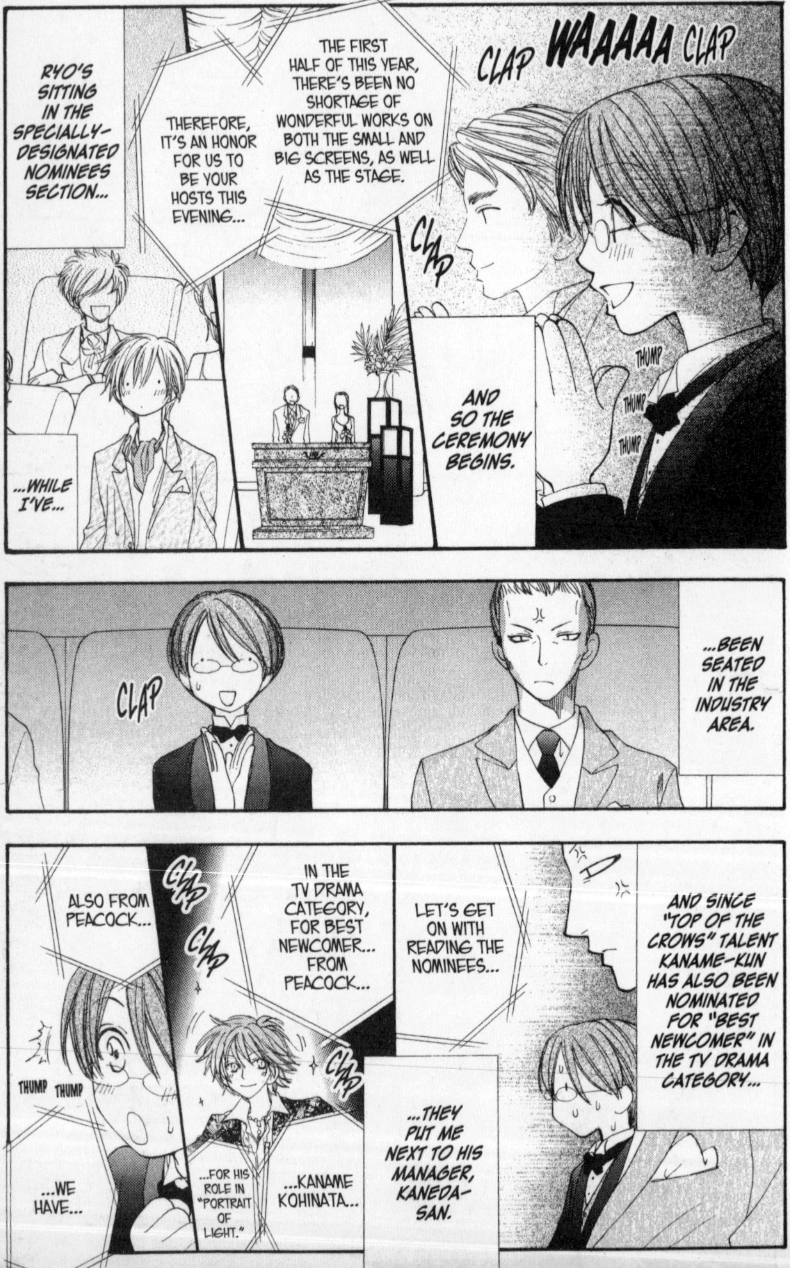
CLAP WAAAAA CLAP
CLAP
THUMP
THUMP
THUMP
AND SO THE CEREMONY BEGINS.
THE FIRST HALF OF THIS YEAR, THERE'S BEEN NO SHORTAGE OF WONDERFUL WORKS ON BOTH THE SMALL AND BIG SCREENS, AS WELL AS THE STAGE.
THEREFORE, IT'S AN HONOR FOR US TO BE YOUR HOSTS THIS EVENING...
RYO'S SITTING IN THE SPECIALLY-DESIGNATED NOMINEES SECTION...
...WHILE I'VE...
...BEEN SEATED IN THE INDUSTRY AREA.
CLAP
AND SINCE "TOP OF THE CROWS" TALENT KANAME-KUN HAS ALSO BEEN NOMINATED FOR "BEST NEWCOMER" IN THE TV DRAMA CATEGORY...
...THEY PUT ME NEXT TO HIS MANAGER, KANEDA-SAN.
LET'S GET ON WITH READING THE NOMINEES...
IN THE TV DRAMA CATEGORY, FOR BEST NEWCOMER... FROM PEACOCK...
CLAP
CLAP
CLAP
...KANAME KOHINATA...
...FOR HIS ROLE IN "PORTRAIT OF LIGHT."
ALSO FROM PEACOCK...
THUMP THUMP
...WE HAVE...

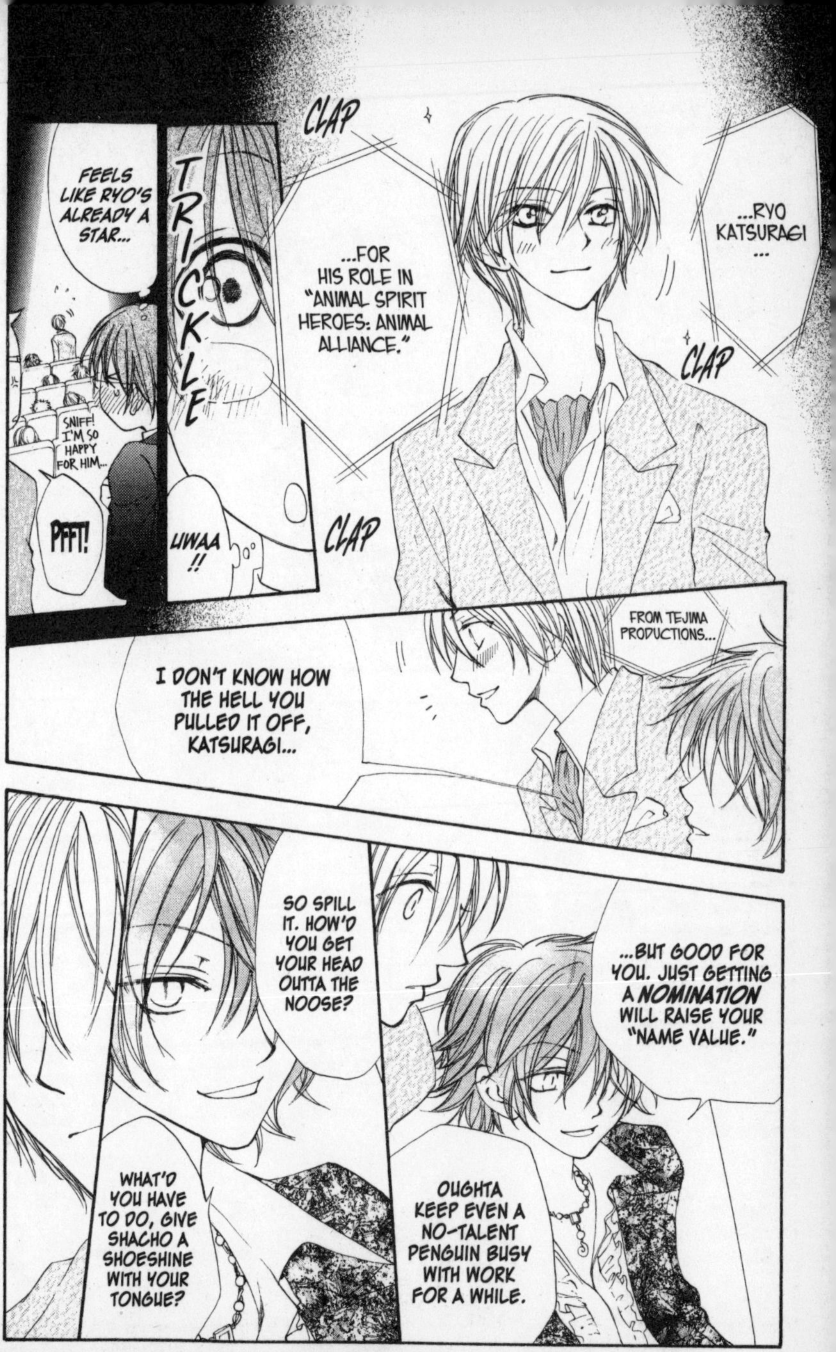
CLAP
...RYO KATSURAGI ...
...FOR HIS ROLE IN "ANIMAL SPIRIT HEROES: ANIMAL ALLIANCE."
CLAP
CLAP
TRICKLE
UWAA!!
FEELS LIKE RYO'S ALREADY A STAR...
SNIFF! I'M SO HAPPY FOR HIM...
PFFT!
FROM TEJIMA PRODUCTIONS...
I DON'T KNOW HOW THE HELL YOU PULLED IT OFF, KATSURAGI...
...BUT GOOD FOR YOU. JUST GETTING A NOMINATION WILL RAISE YOUR "NAME VALUE."
OUGHTA KEEP EVEN A NO-TALENT PENGUIN BUSY WITH WORK FOR A WHILE.
SO SPILL IT. HOW'D YOU GET YOUR HEAD OUTTA THE NOOSE?
WHAT'D YOU HAVE TO DO, GIVE SHACHO A SHOESHINE WITH YOUR TONGUE?

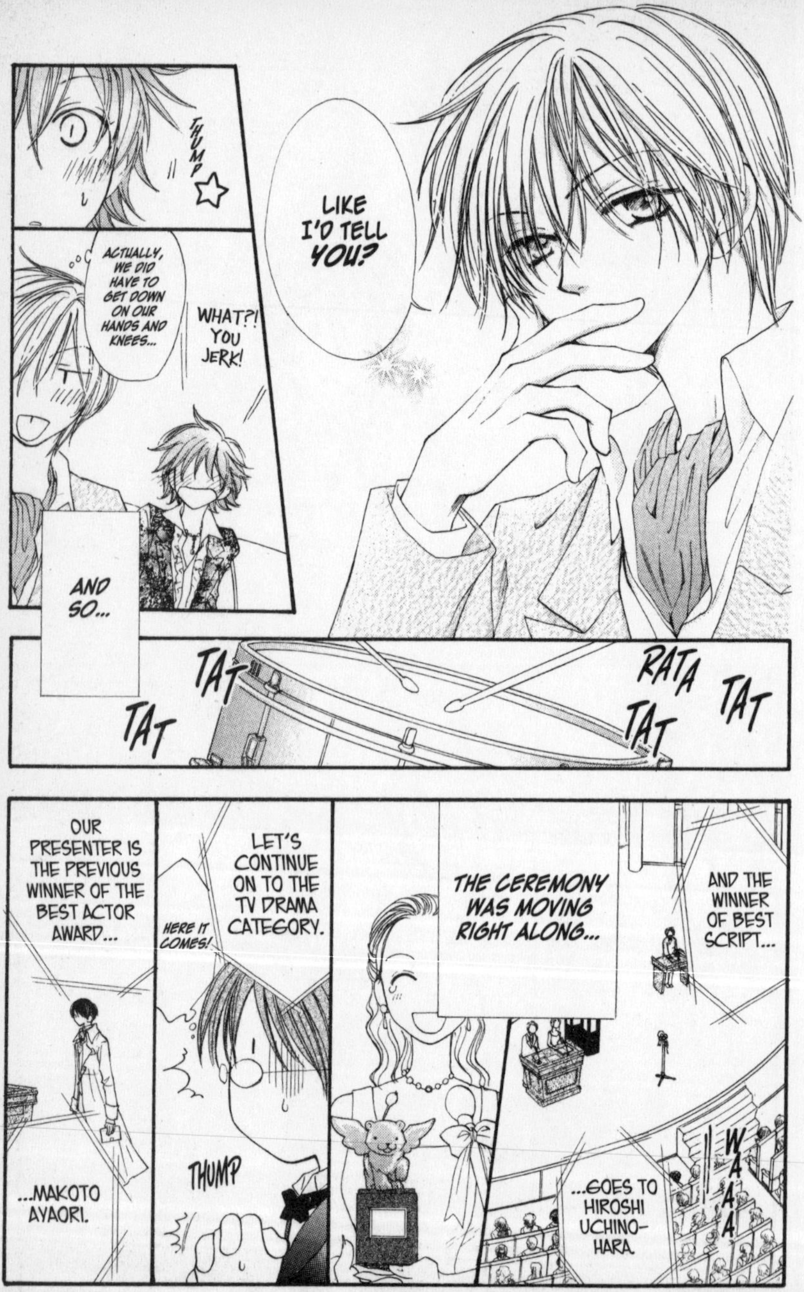
LIKE I'D TELL YOU?
THUMP
ACTUALLY, WE DID HAVE TO GET DOWN ON OUR HANDS AND KNEES...
WHAT?! YOU JERK!
AND SO...
RATA TAT
TAT
TAT
TAT
AND THE WINNER OF BEST SCRIPT...
...GOES TO HIROSHI UCHINO-HARA.
WAAA
THE CEREMONY WAS MOVING RIGHT ALONG...
LET'S CONTINUE ON TO THE TV DRAMA CATEGORY.
HERE IT COMES!
THUMP
OUR PRESENTER IS THE PREVIOUS WINNER OF THE BEST ACTOR AWARD...
...MAKOTO AYAORI.

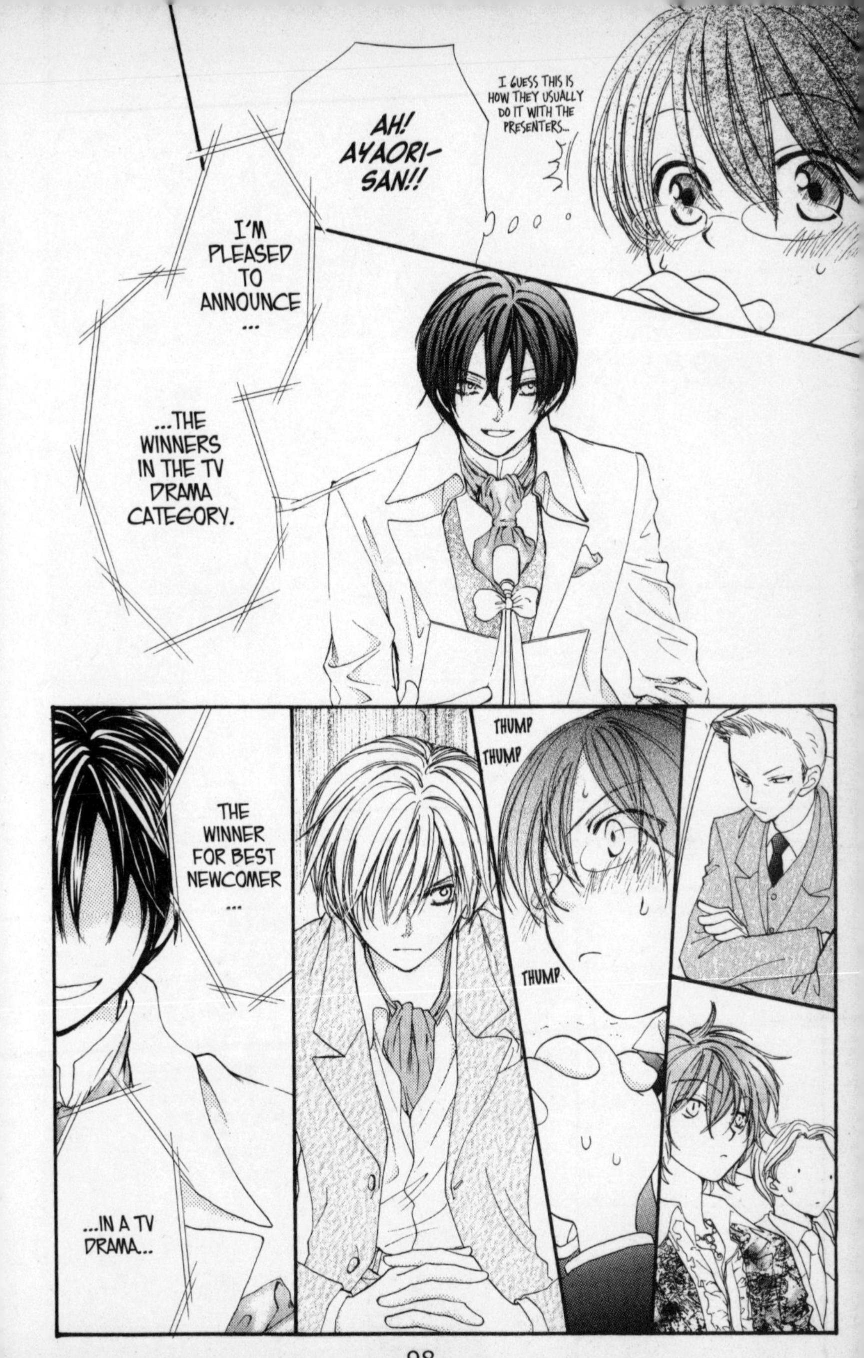
I GUESS THIS IS HOW THEY USUALLY DO IT WITH THE PRESENTERS...
AH! AYAORI-SAN!!
I'M PLEASED TO ANNOUNCE...
...THE WINNERS IN THE TV DRAMA CATEGORY.
THUMP
THUMP
THUMP
THE WINNER FOR BEST NEWCOMER...
...IN A TV DRAMA...

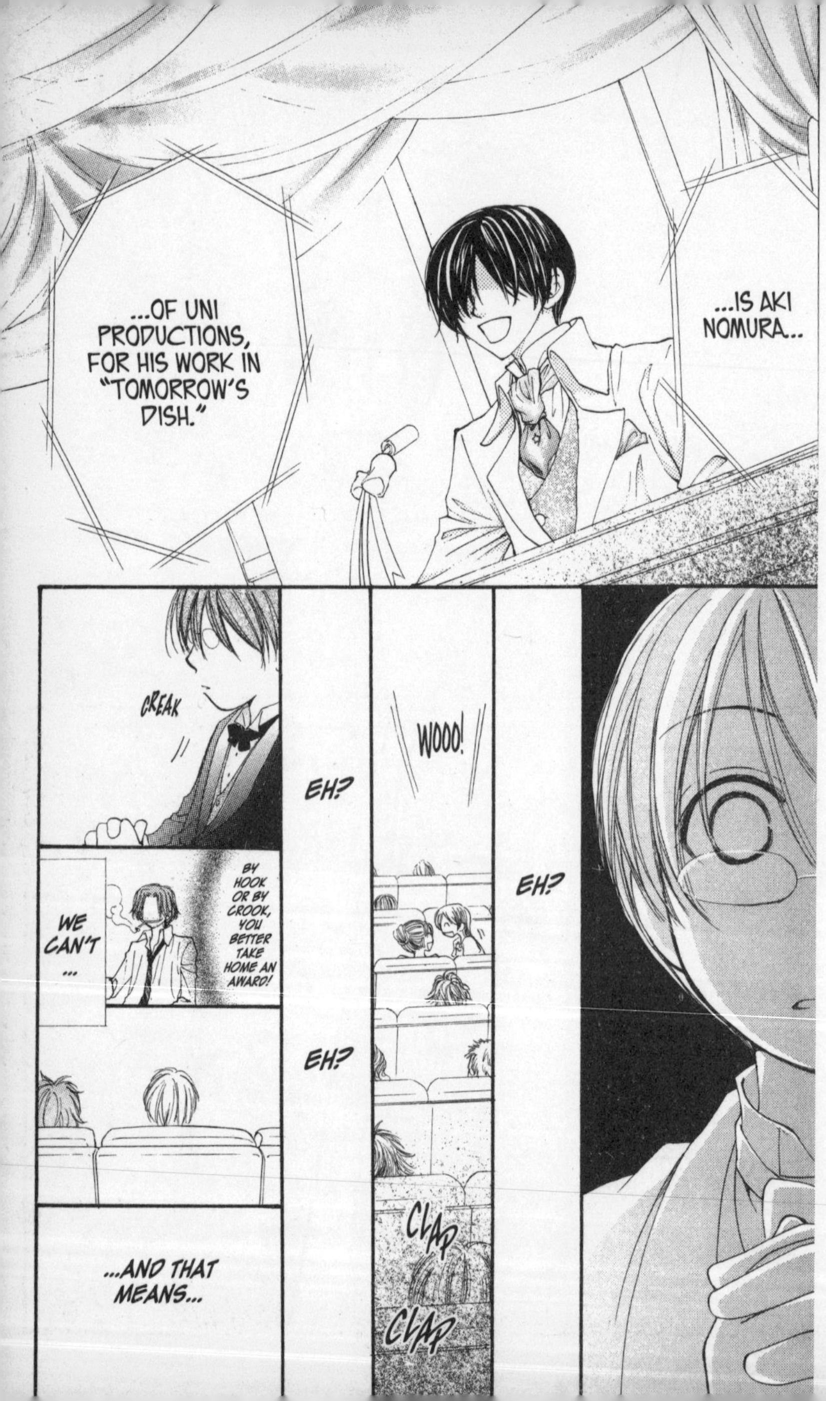
...IS AKI NOMURA...
...OF UNI PRODUCTIONS, FOR HIS WORK IN "TOMORROW'S DISH."
EH?
WOOO!
CLAP
CLAP
EH?
EH?
CREAK
BY HOOK OR BY CROOK, YOU BETTER TAKE HOME AN AWARD!
WE CAN'T ...
...AND THAT MEANS...

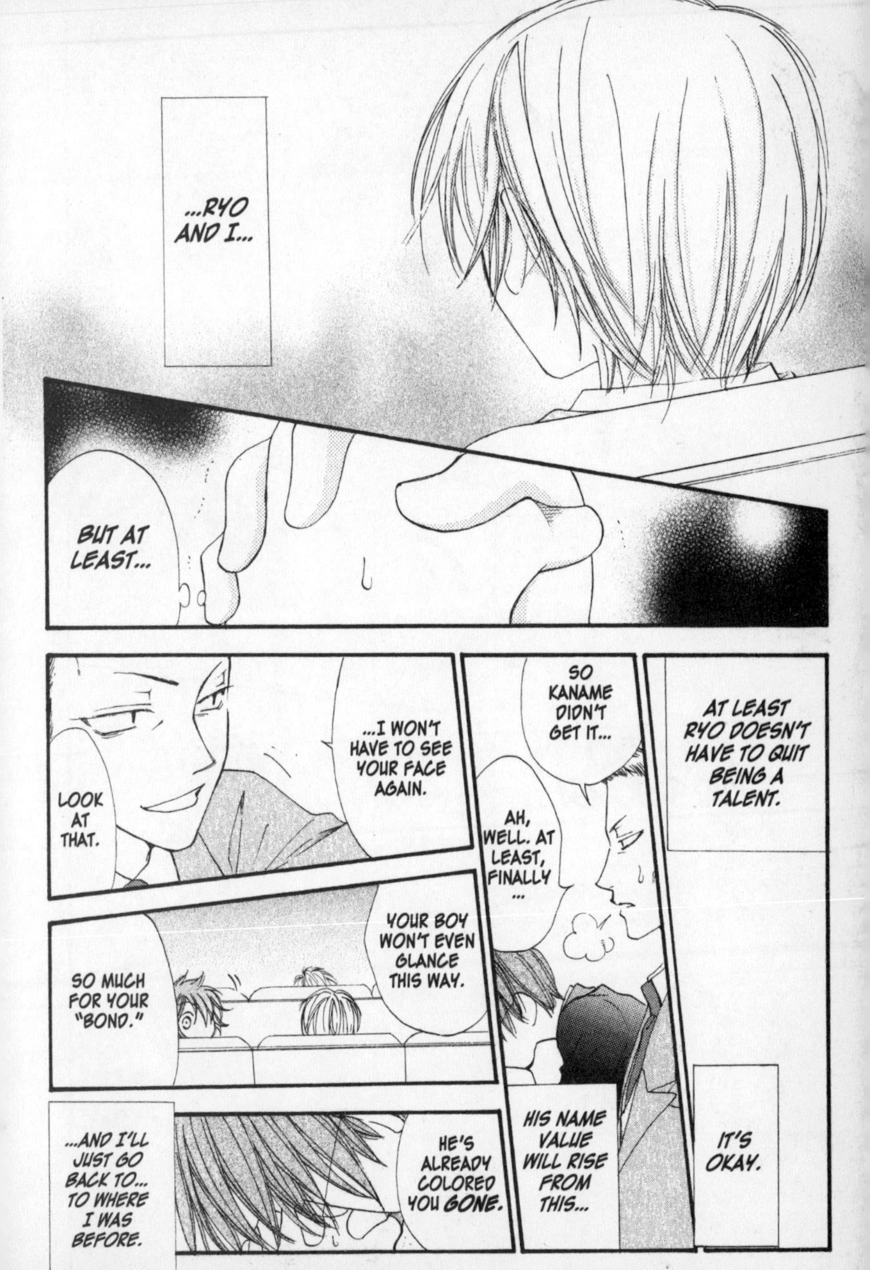
...RYO AND I...
BUT AT LEAST...
AT LEAST RYO DOESN'T HAVE TO QUIT BEING A TALENT.
SO KANAME DIDN'T GET IT...
AH, WELL. AT LEAST, FINALLY...
...I WON'T HAVE TO SEE YOUR FACE AGAIN.
LOOK AT THAT.
YOUR BOY WON'T EVEN GLANCE THIS WAY.
SO MUCH FOR YOUR "BOND."
IT'S OKAY.
HIS NAME VALUE WILL RISE FROM THIS...
HE'S ALREADY COLORED YOU GONE.
...AND I'LL JUST GO BACK TO... TO WHERE I WAS BEFORE.

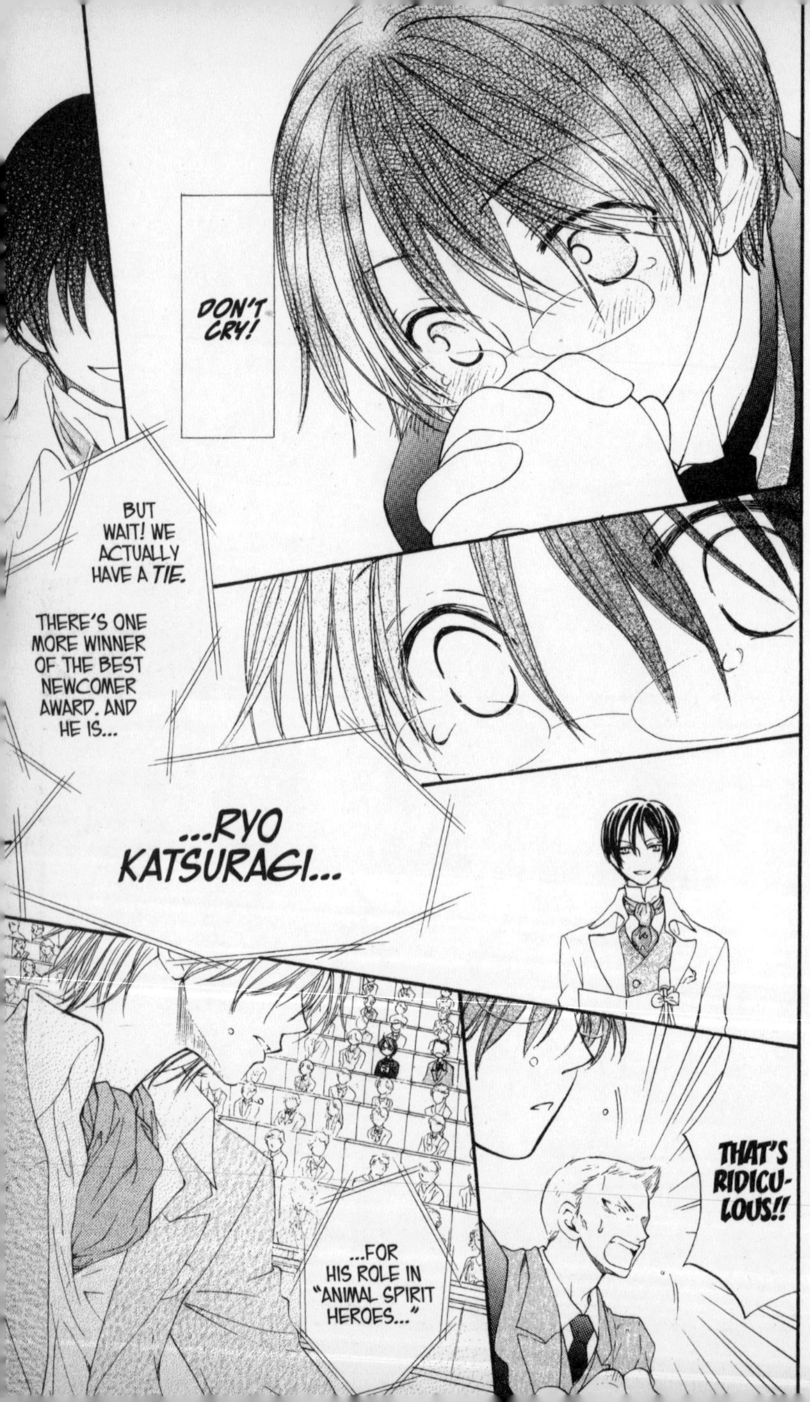
DON'T CRY!
BUT WAIT! WE ACTUALLY HAVE A *TIE*.
THERE'S ONE MORE WINNER OF THE BEST NEWCOMER AWARD. AND HE IS...
...RYO KATSURAGI...
THAT'S RIDICU-LOUS!!
...FOR HIS ROLE IN "ANIMAL SPIRIT HEROES..."

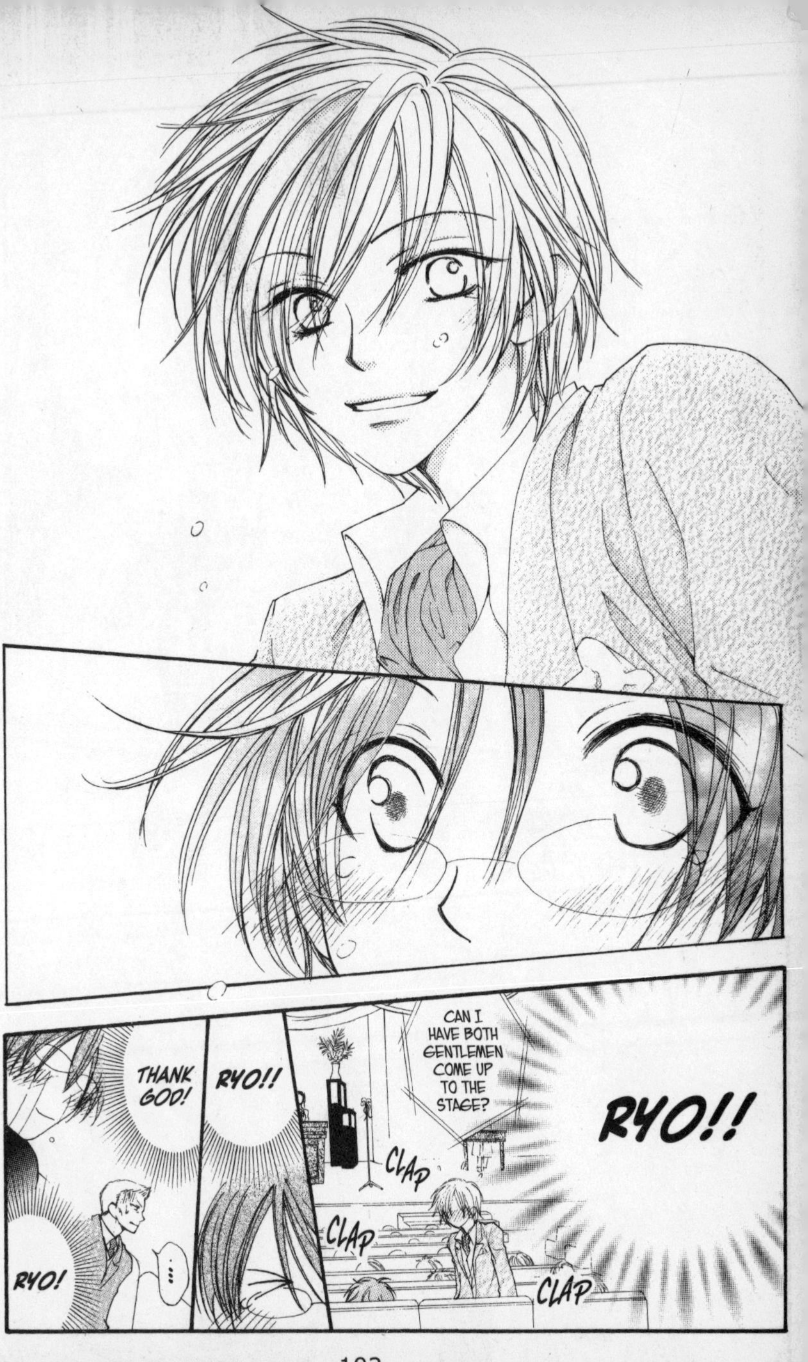
CAN I HAVE BOTH GENTLEMEN COME UP TO THE STAGE?
RYO!!
CLAP
CLAP
CLAP
RYO!!
THANK GOD!
...
RYO!

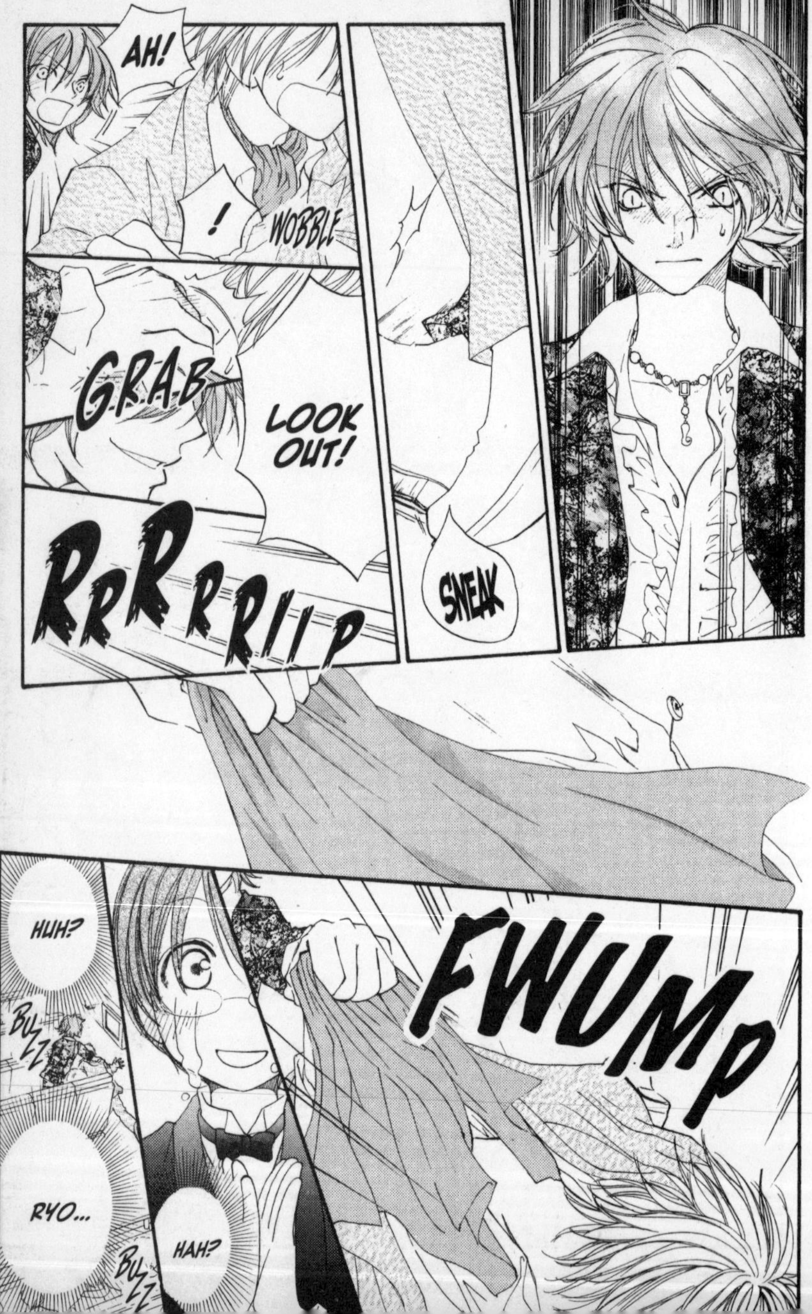
SNEAK
AH!
!
WOBBLE
GRAB
LOOK OUT!
RRRRRIIP
FWUMP
HUH?
BUZZ
RYO...
HAH?
BUZZ

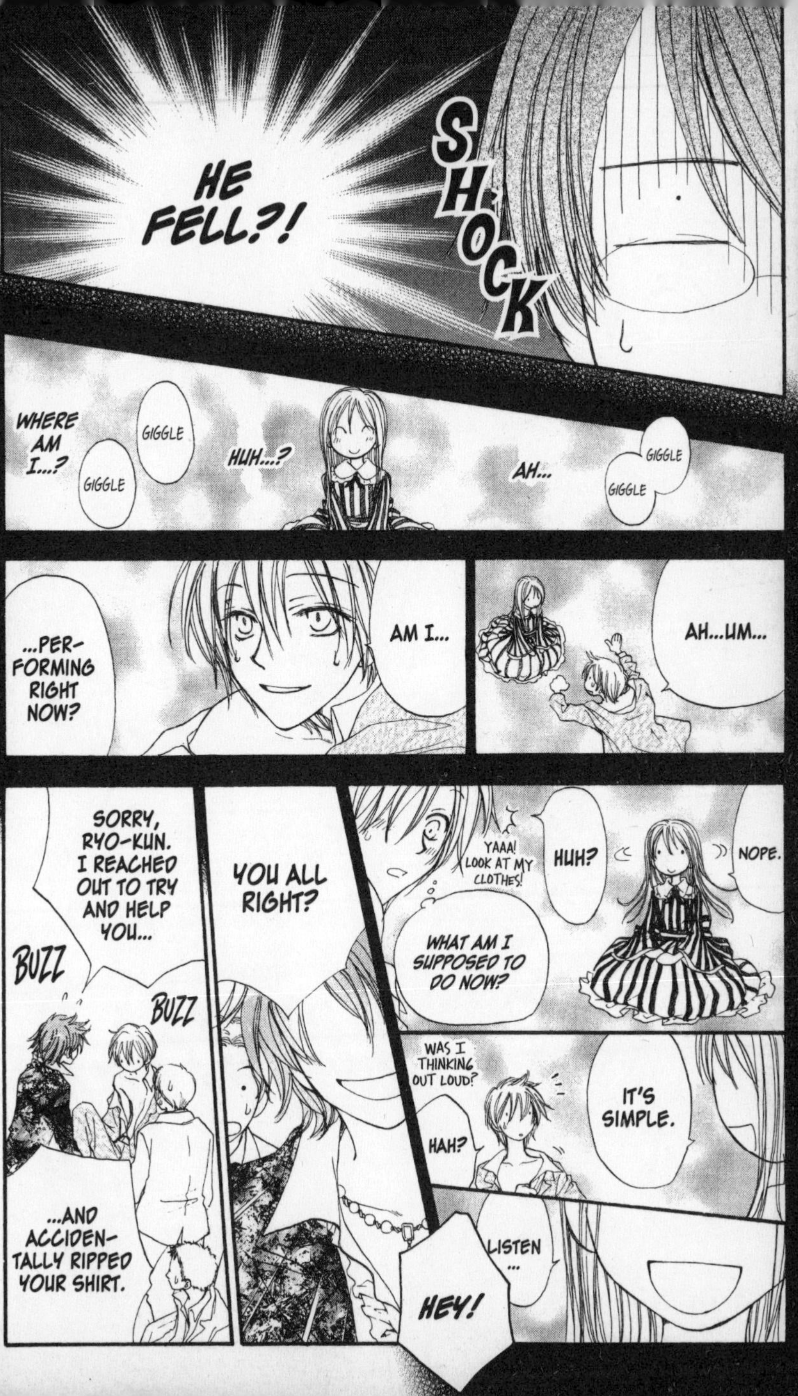
SHOCK
HE FELL?!
GIGGLE
GIGGLE
AH...
HUH...?
GIGGLE
GIGGLE
WHERE AM I...?
AH...UM...
AM I...
...PER-FORMING RIGHT NOW?
NOPE.
HUH?
YAAA! LOOK AT MY CLOTHES!
WHAT AM I SUPPOSED TO DO NOW?
IT'S SIMPLE.
WAS I THINKING OUT LOUD?
HAH?
LISTEN ...
HEY!
YOU ALL RIGHT?
SORRY, RYO-KUN. I REACHED OUT TO TRY AND HELP YOU...
BUZZ
BUZZ
...AND ACCIDEN-TALLY RIPPED YOUR SHIRT.

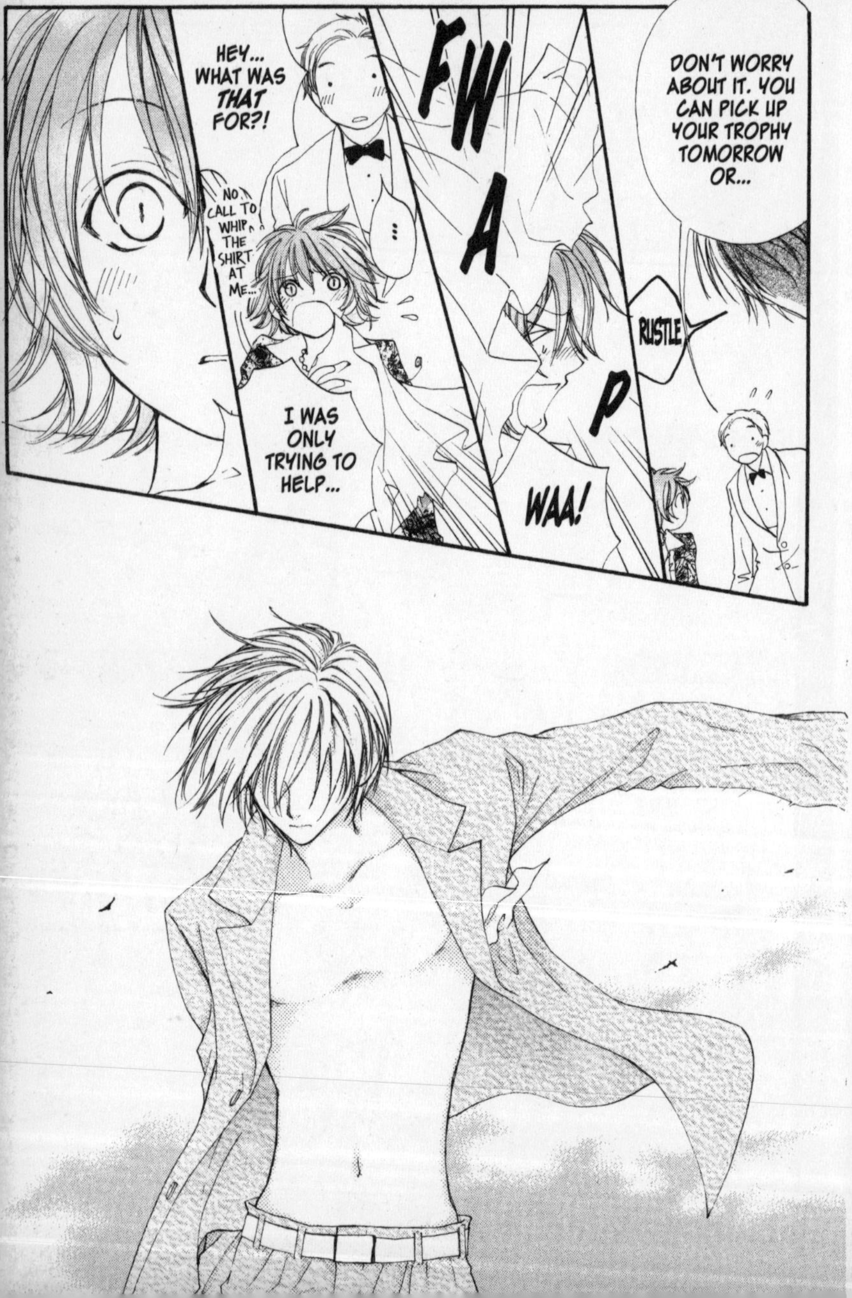
DON'T WORRY ABOUT IT. YOU CAN PICK UP YOUR TROPHY TOMORROW OR...
RUSTLE
FWAP
WAA!
HEY... WHAT WAS THAT FOR?!
...
I WAS ONLY TRYING TO HELP...
NO CALL TO WHIP THE SHIRT AT ME...

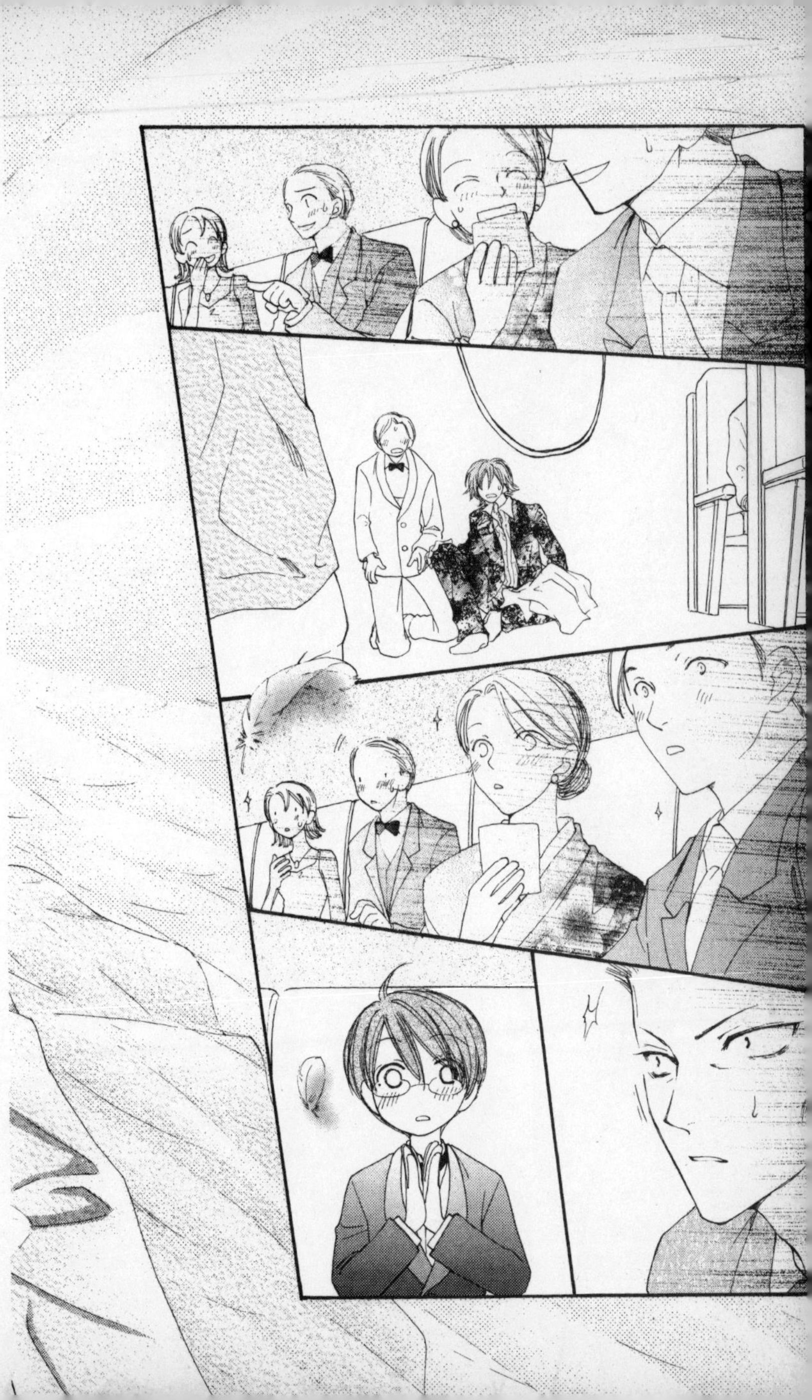

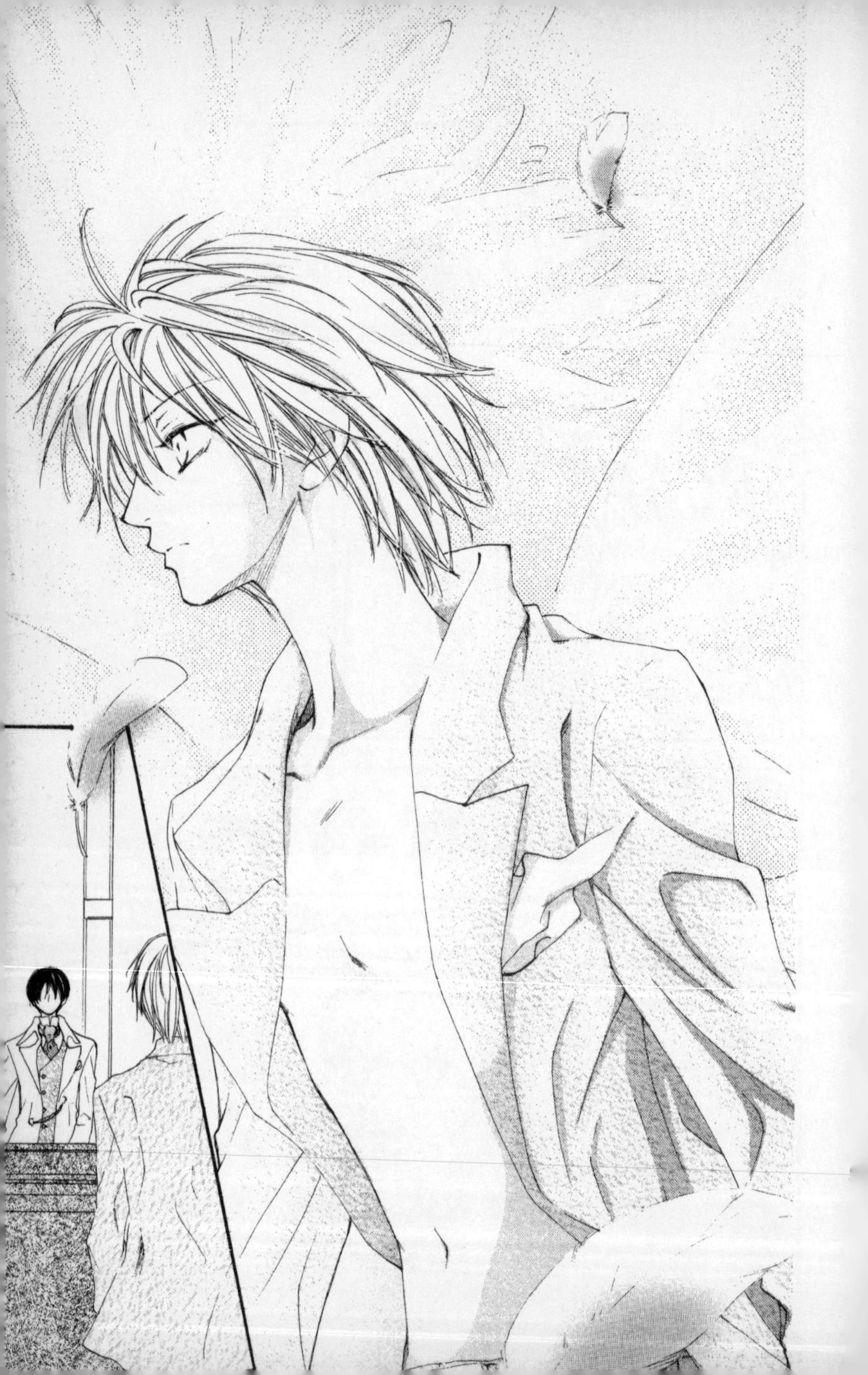

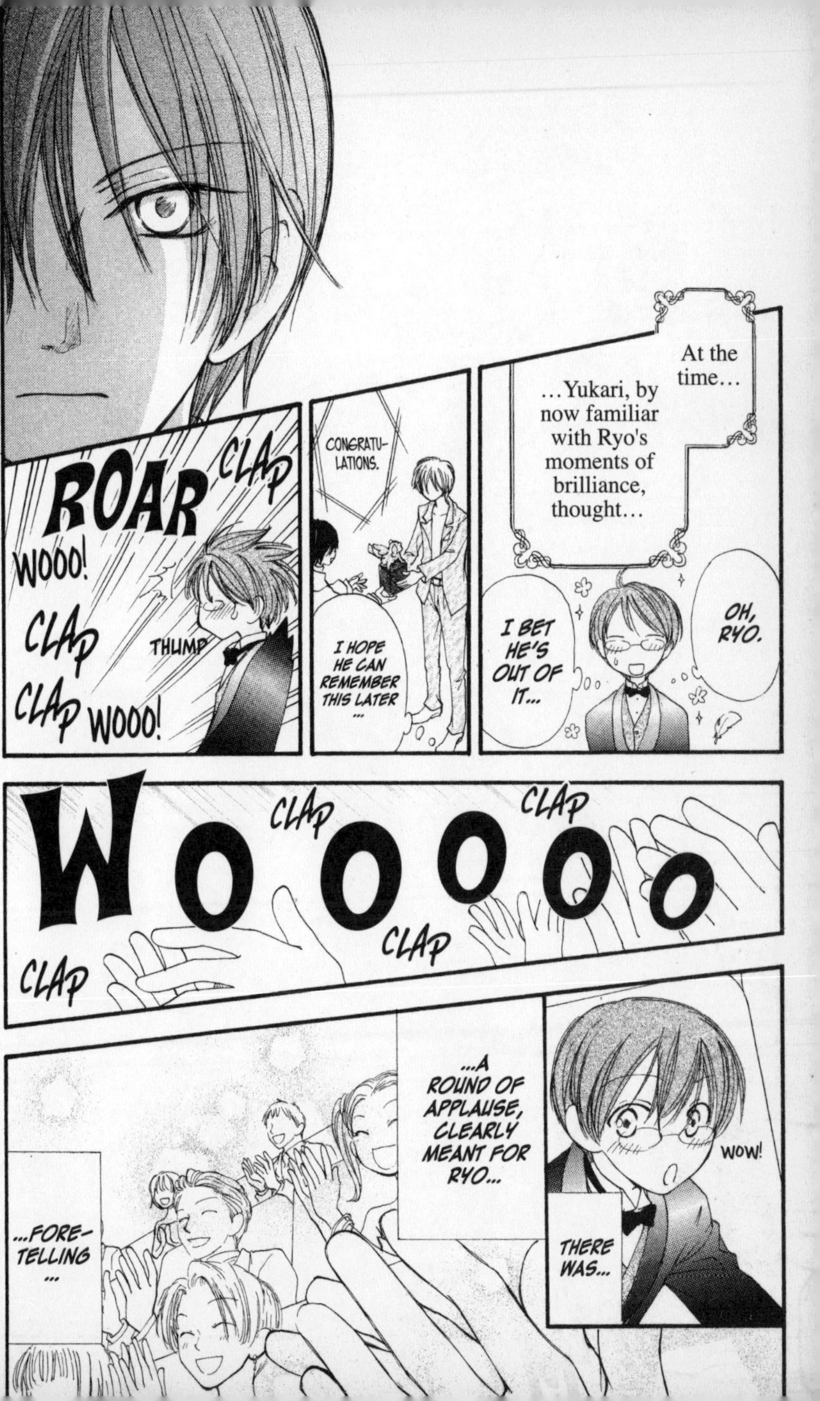
At the time…
…Yukari, by now familiar with Ryo's moments of brilliance, thought…
OH, RYO.
I BET HE'S OUT OF IT...
CONGRATU-LATIONS.
I HOPE HE CAN REMEMBER THIS LATER ...
CLAP
ROAR
WOOO!
CLAP
THUMP
CLAP
WOOO!
CLAP
WOOOOO
CLAP
CLAP
CLAP
WOW!
THERE WAS...
...A ROUND OF APPLAUSE, CLEARLY MEANT FOR RYO...
...FORE-TELLING ...

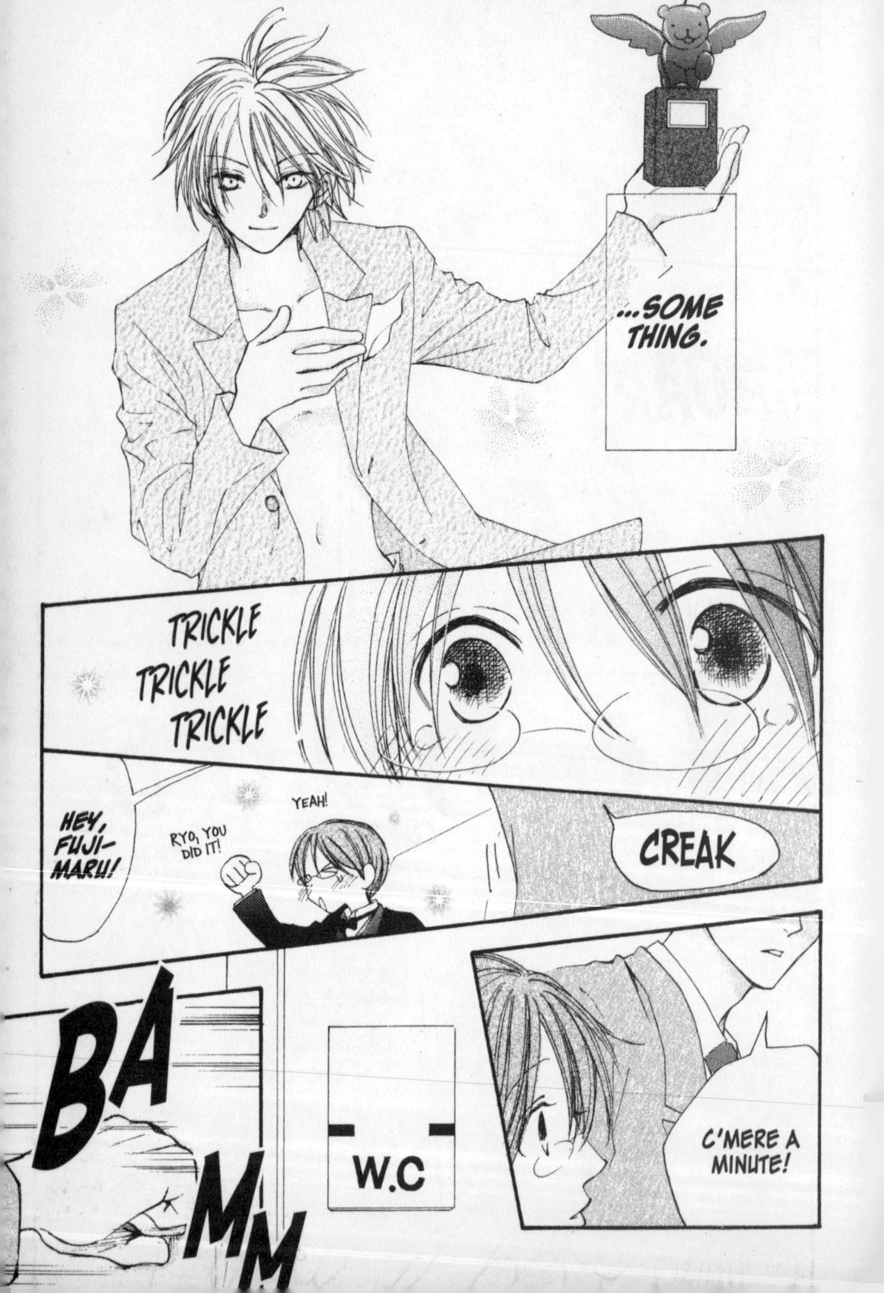
...SOME THING.
TRICKLE
TRICKLE
TRICKLE
CREAK
YEAH!
RYO, YOU DID IT!
HEY, FUJI-MARU!
C'MERE A MINUTE!
W.C
BAMM

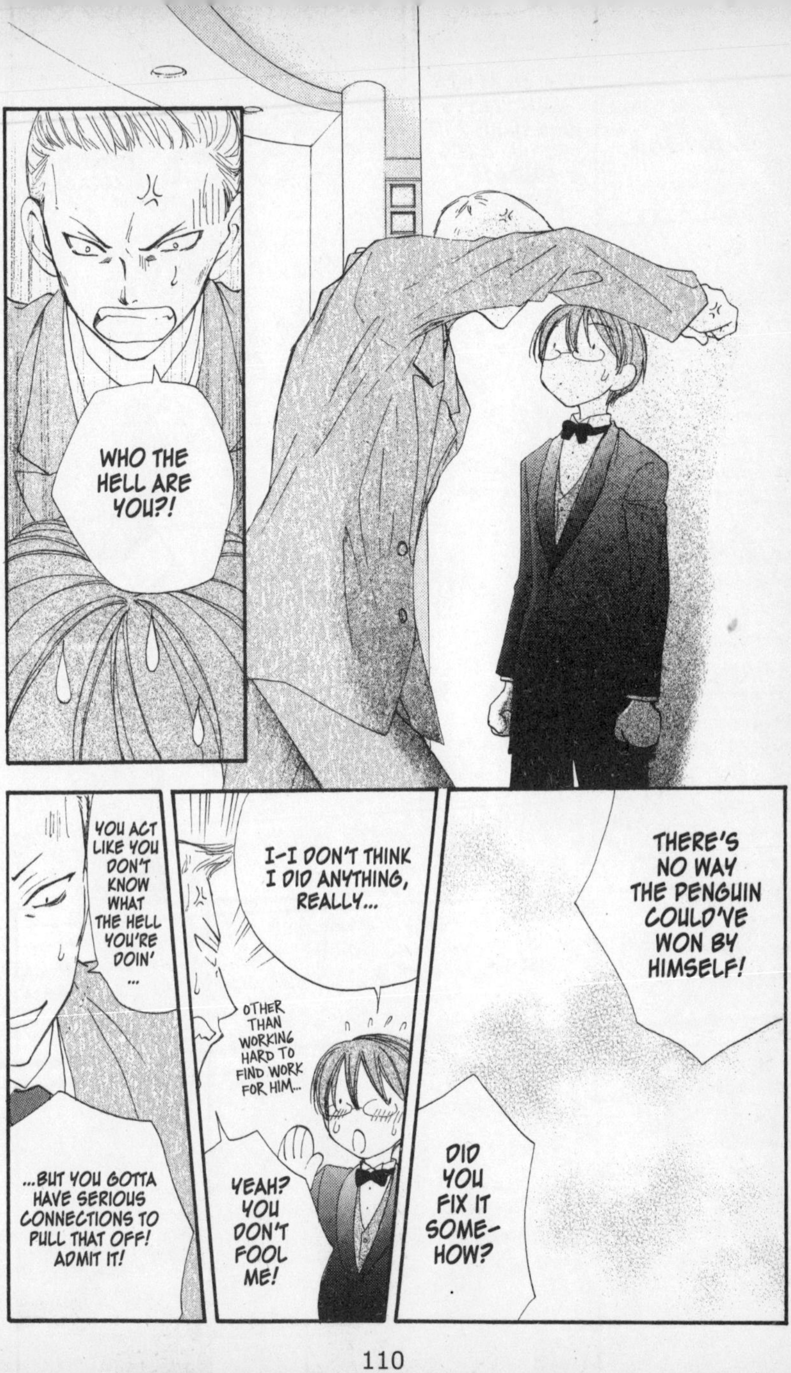
WHO THE HELL ARE YOU?!
THERE'S NO WAY THE PENGUIN COULD'VE WON BY HIMSELF!
DID YOU FIX IT SOME-HOW?
I-I DON'T THINK I DID ANYTHING, REALLY...
OTHER THAN WORKING HARD TO FIND WORK FOR HIM...
YEAH? YOU DON'T FOOL ME!
YOU ACT LIKE YOU DON'T KNOW WHAT THE HELL YOU'RE DOIN' ...
...BUT YOU GOTTA HAVE SERIOUS CONNECTIONS TO PULL THAT OFF! ADMIT IT!

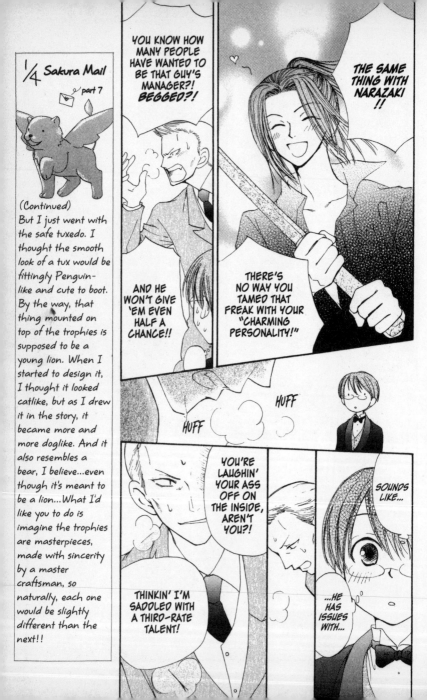

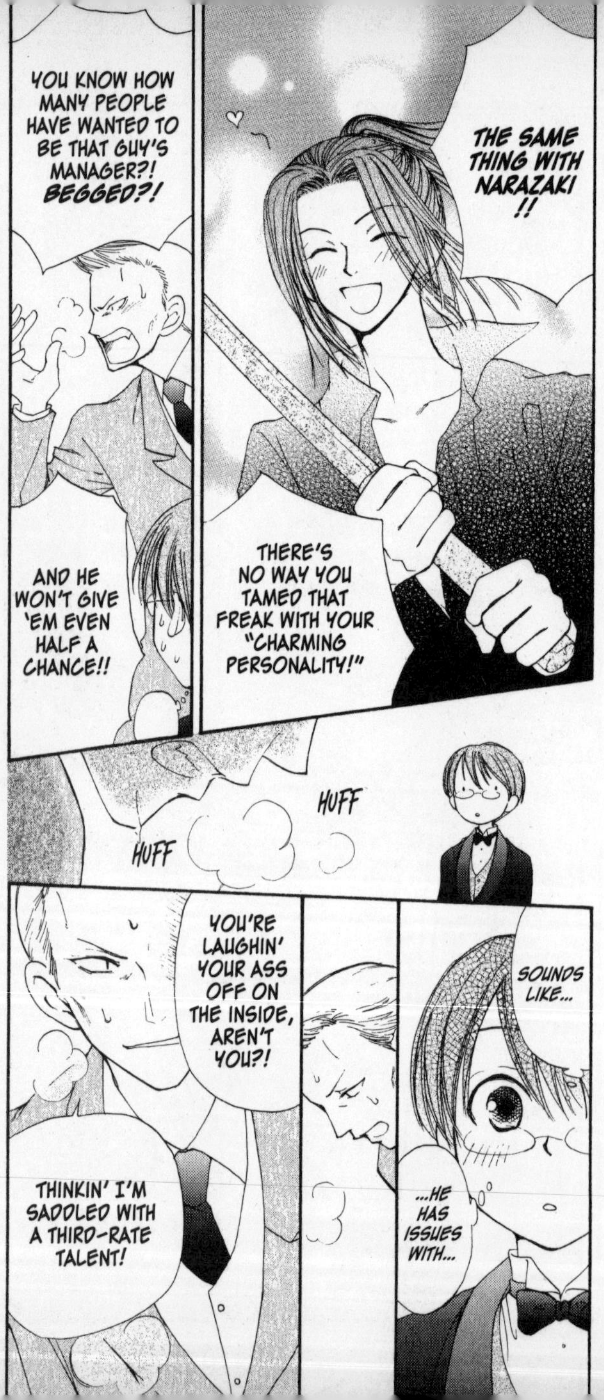
THE SAME THING WITH NARAZAKI!!
THERE'S NO WAY YOU TAMED THAT FREAK WITH YOUR "CHARMING PERSONALITY!"
YOU KNOW HOW MANY PEOPLE HAVE WANTED TO BE THAT GUY'S MANAGER?! BEGGED?!
AND HE WON'T GIVE 'EM EVEN HALF A CHANCE!!
HUFF
HUFF
SOUNDS LIKE...
...HE HAS ISSUES WITH...
YOU'RE LAUGHIN' YOUR ASS OFF ON THE INSIDE, AREN'T YOU?!
THINKIN' I'M SADDLED WITH A THIRD-RATE TALENT!

1/4 Sakura Mail

part 7

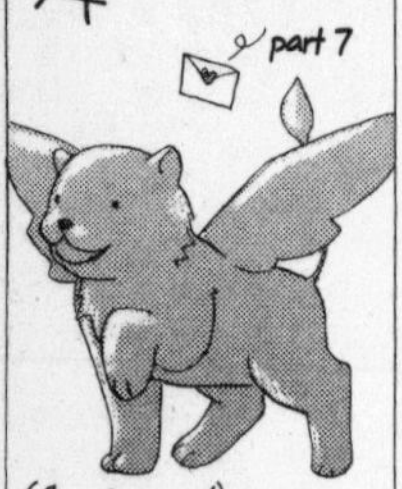

(Continued)

But I just went with the safe tuxedo. I thought the smooth look of a tux would be fittingly Penguin-like and cute to boot. By the way, that thing mounted on top of the trophies is supposed to be a young lion. When I started to design it, I thought it looked catlike, but as I drew it in the story, it became more and more doglike. And it also resembles a bear, I believe...even though it's meant to be a lion...What I'd like you to do is imagine the trophies are masterpieces, made with sincerity by a master craftsman, so naturally, each one would be slightly different than the next!!

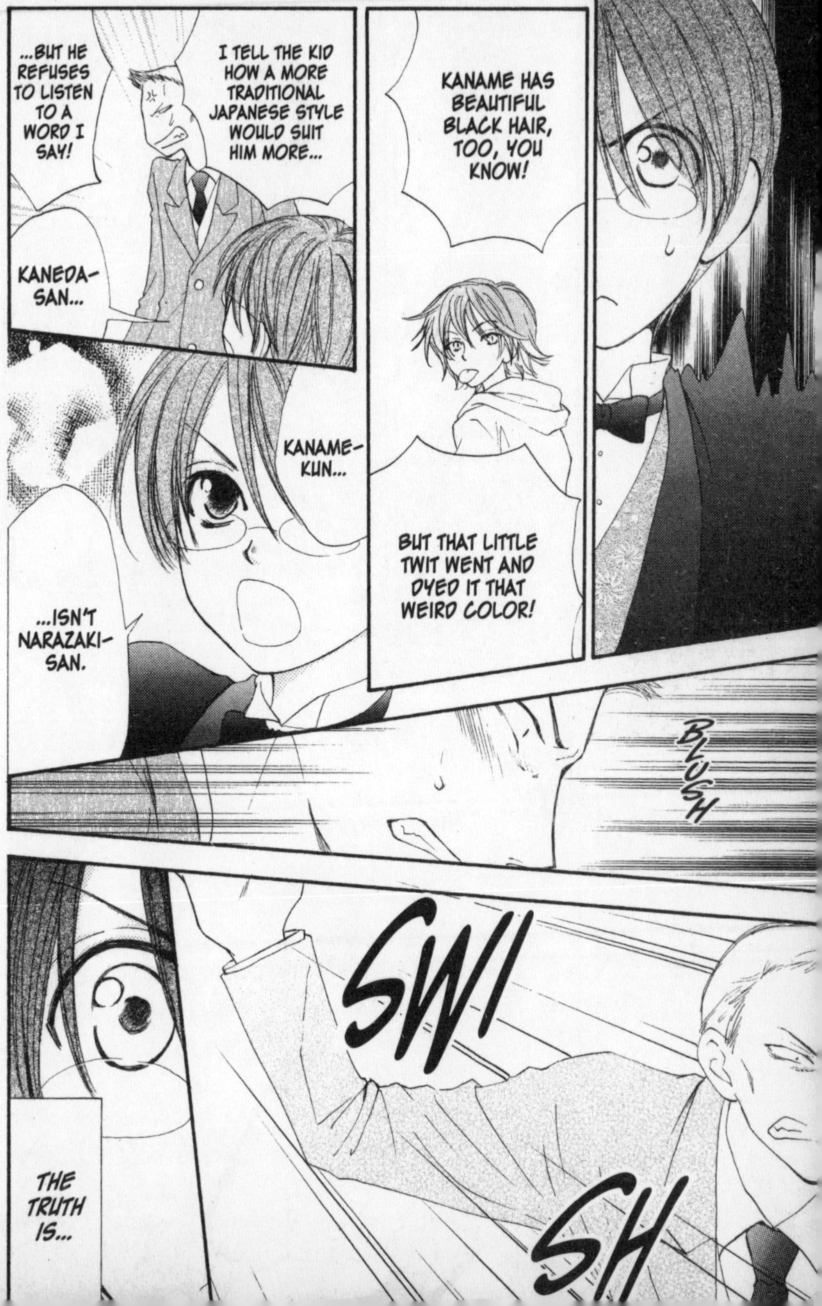
KANAME HAS BEAUTIFUL BLACK HAIR, TOO, YOU KNOW!
BUT THAT LITTLE TWIT WENT AND DYED IT THAT WEIRD COLOR!
I TELL THE KID HOW A MORE TRADITIONAL JAPANESE STYLE WOULD SUIT HIM MORE...
...BUT HE REFUSES TO LISTEN TO A WORD I SAY!
KANEDA-SAN...
KANAME-KUN...
...ISN'T NARAZAKI-SAN.
BLUSH
SWISH
THE TRUTH IS...

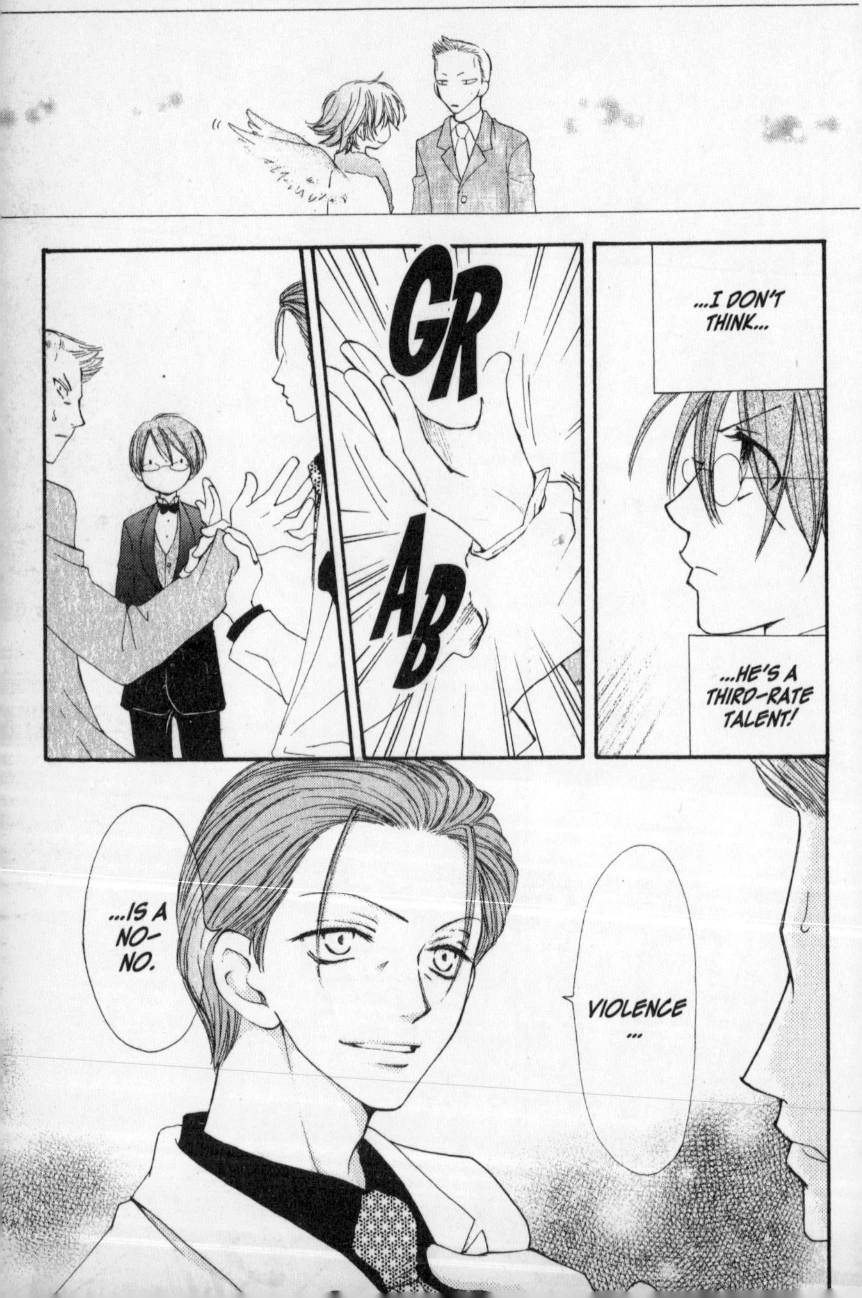
...I DON'T THINK...
...HE'S A THIRD-RATE TALENT!
GRAB
VIOLENCE ...
...IS A NO-NO.

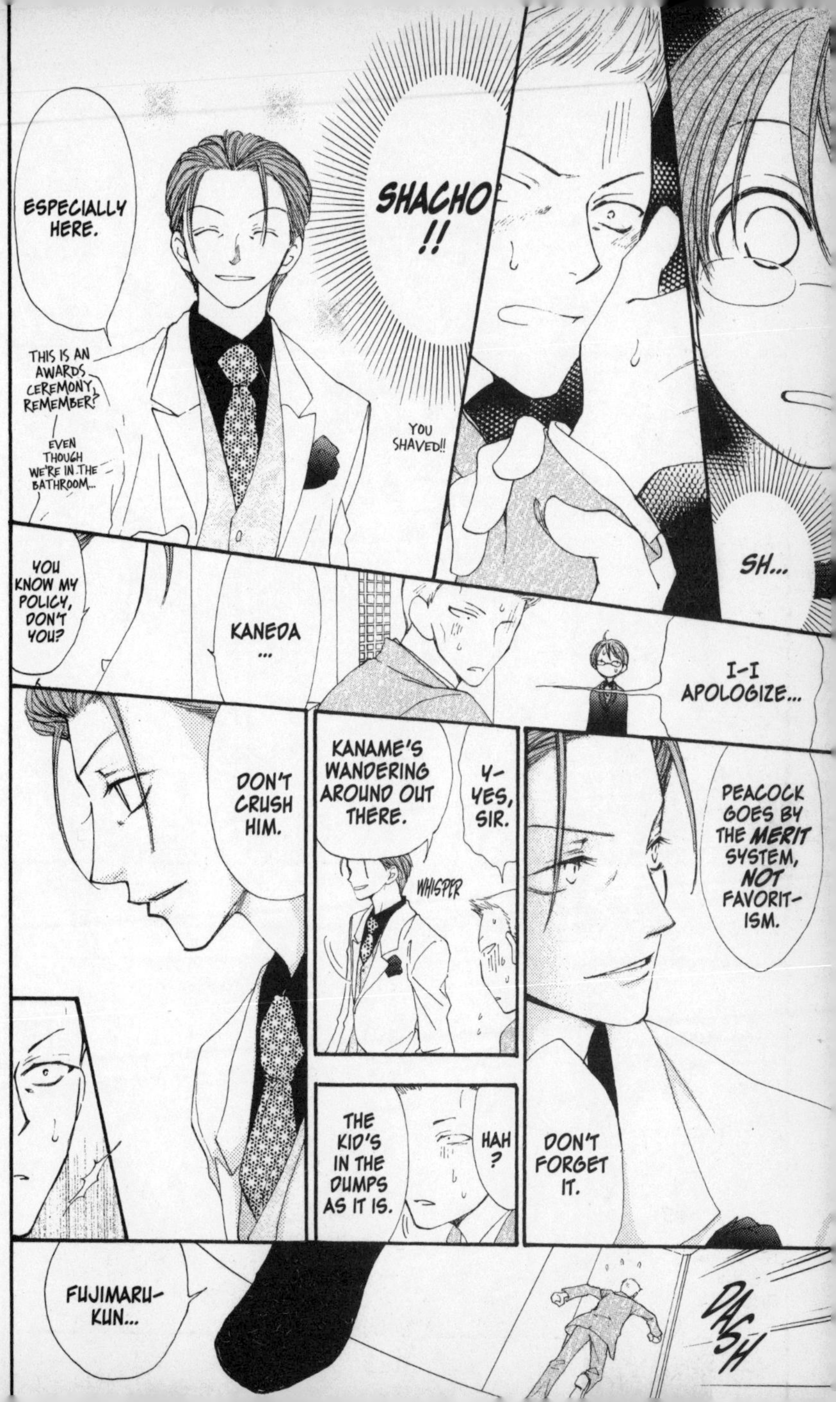
SHACHO !!
SH...
YOU SHAVED!!
ESPECIALLY HERE.
THIS IS AN AWARDS CEREMONY, REMEMBER?
EVEN THOUGH WE'RE IN THE BATHROOM...
I-I APOLOGIZE...
KANEDA ...
YOU KNOW MY POLICY, DON'T YOU?
PEACOCK GOES BY THE *MERIT* SYSTEM, *NOT* FAVORIT-ISM.
DON'T FORGET IT.
Y-YES, SIR.
KANAME'S WANDERING AROUND OUT THERE.
WHISPER
HAH ?
THE KID'S IN THE DUMPS AS IT IS.
DON'T CRUSH HIM.
DASH
FUJIMARU-KUN...

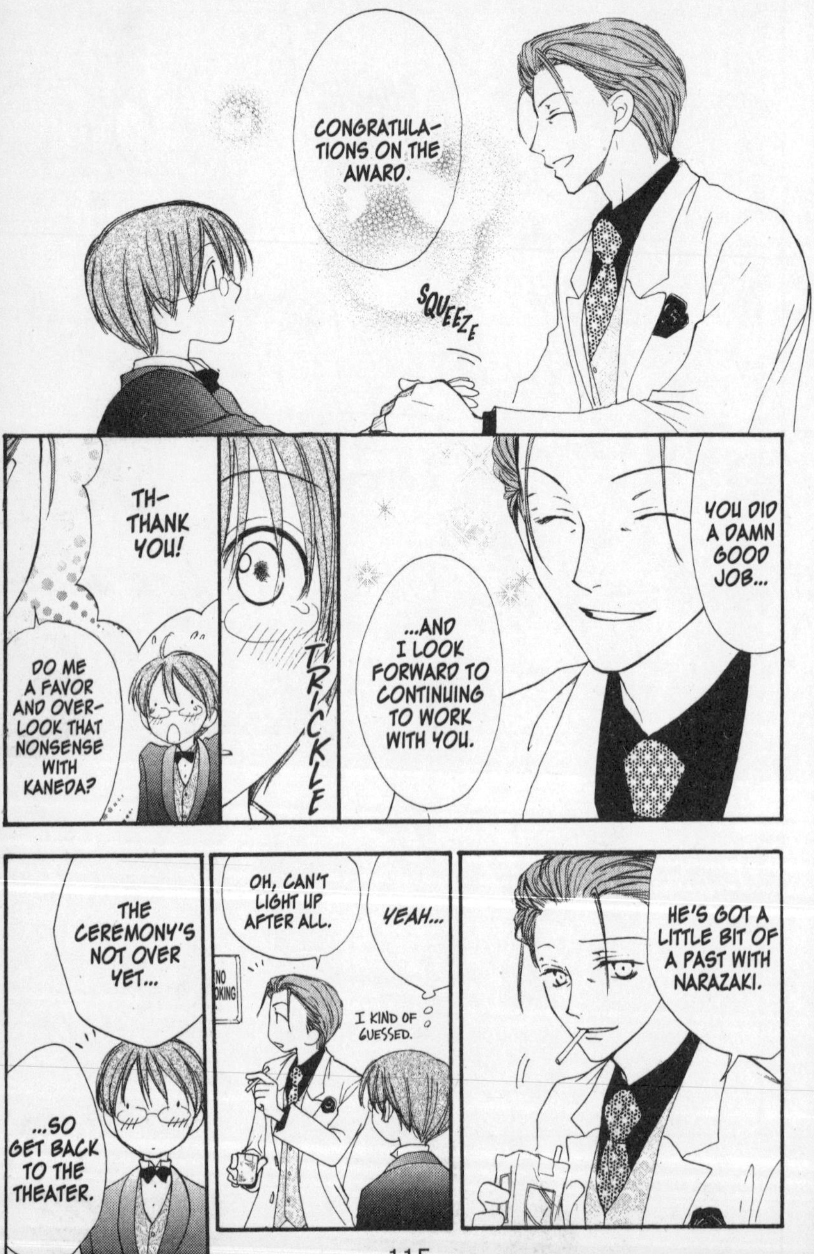
CONGRATULATIONS ON THE AWARD.
SQUEEZE
YOU DID A DAMN GOOD JOB...
...AND I LOOK FORWARD TO CONTINUING TO WORK WITH YOU.
TRICKLE
TH-THANK YOU!
DO ME A FAVOR AND OVERLOOK THAT NONSENSE WITH KANEDA?
HE'S GOT A LITTLE BIT OF A PAST WITH NARAZAKI.
YEAH...
I KIND OF GUESSED.
OH, CAN'T LIGHT UP AFTER ALL.
THE CEREMONY'S NOT OVER YET...
...SO GET BACK TO THE THEATER.

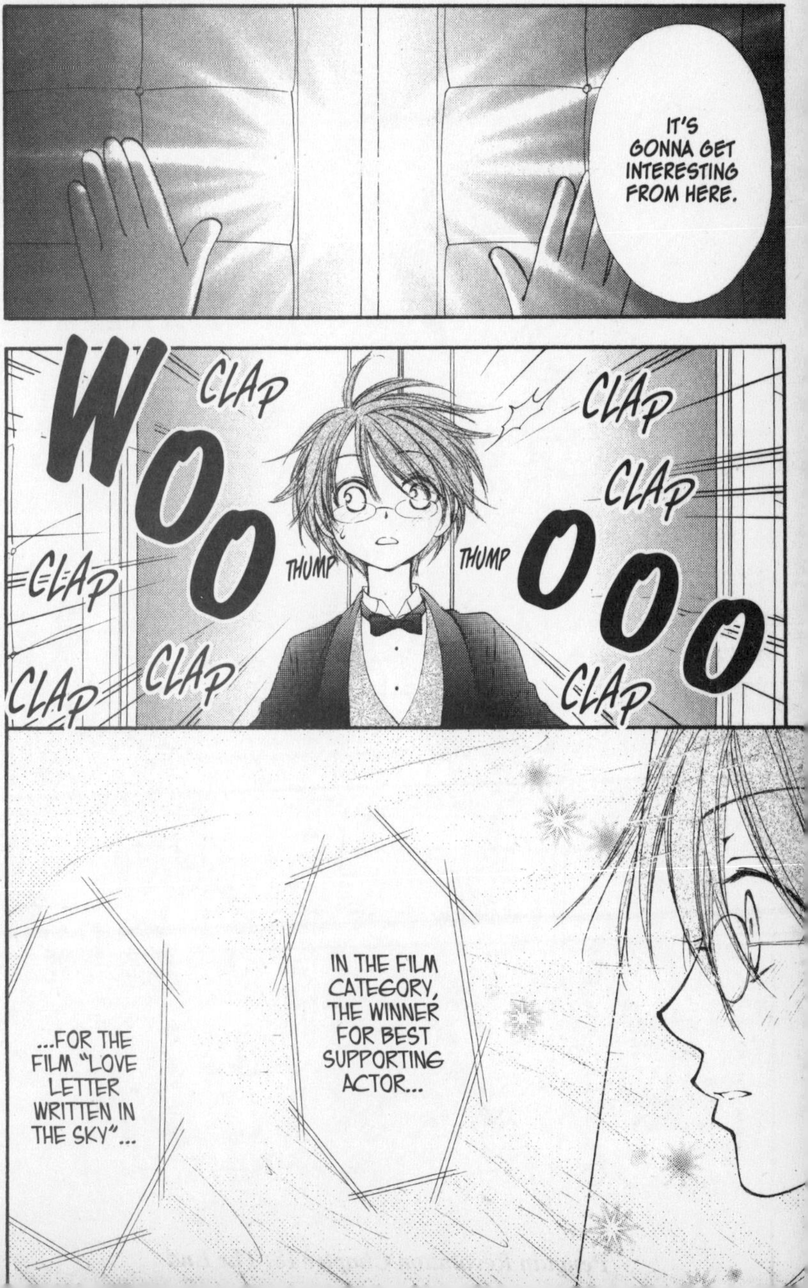
IT'S GONNA GET INTERESTING FROM HERE.
CLAP
CLAP
OOOO
THUMP
CLAP
WOO
THUMP
CLAP
CLAP
CLAP
CLAP
IN THE FILM CATEGORY, THE WINNER FOR BEST SUPPORTING ACTOR...
...FOR THE FILM "LOVE LETTER WRITTEN IN THE SKY"...

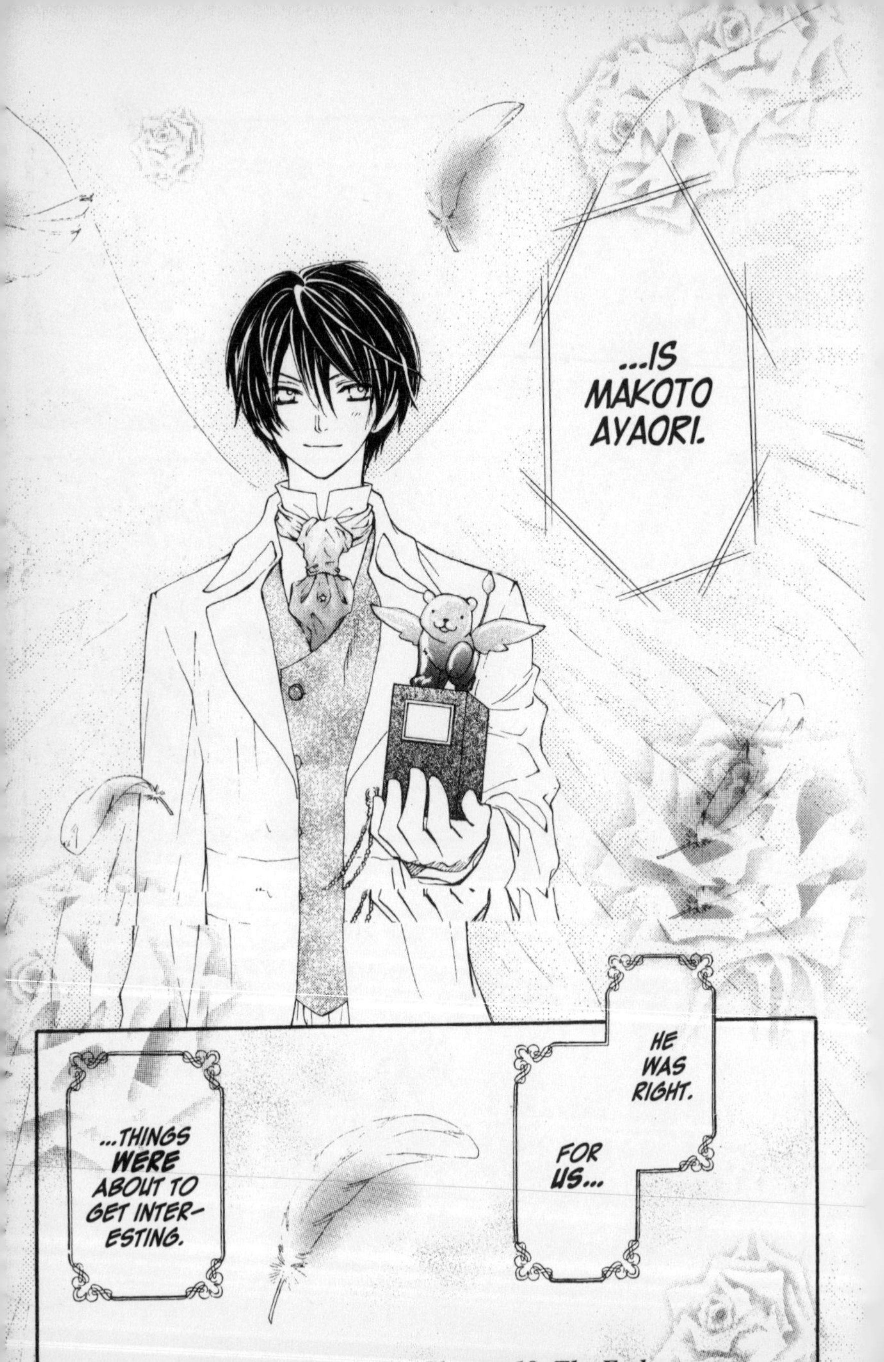
...IS MAKOTO AYAORI.
HE WAS RIGHT.
FOR US...
...THINGS WERE ABOUT TO GET INTER-ESTING.

Penguin Revolution Chapter 18: The End

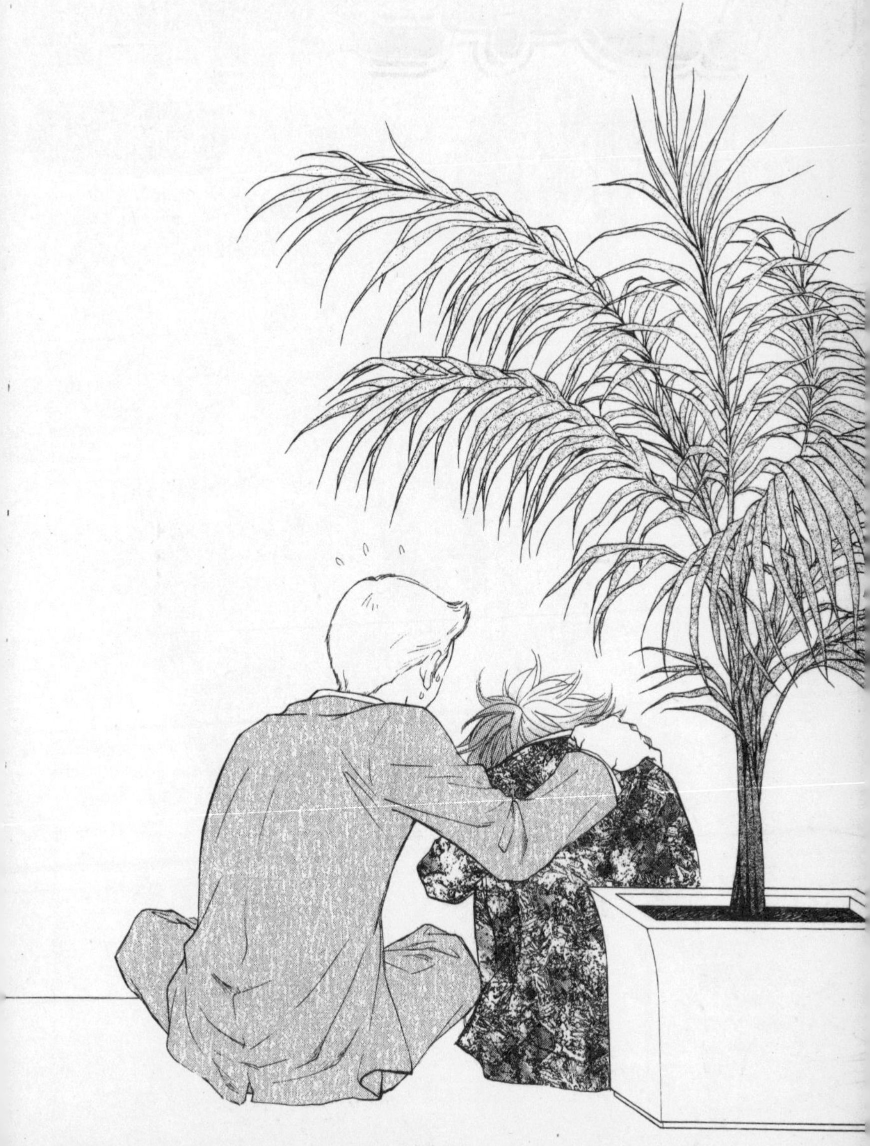

ペンギン革命（かくめい）

PENGUIN REVOLUTION

Episode 19

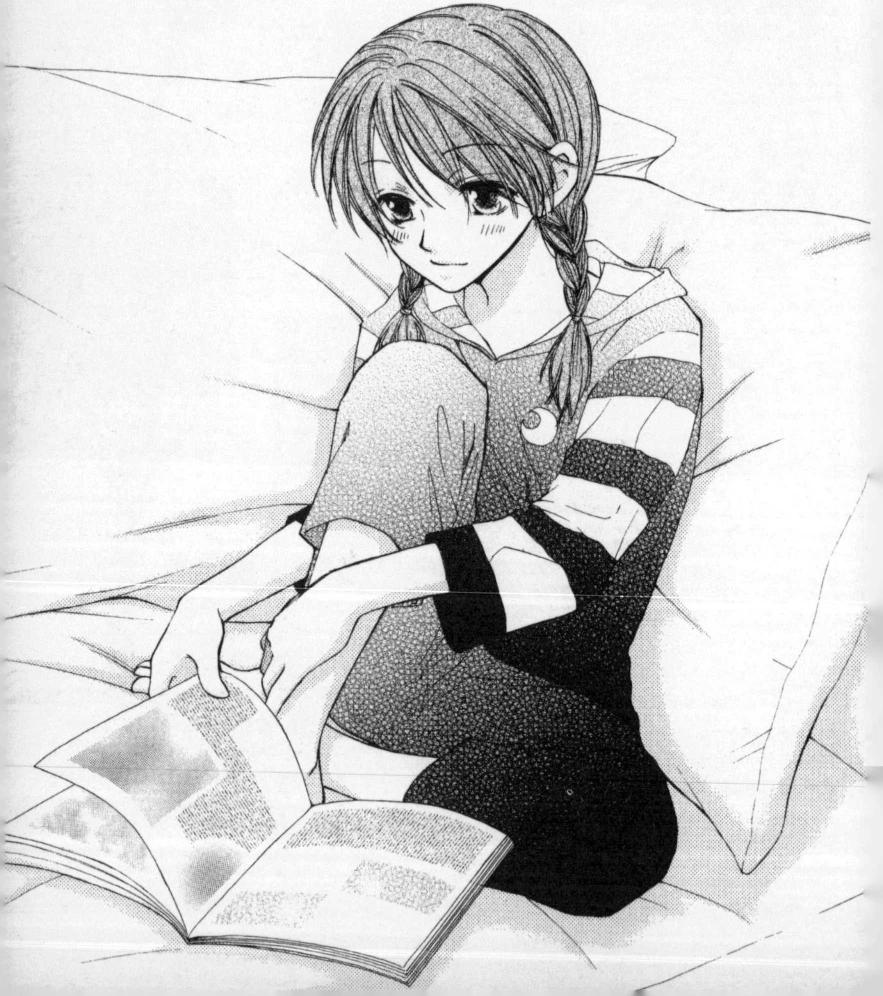

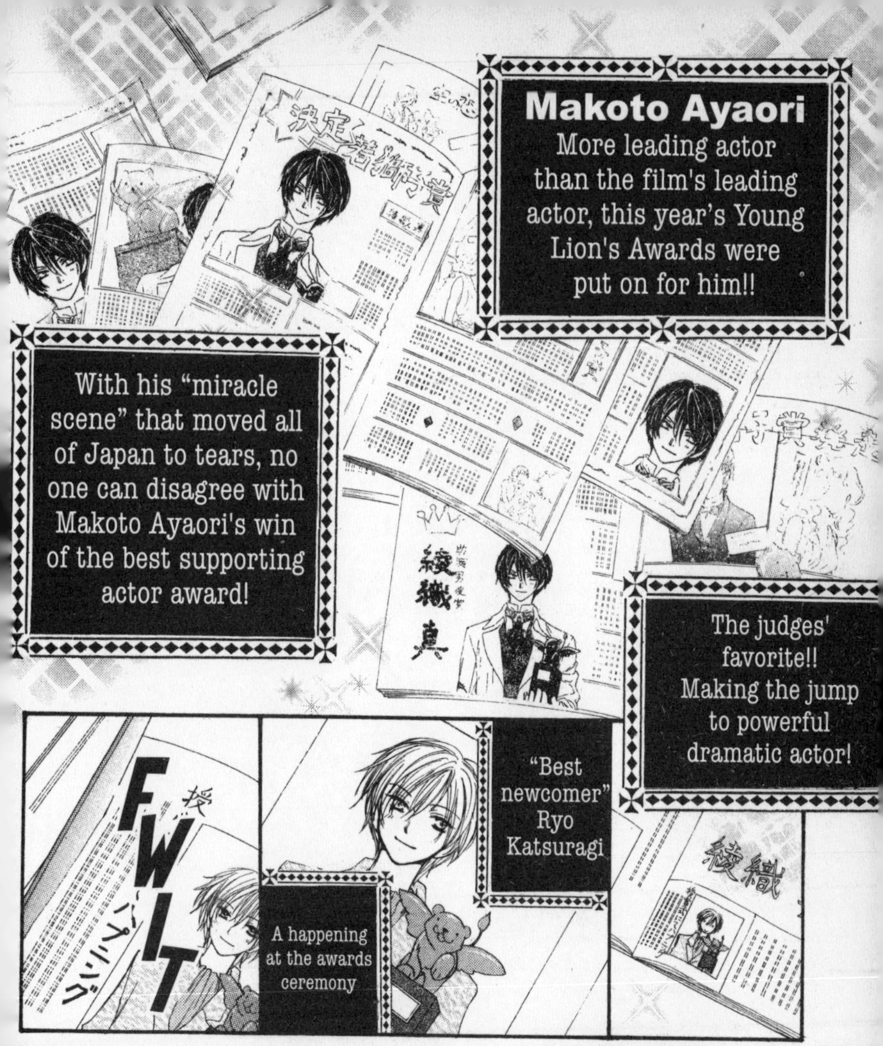
Makoto Ayaori
More leading actor than the film's leading actor, this year's Young Lion's Awards were put on for him!!
With his "miracle scene" that moved all of Japan to tears, no one can disagree with Makoto Ayaori's win of the best supporting actor award!
The judges' favorite!! Making the jump to powerful dramatic actor!
"Best newcomer" Ryo Katsuragi
A happening at the awards ceremony
FWIT

And so, the awards ceremony went off without a hitch (?) and our characters are back into their normal routine. It looks like Yuka-chin is good at scrapbooking. I'm not. I often think that I have to do something like that since my mind always screws up memories, but...Anyway, back to the story, in this episode, we have Narazaki-san filming a movie.
(To be continued...)

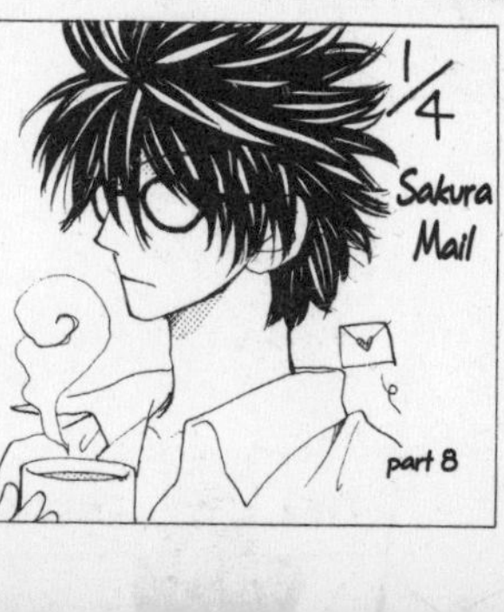
1/4
Sakura Mail
part 8

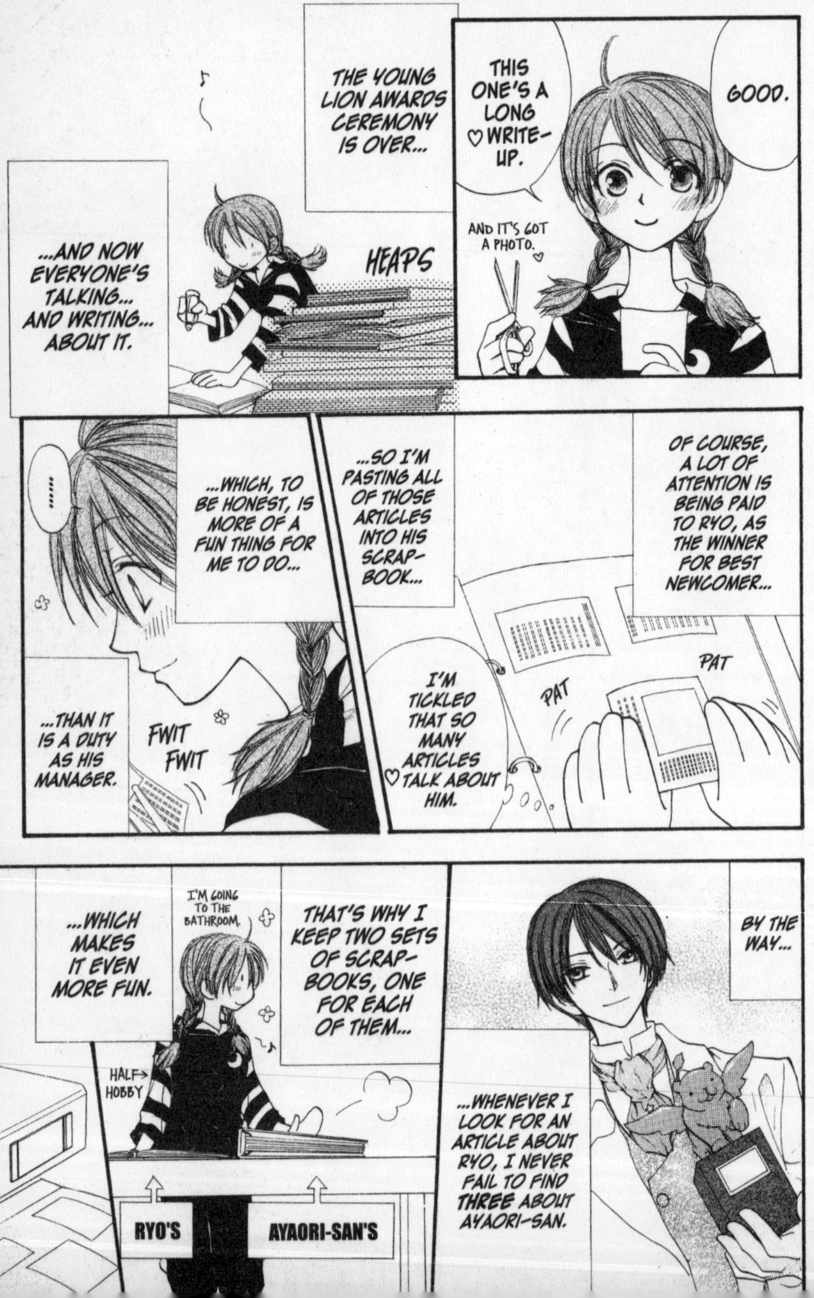
GOOD.
THIS ONE'S A LONG ♡ WRITE-UP.
AND IT'S GOT A PHOTO. ♡
THE YOUNG LION AWARDS CEREMONY IS OVER...
...AND NOW EVERYONE'S TALKING... AND WRITING... ABOUT IT.
HEAPS
OF COURSE, A LOT OF ATTENTION IS BEING PAID TO RYO, AS THE WINNER FOR BEST NEWCOMER...
...SO I'M PASTING ALL OF THOSE ARTICLES INTO HIS SCRAP-BOOK...
PAT
PAT
I'M TICKLED THAT SO MANY ARTICLES ♡ TALK ABOUT HIM.
......
...WHICH, TO BE HONEST, IS MORE OF A FUN THING FOR ME TO DO...
FWIT FWIT
...THAN IT IS A DUTY AS HIS MANAGER.
BY THE WAY...
...WHENEVER I LOOK FOR AN ARTICLE ABOUT RYO, I NEVER FAIL TO FIND THREE ABOUT AYAORI-SAN.
THAT'S WHY I KEEP TWO SETS OF SCRAP-BOOKS, ONE FOR EACH OF THEM...
I'M GOING TO THE BATHROOM.
...WHICH MAKES IT EVEN MORE FUN.
HALF→ HOBBY
RYO'S
AYAORI-SAN'S

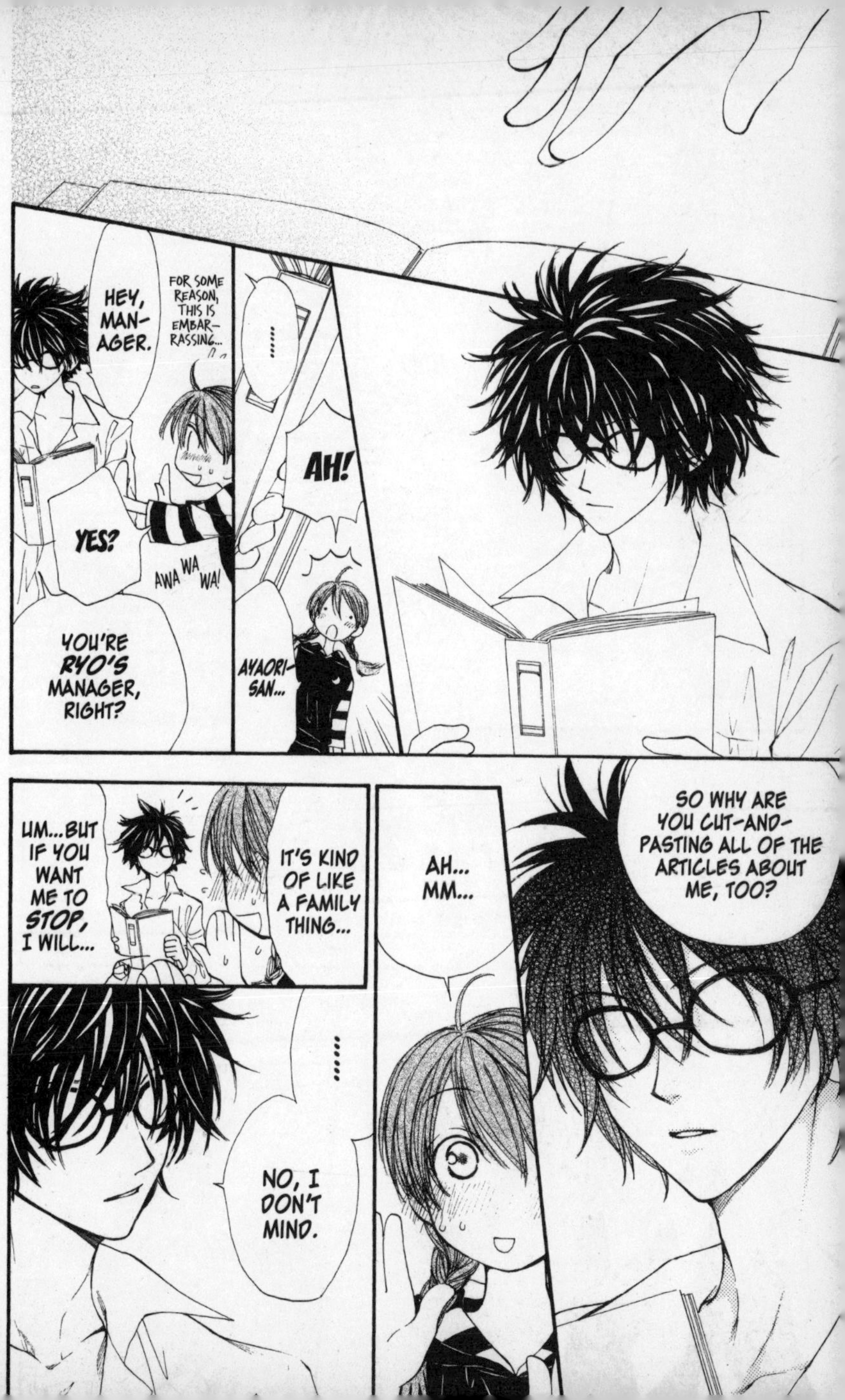
......
AH!
AYAORI-SAN...
HEY, MANAGER.
FOR SOME REASON, THIS IS EMBARRASSING...
YES?
AWA WA WA!
YOU'RE RYO'S MANAGER, RIGHT?
SO WHY ARE YOU CUT-AND-PASTING ALL OF THE ARTICLES ABOUT ME, TOO?
AH... MM...
IT'S KIND OF LIKE A FAMILY THING...
UM...BUT IF YOU WANT ME TO STOP, I WILL...
......
NO, I DON'T MIND.

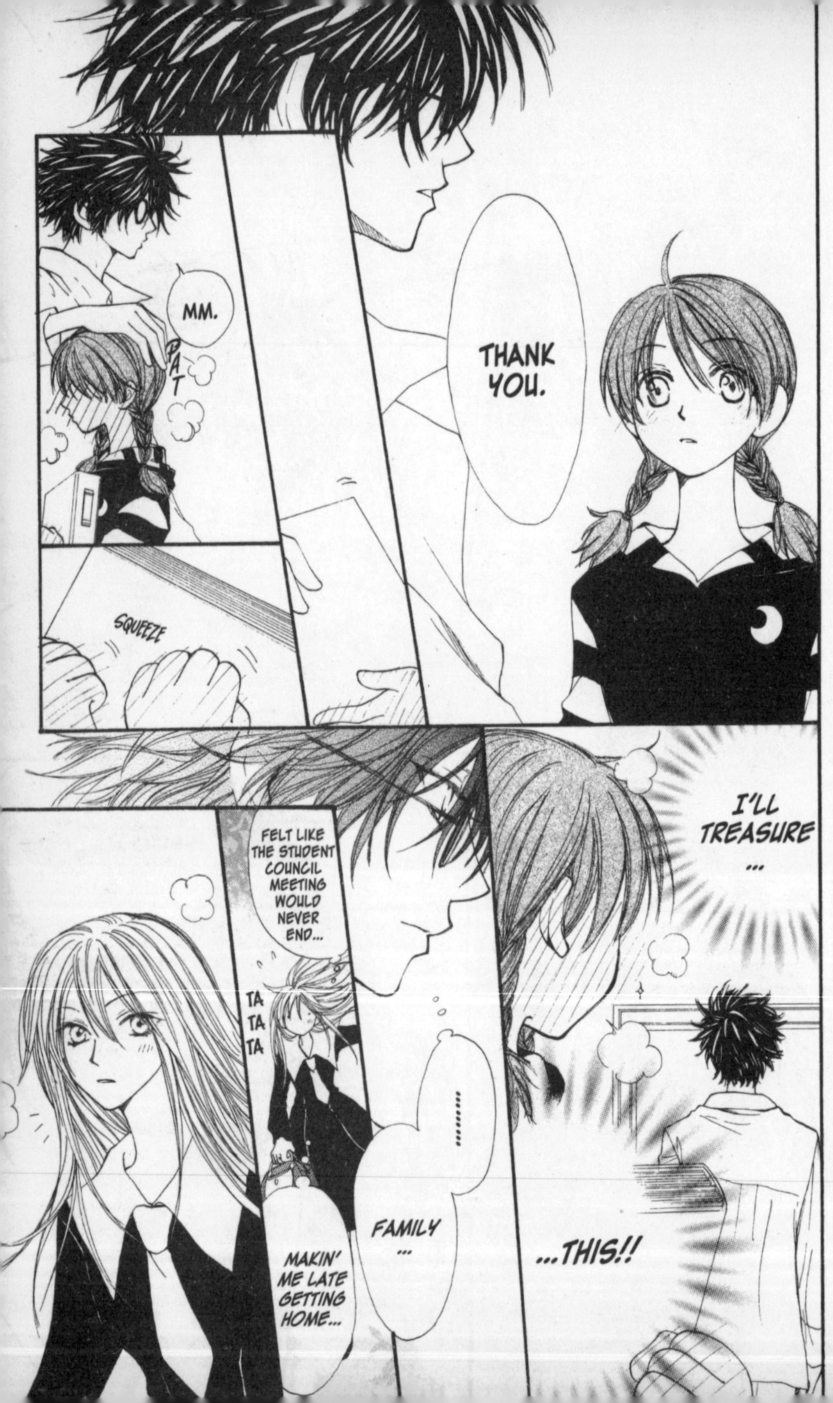
THANK YOU.
MM.
PAT
SQUEEZE
I'LL TREASURE ...
...THIS!!
....
FAMILY ...
MAKIN' ME LATE GETTING HOME...
FELT LIKE THE STUDENT COUNCIL MEETING WOULD NEVER END...
TA TA TA

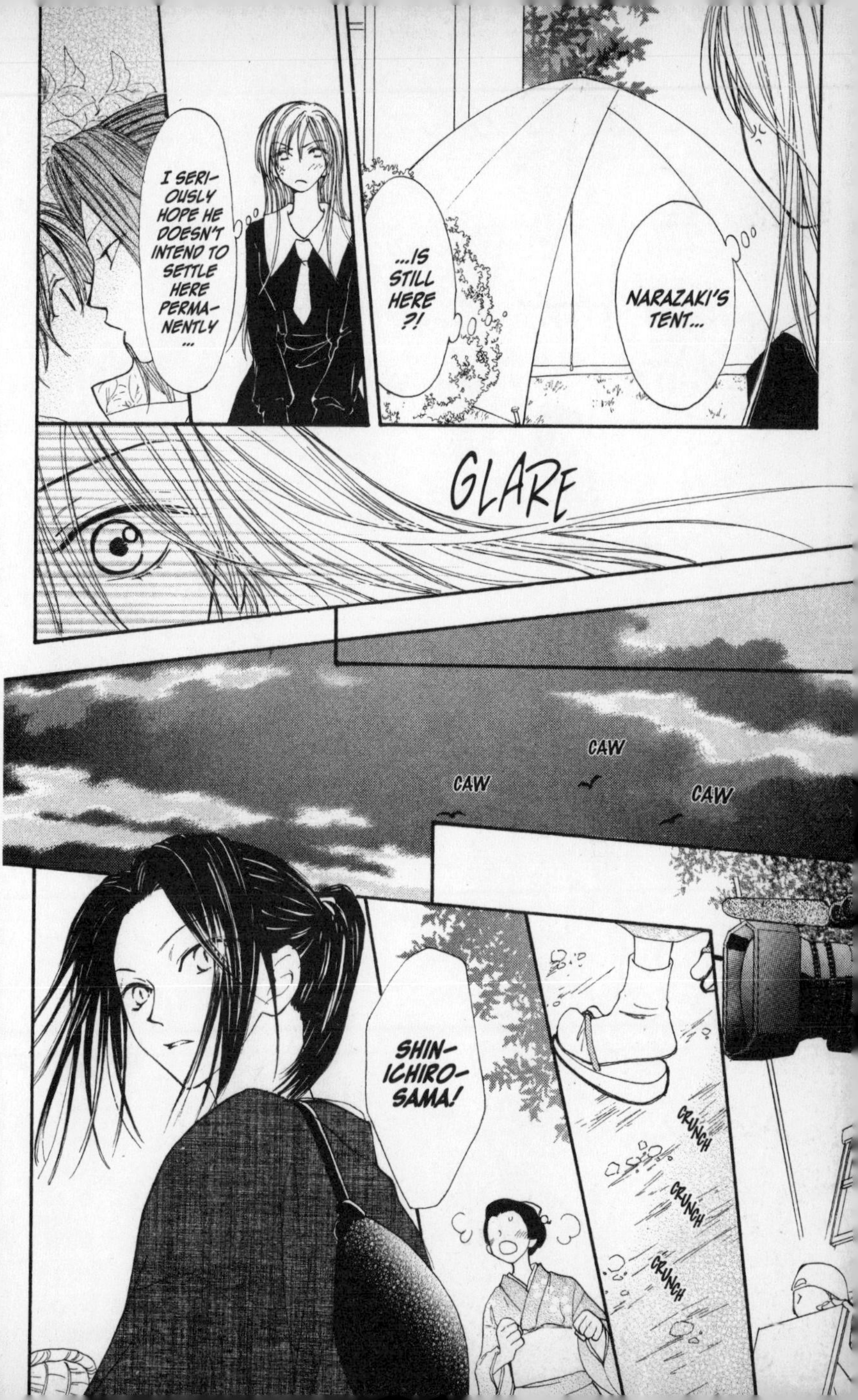
NARAZAKI'S TENT...
...IS STILL HERE?!
I SERIOUSLY HOPE HE DOESN'T INTEND TO SETTLE HERE PERMANENTLY...
GLARE
CAW
CAW
CAW
CRUNCH
CRUNCH
CRUNCH
SHIN-ICHIRO-SAMA!

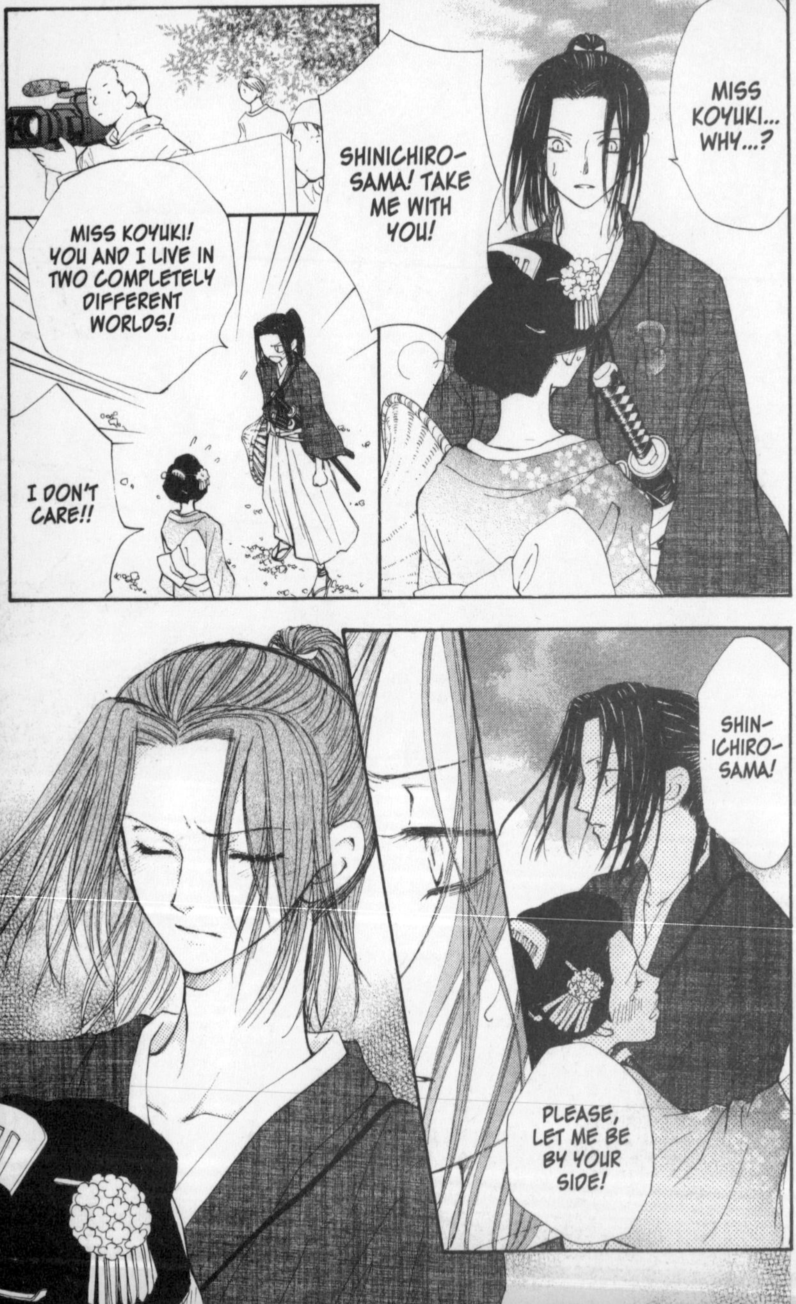
MISS KOYUKI... WHY...?
SHINICHIRO-SAMA! TAKE ME WITH YOU!
MISS KOYUKI! YOU AND I LIVE IN TWO COMPLETELY DIFFERENT WORLDS!
I DON'T CARE!!
SHIN-ICHIRO-SAMA!
PLEASE, LET ME BE BY YOUR SIDE!

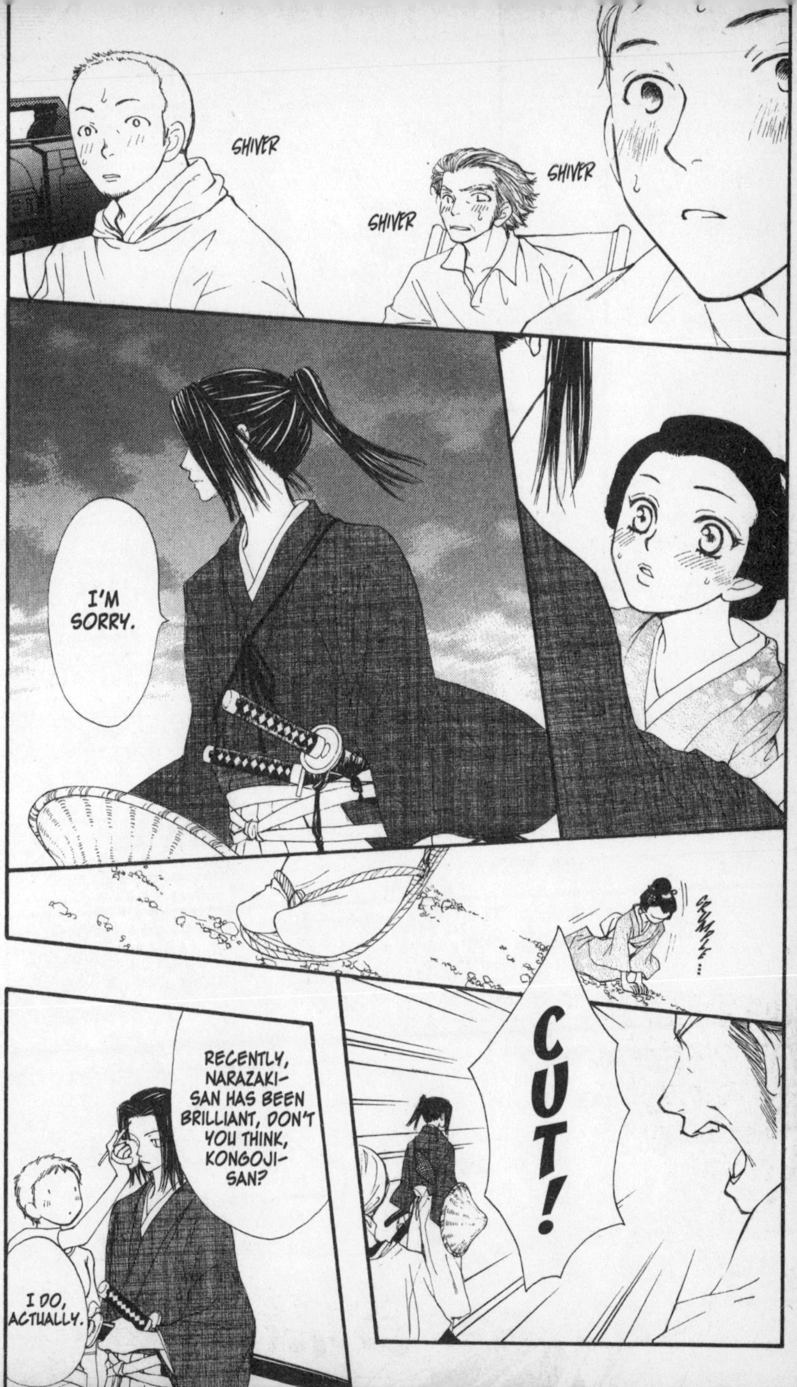
SHIVER
SHIVER
SHIVER
I'M SORRY.
CRUMPLE...
CUT!
RECENTLY, NARAZAKI-SAN HAS BEEN BRILLIANT, DON'T YOU THINK, KONGOJI-SAN?
I DO, ACTUALLY.

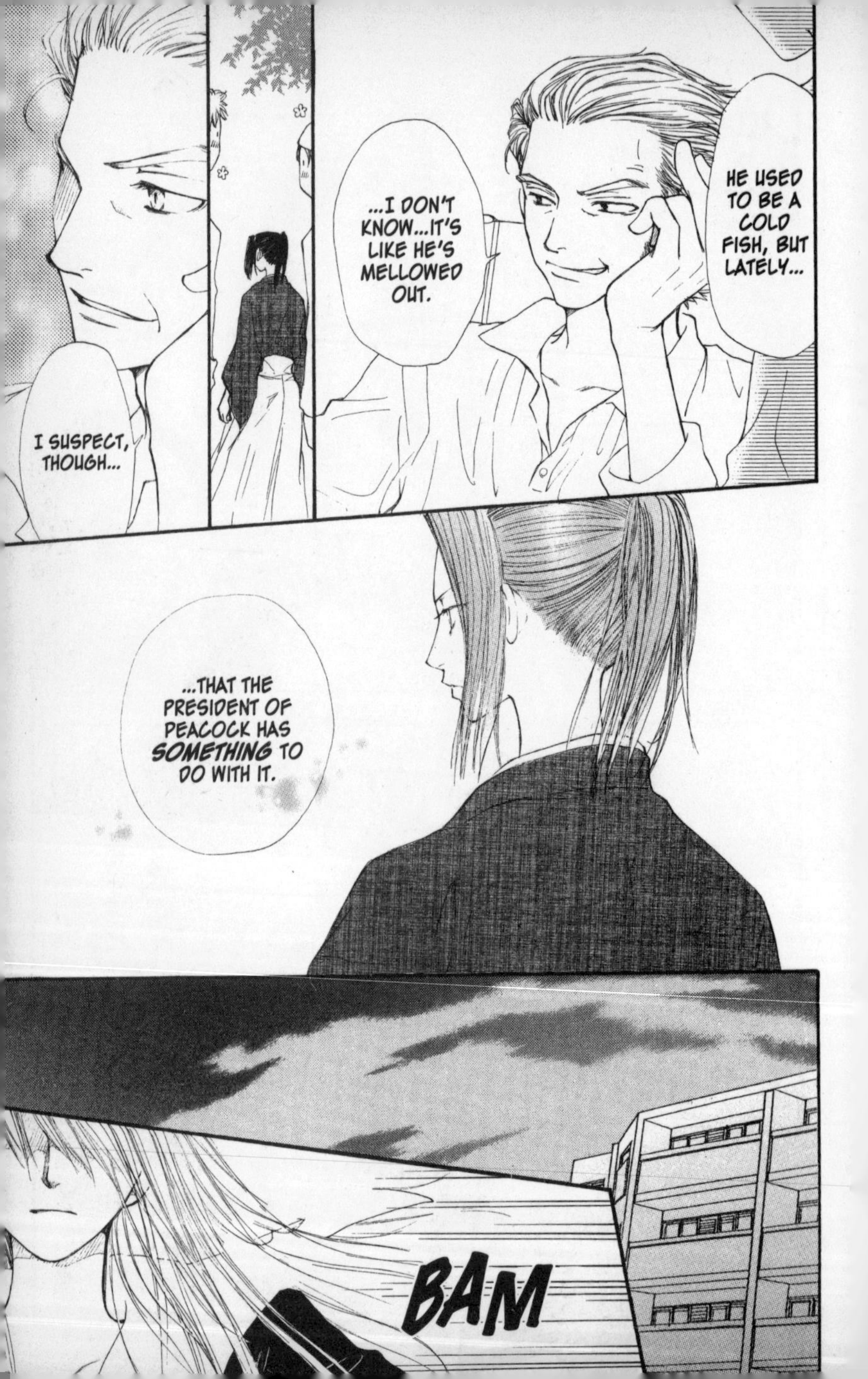
HE USED TO BE A COLD FISH, BUT LATELY...
...I DON'T KNOW...IT'S LIKE HE'S MELLOWED OUT.
I SUSPECT, THOUGH...
...THAT THE PRESIDENT OF PEACOCK HAS SOMETHING TO DO WITH IT.
BAM

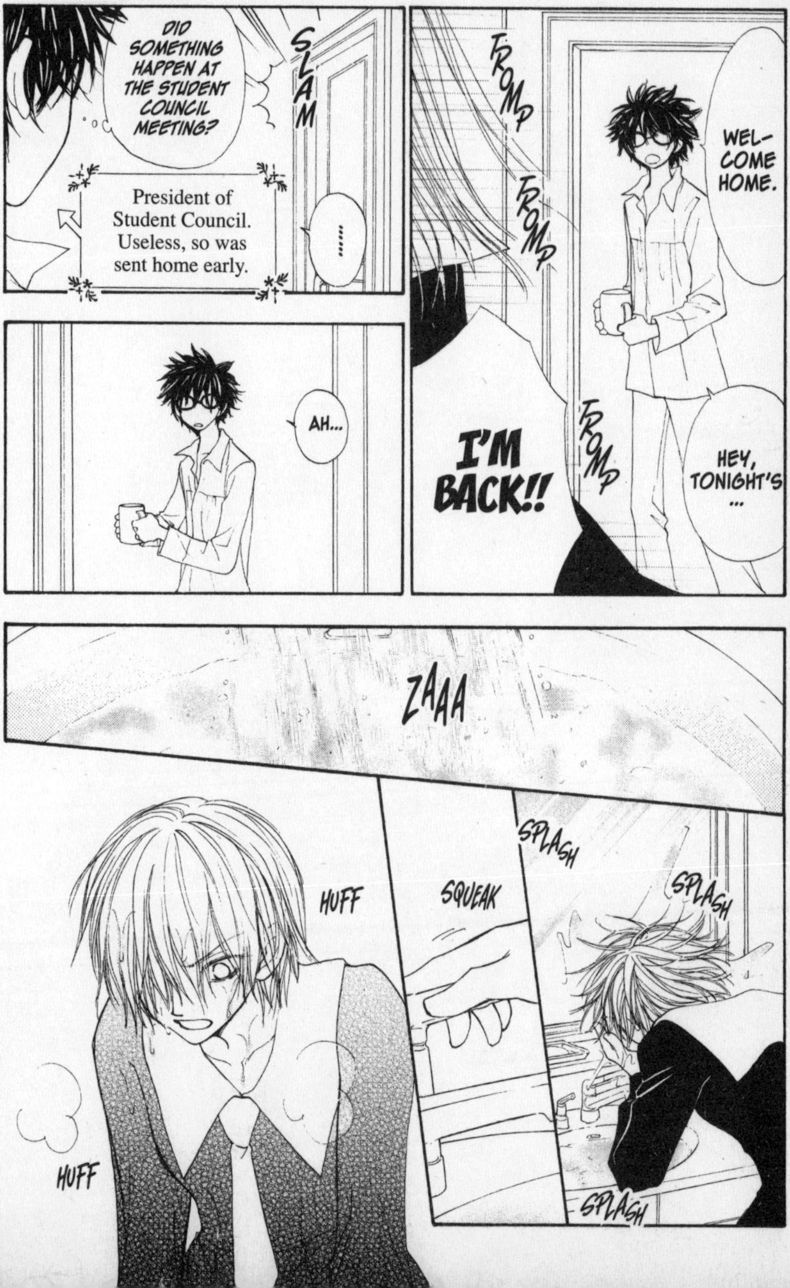

WEL-COME HOME.
TROMP
TROMP
HEY, TONIGHT'S ...
TROMP
I'M BACK!!
SLAM
......
DID SOMETHING HAPPEN AT THE STUDENT COUNCIL MEETING?
President of Student Council. Useless, so was sent home early.
AH...
ZAAA
SPLASH
SPLASH
SPLASH
SQUEAK
HUFF
HUFF

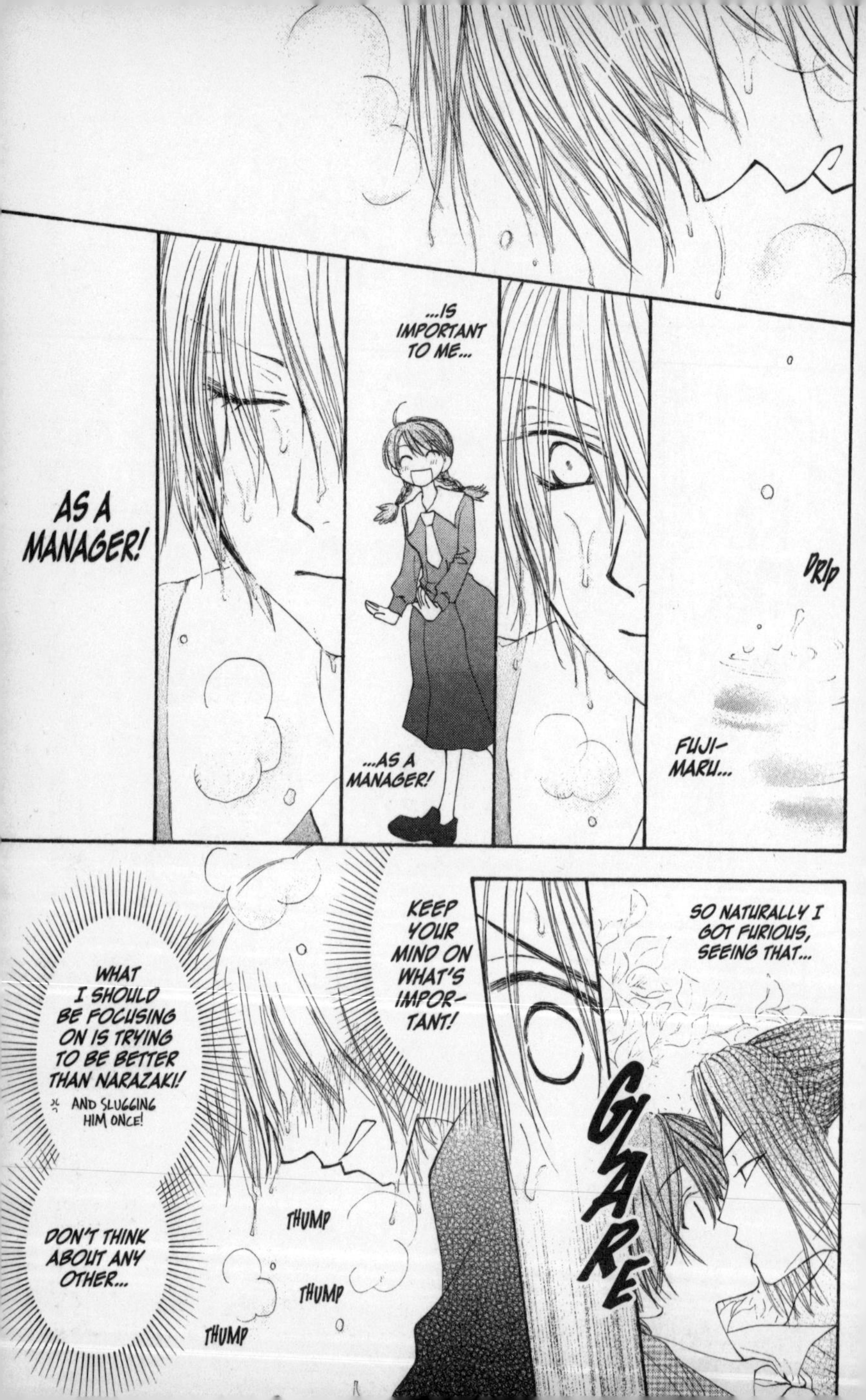
DRIP
FUJI-MARU...
...IS IMPORTANT TO ME...
...AS A MANAGER!
AS A MANAGER!
SO NATURALLY I GOT FURIOUS, SEEING THAT...
GLARE
KEEP YOUR MIND ON WHAT'S IMPOR-TANT!
WHAT I SHOULD BE FOCUSING ON IS TRYING TO BE BETTER THAN NARAZAKI!
AND SLUGGING HIM ONCE!
THUMP
THUMP
THUMP
DON'T THINK ABOUT ANY OTHER...

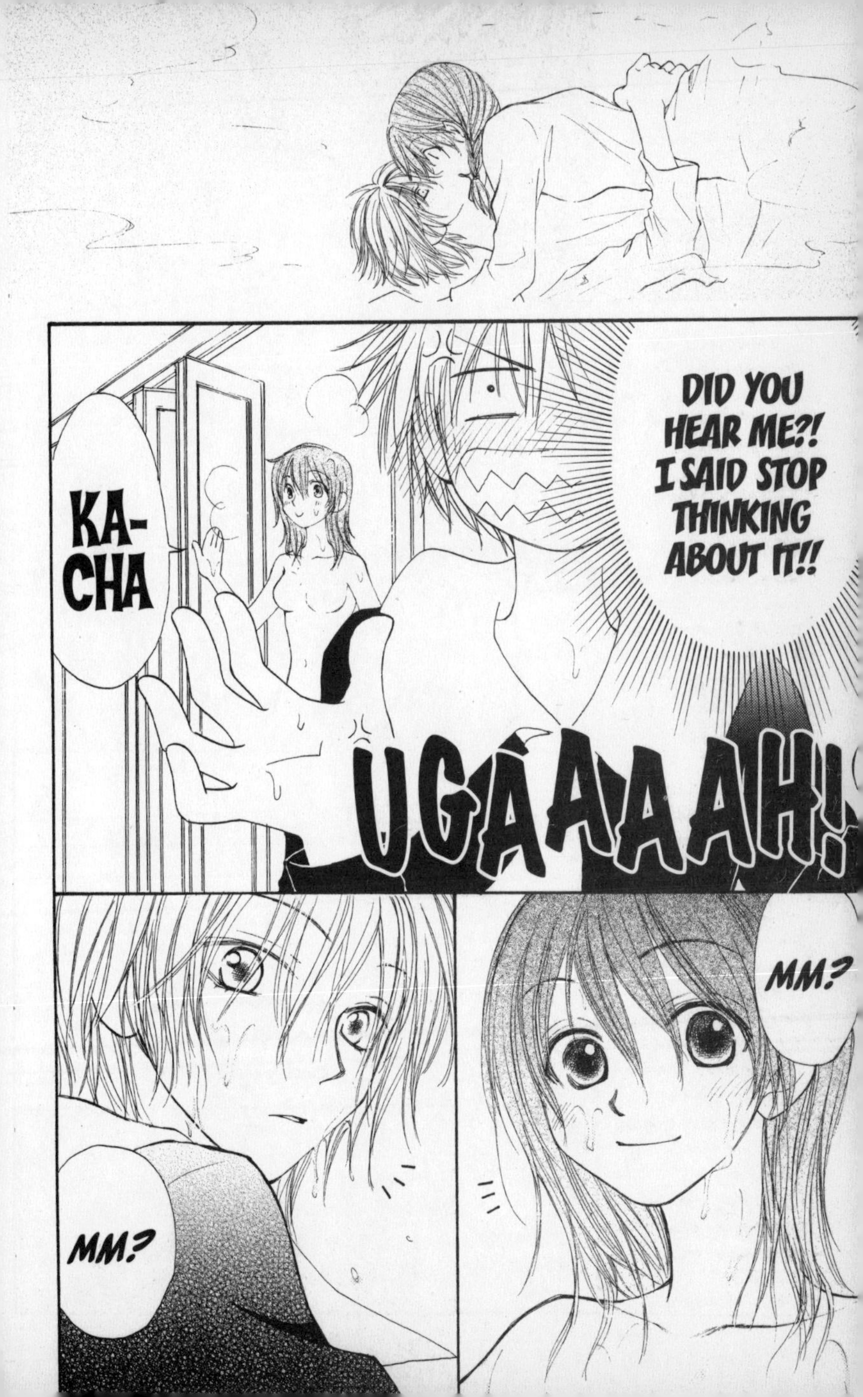
DID YOU HEAR ME?! I SAID STOP THINKING ABOUT IT!!
UGÁAAAAH!
KA-CHA
MM?
MM?

1/4 Sakura Mail

part 9

(Continued)
Regarding "Animal Alliance," I wanted to have a director who was more "craftsman" than "movie director"-like director, and ended up with kind of an old man. My image was a guy who translates the visuals in his head pretty much exactly the way he sees them to little drawings on paper, like storyboards. Now, the only problem is that I couldn't seem to get him down on paper...not well at least!! Everyone who wanted to help showed me the original memo I had on him and said that my very first sketch of the guy was the best. GROAN... So, I tried my best to get him down in the manuscript. He didn't exactly come out the way I wanted, but it's the best I could do. That happens to me a lot, where the best drawings are the ones that I just sketch off the top of my head...Maybe because I don't really expect anything when I draw them?

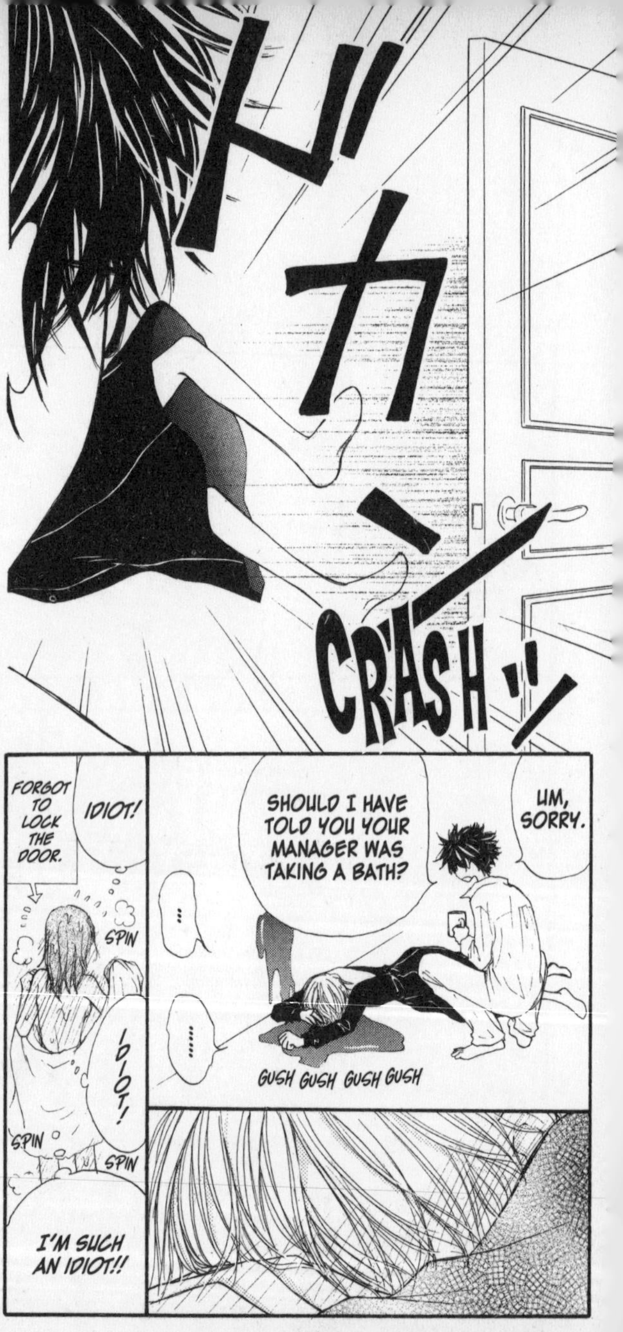
ドカッ
CRASH!!
UM, SORRY.
SHOULD I HAVE TOLD YOU YOUR MANAGER WAS TAKING A BATH?
...
......
GUSH GUSH GUSH GUSH
IDIOT!
FORGOT TO LOCK THE DOOR.
SPIN
IDIOT!
SPIN
SPIN
I'M SUCH AN IDIOT!!

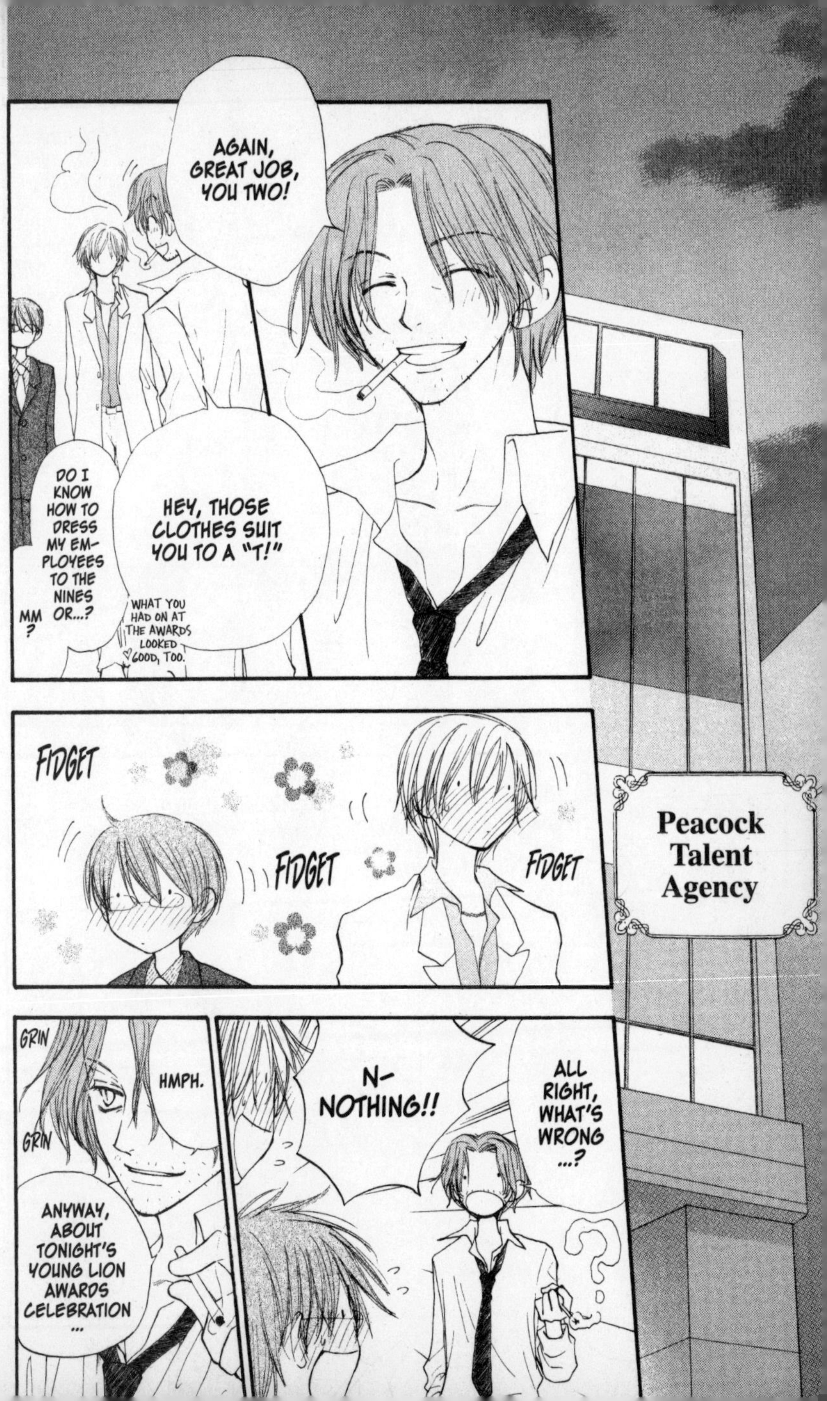
AGAIN, GREAT JOB, YOU TWO!
HEY, THOSE CLOTHES SUIT YOU TO A "T!"
WHAT YOU HAD ON AT THE AWARDS LOOKED ♡GOOD, TOO.
DO I KNOW HOW TO DRESS MY EM-PLOYEES TO THE NINES OR...?
MM ?
Peacock Talent Agency
FIDGET
FIDGET
FIDGET
ALL RIGHT, WHAT'S WRONG ...?
N- NOTHING!!
GRIN
GRIN
HMPH.
ANYWAY, ABOUT TONIGHT'S YOUNG LION AWARDS CELEBRATION ...

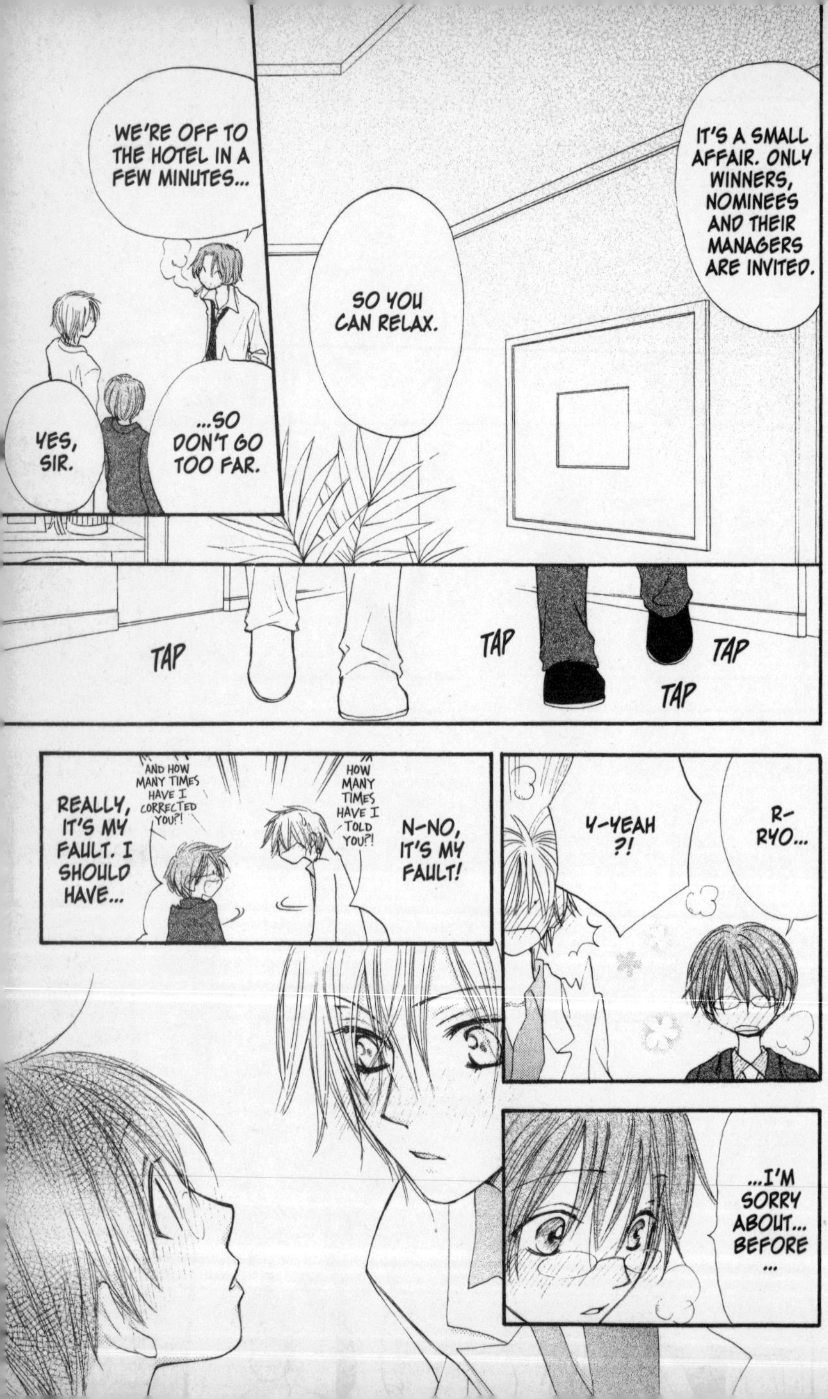
IT'S A SMALL AFFAIR. ONLY WINNERS, NOMINEES AND THEIR MANAGERS ARE INVITED.
SO YOU CAN RELAX.
WE'RE OFF TO THE HOTEL IN A FEW MINUTES...
...SO DON'T GO TOO FAR.
YES, SIR.
TAP
TAP
TAP
TAP
R-RYO...
Y-YEAH?!
N-NO, IT'S MY FAULT!
HOW MANY TIMES HAVE I TOLD YOU?!
AND HOW MANY TIMES HAVE I CORRECTED YOU?!
REALLY, IT'S MY FAULT. I SHOULD HAVE...
...I'M SORRY ABOUT... BEFORE ...

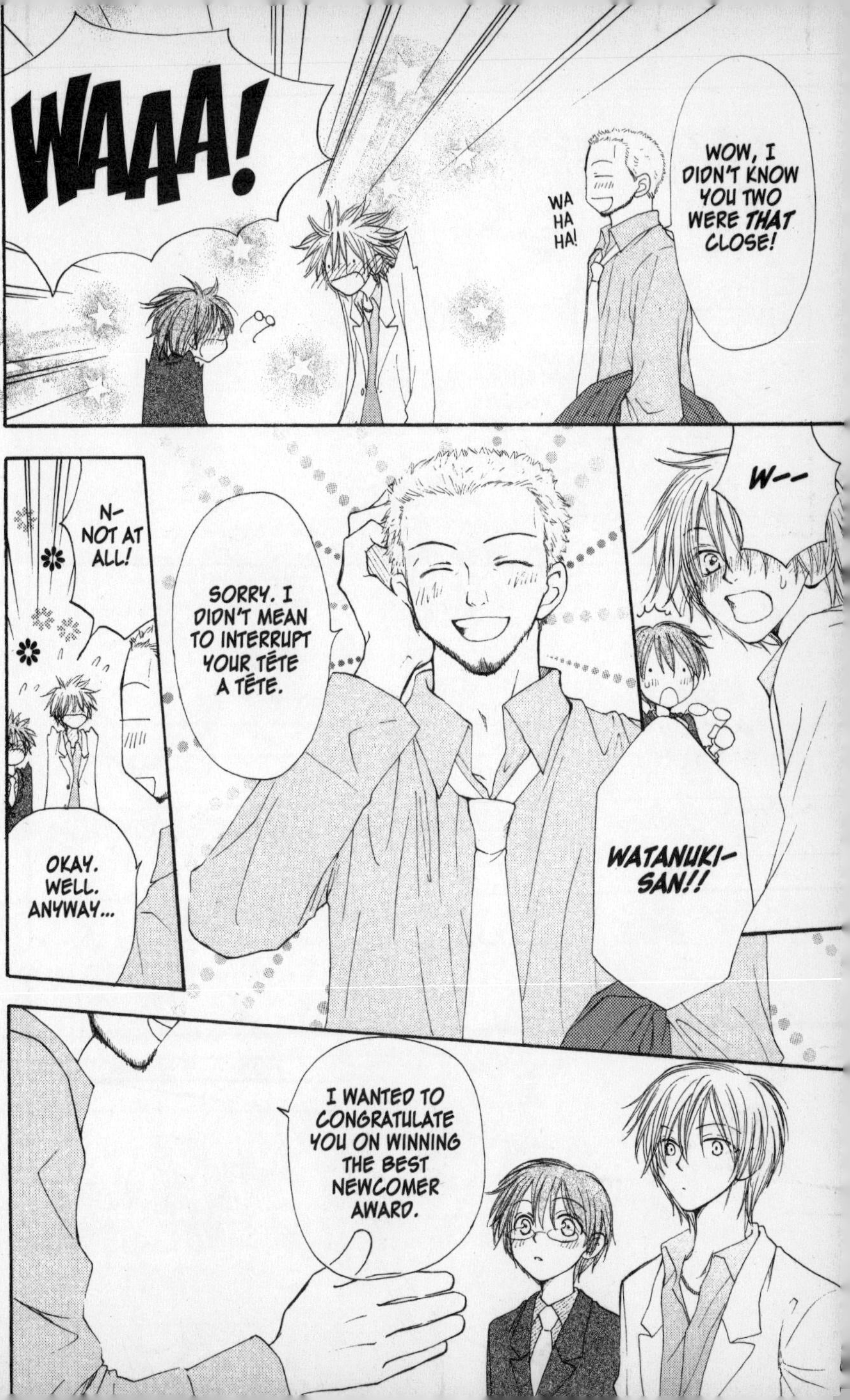
WOW, I DIDN'T KNOW YOU TWO WERE *THAT* CLOSE!
WA HA HA!
WAAAA!
W--
WATANUKI-SAN!!
SORRY. I DIDN'T MEAN TO INTERRUPT YOUR TÊTE A TÊTE.
N-NOT AT ALL!
OKAY. WELL. ANYWAY...
I WANTED TO CONGRATULATE YOU ON WINNING THE BEST NEWCOMER AWARD.

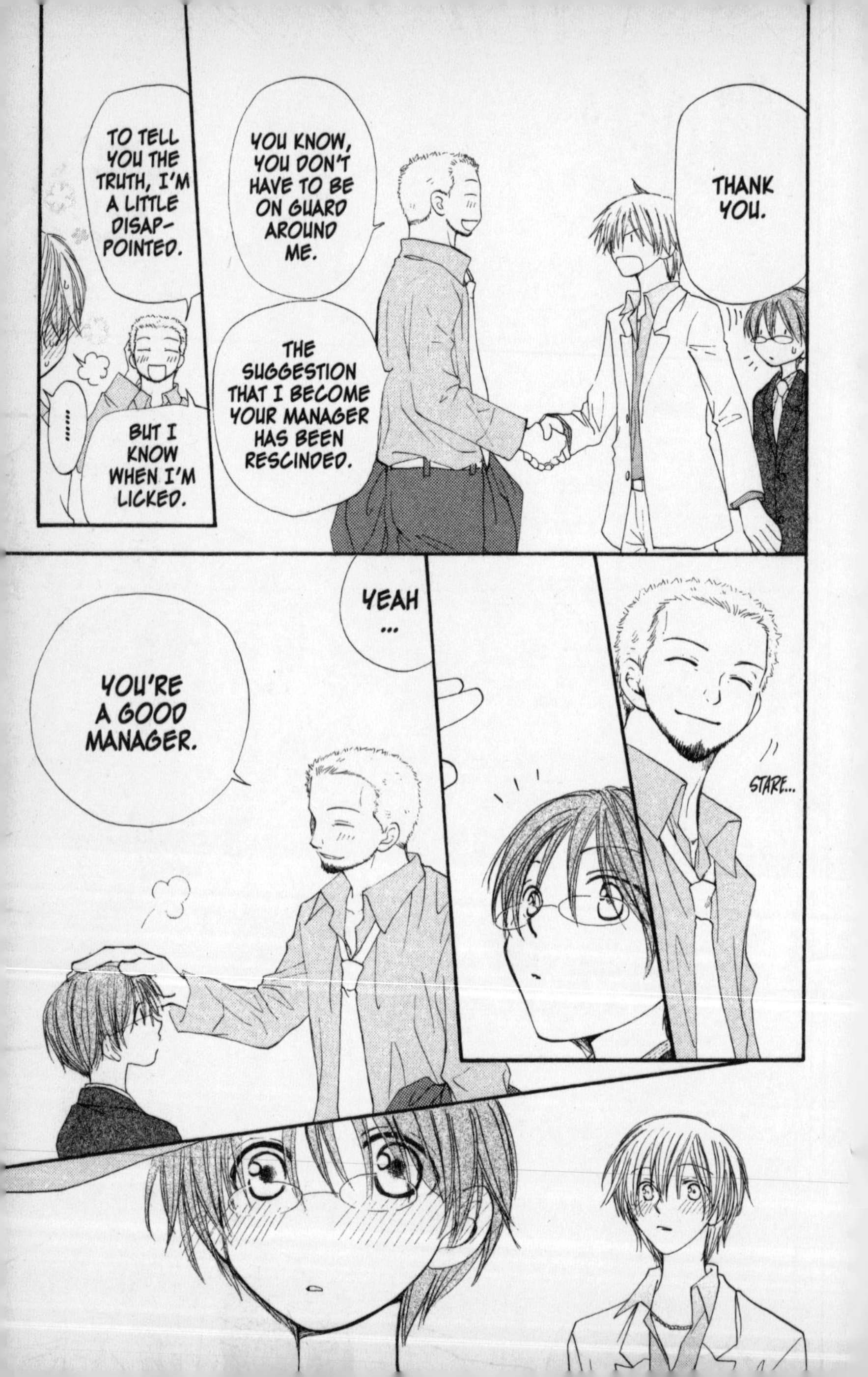
THANK YOU.
YOU KNOW, YOU DON'T HAVE TO BE ON GUARD AROUND ME.
THE SUGGESTION THAT I BECOME YOUR MANAGER HAS BEEN RESCINDED.
TO TELL YOU THE TRUTH, I'M A LITTLE DISAP-POINTED.
BUT I KNOW WHEN I'M LICKED.
......
STARE...
YEAH ...
YOU'RE A GOOD MANAGER.

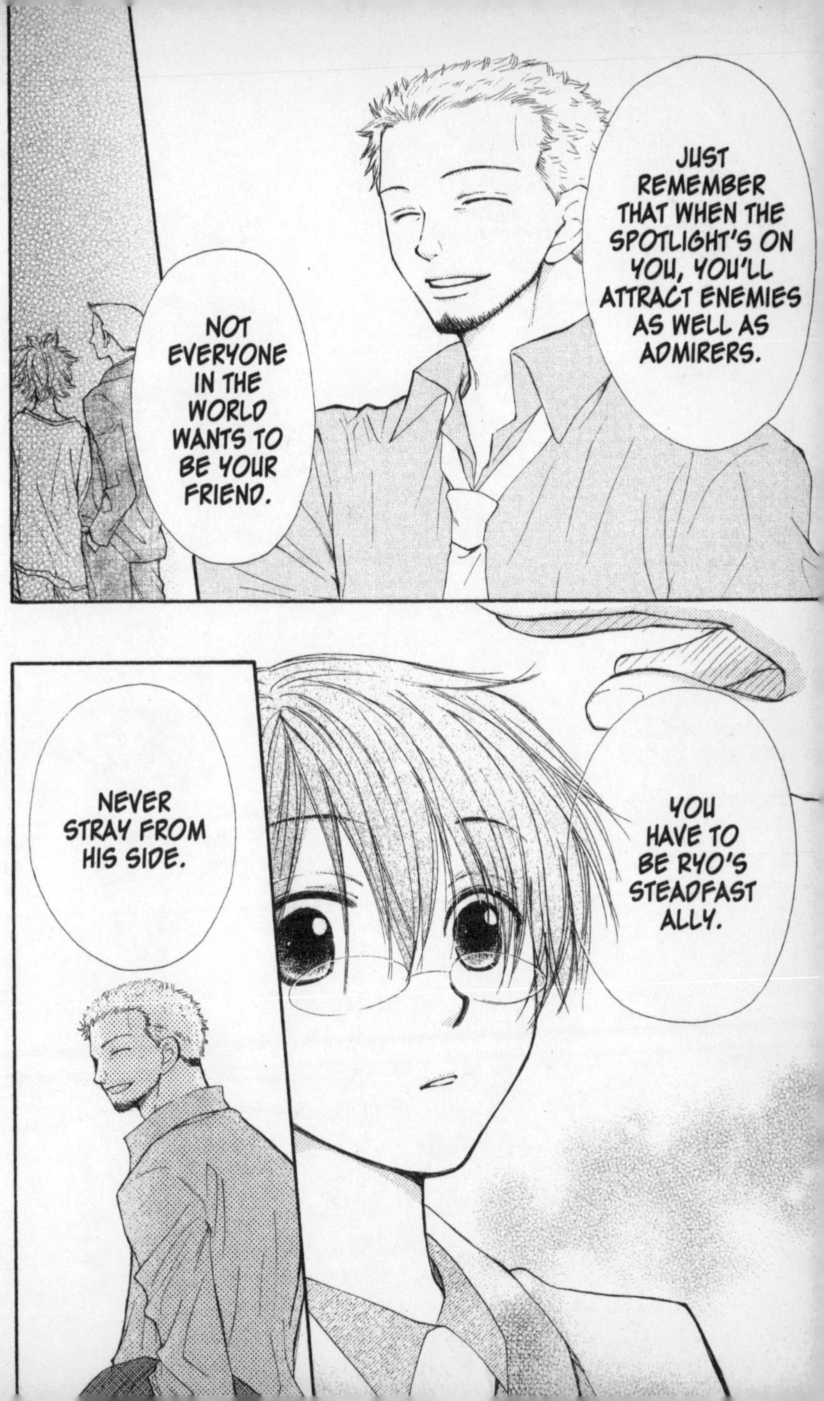
JUST REMEMBER THAT WHEN THE SPOTLIGHT'S ON YOU, YOU'LL ATTRACT ENEMIES AS WELL AS ADMIRERS.
NOT EVERYONE IN THE WORLD WANTS TO BE YOUR FRIEND.
YOU HAVE TO BE RYO'S STEADFAST ALLY.
NEVER STRAY FROM HIS SIDE.

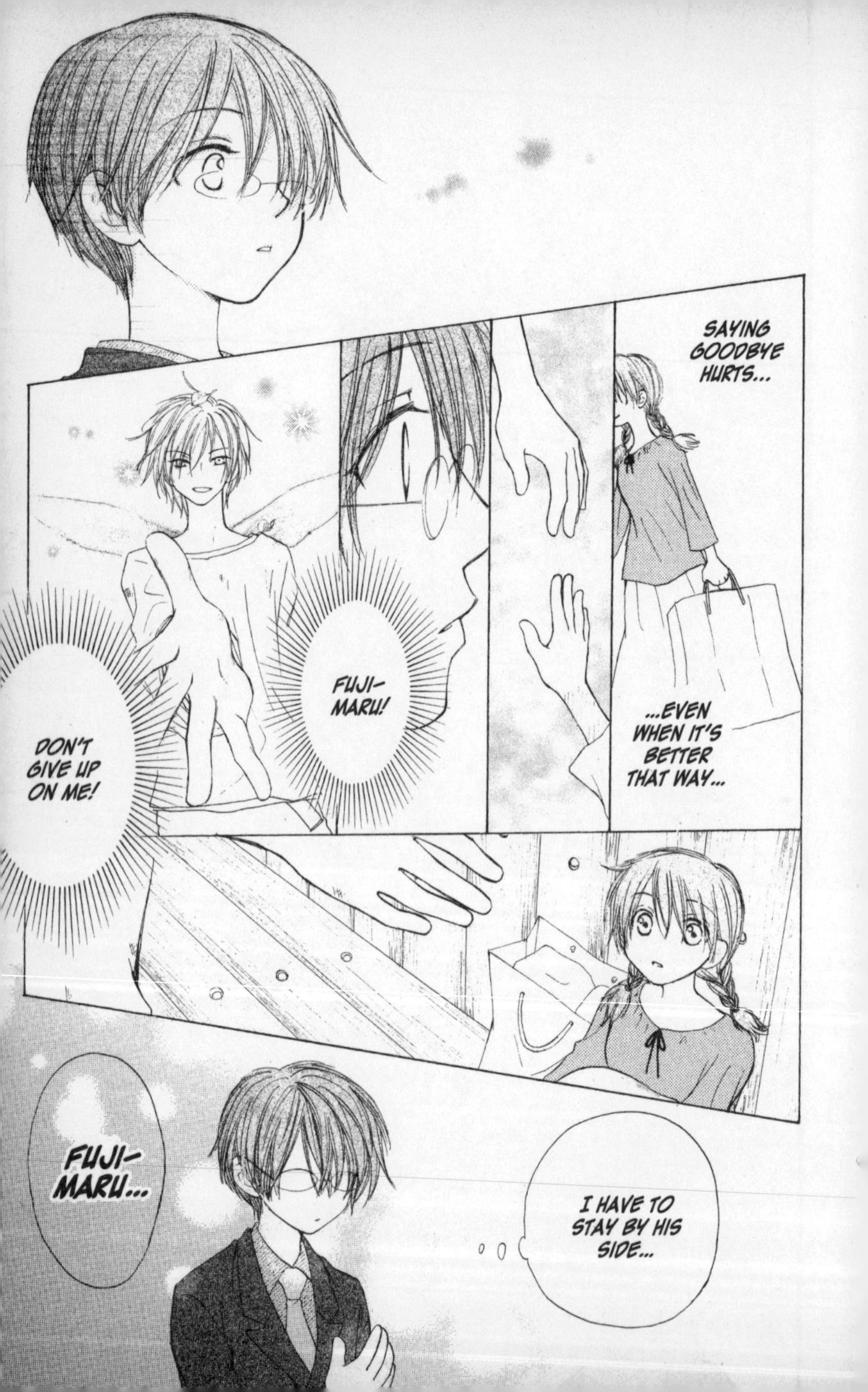
SAYING GOODBYE HURTS...
...EVEN WHEN IT'S BETTER THAT WAY...
FUJI-MARU!
DON'T GIVE UP ON ME!
I HAVE TO STAY BY HIS SIDE...
FUJI-MARU...

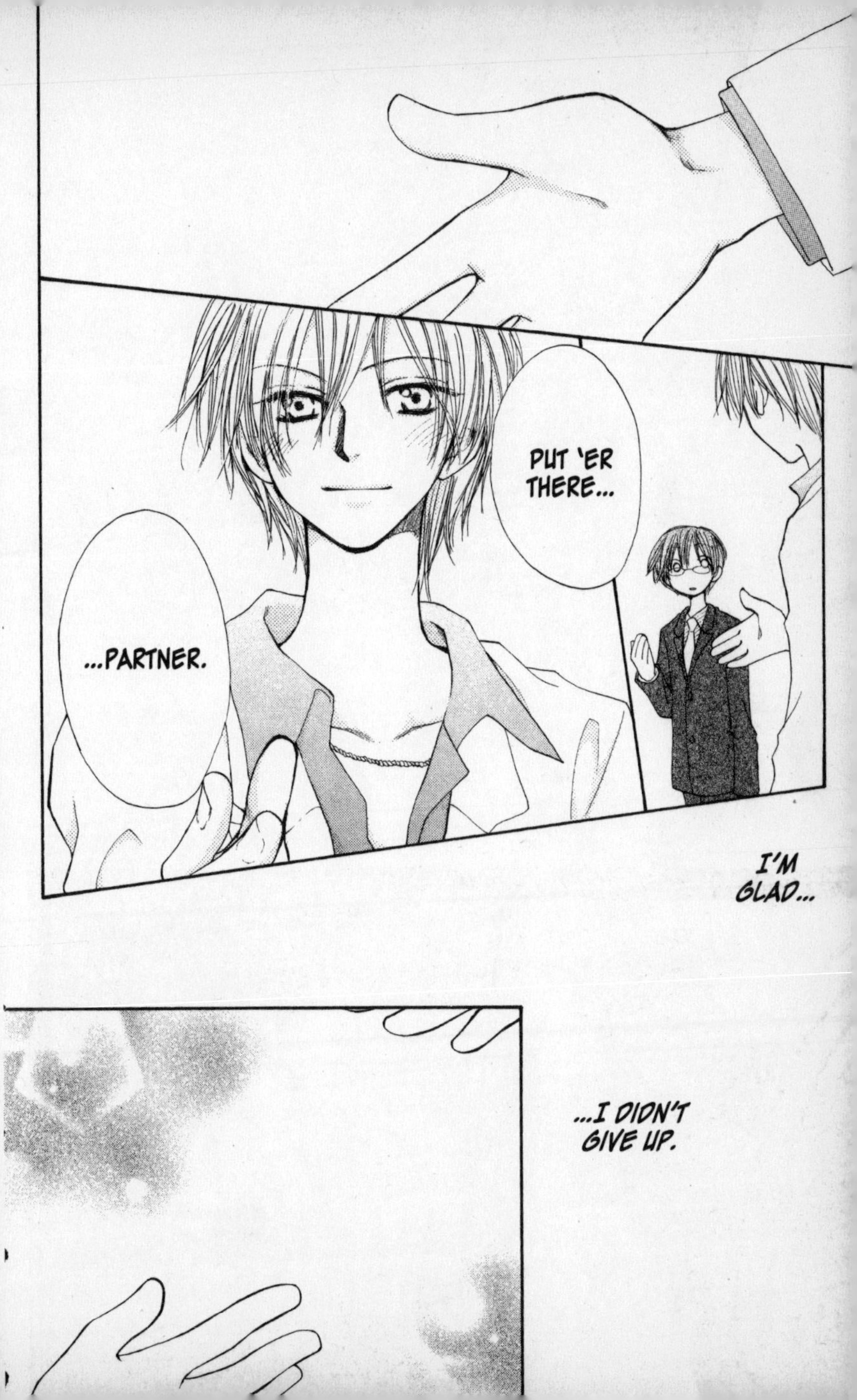
PUT 'ER THERE...
...PARTNER.
I'M GLAD...
...I DIDN'T GIVE UP.

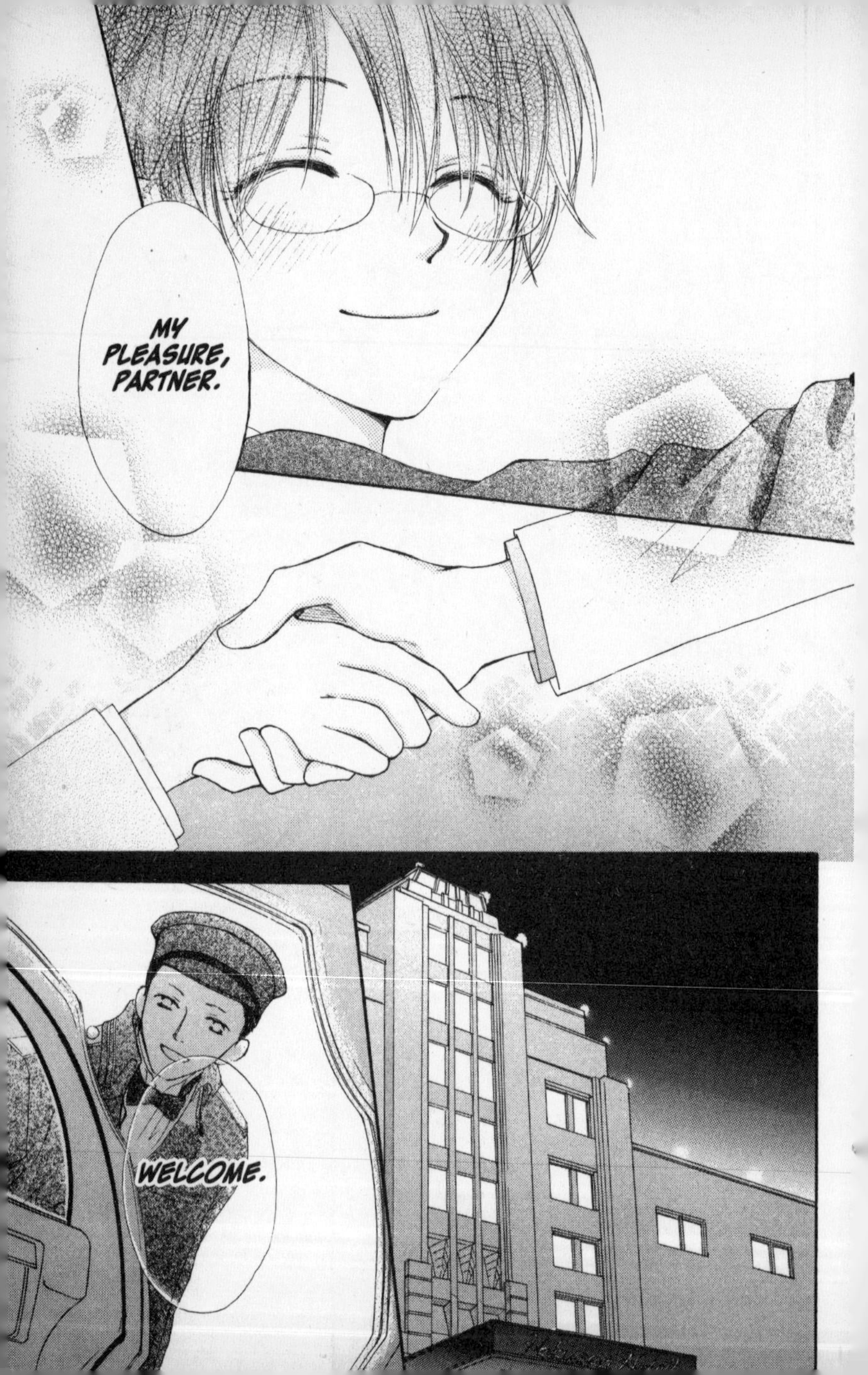
MY PLEASURE, PARTNER.
WELCOME.

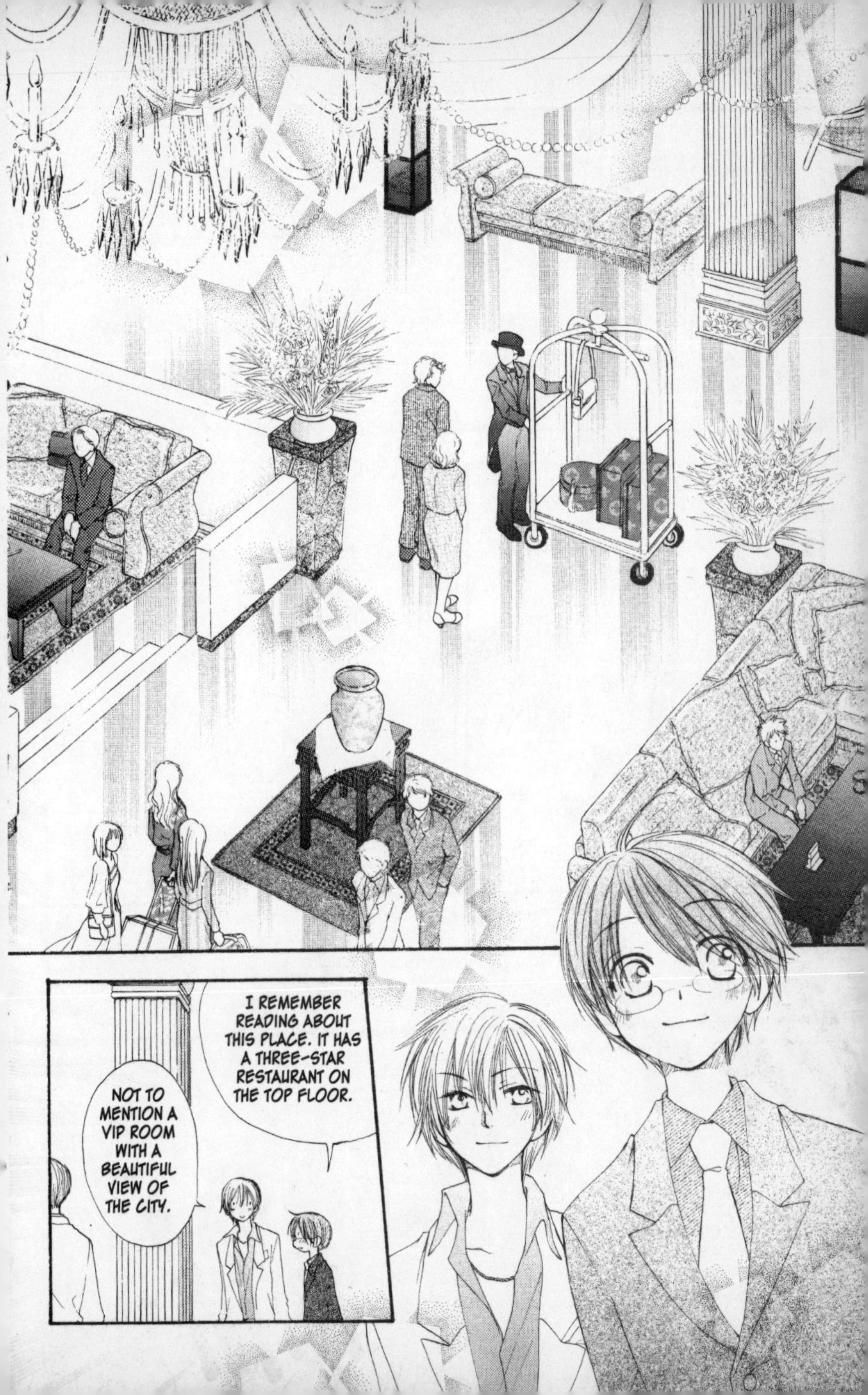
I REMEMBER READING ABOUT THIS PLACE. IT HAS A THREE-STAR RESTAURANT ON THE TOP FLOOR.
NOT TO MENTION A VIP ROOM WITH A BEAUTIFUL VIEW OF THE CITY.

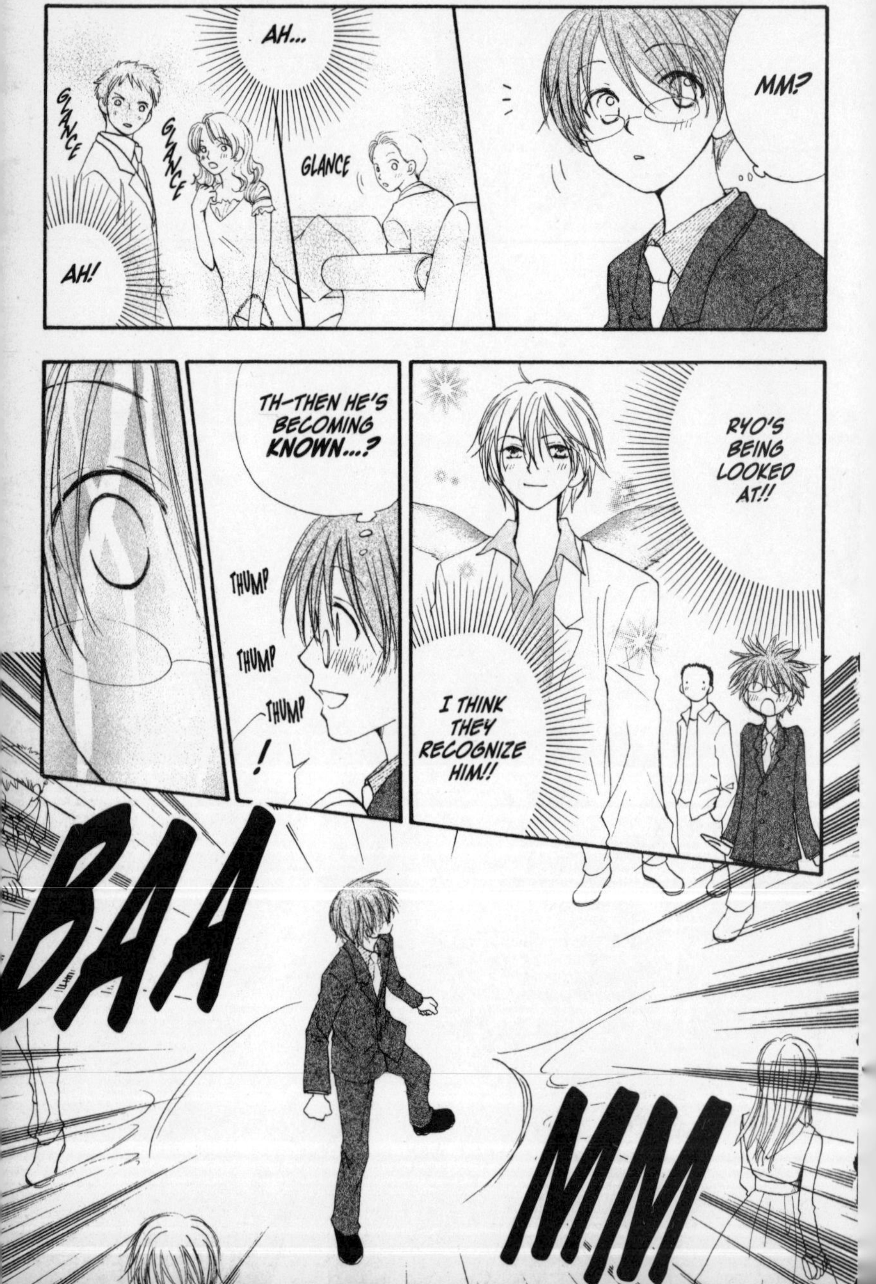

MM?
GLANCE
AH...
GLANCE
GLANCE
AH!
RYO'S BEING LOOKED AT!!
I THINK THEY RECOGNIZE HIM!!
TH-THEN HE'S BECOMING KNOWN...?
THUMP
THUMP
THUMP
!
BAA
MM

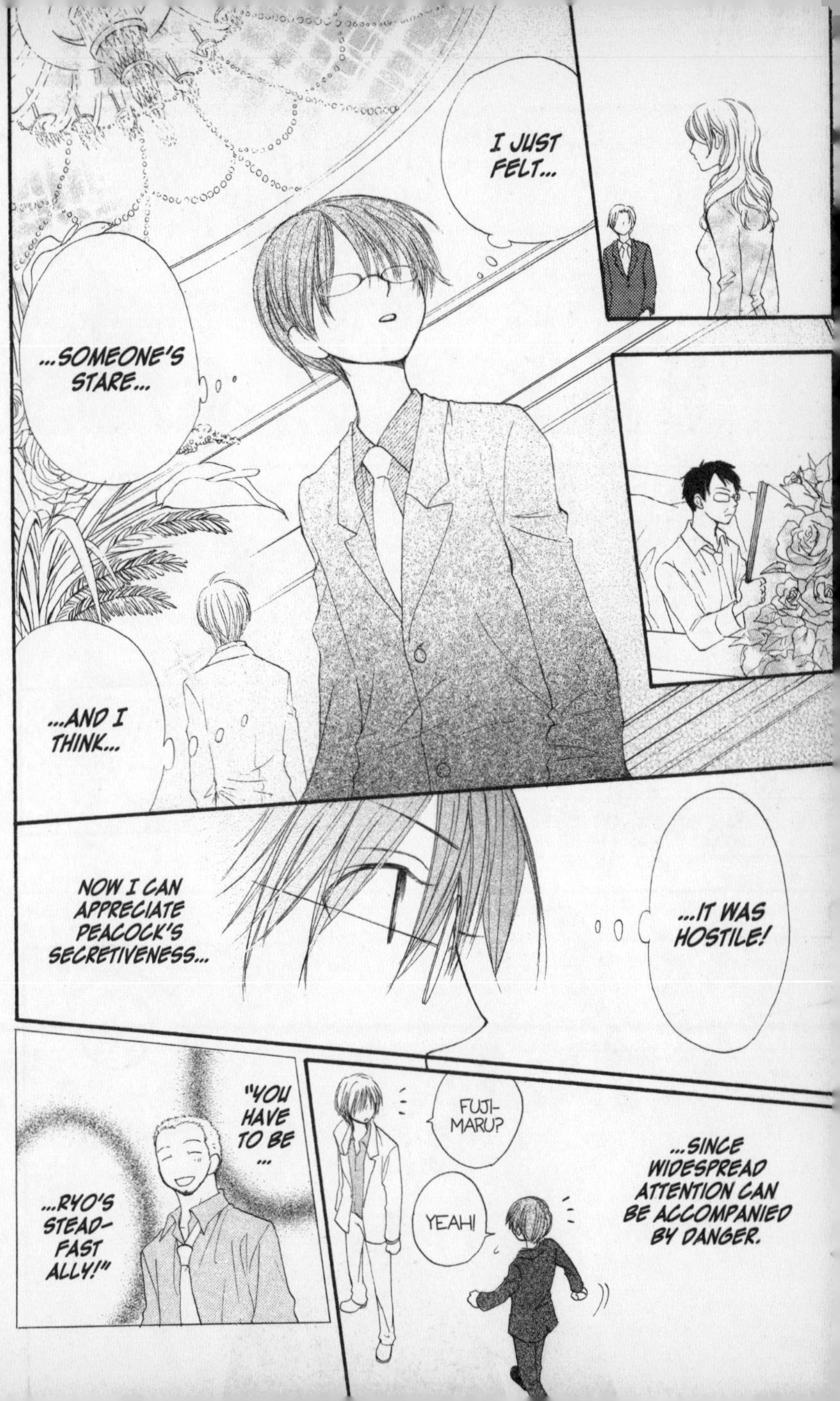
I JUST FELT...
...SOMEONE'S STARE...
...AND I THINK...
...IT WAS HOSTILE!
NOW I CAN APPRECIATE PEACOCK'S SECRETIVENESS...
FUJI-MARU?
...SINCE WIDESPREAD ATTENTION CAN BE ACCOMPANIED BY DANGER.
YEAH!
"YOU HAVE TO BE ...
...RYO'S STEAD-FAST ALLY!"

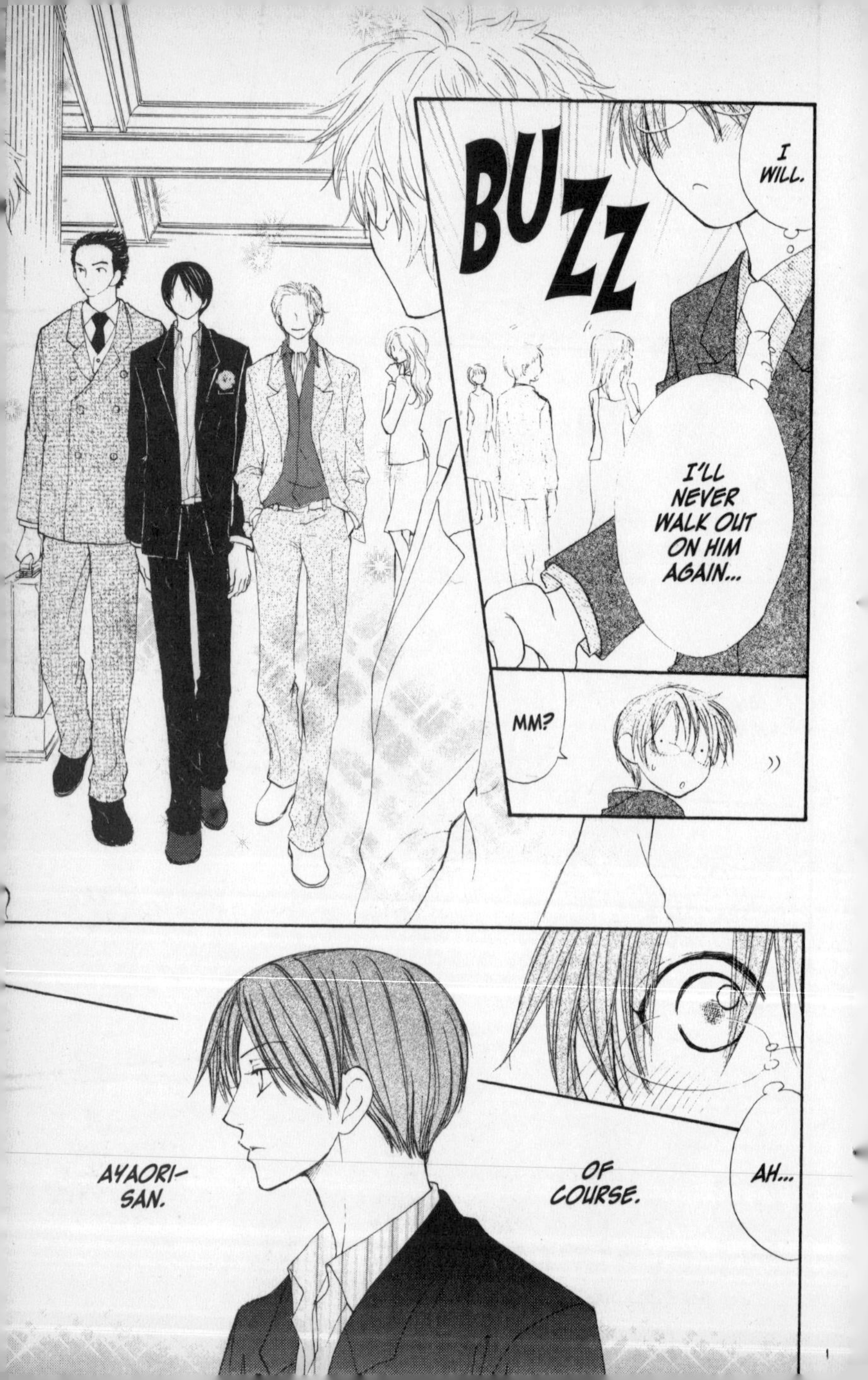
I WILL.
BUZZ
I'LL NEVER WALK OUT ON HIM AGAIN...
MM?
AH...
OF COURSE.
AYAORI-SAN.

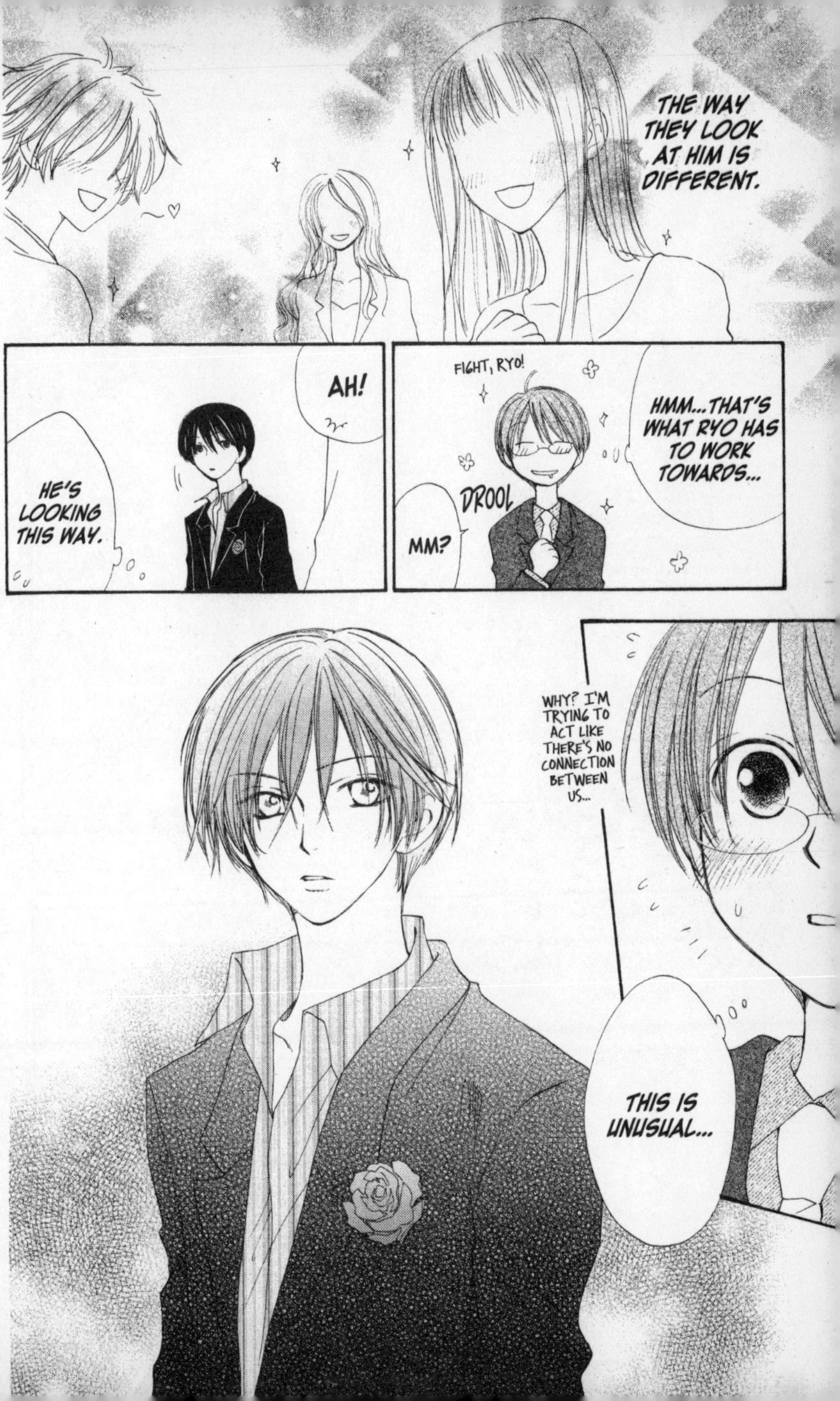
THE WAY THEY LOOK AT HIM IS DIFFERENT.
HMM...THAT'S WHAT RYO HAS TO WORK TOWARDS...
FIGHT, RYO!
DROOL
MM?
AH!
HE'S LOOKING THIS WAY.
WHY? I'M TRYING TO ACT LIKE THERE'S NO CONNECTION BETWEEN US...
THIS IS UNUSUAL...

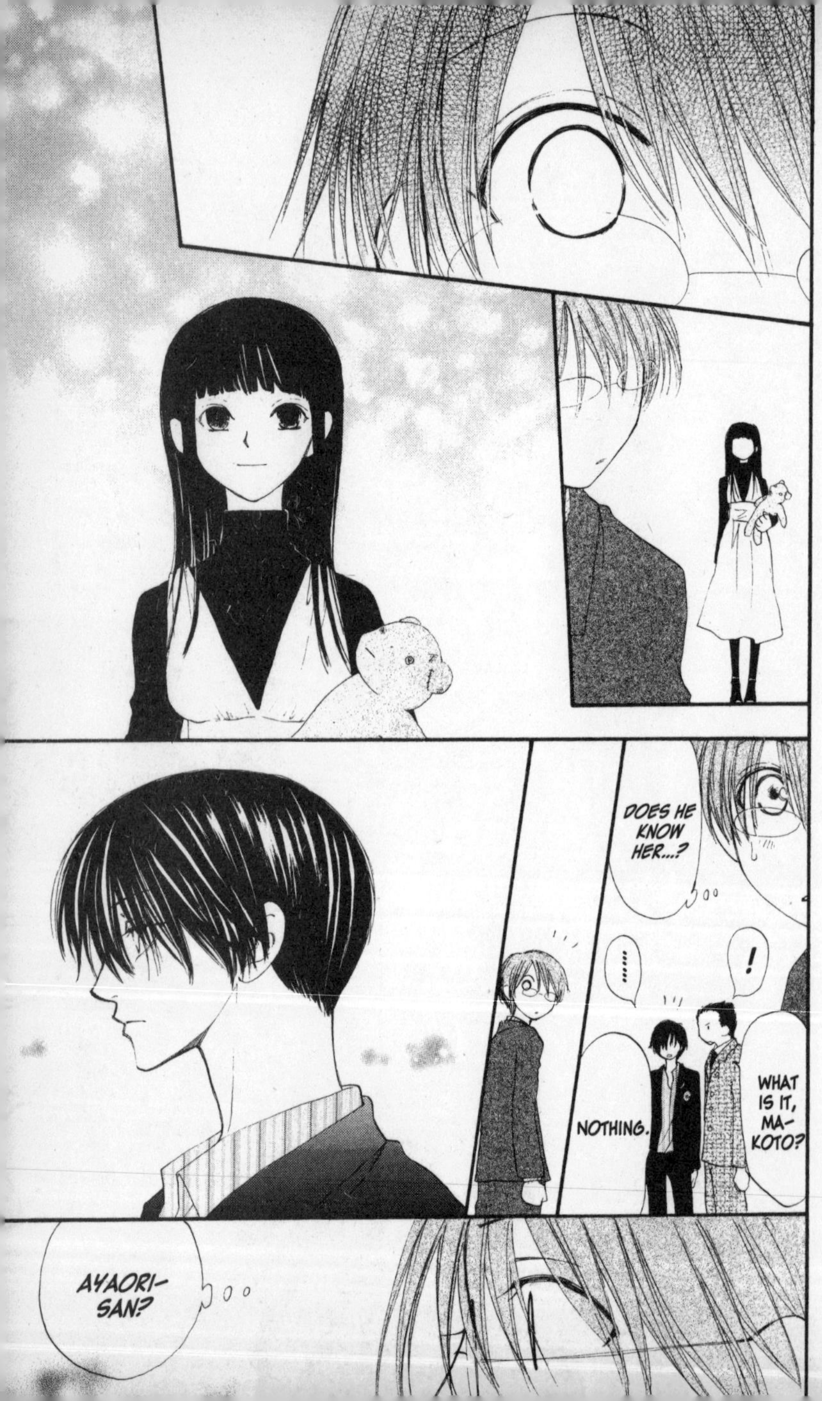

DOES HE KNOW HER...?
!
......
WHAT IS IT, MA-KOTO?
NOTHING.
AYAORI-SAN?

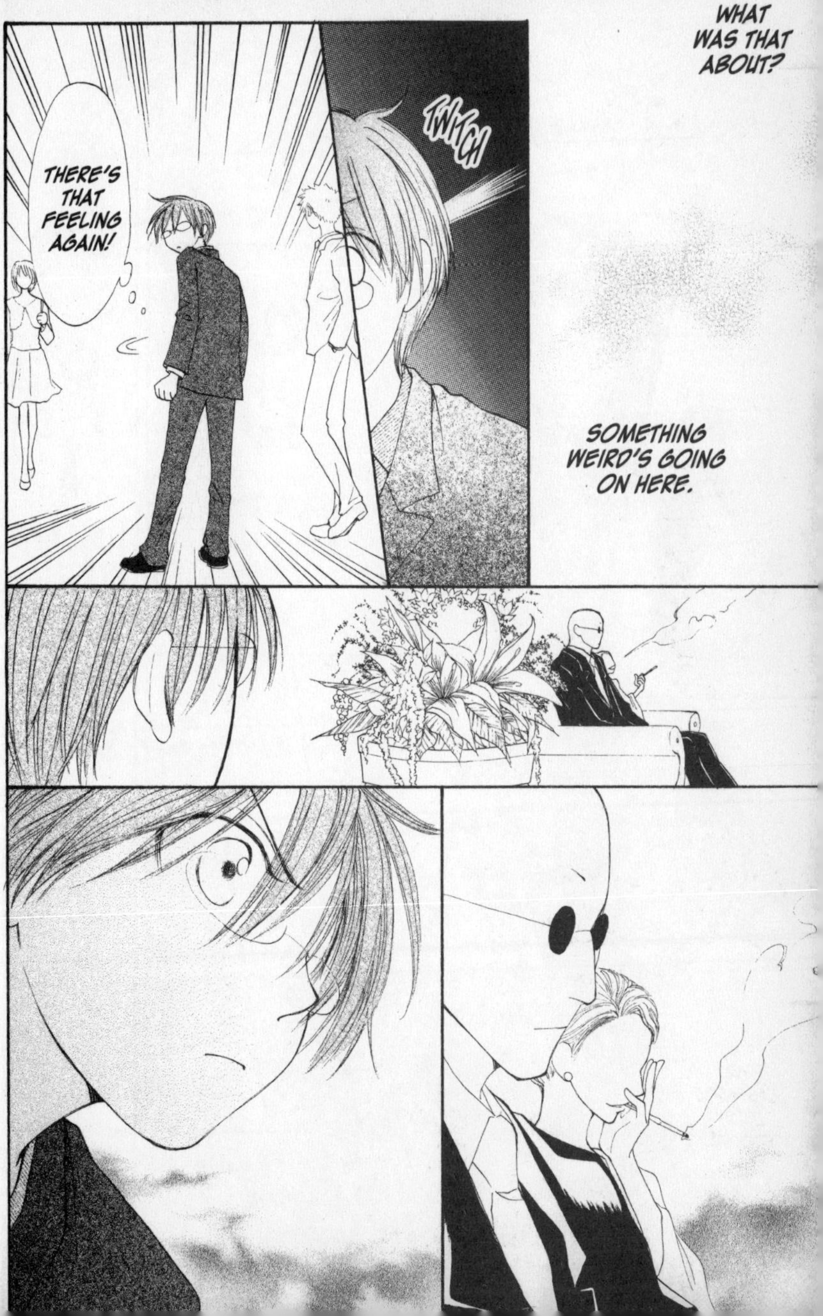
WHAT WAS THAT ABOUT?
SOMETHING WEIRD'S GOING ON HERE.
TWITCH
THERE'S THAT FEELING AGAIN!

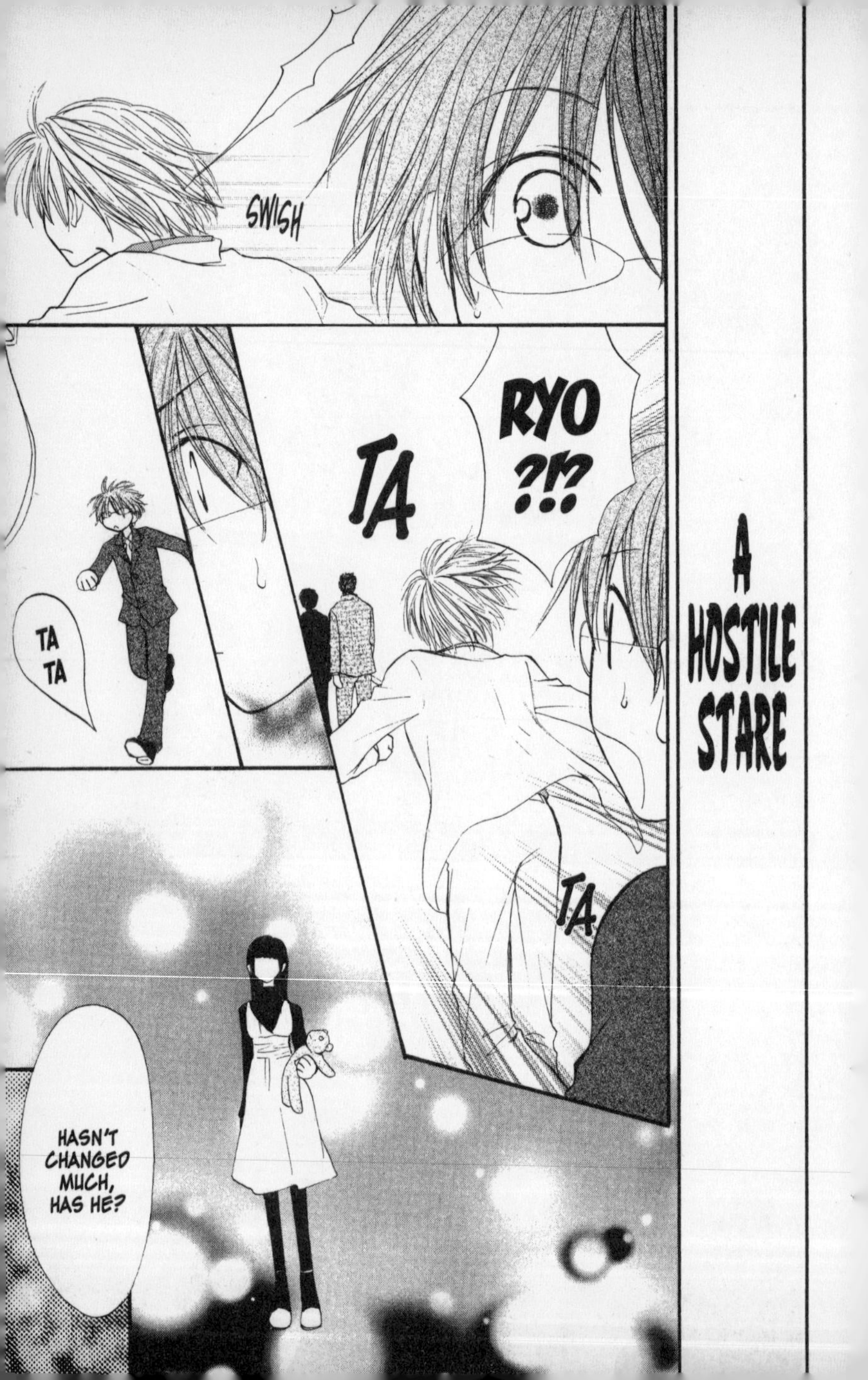
A HOSTILE STARE
SWISH
RYO ?!?
TA
TA
TA TA
HASN'T CHANGED MUCH, HAS HE?

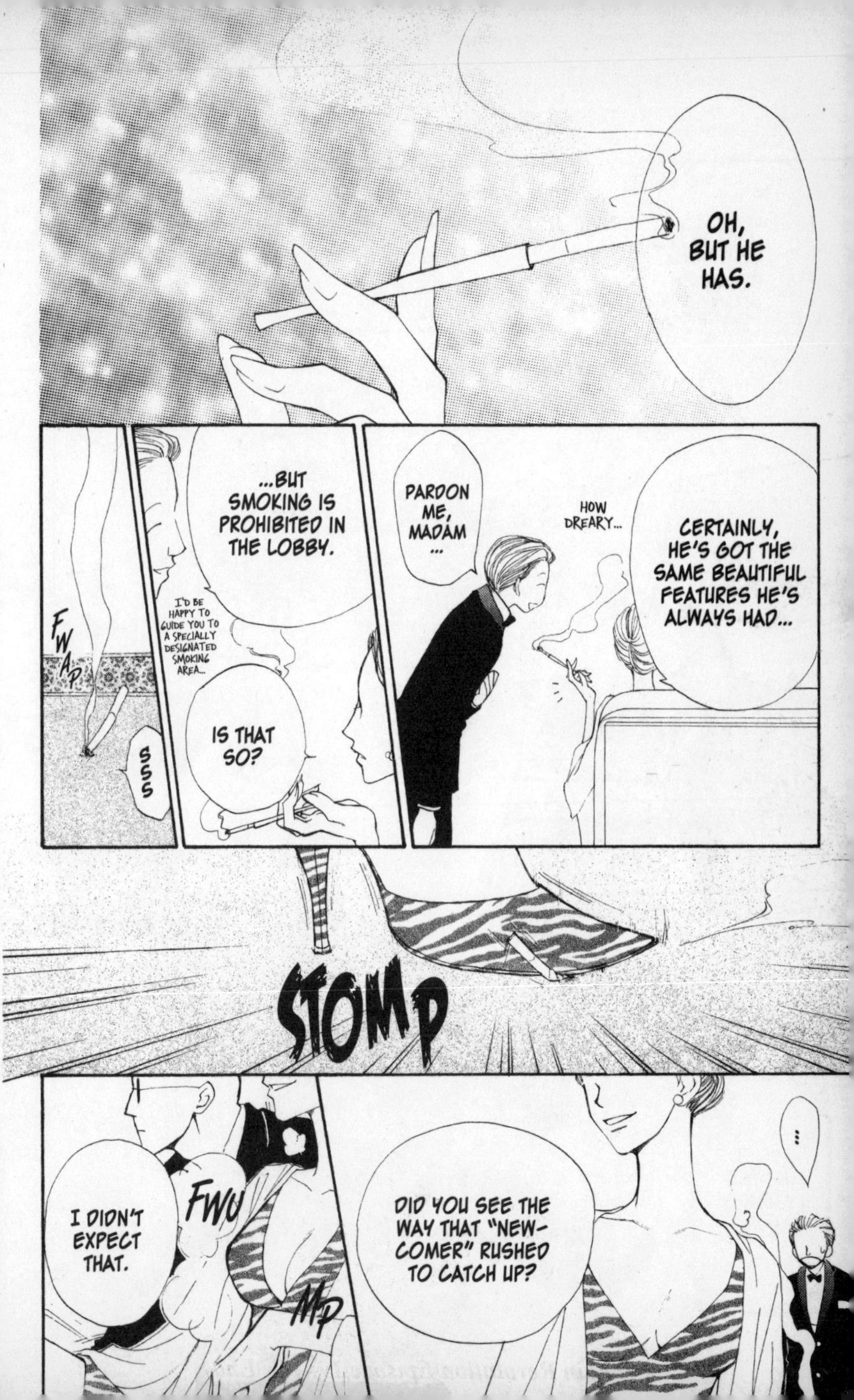
OH, BUT HE HAS.
CERTAINLY, HE'S GOT THE SAME BEAUTIFUL FEATURES HE'S ALWAYS HAD...
HOW DREARY...
PARDON ME, MADAM ...
...BUT SMOKING IS PROHIBITED IN THE LOBBY.
I'D BE HAPPY TO GUIDE YOU TO A SPECIALLY DESIGNATED SMOKING AREA...
IS THAT SO?
FWAP
SSS
STOMP
...
DID YOU SEE THE WAY THAT "NEW-COMER" RUSHED TO CATCH UP?
FWU
I DIDN'T EXPECT THAT.
MP

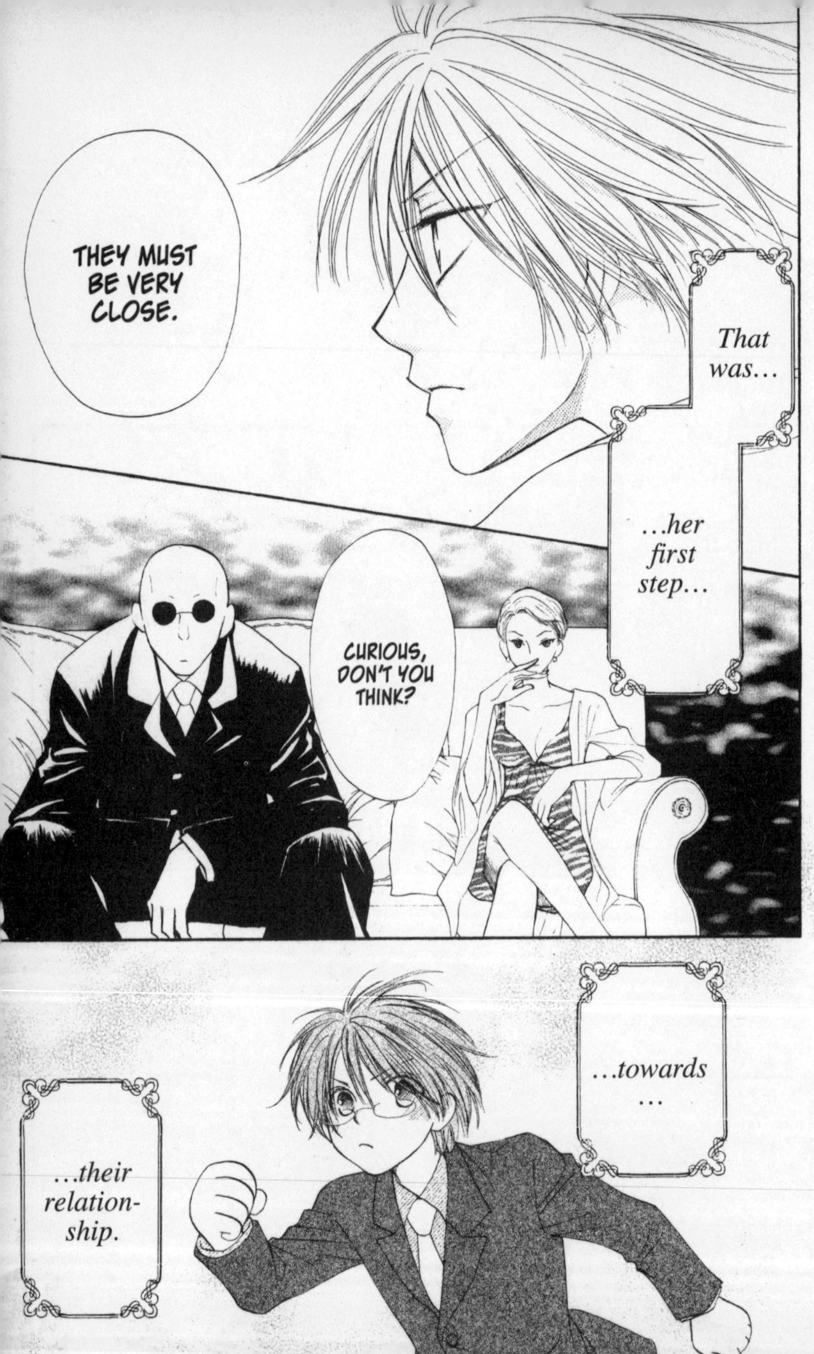
That was…
THEY MUST BE VERY CLOSE.
…her first step…
CURIOUS, DON'T YOU THINK?
…towards …
…their relationship.

Penguin Revolution Episode 19: The End

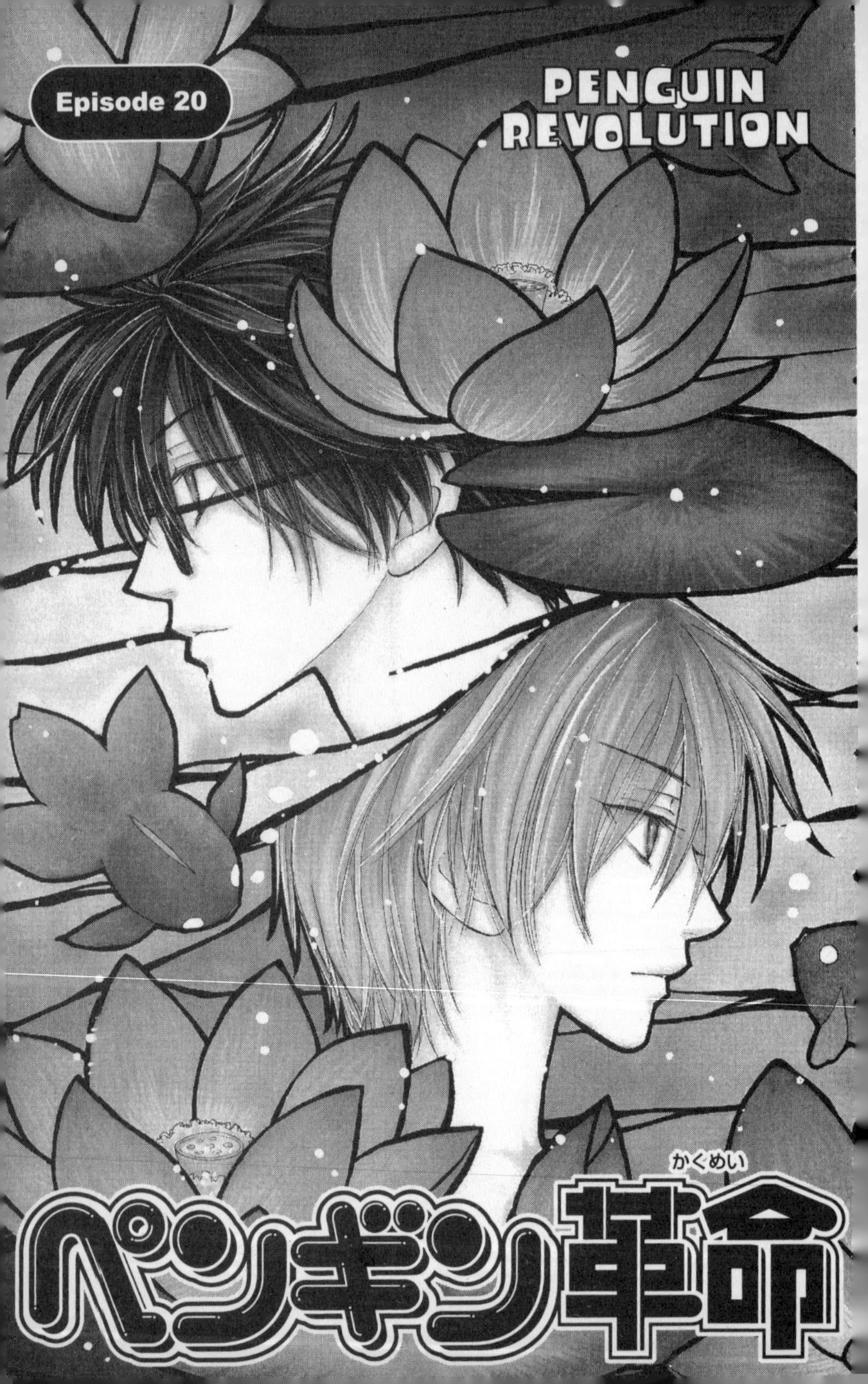
Episode 20
PENGUIN REVOLUTION
かくめい
ペンギン革命

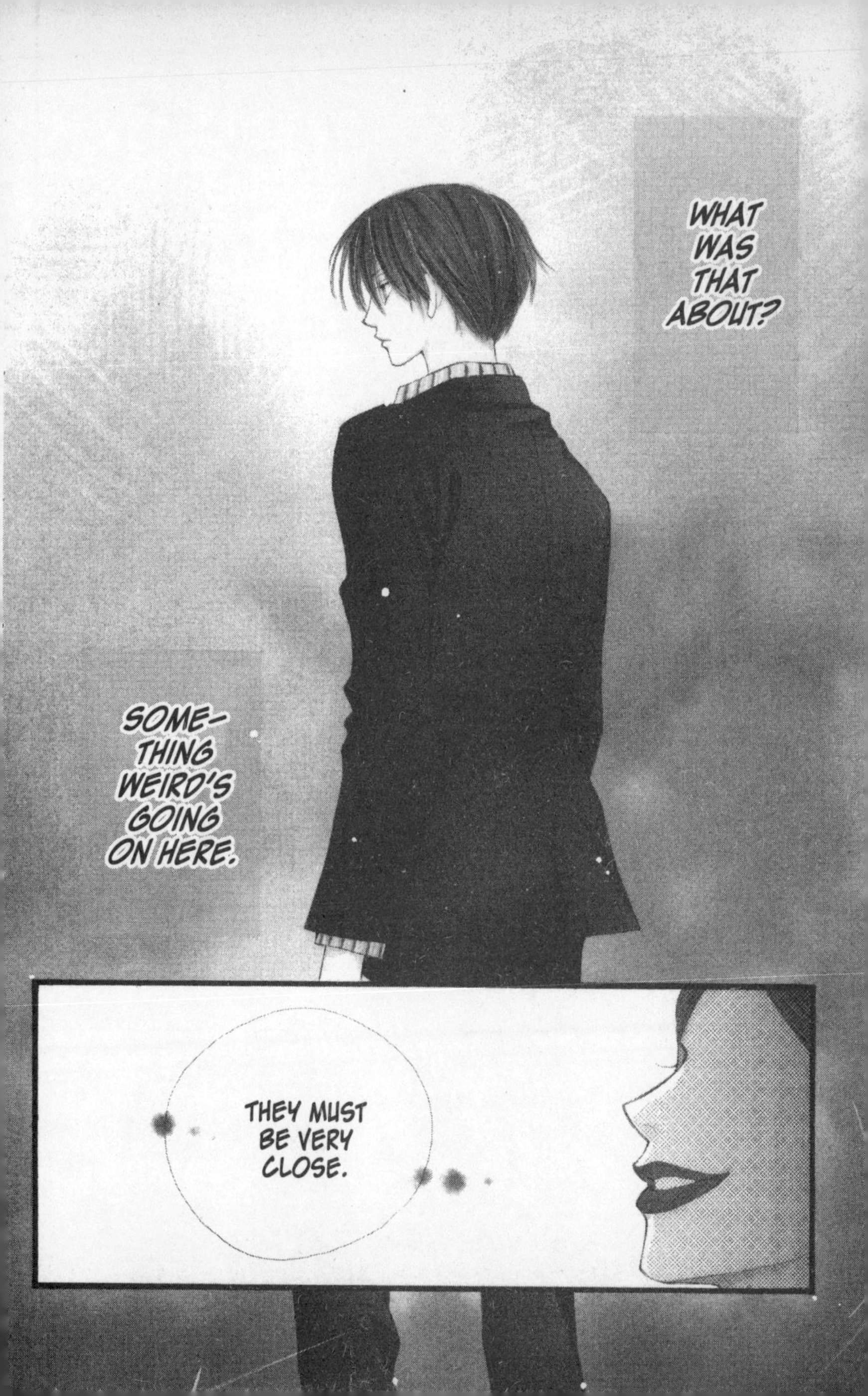
WHAT WAS THAT ABOUT?
SOME-THING WEIRD'S GOING ON HERE.
THEY MUST BE VERY CLOSE.

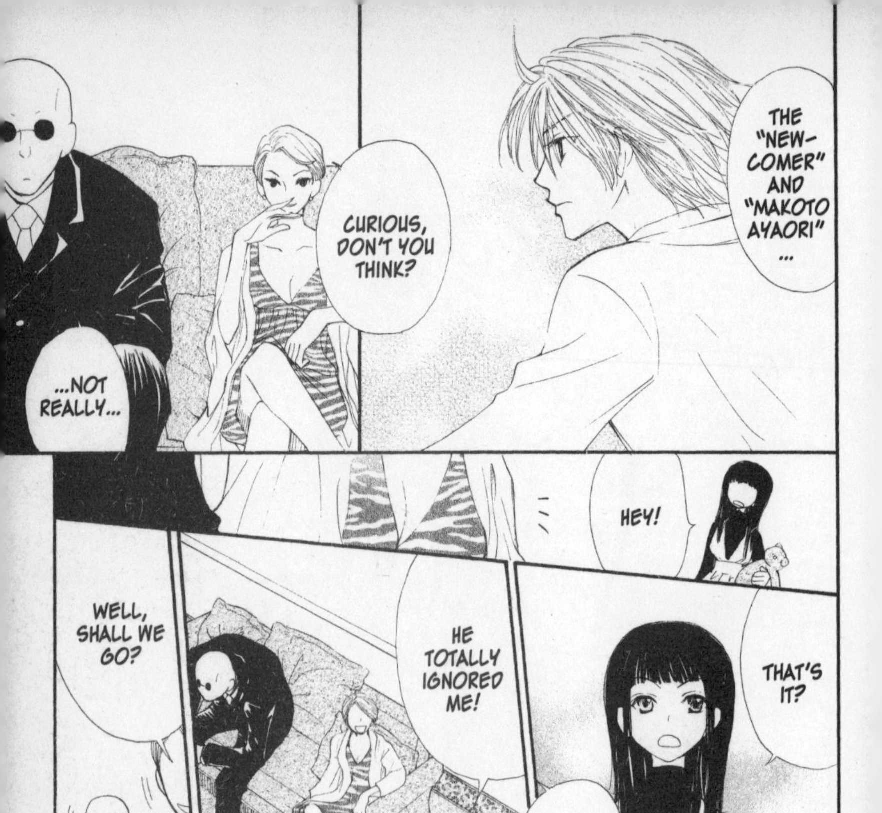
THE "NEW-COMER" AND "MAKOTO AYAORI"...
CURIOUS, DON'T YOU THINK?
...NOT REALLY...
HEY!
THAT'S IT?
YOU WERE BRILLIANT.
HE TOTALLY IGNORED ME!
EVEN THOUGH I KNOW HE NOTICED!
HE CERTAINLY DID.
WELL, SHALL WE GO?
CREAK
SURE.
......

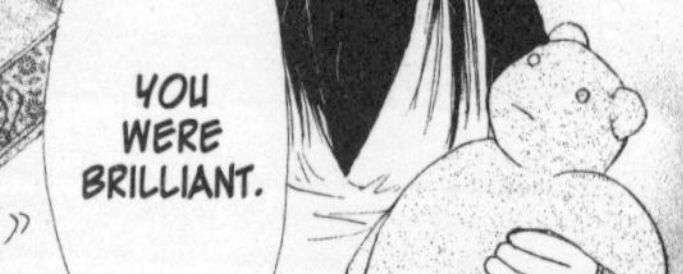

Sakura Mail

From here, we get into a storyline involving Aya's past. Things are going to get a little rough, so I'm committed to raising the tension and working harder than ever!! Uwaaa! By the way, the page opposite this was printed in color in the magazine. Even though it was only one page, coloring it was difficult for me, as always... (To be continued)

part 10

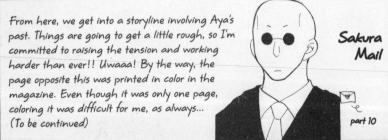

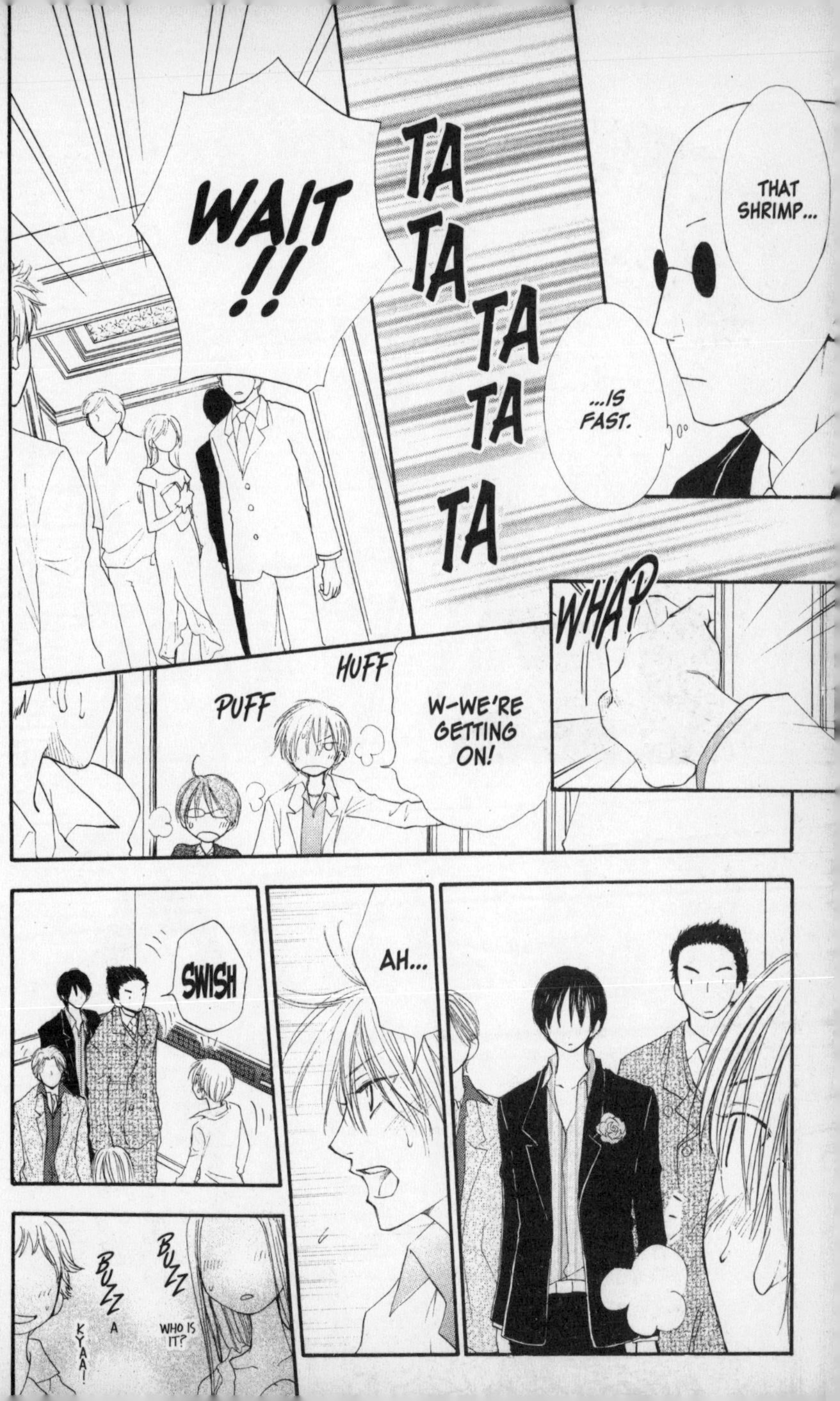
THAT SHRIMP...
...IS FAST.
WHAP
TA TA TA TA TA
WAIT!!
W-WE'RE GETTING ON!
HUFF
PUFF
AH...
SWISH
BUZZ
WHO IS IT?
BUZZ
A
KYAA!

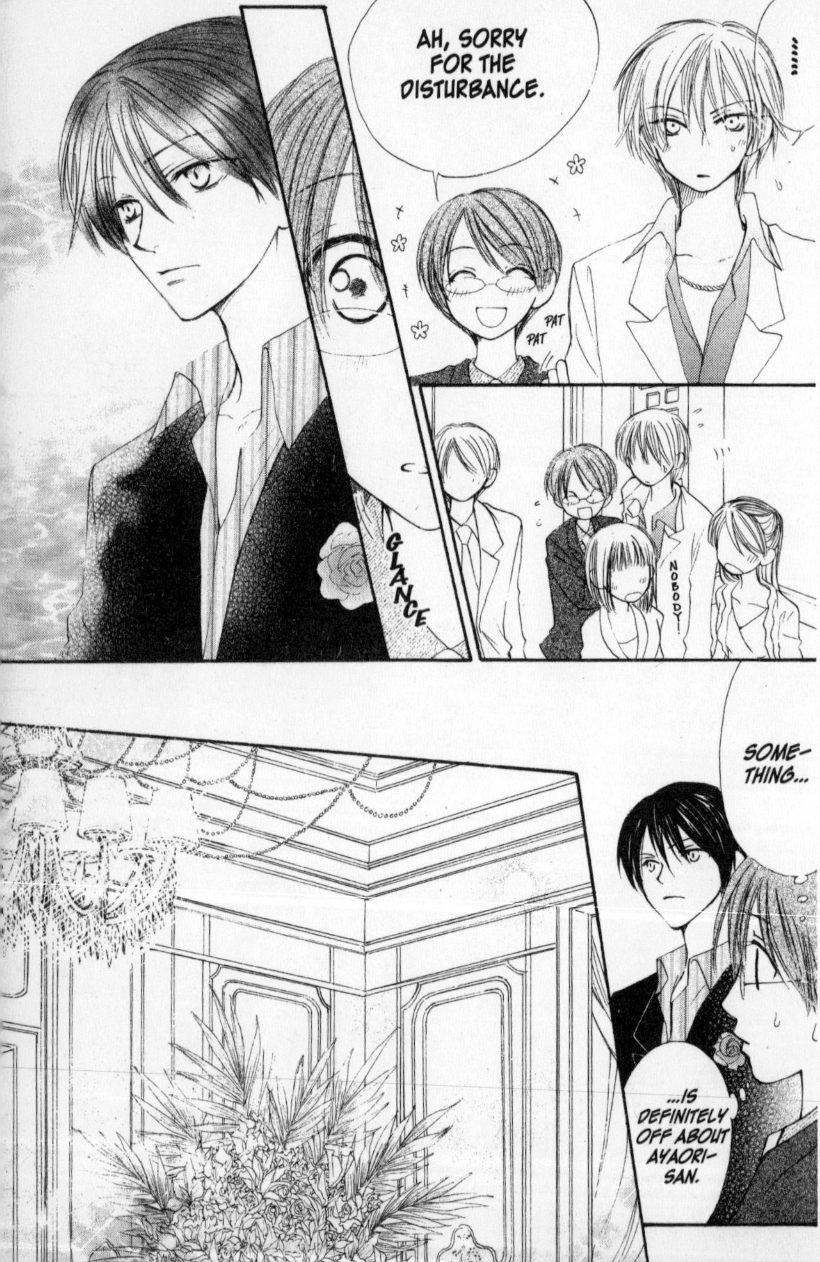
......
AH, SORRY FOR THE DISTURBANCE.
PAT PAT
NOBODY!
GLANCE
SOME-THING...
...IS DEFINITELY OFF ABOUT AYAORI-SAN.

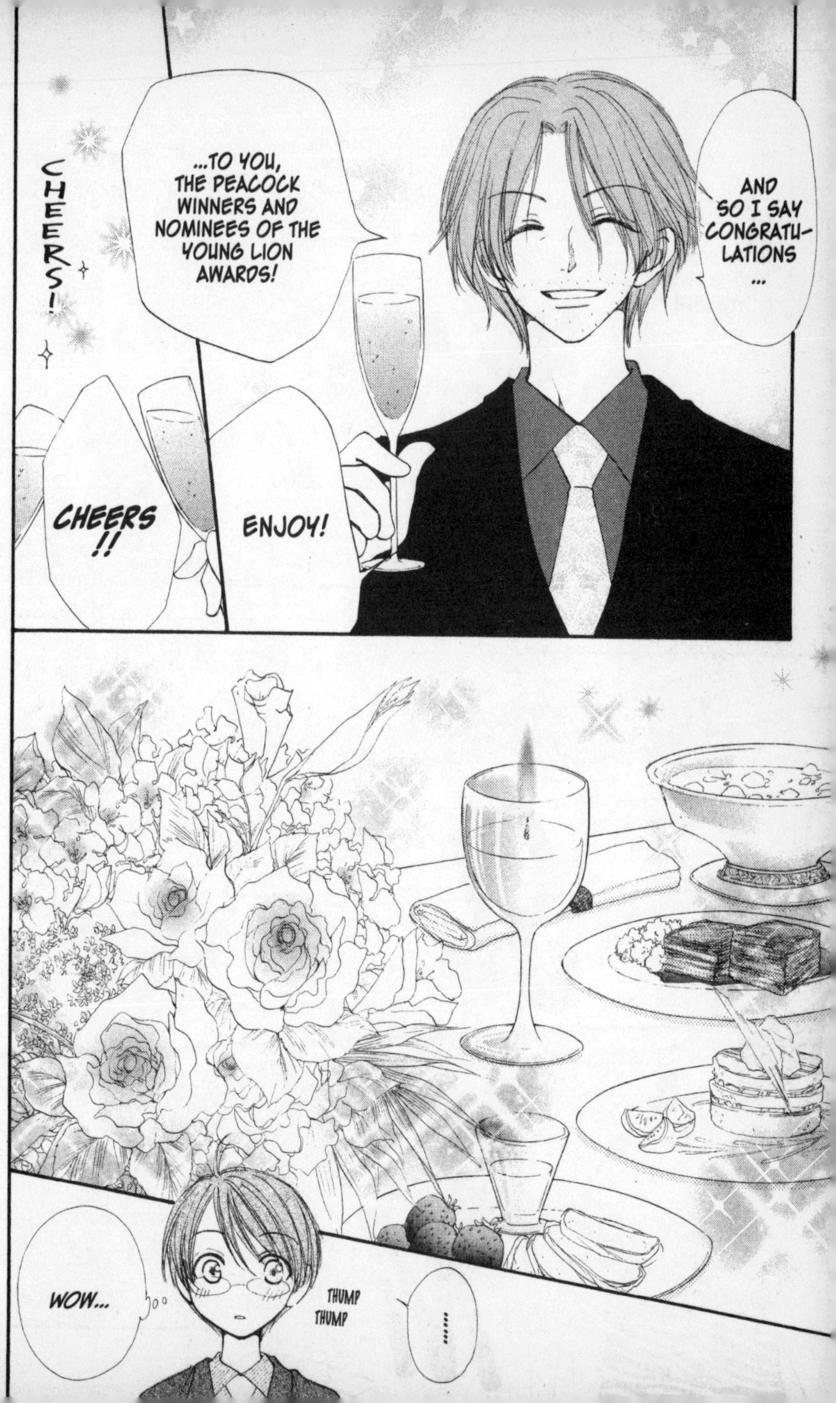
AND SO I SAY CONGRATULATIONS...
...TO YOU, THE PEACOCK WINNERS AND NOMINEES OF THE YOUNG LION AWARDS!
ENJOY!
CHEERS!!
CHEERS!
......
THUMP THUMP
WOW...

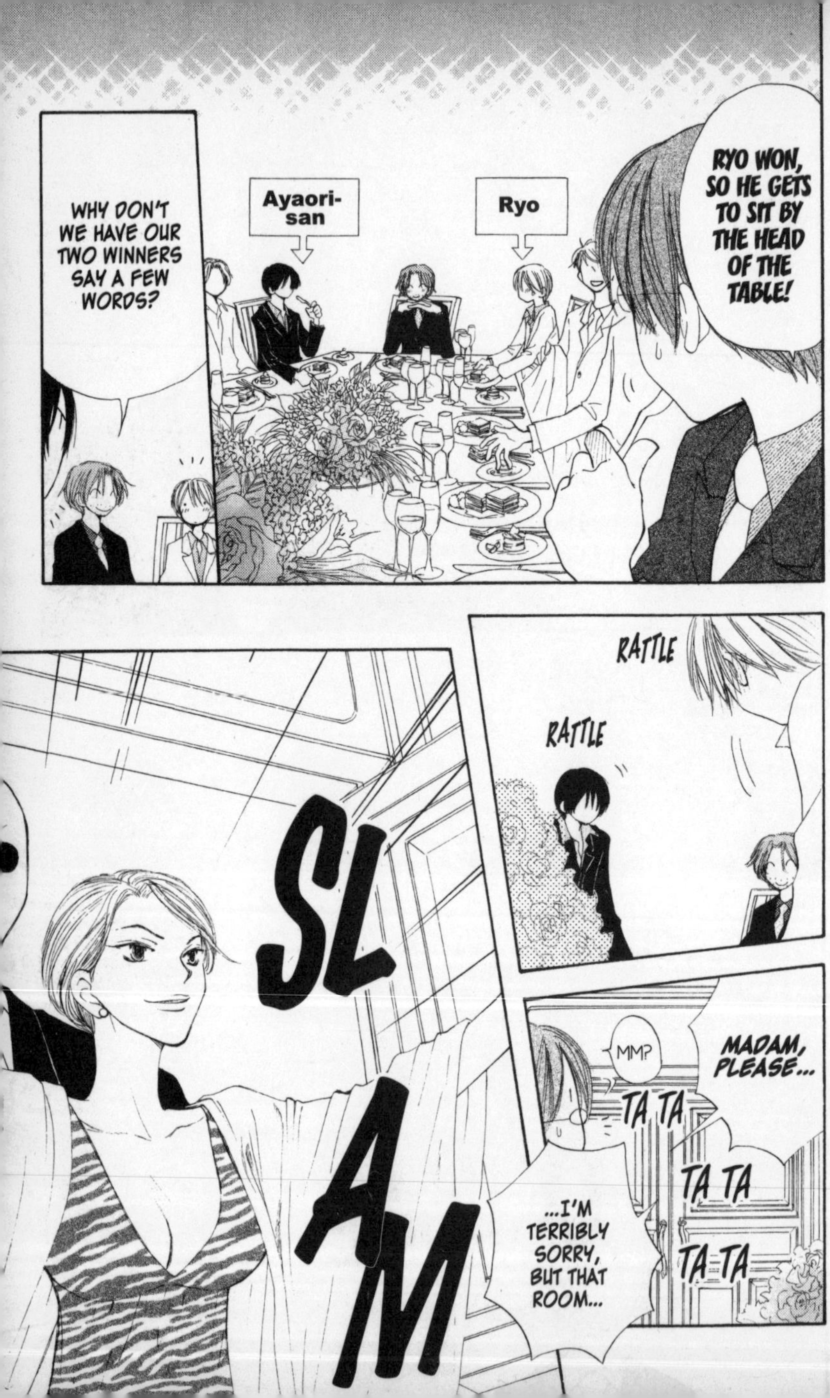
RYO WON, SO HE GETS TO SIT BY THE HEAD OF THE TABLE!
Ryo
Ayaori-san
WHY DON'T WE HAVE OUR TWO WINNERS SAY A FEW WORDS?
RATTLE
RATTLE
MADAM, PLEASE...
MM?
TA TA
TA TA
TA TA
...I'M TERRIBLY SORRY, BUT THAT ROOM...
SLAM

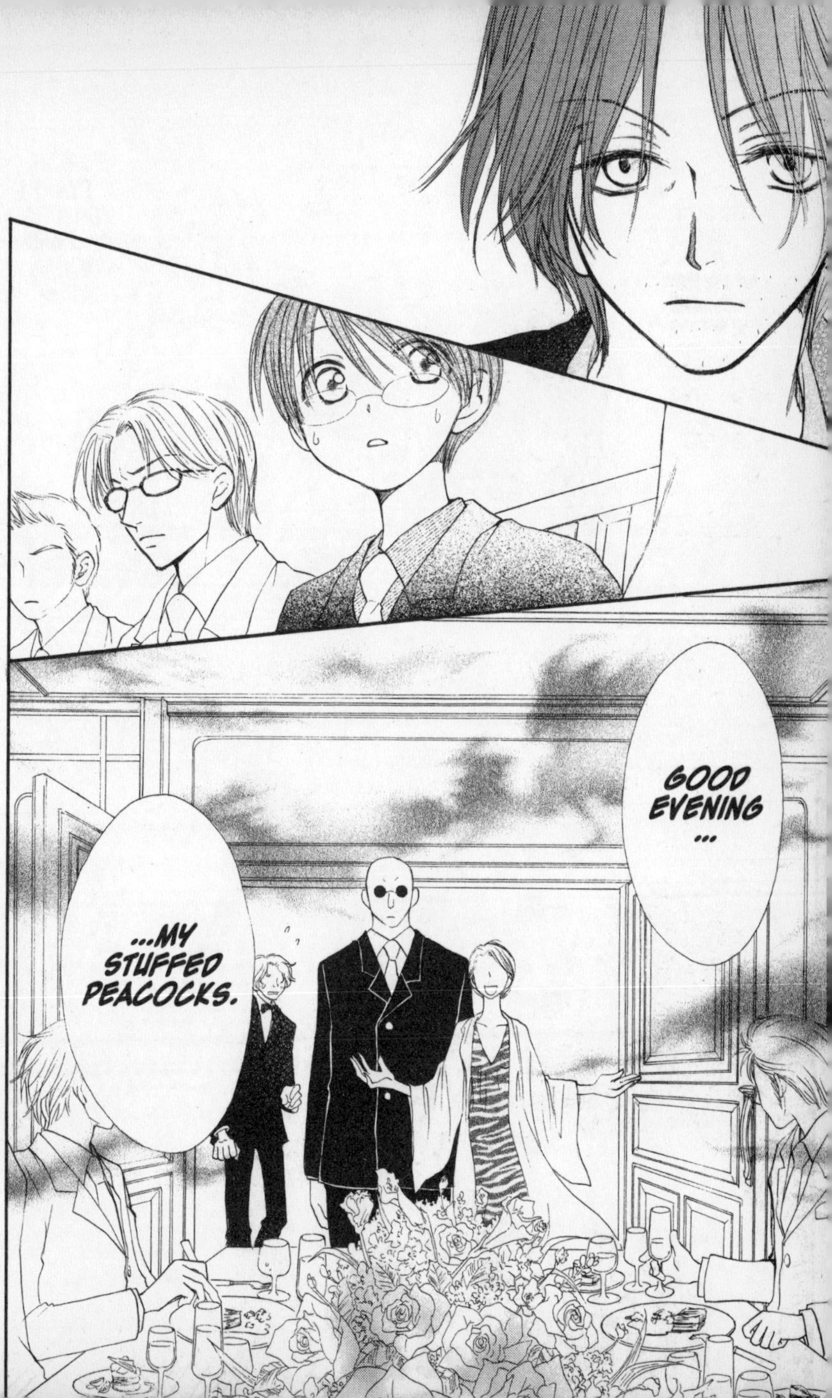
GOOD EVENING ...
...MY STUFFED PEACOCKS.

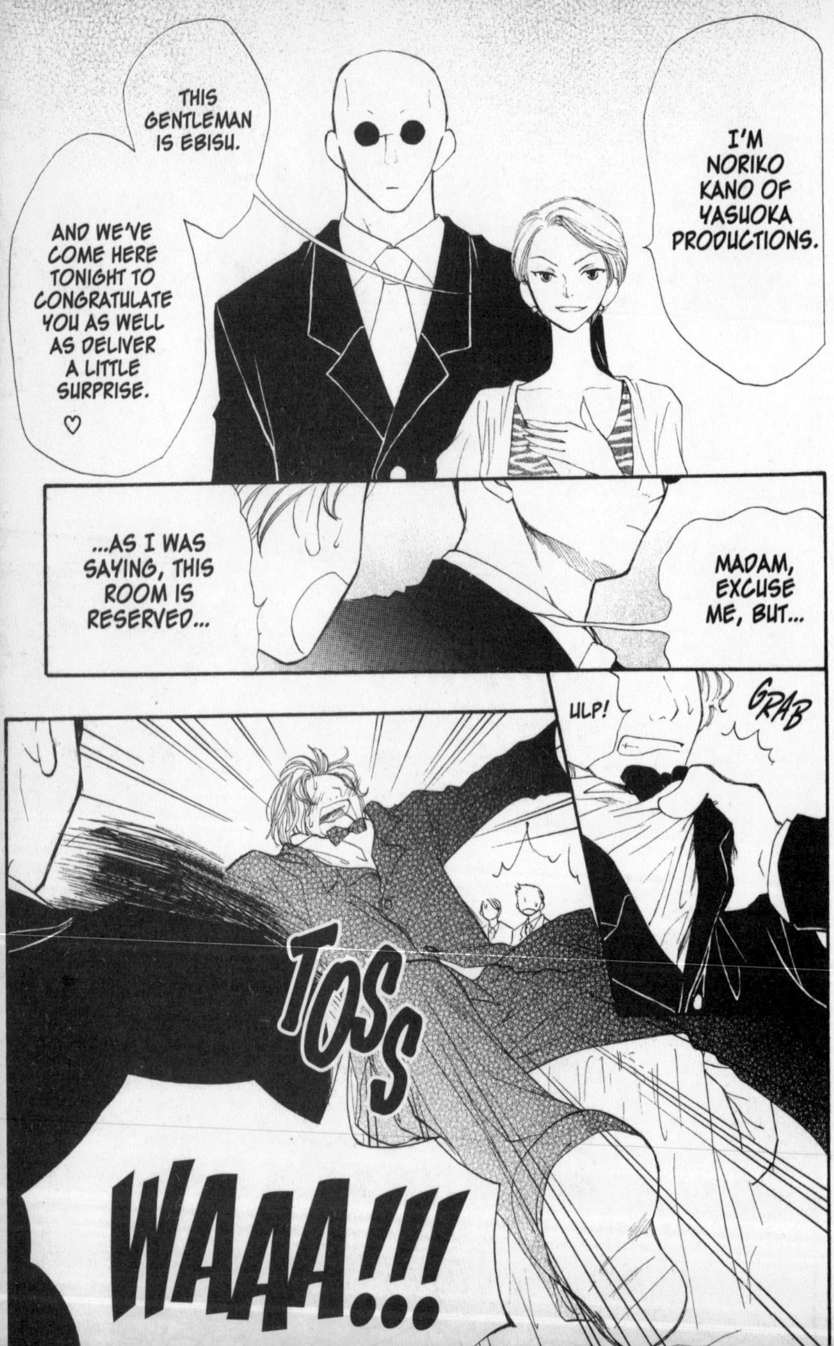
I'M NORIKO KANO OF YASUOKA PRODUCTIONS.
THIS GENTLEMAN IS EBISU.
AND WE'VE COME HERE TONIGHT TO CONGRATULATE YOU AS WELL AS DELIVER A LITTLE SURPRISE. ♡
MADAM, EXCUSE ME, BUT...
...AS I WAS SAYING, THIS ROOM IS RESERVED...
GRAB
ULP!
TOSS
WAAA!!!

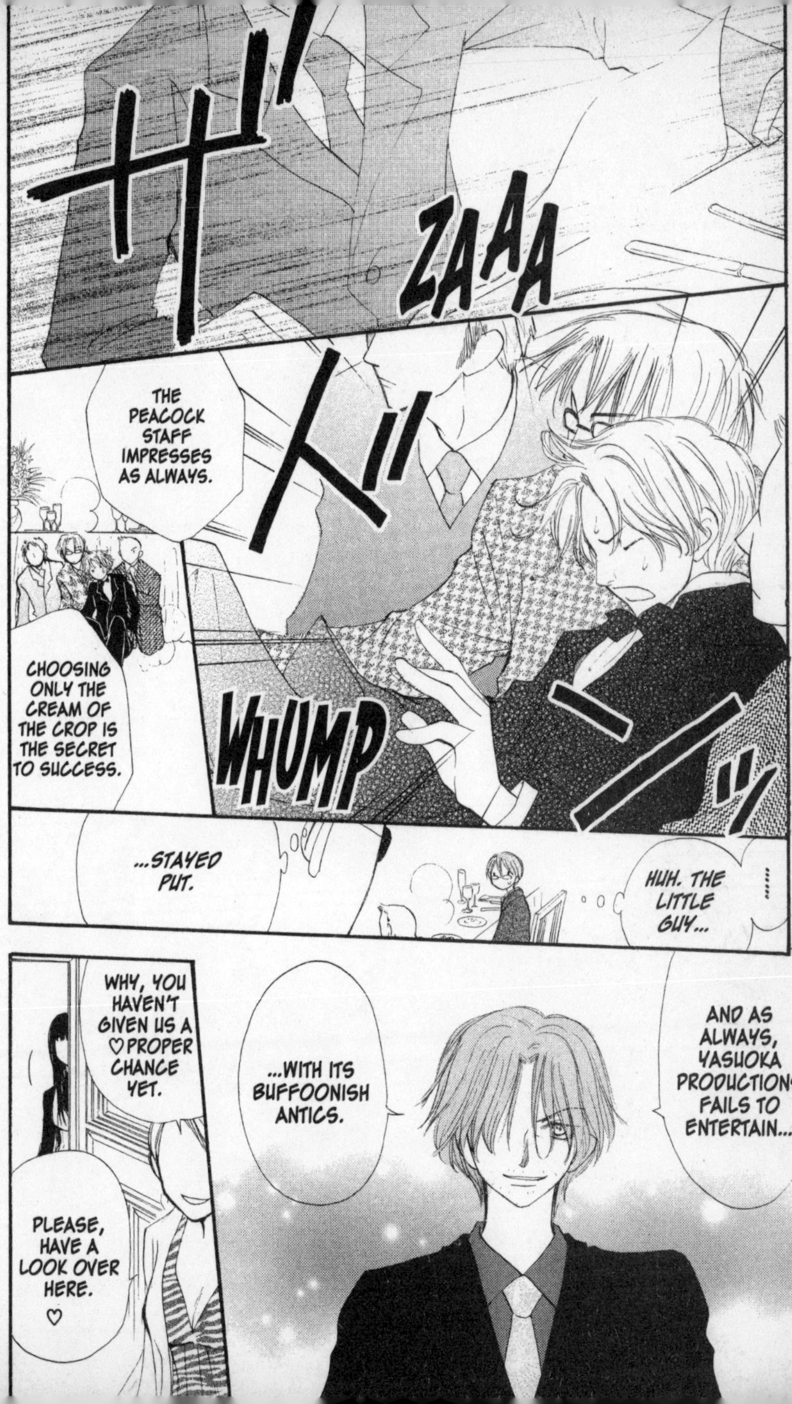
ZAAA
WHUMP
THE PEACOCK STAFF IMPRESSES AS ALWAYS.
CHOOSING ONLY THE CREAM OF THE CROP IS THE SECRET TO SUCCESS.
......
HUH. THE LITTLE GUY...
...STAYED PUT.
AND AS ALWAYS, YASUOKA PRODUCTIONS FAILS TO ENTERTAIN...
...WITH ITS BUFFOONISH ANTICS.
WHY, YOU HAVEN'T GIVEN US A ♡ PROPER CHANCE YET.
PLEASE, HAVE A LOOK OVER HERE. ♡

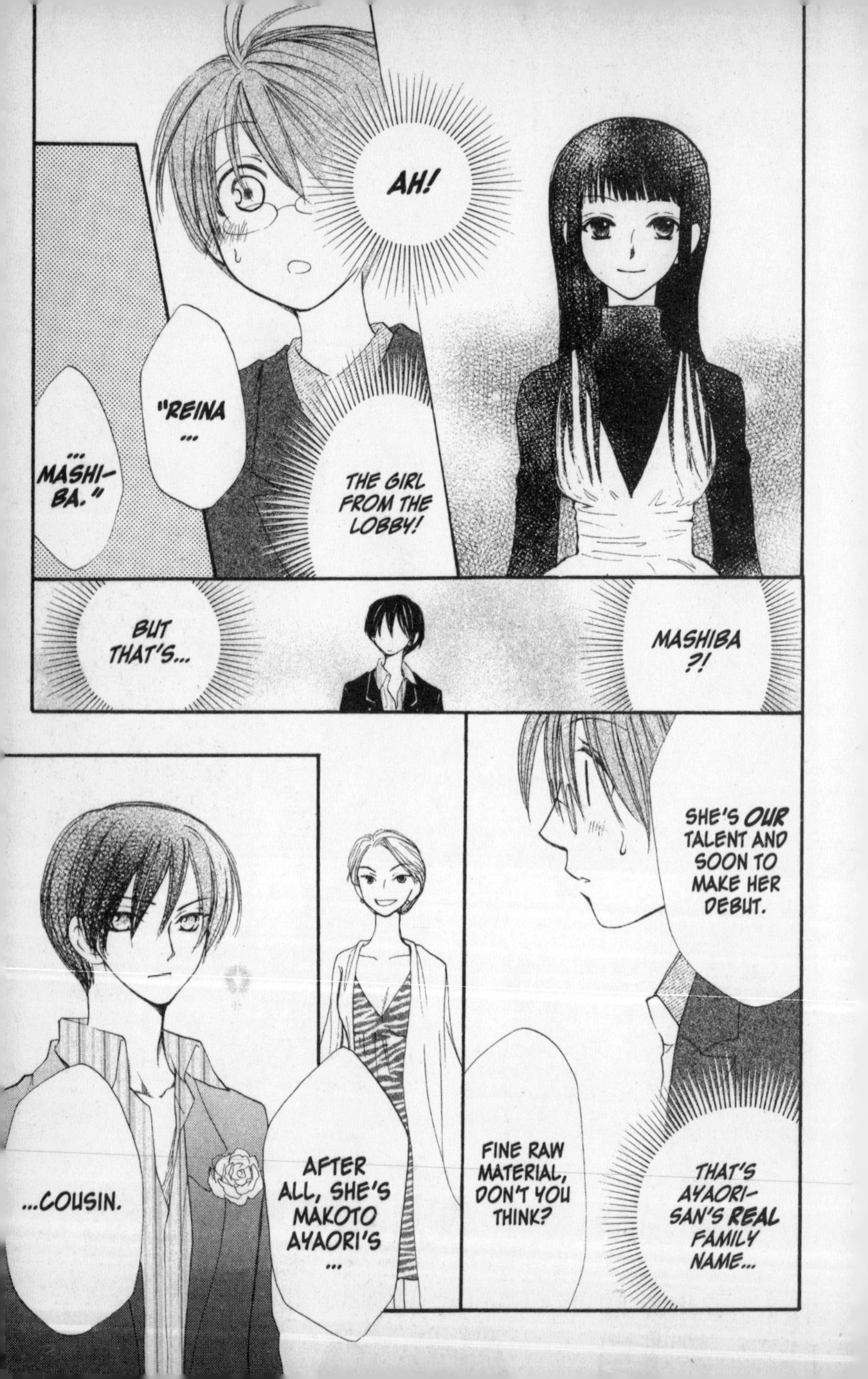
AH!
THE GIRL FROM THE LOBBY!
"REINA ...
... MASHIBA."
MASHIBA ?!
BUT THAT'S...
SHE'S *OUR* TALENT AND SOON TO MAKE HER DEBUT.
THAT'S AYAORI-SAN'S *REAL* FAMILY NAME...
FINE RAW MATERIAL, DON'T YOU THINK?
AFTER ALL, SHE'S MAKOTO AYAORI'S ...
...COUSIN.

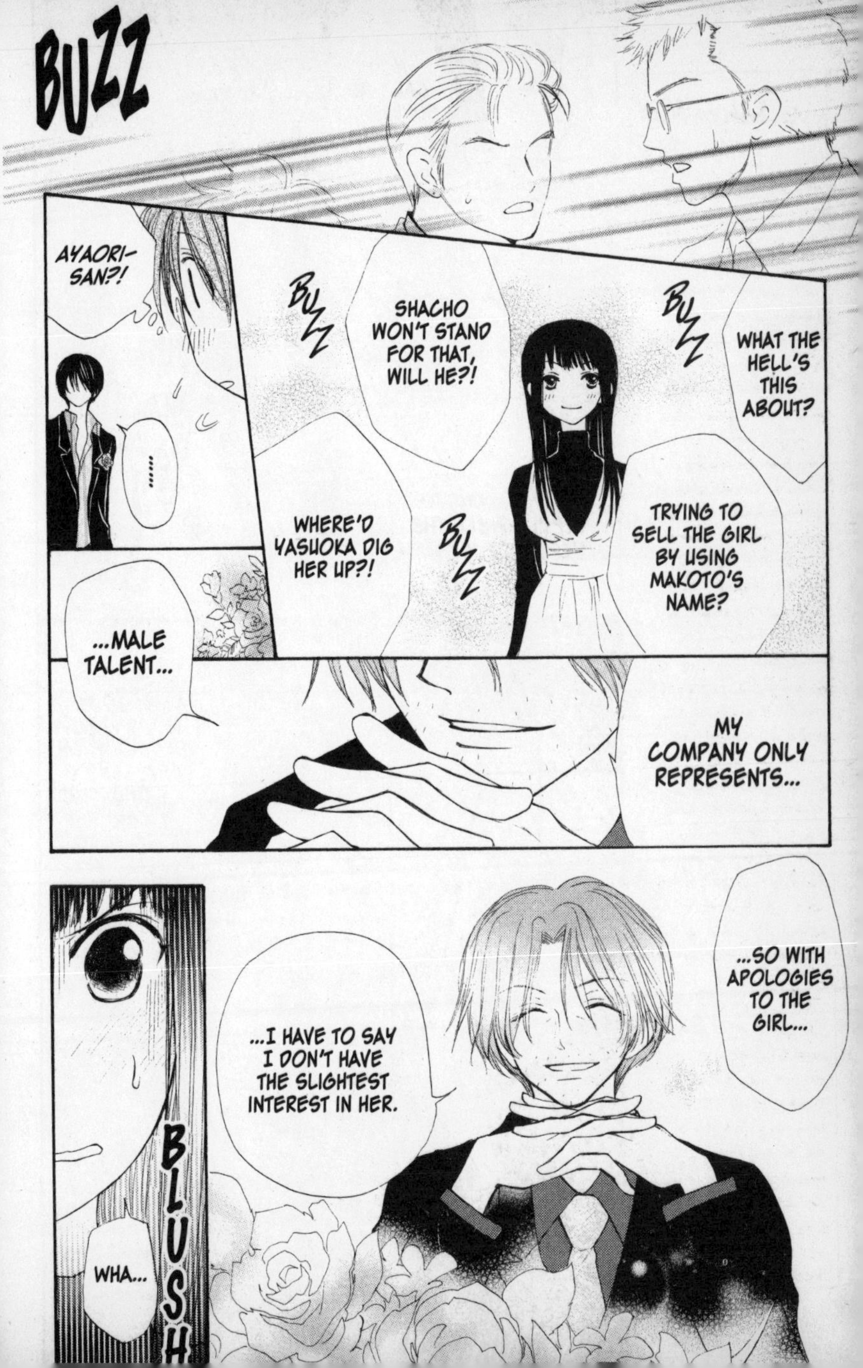
BUZZ
WHAT THE HELL'S THIS ABOUT?
BUZZ
TRYING TO SELL THE GIRL BY USING MAKOTO'S NAME?
SHACHO WON'T STAND FOR THAT, WILL HE?!
BUZZ
WHERE'D YASUOKA DIG HER UP?!
BUZZ
AYAORI-SAN?!
......
MY COMPANY ONLY REPRESENTS...
...MALE TALENT...
...SO WITH APOLOGIES TO THE GIRL...
...I HAVE TO SAY I DON'T HAVE THE SLIGHTEST INTEREST IN HER.
BLUSH
WHA...

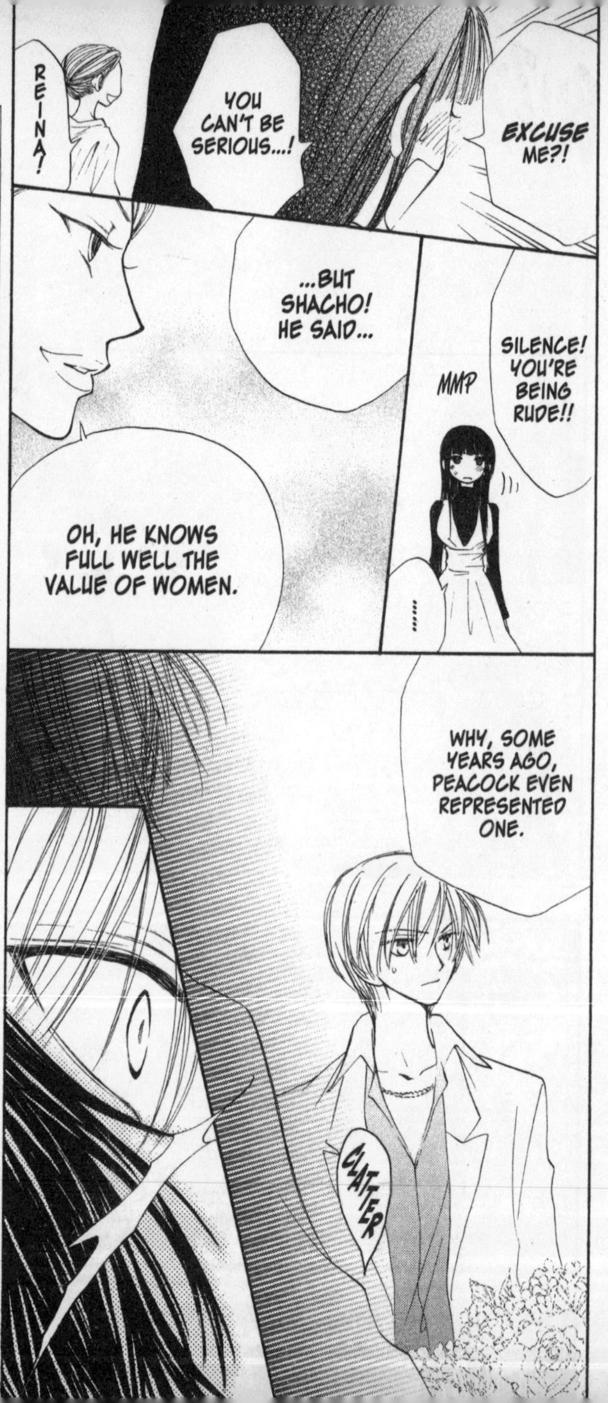
EXCUSE ME?!
YOU CAN'T BE SERIOUS...!
REINA!
SILENCE! YOU'RE BEING RUDE!!
MMP
......
...BUT SHACHO! HE SAID...
OH, HE KNOWS FULL WELL THE VALUE OF WOMEN.
WHY, SOME YEARS AGO, PEACOCK EVEN REPRESENTED ONE.
CLATTER

1/4 Sakura Mail

part 11

(Continued)
It's even more difficult to color the art when it's part of the story and has more than one panel!! I've gotten a little used to coloring my art, but I'm still not very good at it... I want to make more progress!! When I was a child, I wanted the manga volumes I read to be in color so much that one time I tried to color it myself with colored pencils. See, I used to love coloring books, so I thought that would make me able to do a good job, but sadly, after not even finishing a page, I realized that it wasn't coming out as I'd imagined, so I abandoned that little project. As it happens, that was one of my favorite manga books, and even though I screwed a page up myself, I wailed like a baby about it. Flash-forward to now, I've got to deal with ink and tones already, so a part of me always thinks I'd do better not to mess with color at all...it's kind of a bitter memory for me... Well, I'm out of space, so I'll sign off here!! See you next time!
Sakura Tsukuba

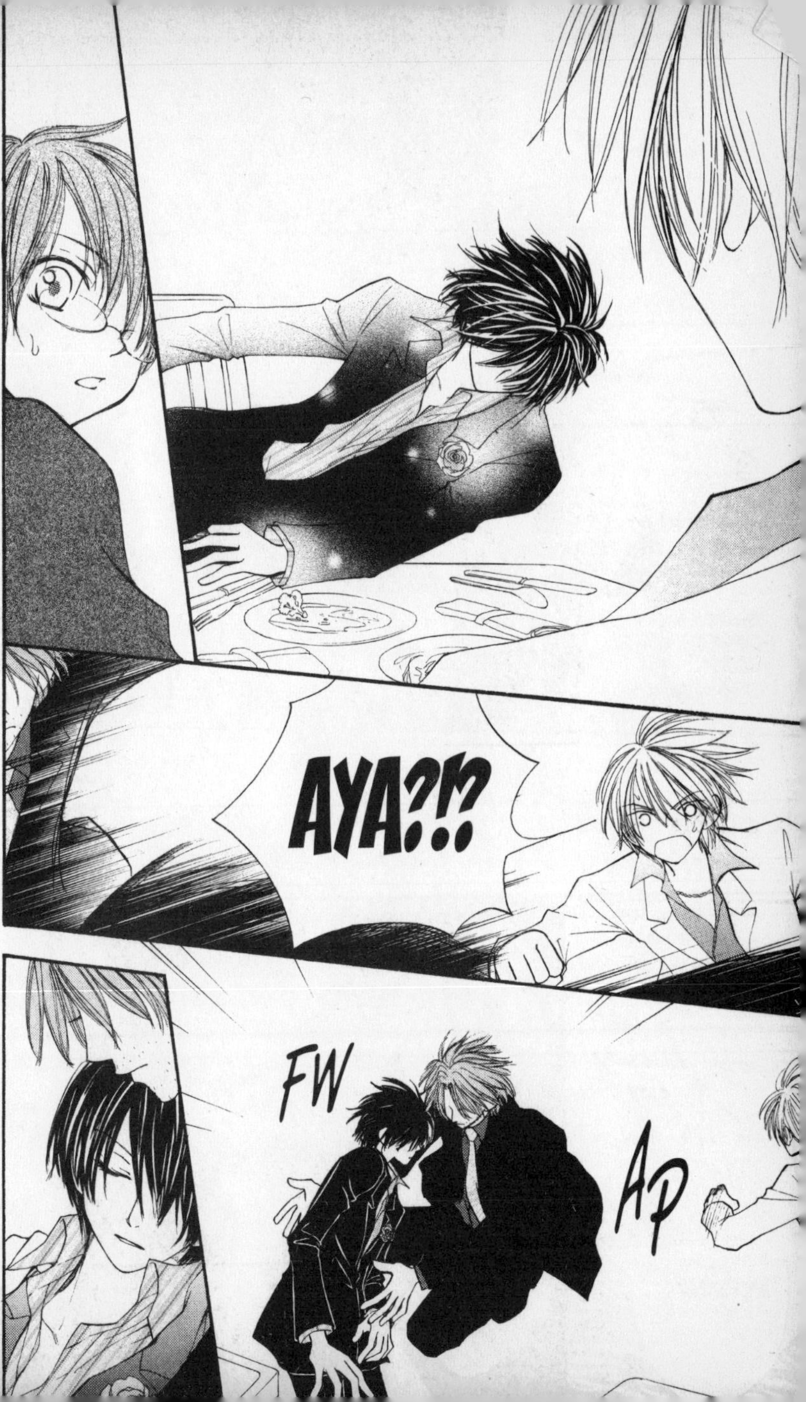
AYA?!?
AP
FW

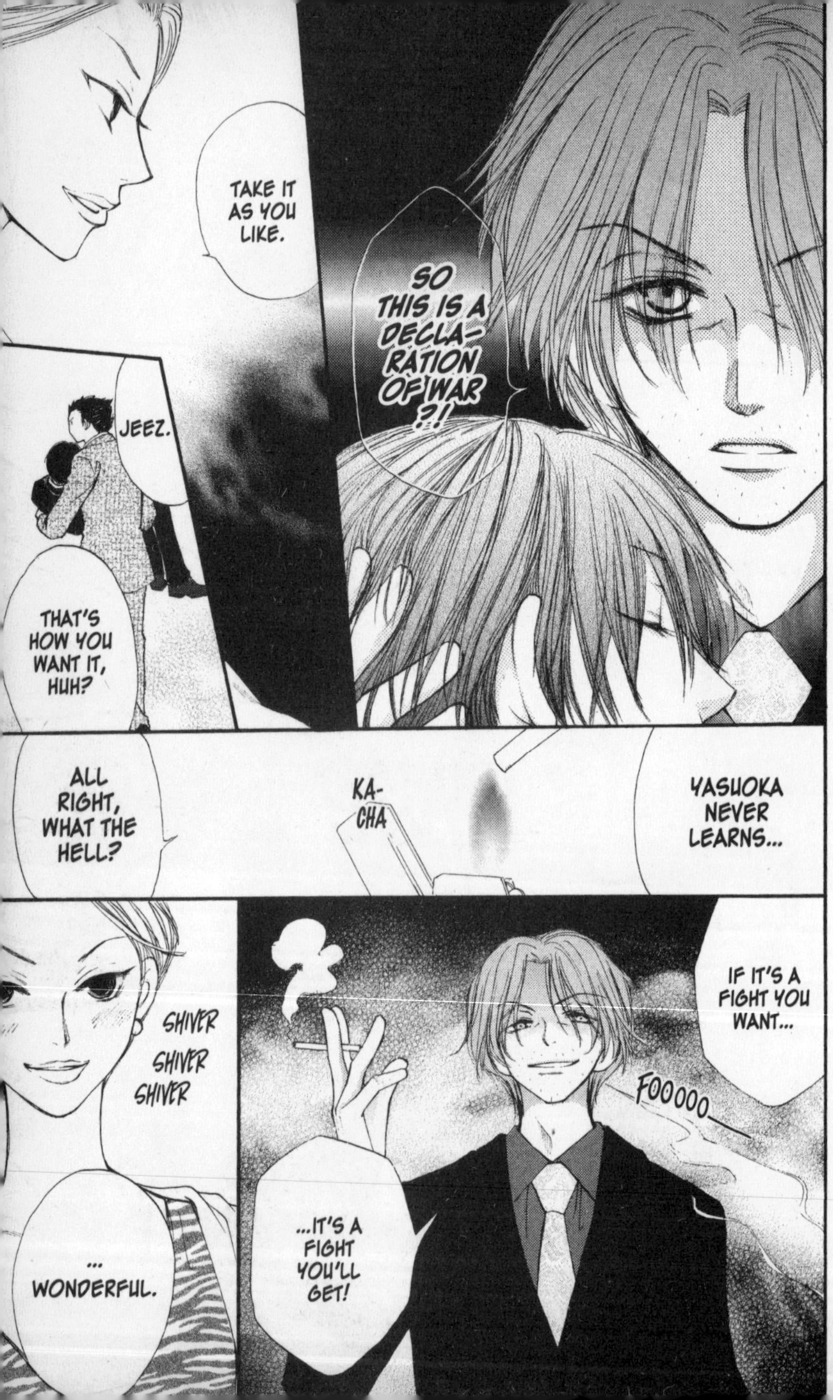
SO THIS IS A DECLARATION OF WAR?!
TAKE IT AS YOU LIKE.
JEEZ.
THAT'S HOW YOU WANT IT, HUH?
YASUOKA NEVER LEARNS...
KA-CHA
ALL RIGHT, WHAT THE HELL?
IF IT'S A FIGHT YOU WANT...
FOOOOO—
...IT'S A FIGHT YOU'LL GET!
SHIVER SHIVER SHIVER
... WONDERFUL.

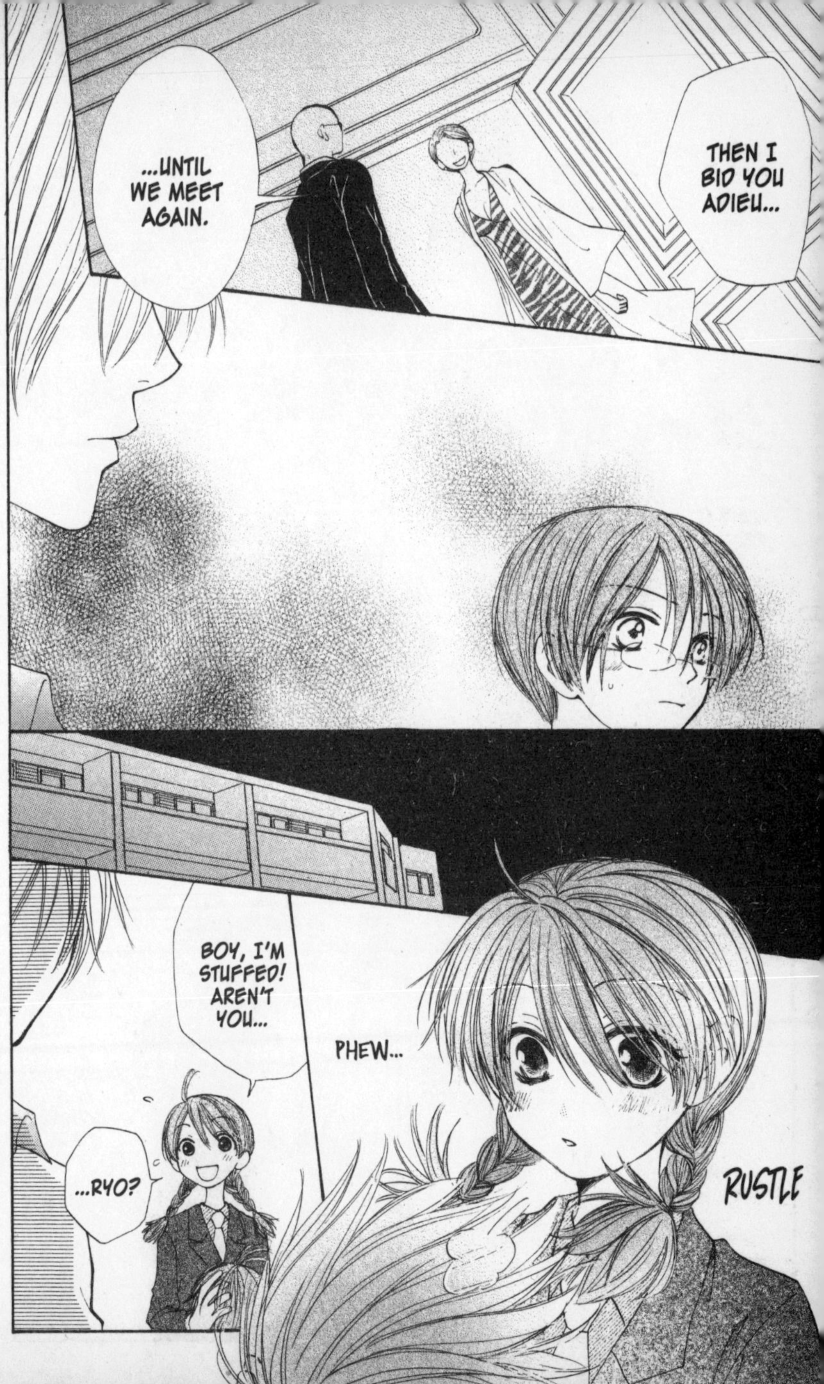
THEN I BID YOU ADIEU...
...UNTIL WE MEET AGAIN.
RUSTLE
PHEW...
BOY, I'M STUFFED! AREN'T YOU...
...RYO?

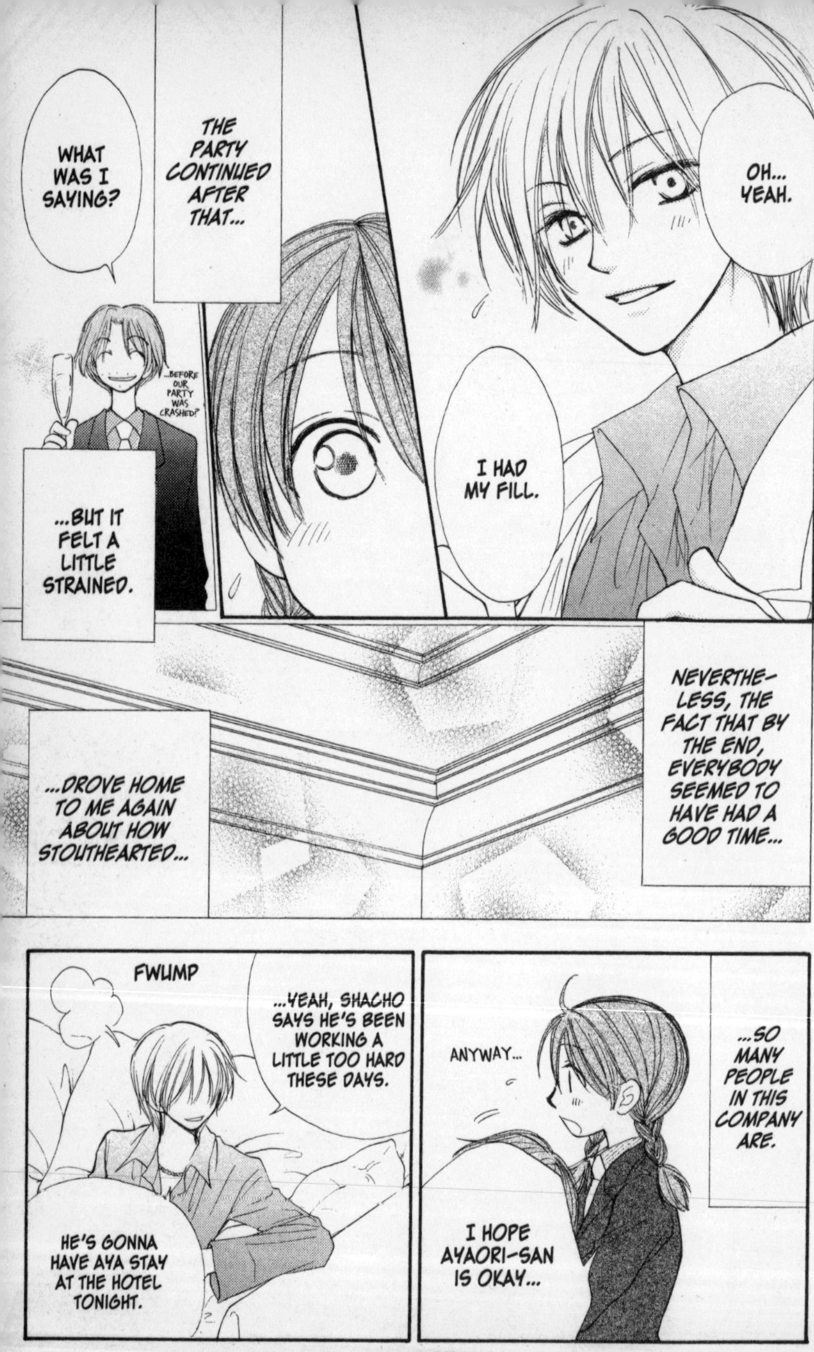
OH... YEAH.
I HAD MY FILL.
THE PARTY CONTINUED AFTER THAT...
WHAT WAS I SAYING?
...BEFORE OUR PARTY WAS CRASHED?
...BUT IT FELT A LITTLE STRAINED.
NEVERTHE-LESS, THE FACT THAT BY THE END, EVERYBODY SEEMED TO HAVE HAD A GOOD TIME...
...DROVE HOME TO ME AGAIN ABOUT HOW STOUTHEARTED...
...SO MANY PEOPLE IN THIS COMPANY ARE.
ANYWAY...
I HOPE AYAORI-SAN IS OKAY...
FWUMP
...YEAH, SHACHO SAYS HE'S BEEN WORKING A LITTLE TOO HARD THESE DAYS.
HE'S GONNA HAVE AYA STAY AT THE HOTEL TONIGHT.

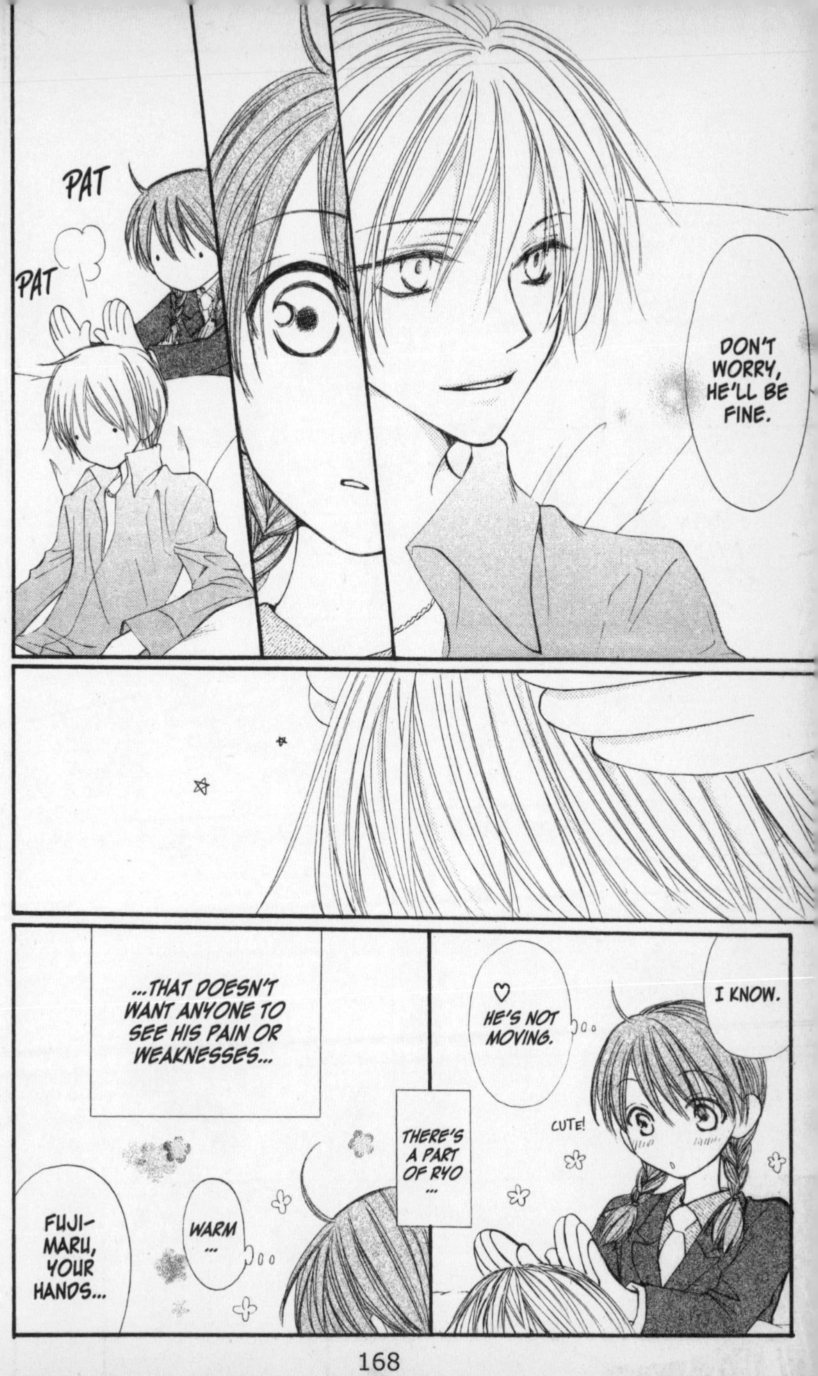
DON'T WORRY, HE'LL BE FINE.
PAT
PAT
I KNOW.
HE'S NOT MOVING.
CUTE!
THERE'S A PART OF RYO ...
...THAT DOESN'T WANT ANYONE TO SEE HIS PAIN OR WEAKNESSES...
WARM ...
FUJI-MARU, YOUR HANDS...

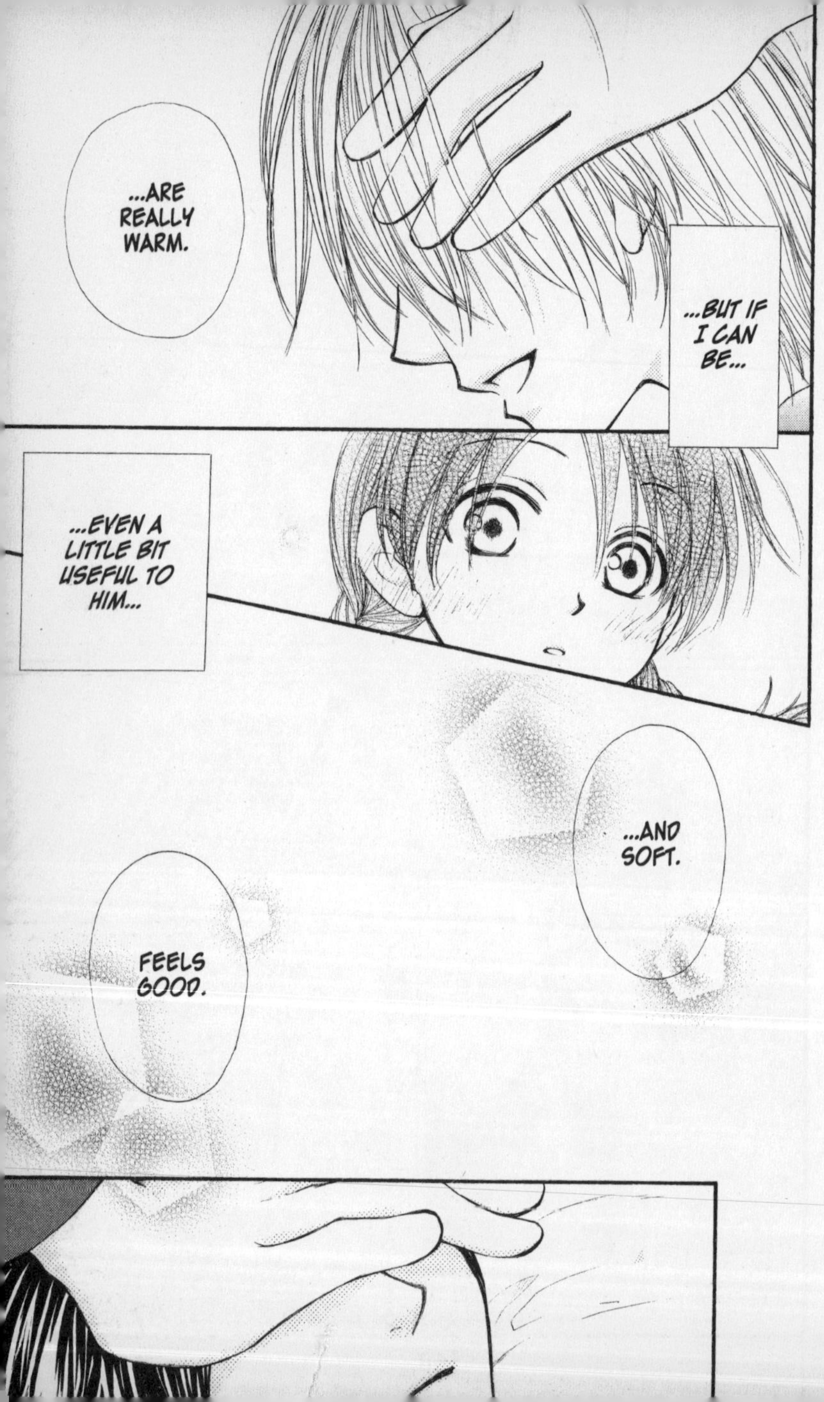
...ARE REALLY WARM.
...BUT IF I CAN BE...
...EVEN A LITTLE BIT USEFUL TO HIM...
...AND SOFT.
FEELS GOOD.

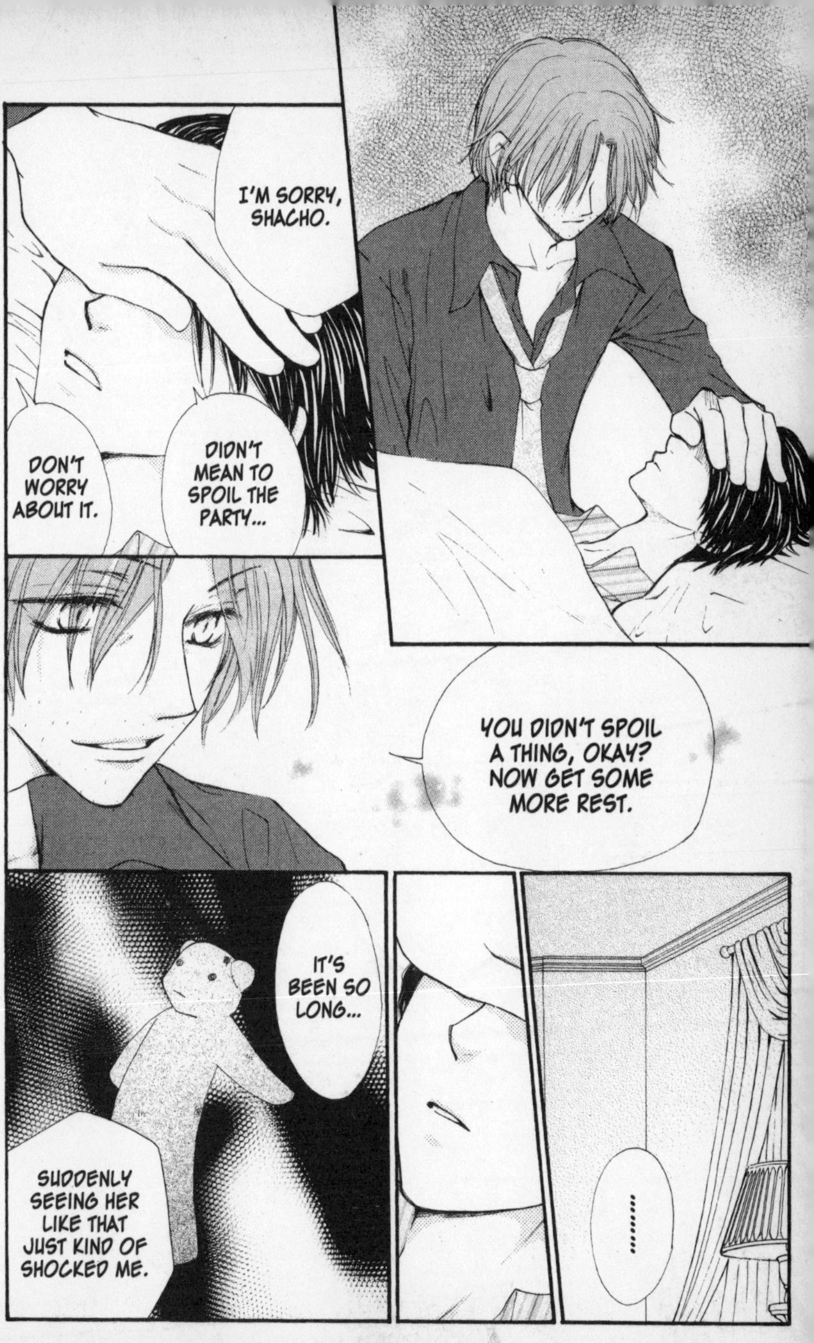
I'M SORRY, SHACHO.
DIDN'T MEAN TO SPOIL THE PARTY...
DON'T WORRY ABOUT IT.
YOU DIDN'T SPOIL A THING, OKAY? NOW GET SOME MORE REST.
......
IT'S BEEN SO LONG...
SUDDENLY SEEING HER LIKE THAT JUST KIND OF SHOCKED ME.

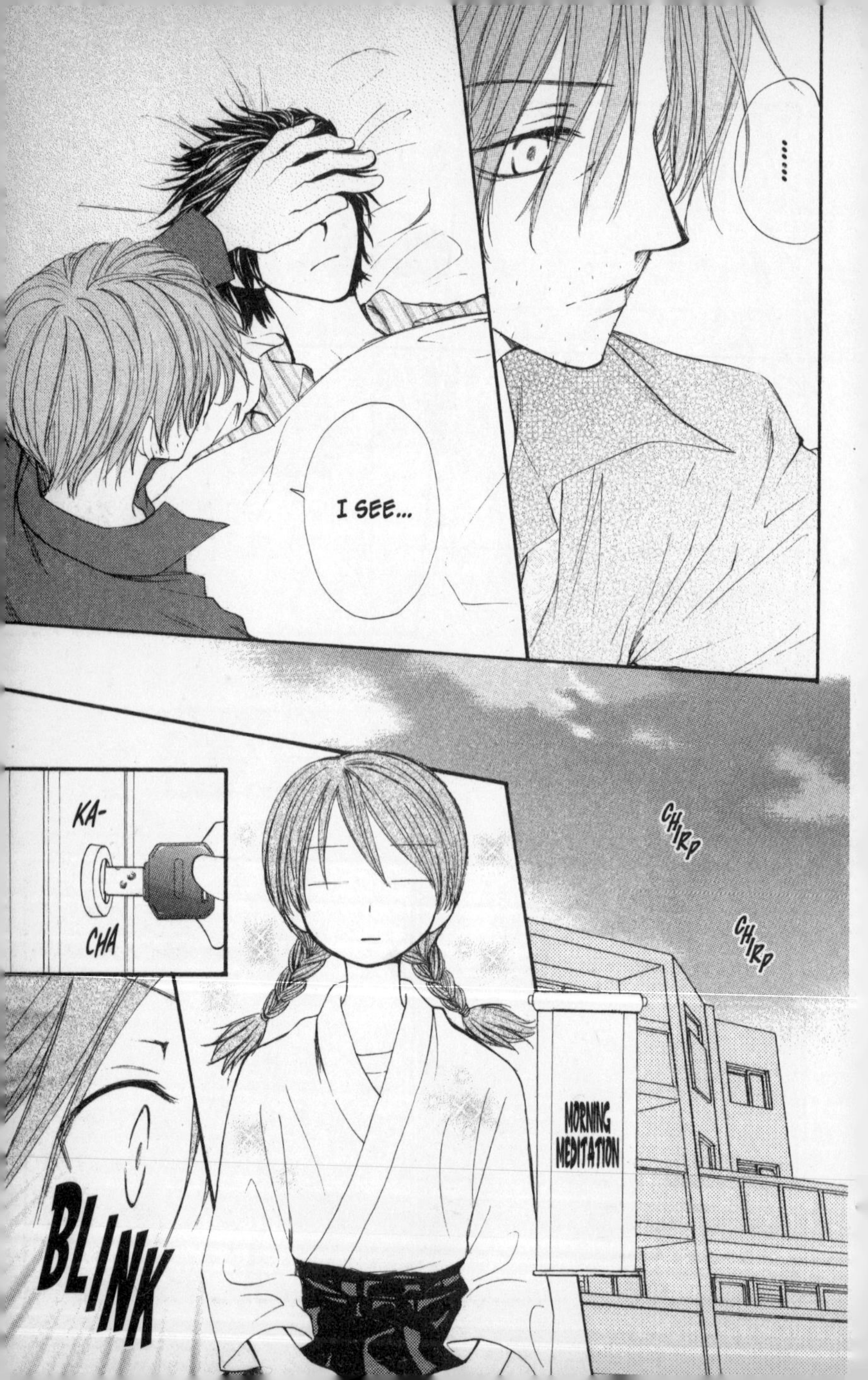
......
I SEE...
CHIRP
CHIRP
MORNING MEDITATION
KA-
CHA
BLINK

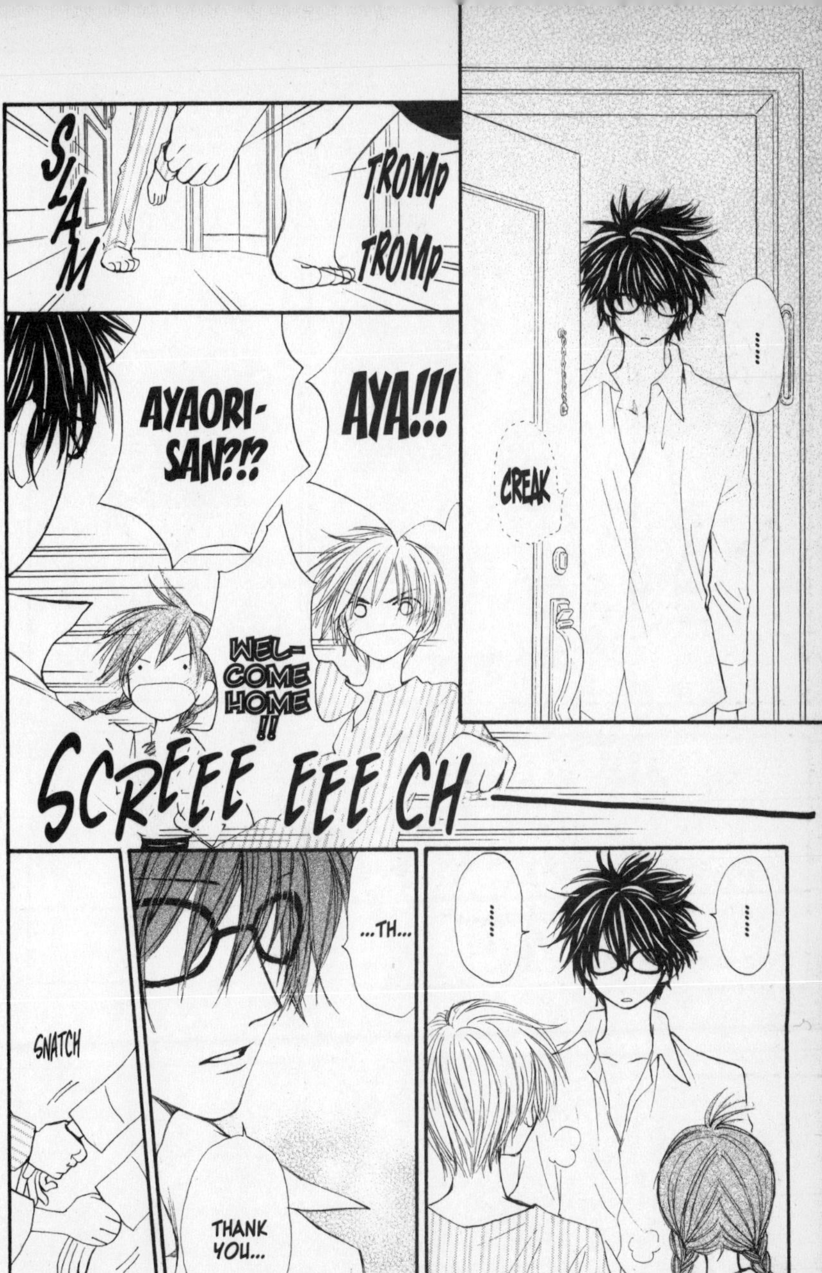
......
CREAK
SLAM
TROMP TROMP
AYA!!!
AYAORI-SAN?!?
WEL-COME HOME !!
SCREEE EEECH
......
......
...TH...
THANK YOU...
SNATCH
SNATCH

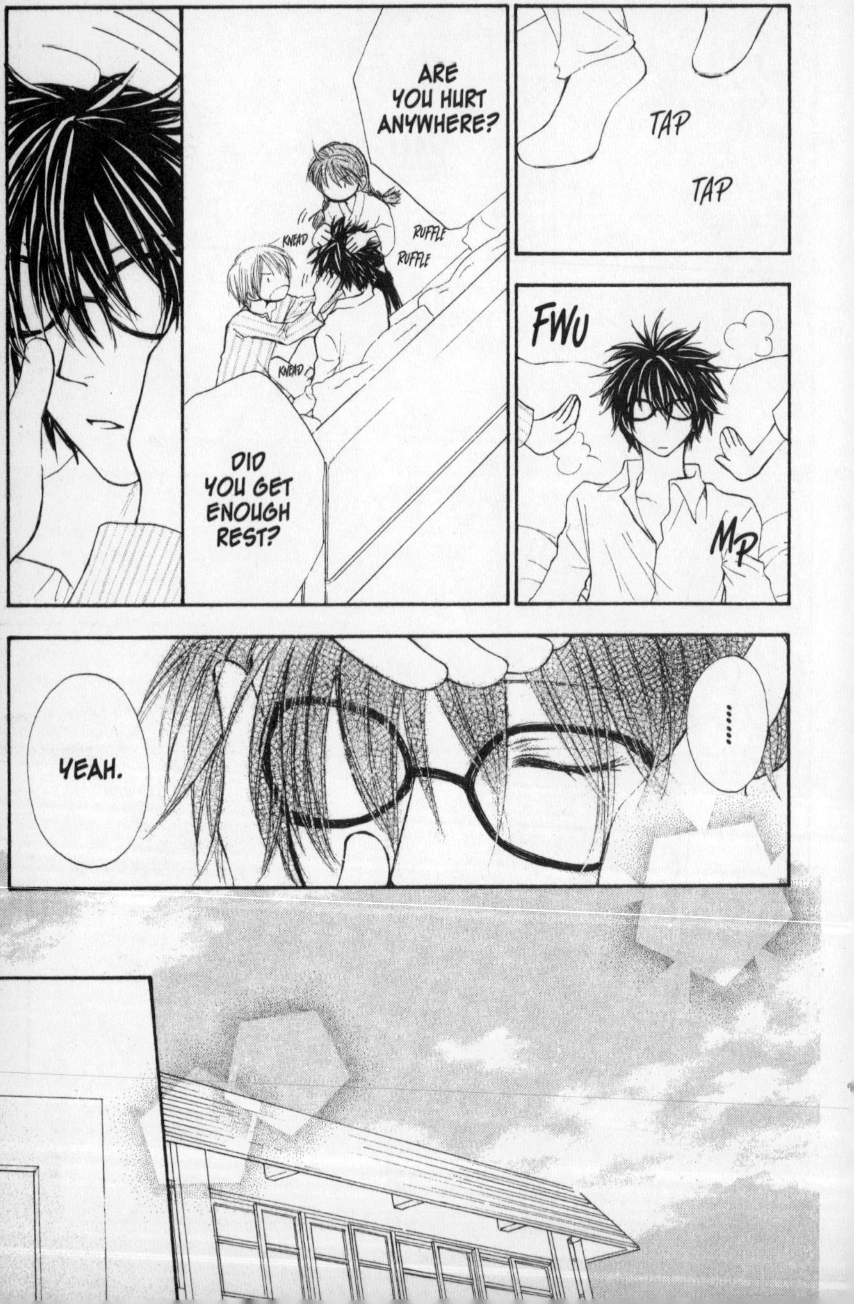
TAP
TAP
FWU
MP
ARE YOU HURT ANYWHERE?
RUFFLE
RUFFLE
KNEAD
KNEAD
DID YOU GET ENOUGH REST?
......
YEAH.

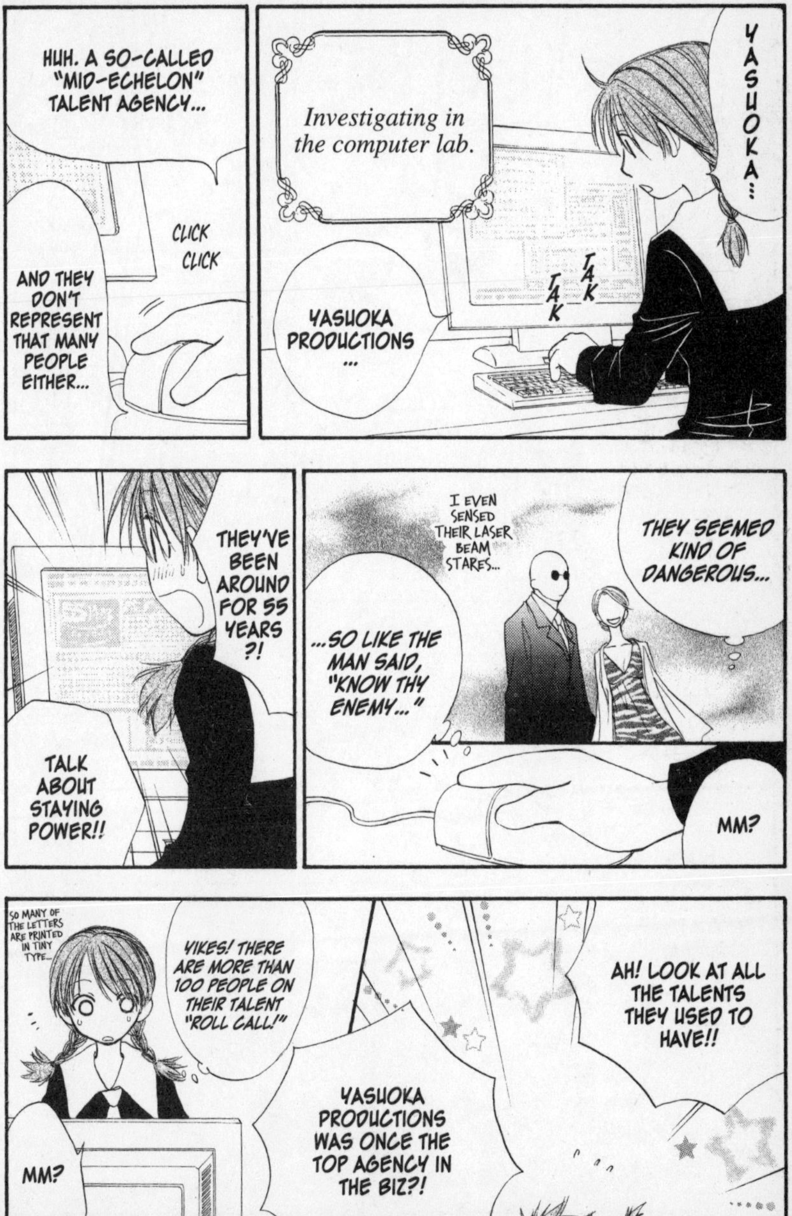
YASUOKA...
Investigating in the computer lab.
YASUOKA PRODUCTIONS ...
TAK TAK
HUH. A SO-CALLED "MID-ECHELON" TALENT AGENCY...
CLICK CLICK
AND THEY DON'T REPRESENT THAT MANY PEOPLE EITHER...
THEY SEEMED KIND OF DANGEROUS...
I EVEN SENSED THEIR LASER BEAM STARES...
...SO LIKE THE MAN SAID, "KNOW THY ENEMY..."
MM?
THEY'VE BEEN AROUND FOR 55 YEARS ?!
TALK ABOUT STAYING POWER!!
AH! LOOK AT ALL THE TALENTS THEY USED TO HAVE!!
YASUOKA PRODUCTIONS WAS ONCE THE TOP AGENCY IN THE BIZ?!
YIKES! THERE ARE MORE THAN 100 PEOPLE ON THEIR TALENT "ROLL CALL!"
SO MANY OF THE LETTERS ARE PRINTED IN TINY TYPE...
MM?

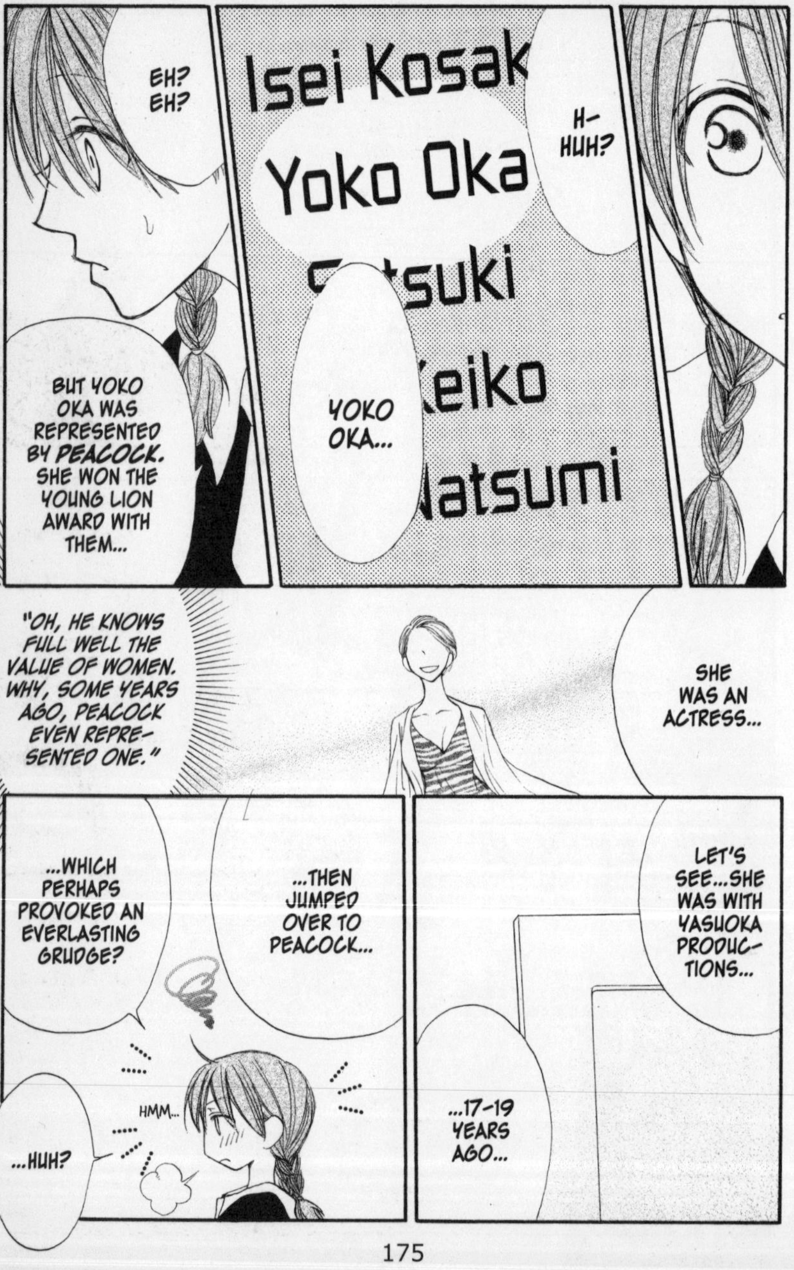
H-HUH?
Isei Kosak
Yoko Oka
YOKO OKA...
EH? EH?
BUT YOKO OKA WAS REPRESENTED BY *PEACOCK*. SHE WON THE YOUNG LION AWARD WITH THEM...
SHE WAS AN ACTRESS...
"OH, HE KNOWS FULL WELL THE VALUE OF WOMEN. WHY, SOME YEARS AGO, PEACOCK EVEN REPRE-SENTED ONE."
LET'S SEE...SHE WAS WITH YASUOKA PRODUC-TIONS...
...17-19 YEARS AGO...
...THEN JUMPED OVER TO PEACOCK...
...WHICH PERHAPS PROVOKED AN EVERLASTING GRUDGE?
HMM...
...HUH?

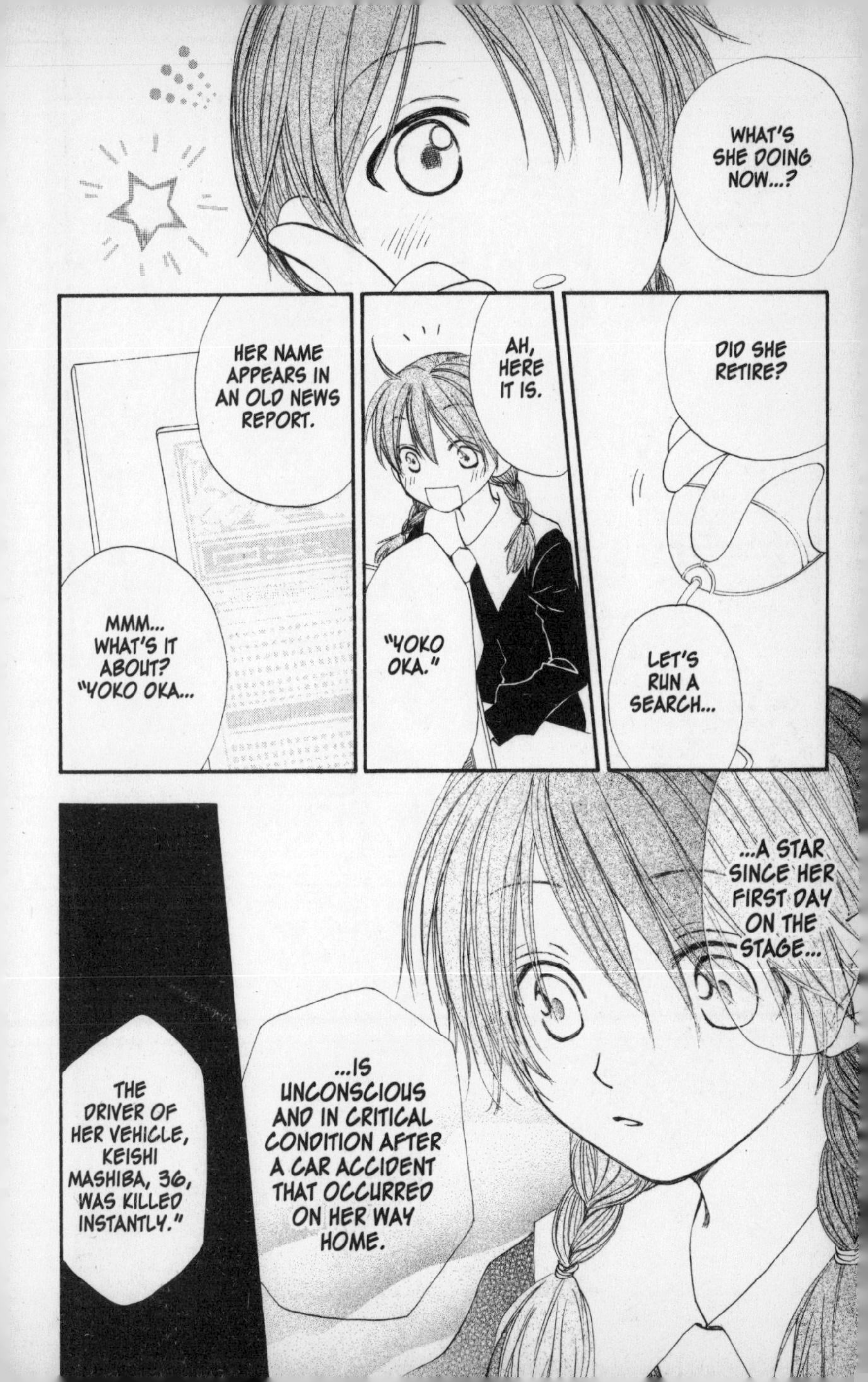
WHAT'S SHE DOING NOW...?
DID SHE RETIRE?
LET'S RUN A SEARCH...
AH, HERE IT IS.
"YOKO OKA."
HER NAME APPEARS IN AN OLD NEWS REPORT.
MMM... WHAT'S IT ABOUT? "YOKO OKA...
...A STAR SINCE HER FIRST DAY ON THE STAGE...
...IS UNCONSCIOUS AND IN CRITICAL CONDITION AFTER A CAR ACCIDENT THAT OCCURRED ON HER WAY HOME.
THE DRIVER OF HER VEHICLE, KEISHI MASHIBA, 36, WAS KILLED INSTANTLY."

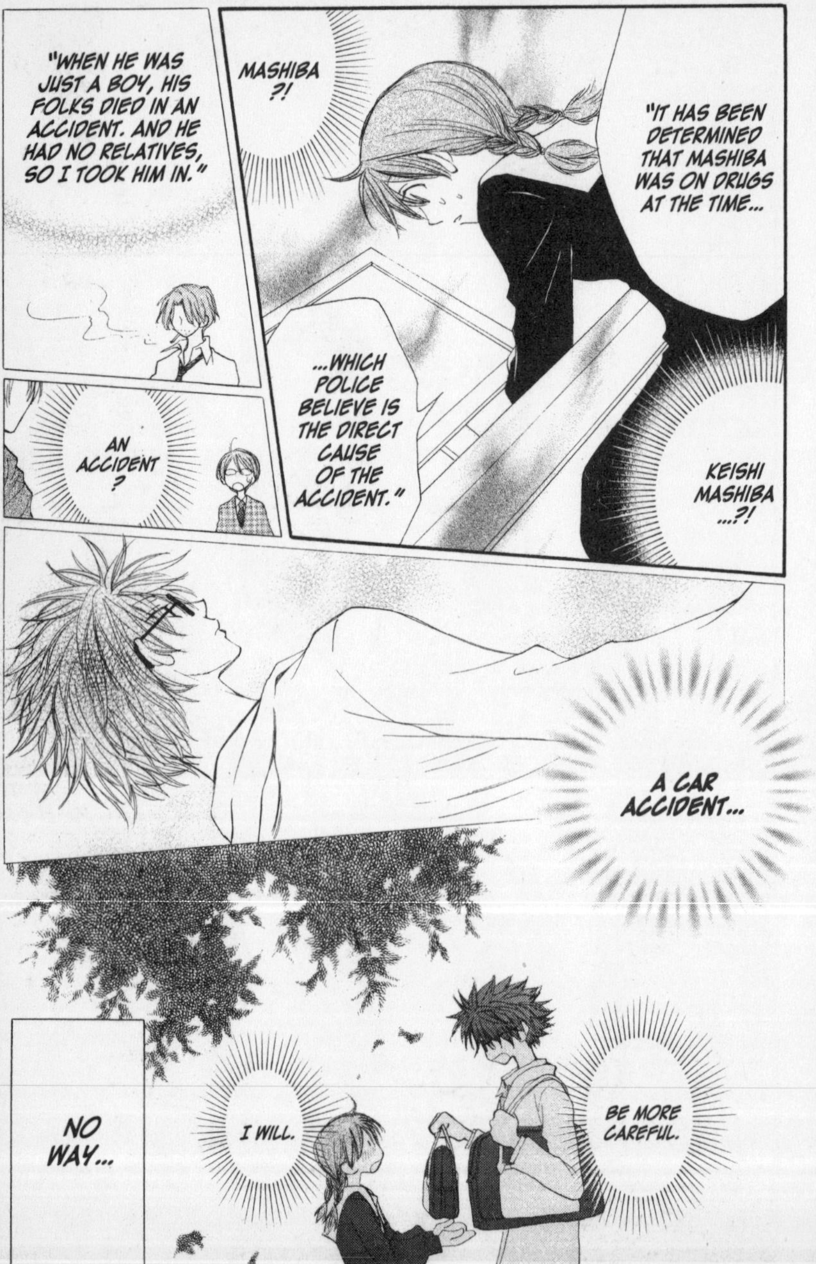
"IT HAS BEEN DETERMINED THAT MASHIBA WAS ON DRUGS AT THE TIME...
MASHIBA ?!
...WHICH POLICE BELIEVE IS THE DIRECT CAUSE OF THE ACCIDENT."
KEISHI MASHIBA ...?!
"WHEN HE WAS JUST A BOY, HIS FOLKS DIED IN AN ACCIDENT. AND HE HAD NO RELATIVES, SO I TOOK HIM IN."
AN ACCIDENT ?
A CAR ACCIDENT...
BE MORE CAREFUL.
I WILL.
NO WAY...

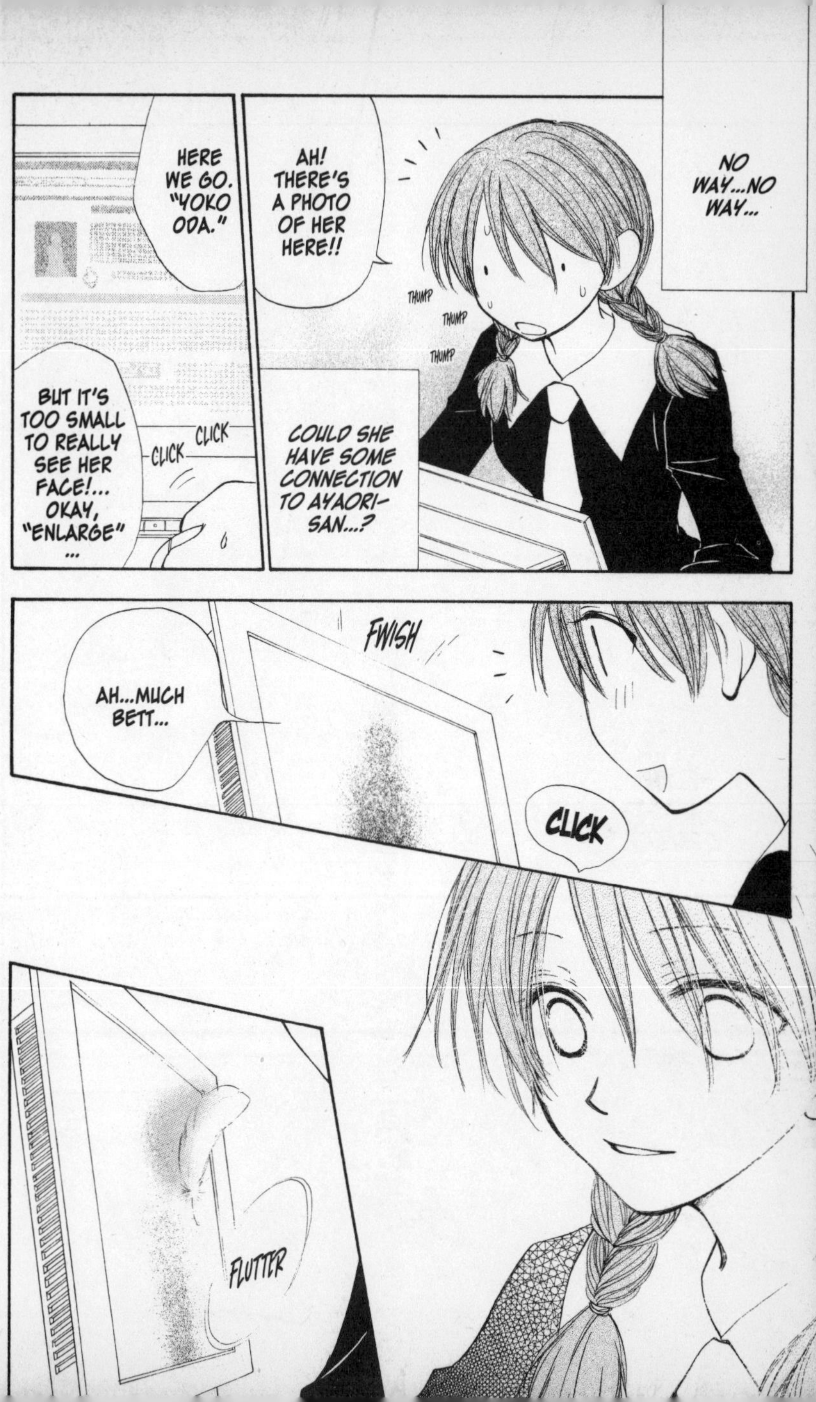
NO WAY...NO WAY...
AH! THERE'S A PHOTO OF HER HERE!!
THUMP
THUMP
THUMP
COULD SHE HAVE SOME CONNECTION TO AYAORI-SAN...?
HERE WE GO. "YOKO ODA."
BUT IT'S TOO SMALL TO REALLY SEE HER FACE!... OKAY, "ENLARGE" ...
CLICK
CLICK
FWISH
CLICK
AH...MUCH BETT...
FLUTTER

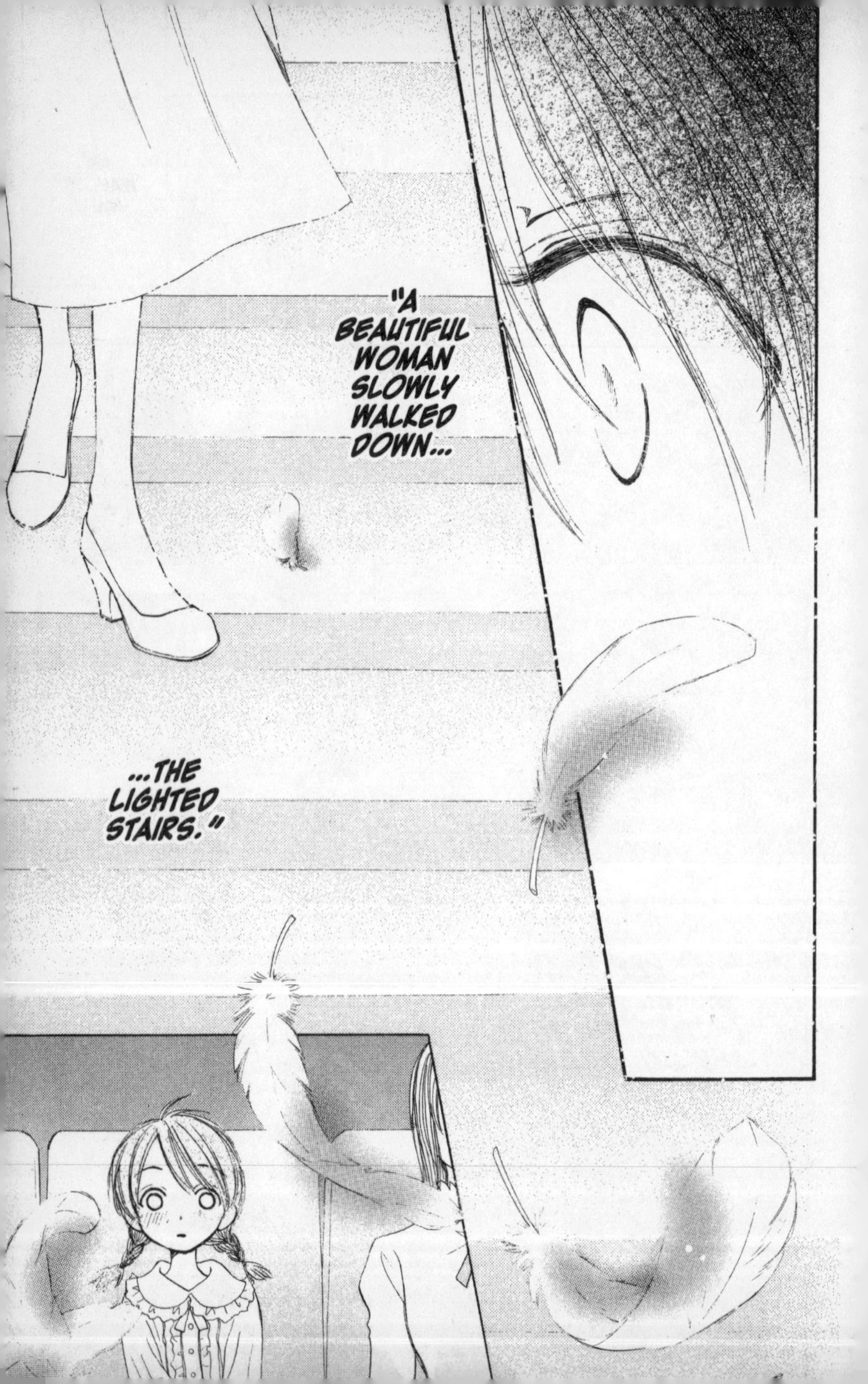
"A BEAUTIFUL WOMAN SLOWLY WALKED DOWN...
...THE LIGHTED STAIRS."

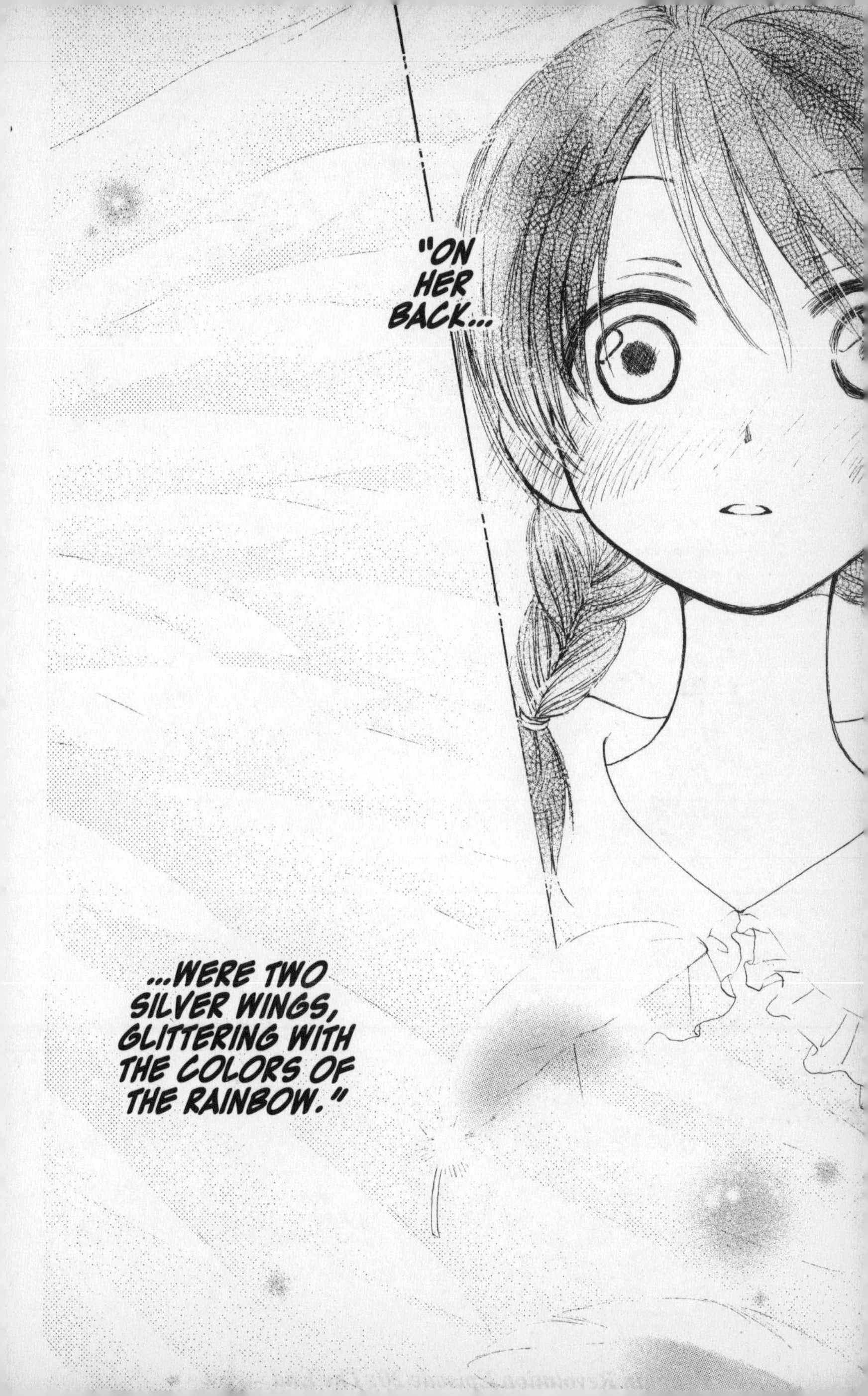
"ON HER BACK...
...WERE TWO SILVER WINGS, GLITTERING WITH THE COLORS OF THE RAINBOW."

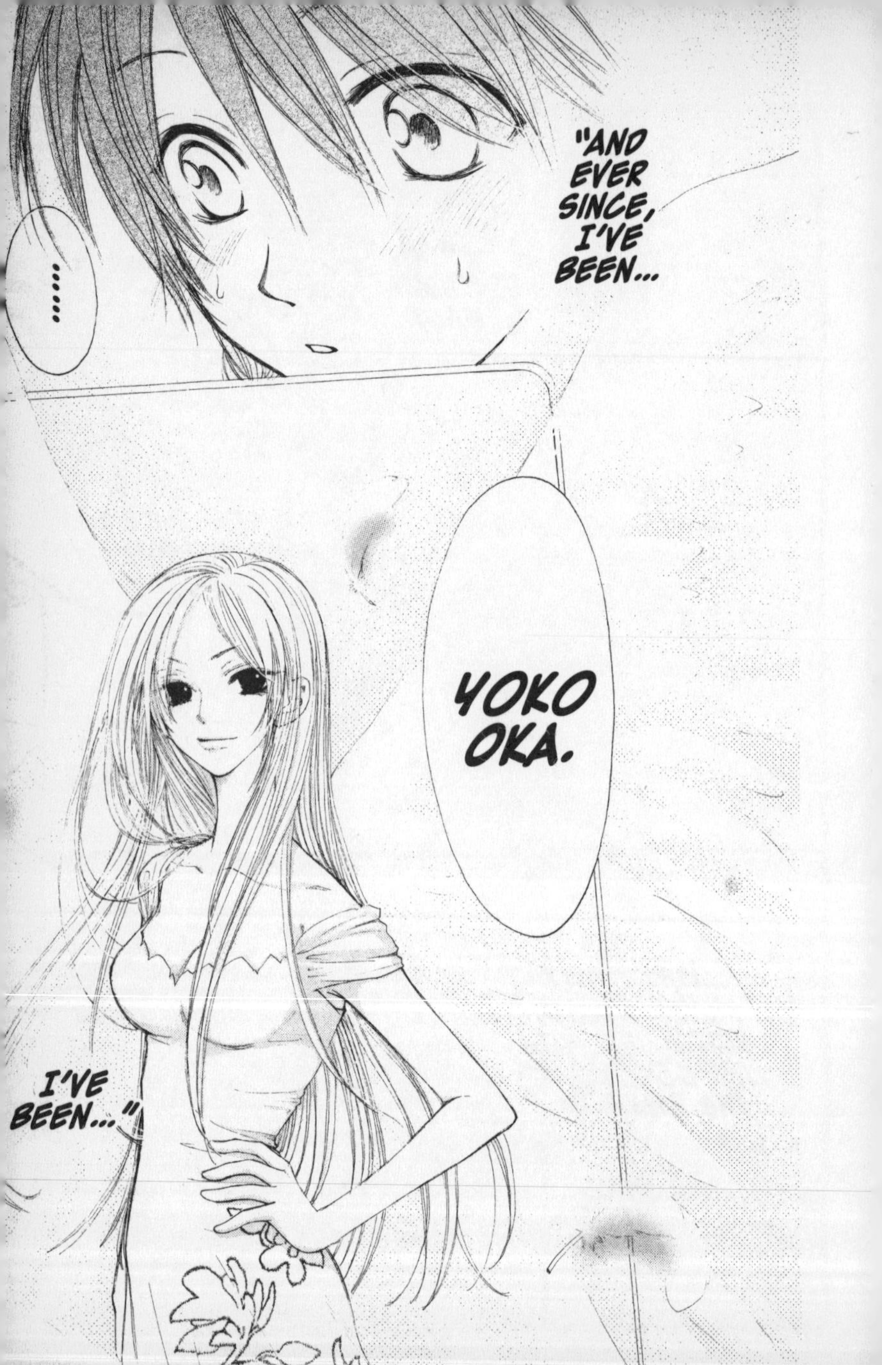
"AND EVER SINCE, I'VE BEEN...
......
YOKO OKA.
I'VE BEEN..."

Penguin Revolution Episode 20: The End

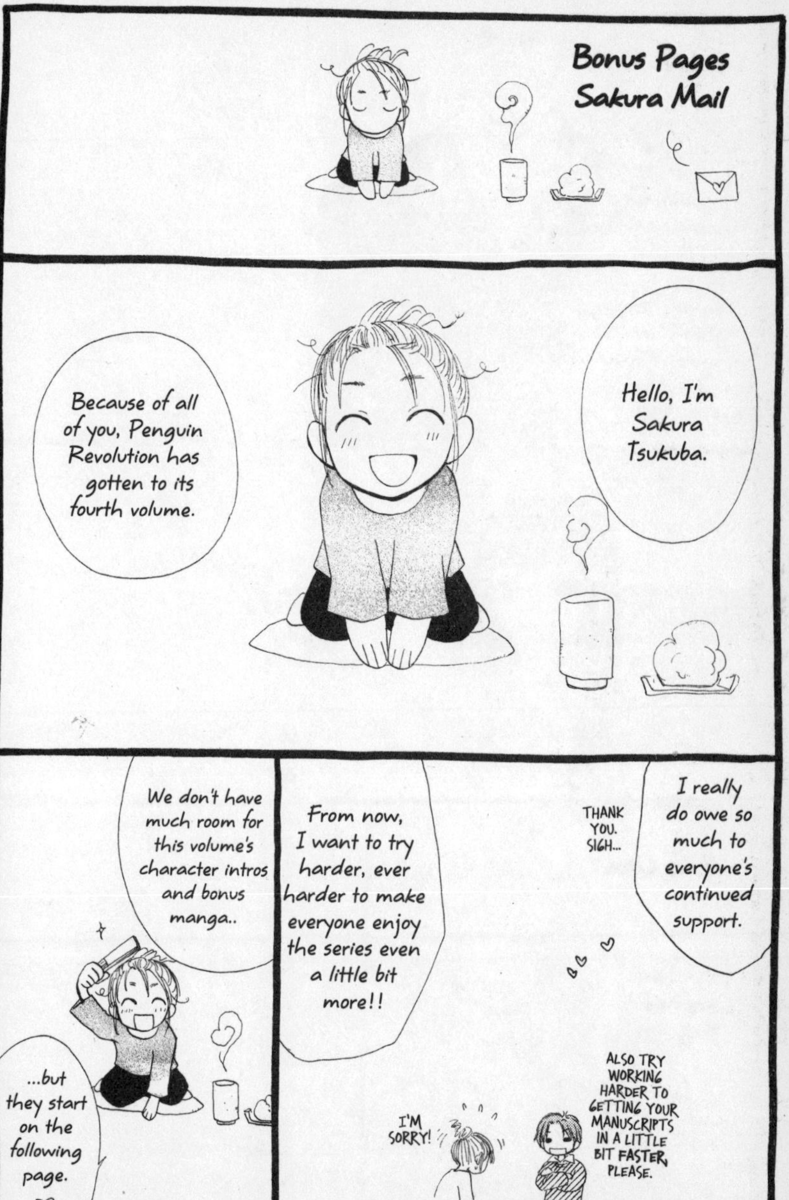

Bonus Pages
Sakura Mail
Hello, I'm Sakura Tsukuba.
Because of all of you, Penguin Revolution has gotten to its fourth volume.
I really do owe so much to everyone's continued support.
THANK YOU. SIGH...
From now, I want to try harder, ever harder to make everyone enjoy the series even a little bit more!!
ALSO TRY WORKING HARDER TO GETTING YOUR MANUSCRIPTS IN A LITTLE BIT FASTER, PLEASE.
I'M SORRY!
ICHIKAWA-SAMA, MY EDITOR
We don't have much room for this volume's character intros and bonus manga..
...but they start on the following page.

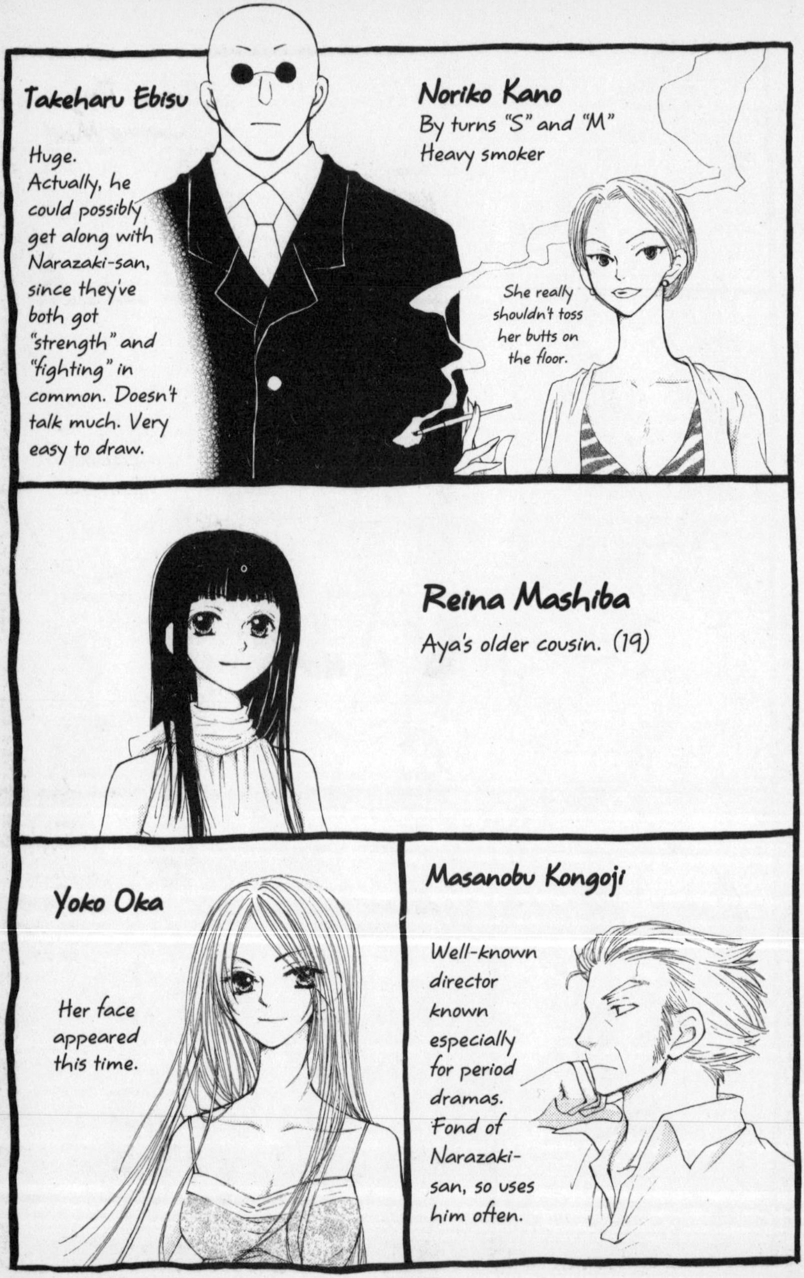
Noriko Kano
By turns "S" and "M"
Heavy smoker
She really shouldn't toss her butts on the floor.
Takeharu Ebisu
Huge. Actually, he could possibly get along with Narazaki-san, since they've both got "strength" and "fighting" in common. Doesn't talk much. Very easy to draw.
Reina Mashiba
Aya's older cousin. (19)
Masanobu Kongoji
Well-known director known especially for period dramas. Fond of Narazaki-san, so uses him often.
Yoko Oka
Her face appeared this time.

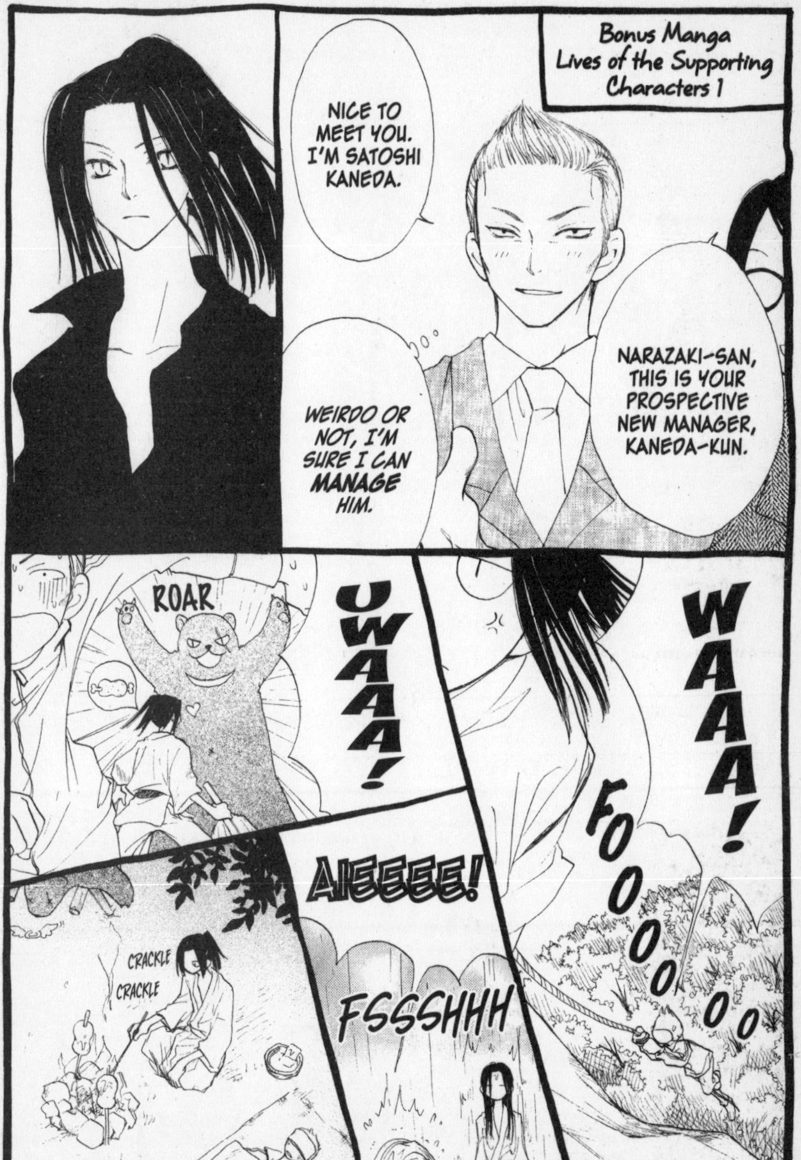
Bonus Manga
Lives of the Supporting Characters 1
NARAZAKI-SAN, THIS IS YOUR PROSPECTIVE NEW MANAGER, KANEDA-KUN.
NICE TO MEET YOU. I'M SATOSHI KANEDA.
WEIRDO OR NOT, I'M SURE I CAN MANAGE HIM.
WAAAA!
FOOOOOOO
UWAAA!
ROAR
AIEEEEE!
FSSSHHH
CRACKLE
CRACKLE

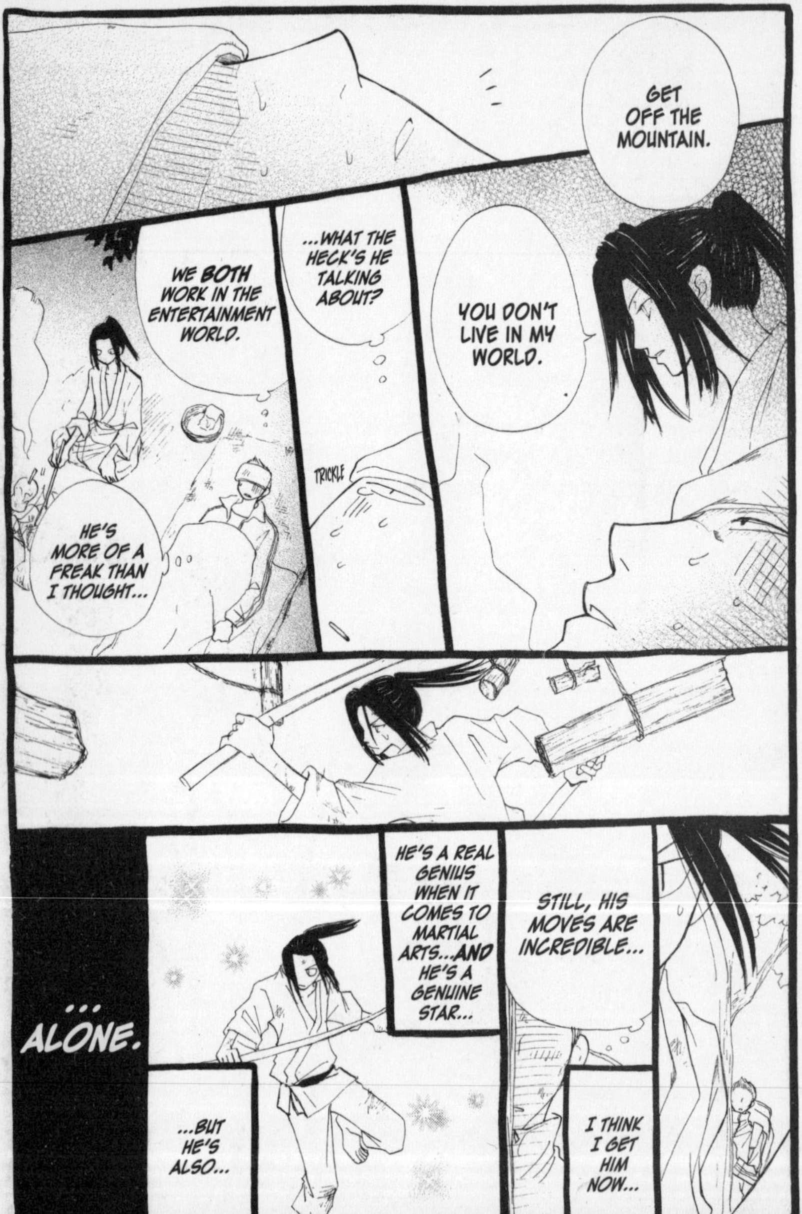
GET OFF THE MOUNTAIN.
YOU DON'T LIVE IN MY WORLD.
...WHAT THE HECK'S HE TALKING ABOUT?
TRICKLE
WE BOTH WORK IN THE ENTERTAINMENT WORLD.
HE'S MORE OF A FREAK THAN I THOUGHT...
STILL, HIS MOVES ARE INCREDIBLE...
I THINK I GET HIM NOW...
HE'S A REAL GENIUS WHEN IT COMES TO MARTIAL ARTS...AND HE'S A GENUINE STAR...
...BUT HE'S ALSO...
...ALONE.

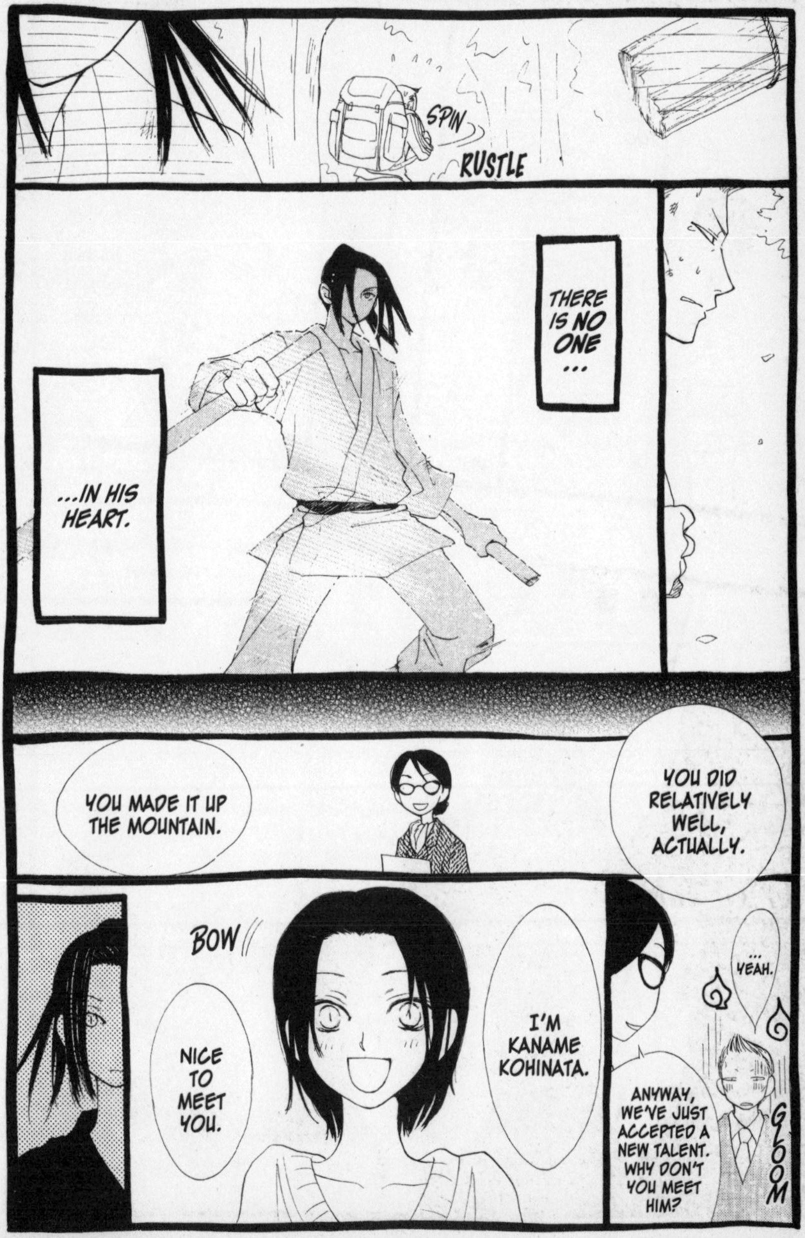

SPIN
RUSTLE
THERE IS NO ONE...
...IN HIS HEART.
YOU DID RELATIVELY WELL, ACTUALLY.
YOU MADE IT UP THE MOUNTAIN.
...YEAH.
ANYWAY, WE'VE JUST ACCEPTED A NEW TALENT. WHY DON'T YOU MEET HIM?
GLOOM
I'M KANAME KOHINATA.
BOW
NICE TO MEET YOU.

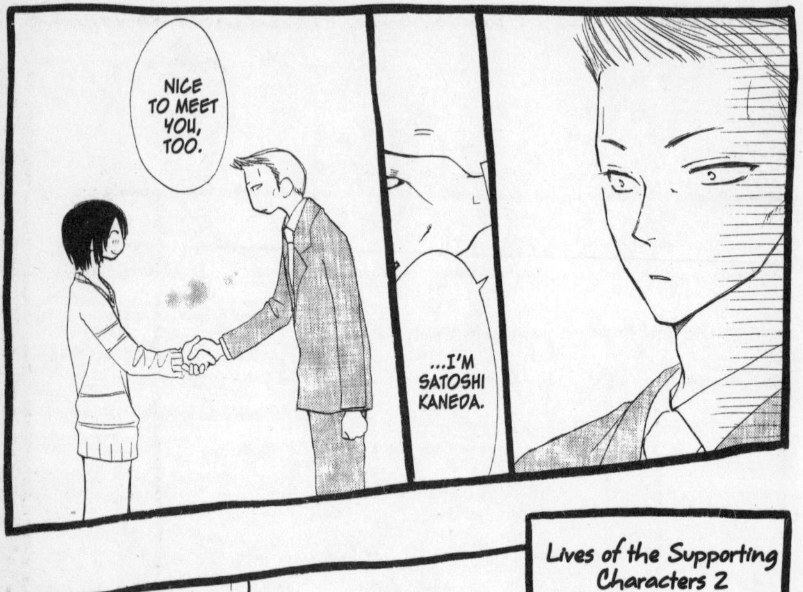
...I'M SATOSHI KANEDA.
NICE TO MEET YOU, TOO.

Lives of the Supporting Characters 2

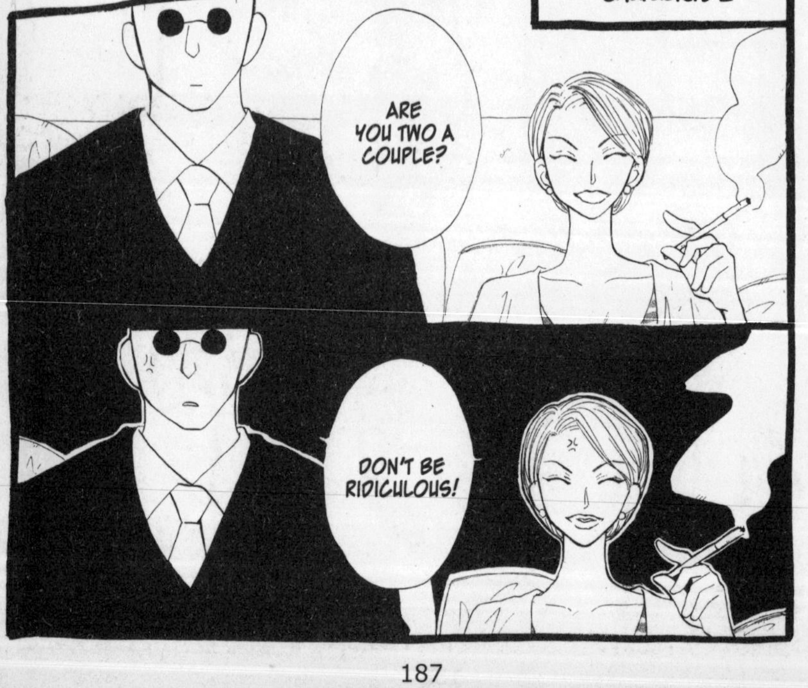
ARE YOU TWO A COUPLE?
DON'T BE RIDICULOUS!

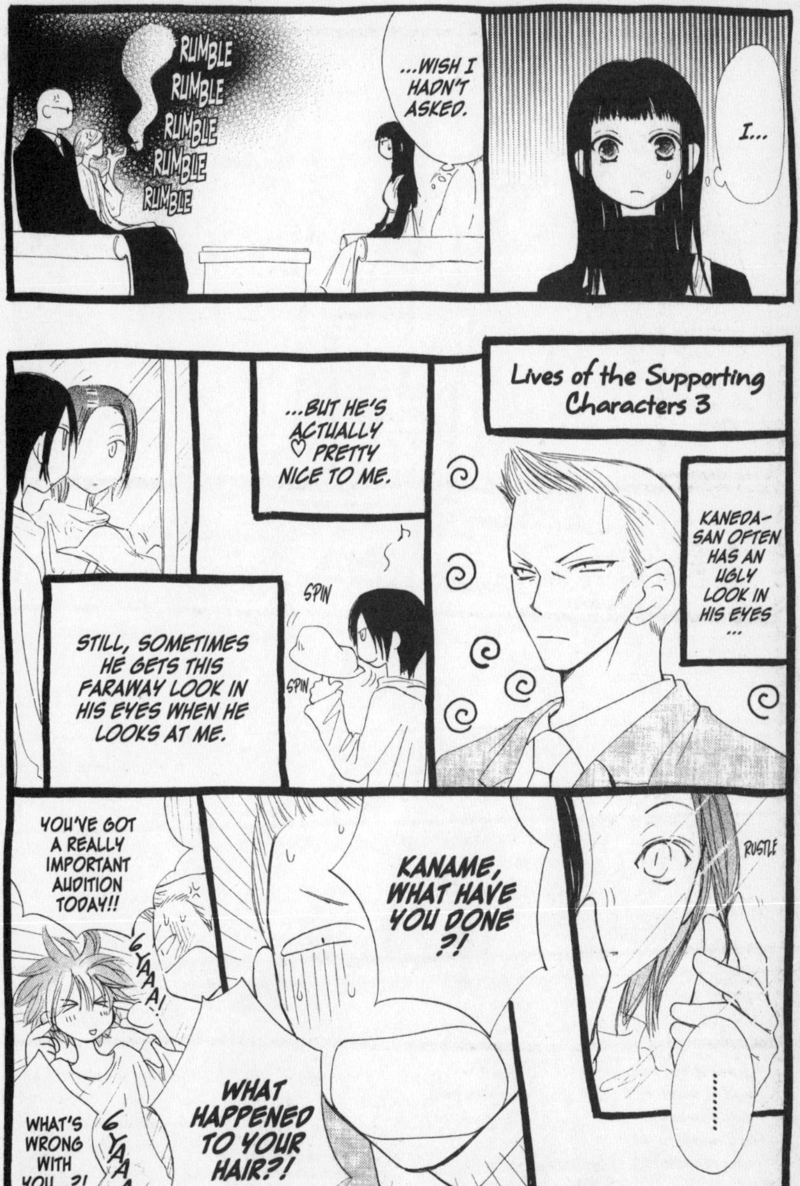
I...
...WISH I HADN'T ASKED.
RUMBLE RUMBLE RUMBLE RUMBLE RUMBLE
Lives of the Supporting Characters 3
KANEDA-SAN OFTEN HAS AN UGLY LOOK IN HIS EYES...
...BUT HE'S ACTUALLY ♡ PRETTY NICE TO ME.
SPIN
SPIN
STILL, SOMETIMES HE GETS THIS FARAWAY LOOK IN HIS EYES WHEN HE LOOKS AT ME.
RUSTLE
......
KANAME, WHAT HAVE YOU DONE?!
WHAT HAPPENED TO YOUR HAIR?!
YOU'VE GOT A REALLY IMPORTANT AUDITION TODAY!!
GYAAA!
WHAT'S WRONG WITH YOU...?!
GYAAA!

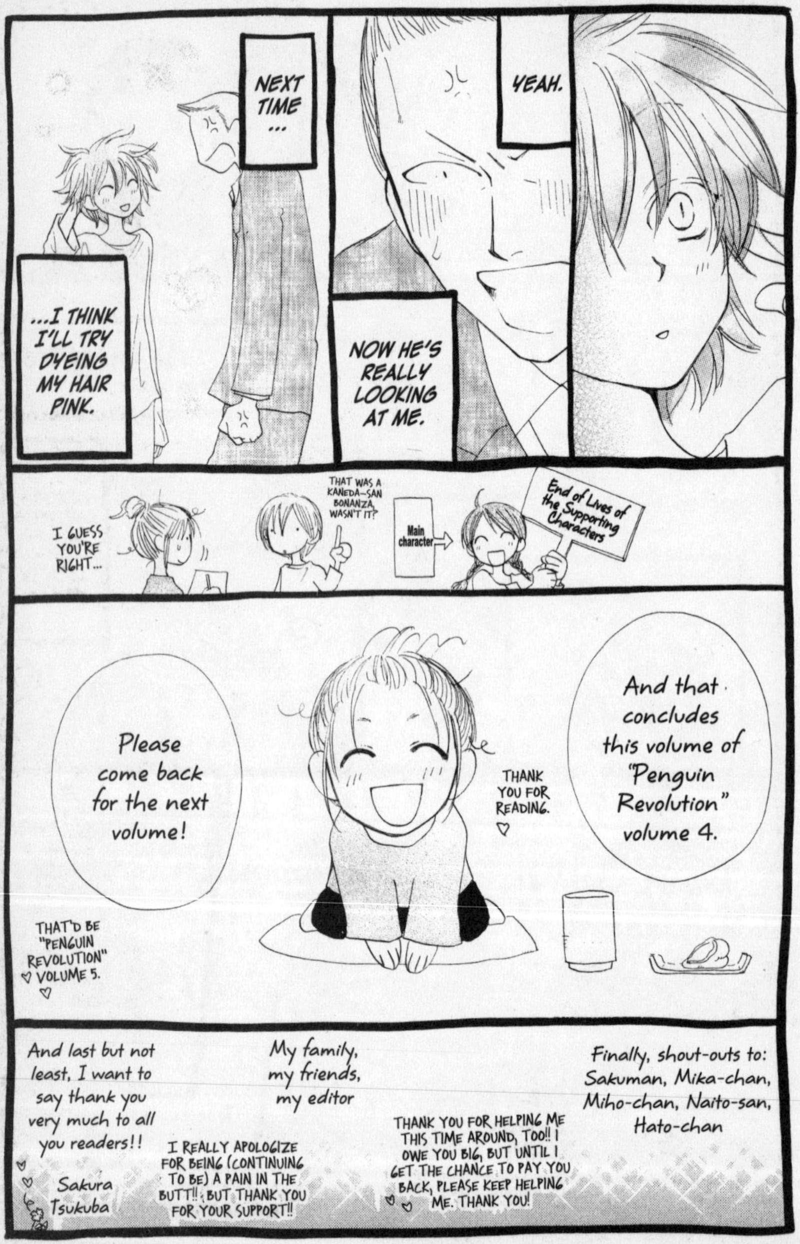
YEAH.
NOW HE'S REALLY LOOKING AT ME.
NEXT TIME...
...I THINK I'LL TRY DYEING MY HAIR PINK.
End of Lives of the Supporting Characters
Main character
THAT WAS A KANEDA-SAN BONANZA, WASN'T IT?
I GUESS YOU'RE RIGHT...
And that concludes this volume of "Penguin Revolution" volume 4.
THANK YOU FOR READING. ♡
Please come back for the next volume!
THAT'D BE "PENGUIN REVOLUTION" ♡ VOLUME 5. ♡
Finally, shout-outs to: Sakuman, Mika-chan, Miho-chan, Naito-san, Hato-chan
THANK YOU FOR HELPING ME THIS TIME AROUND, TOO!! I OWE YOU BIG, BUT UNTIL I GET THE CHANCE TO PAY YOU BACK, PLEASE KEEP HELPING ME. THANK YOU! ♡
My family, my friends, my editor
I REALLY APOLOGIZE FOR BEING (CONTINUING TO BE) A PAIN IN THE BUTT!! BUT THANK YOU FOR YOUR SUPPORT!!
And last but not least, I want to say thank you very much to all you readers!!
Sakura Tsukuba

Sakura Mail Bonus Pages: The End

JOIN THE PENGUIN REVOLUTION TODAY!

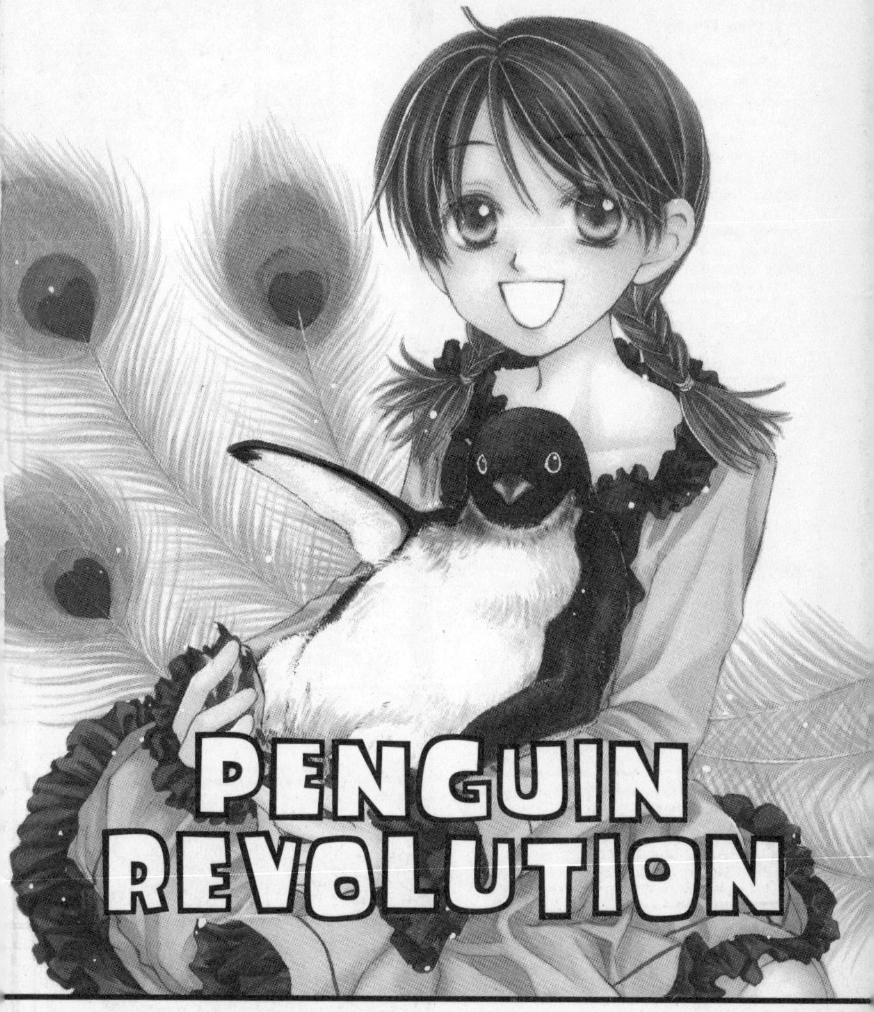
PENGUIN
REVOLUTION

By Sakura Tsukuba. If you've missed any of the three previous volumes in this series, now is the time to catch up! See how Yukari first discovered her magical ability to see wings on people with real talent. Find out how she first got connected with the Peacock agency and why she had to assume the identity of a male talent agent. Then be sure to come back and join us for Penguin Revolution volume 5 in 2008!

Jim Lee
    Editorial Director
John Nee
    VP—Business Development
Hank Kanalz
    VP—General Manager, WildStorm
Paul Levitz
    President & Publisher
Georg Brewer
    VP—Design & DC Direct Creative
Richard Bruning
    Senior VP—Creative Director
Patrick Caldon
    Executive VP—Finance & Operations
Chris Caramalis
    VP—Finance
John Cunningham
    VP—Marketing
Terri Cunningham
    VP—Managing Editor
Alison Gill
    VP—Manufacturing
Paula Lowitt
    Senior VP—Business & Legal Affairs
Gregory Noveck
    Senior VP—Creative Affairs
Sue Pohja
    VP—Book Trade Sales
Cheryl Rubin
    Senior VP—Brand Management
Jeff Trojan
    VP—Business Development, DC Direct
Bob Wayne
    VP—Sales

PENGUIN KAKUMEI Volume 4 © 2006 Sakura Tsukuba.
All Rights Reserved. First published in Japan in 2006
by HAKUSENSHA, INC., Tokyo.

PENGUIN REVOLUTION Volume 4, published by WildStorm
Productions, an imprint of DC Comics, 888 Prospect St.
#240, La Jolla, CA 92037. English Translation © 2007. All
Rights Reserved. English translation rights in U.S.A. and
Canada arranged by HAKUSENSHA, INC., through
Tuttle-Mori Agency Inc., Tokyo. CMX is trademark of DC
Comics. The stories, characters, and incidents mentioned in
this magazine are entirely fictional. Printed on recyclable
paper. WildStorm does not read or accept unsolicited
submissions of ideas, stories or artwork. Printed in Canada.

DC Comics, a Warner Bros. Entertainment Company.

Sheldon Drzka – Translation and Adaptation

AndWorld Design – Lettering

Larry Berry – Design

Jim Chadwick – Editor

ISBN:1-4012-1306-5
ISBN-13: 978-1-4012-1306-0

All the pages in this book were created [so they use] RIGHT-to-LEFT format. No artwork h[as been ...so you] can read the stories the way the cr[eators...]

WITHDRAWN
Sno-Isle Libraries

FLIP IT!

RIGHT TO LEFT?!

Traditional Japanese manga starts at the upper right-hand corner, and moves right-to-left as it goes down the page. Follow this guide for an easy understanding.

For more information and sneak previews, visit cmxmanga.com. Call 1-888-COMIC BOOK for the nearest comics shop or head to your local book store.